Back to the Essence

Design Guidelines for Minimalist Graphics

©2020 SendPoints Publishing Co., Ltd.
First printing of the first edition, January 2020

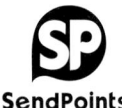

EDITED & PUBLISHED BY SendPoints Publishing Co., Ltd.
PUBLISHER: Lin Gengli
PUBLISHING DIRECTOR: Lin Shijian
CHIEF EDITOR: Lin Shijian
DESIGN ADVISOR: Chen Ting
EXECUTIVE EDITOR: Li Weiji
EXECUTIVE ART EDITOR: Chen Ting
PROOFREADING: Li Weiji

REGISTERED ADDRESS: Room 15A Block 9 Tsui Chuk Garden, Wong Tai Sin, Kowloon, Hong Kong
TEL: +852-35832323 / **FAX:** +852-35832448
OFFICE ADDRESS: 7F, 9th Anning Street, Jinshazhou, Baiyun District, Guangzhou, China
TEL: +86-20-89095121 / **FAX:** +86-20-89095206
BEIJING OFFICE: Room 107, Floor 1, Xiyingfang Alley, Ande Road, Dongcheng District, Beijing, China
TEL: +86-10-84139071 / **FAX:** +86-10-84139071
SHANGHAI OFFICE: Room 307, Building 1, Hong Qiang Creative Zhabei District, Shanghai, China
TEL: +86-21-63523469 / **FAX:** +86-21-63523469

SALES TEAM
UK, Europe, Africa, Oceania: Sunnie   sales02@sendpoints.cn
America, the Middle East: Mia   sales03@sendpoints.cn
Asia: Hedy   sales01@sendpoints.cn
TEL: +86-20-81007895
EMAIL: sales@sendpoints.cn
WEBSITE: www.sendpoints.cn / www.spbooks.cn

ISBN 978-988-79284-1-6

All rights reserved. No part of this publication may be reproduced, stored in a retrieval system or transmitted in any form or by any means, electronic, mechanical, photocopying, recording or otherwise, without prior permission in writing from the publisher. For more information, please contact SendPoints Publishing Co., Ltd.
Printed and bound in China.

Back to the Essence

Design Guidelines for Minimalist Graphics

引き算のデザイン

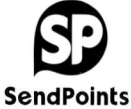

Back to the Essence

Design Guidelines for Minimalist Graphics

©2020 SendPoints Publishing Co., Ltd.
First printing of the first edition, January 2020

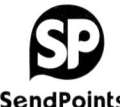

EDITED & PUBLISHED BY SendPoints Publishing Co., Ltd.
PUBLISHER: Lin Gengli
PUBLISHING DIRECTOR: Lin Shijian
CHIEF EDITOR: Lin Shijian
DESIGN ADVISOR: Chen Ting
EXECUTIVE EDITOR: Li Weiji
EXECUTIVE ART EDITOR: Chen Ting
PROOFREADING: Li Weiji

REGISTERED ADDRESS: Room 15A Block 9 Tsui Chuk Garden, Wong Tai Sin, Kowloon, Hong Kong
TEL: +852-35832323 / **FAX:** +852-35832448
OFFICE ADDRESS: 7F, 9th Anning Street, Jinshazhou, Baiyun District, Guangzhou, China
TEL: +86-20-89095121 / **FAX:** +86-20-89095206
BEIJING OFFICE: Room 107, Floor 1, Xiyingfang Alley, Ande Road, Dongcheng District, Beijing, China
TEL: +86-10-84139071 / **FAX:** +86-10-84139071
SHANGHAI OFFICE: Room 307, Building 1, Hong Qiang Creative Zhabei District, Shanghai, China
TEL: +86-21-63523469 / **FAX:** +86-21-63523469

SALES TEAM
UK, Europe, Africa, Oceania: Sunnie sales02@sendpoints.cn
America, the Middle East: Mia sales03@sendpoints.cn
Asia: Hedy sales01@sendpoints.cn
TEL: +86-20-81007895
EMAIL: sales@sendpoints.cn
WEBSITE: www.sendpoints.cn / www.spbooks.cn

ISBN 978-988-79284-1-6

All rights reserved. No part of this publication may be reproduced, stored in a retrieval system or transmitted in any form or by any means, electronic, mechanical, photocopying, recording or otherwise, without prior permission in writing from the publisher. For more information, please contact SendPoints Publishing Co., Ltd.
Printed and bound in China.

Contents

The Origins of "Less is More"	5
Development of Minimalism	8
Minimalism in "Less is More"	10
Minimalist Design in Germany	14
Minimalist Design in Japan	16
Minimalist Design in Switzerland	18
30 Designers // Less is More	20
The Hidden World, by Daigo Daikoku	22
The Power of Limitations, by Lars Kjelsnes	30
Design Projects	37
Index	206

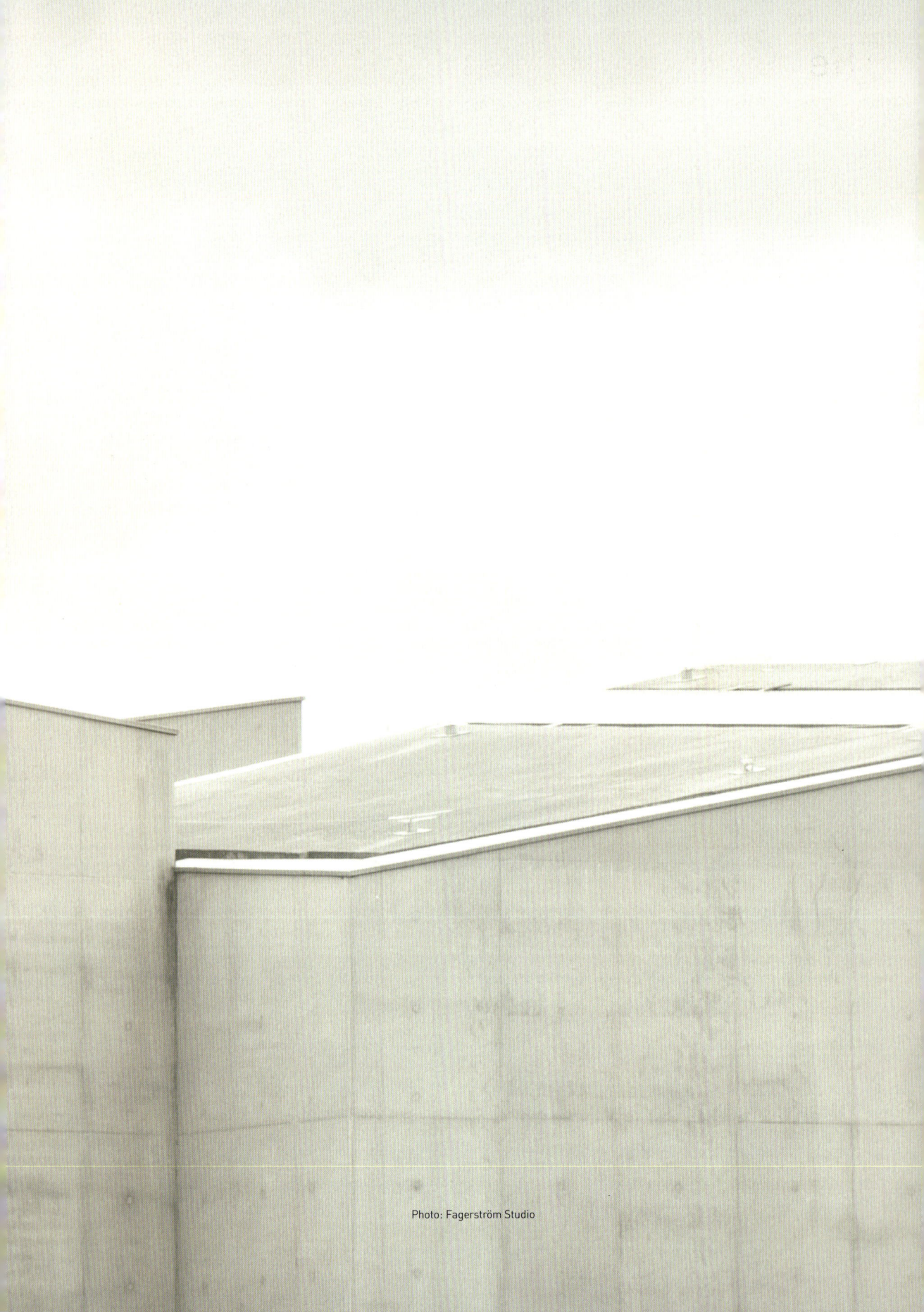
Photo: Fagerström Studio

The Origins of "Less is More"

Started in 1917 and lasted till roughly the early 1930s, De Stijl was an artistic movement in Netherlands that espoused the abstract expressionism art, using only the rudimentary geometric shapes in their works without being over decorated. "De Stijl" is Dutch for "The Style". The movement was a major influence on painting, sculpture, architecture and design.

De Stijl pushed for simplicity and abstraction by reducing designs only to its essential form and color, sticking only to horizontal and vertical lines, rectangular forms, primary colors and noncolors: white, black, gray, blue, red and yellow. Furthermore, many of the elements or layers don't intersect, each independent of other elements.

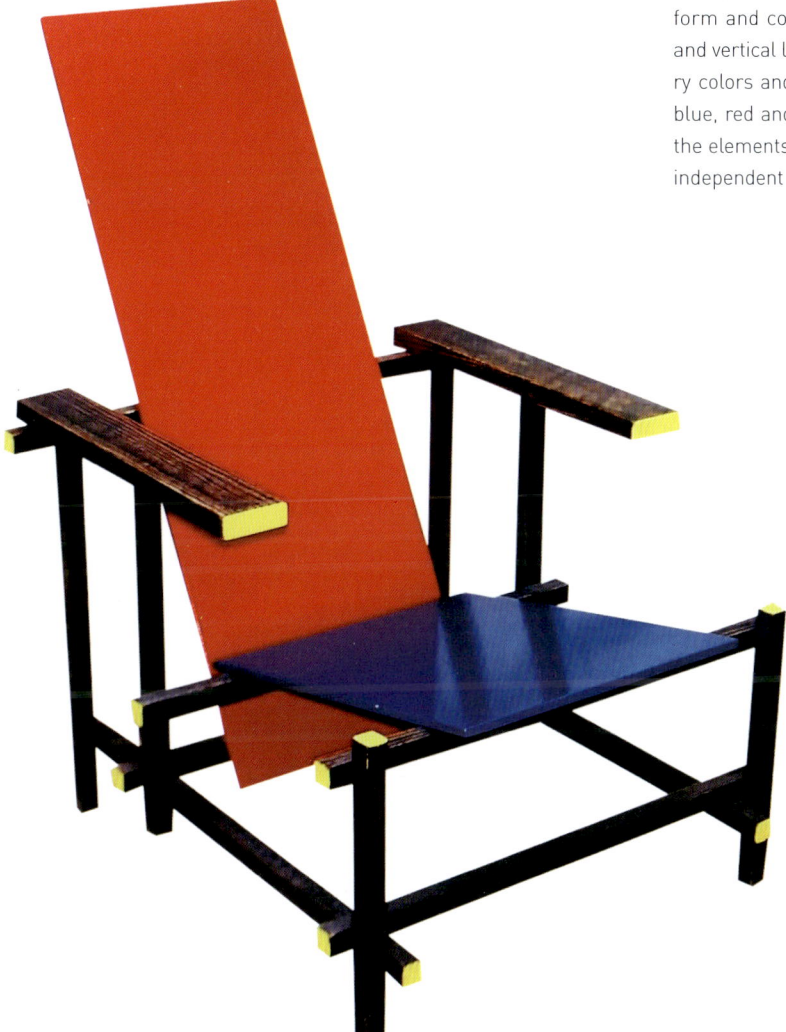

Red Blue Chair, by Gerrit Rietveld

Less is More

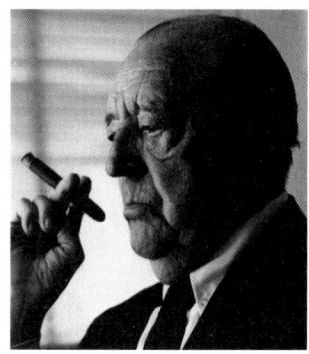

Ludwig Mies van der Rohe

1886 / 1969

This aphorism favored by a great many designers was proposed by Ludwig Mies van der Rohe.

Ludwig Mies van der Rohe was considered a pioneer of modern architecture and his architectural style during post-World War I laid the groundwork for Minimalist design. He had designed many landmark buildings, including Chicago's Crown Hall and New York's Seagram Building.

Van der Rohe's architectural designs are known for their simplicity and clarity. Made up of modern materials like steel and plates of glass, these architectural designs have a minimal structural framework which often includes lots of open space.

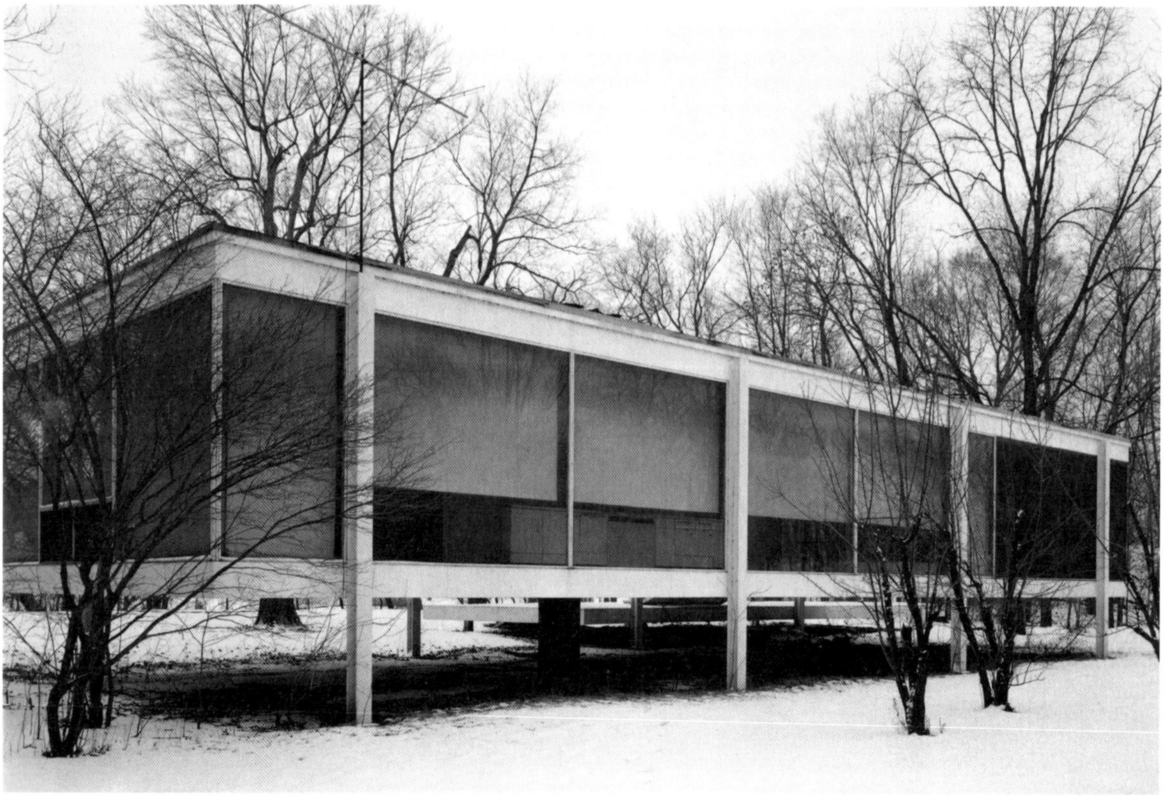

One of the influential works by Mies van der Rohe: Farnsworth House

Traditional Japanese Design

Traditional Japanese design demonstrates best what Minimalist design is all about: to strip the unnecessary parts and keep the essence, that is, the mission statement of Ludwig Mies van der Rohe--less is more. To the Japanese, design is an activity of making things, an activity that originates in human senses rather than being stimulated by new materials. It is the sense of touch. Traditional Japanese designs are characterized by simple color and design elements, clean lines and form, and few flourishes.

The connection between Japanese design and Japanese culture is such that one cannot talk of one without mentioning the other. Japanese culture is infused with Zen and simplicity. From ikebana to tea ceremony, it is the process rather than the result that the Japanese pay attention to.

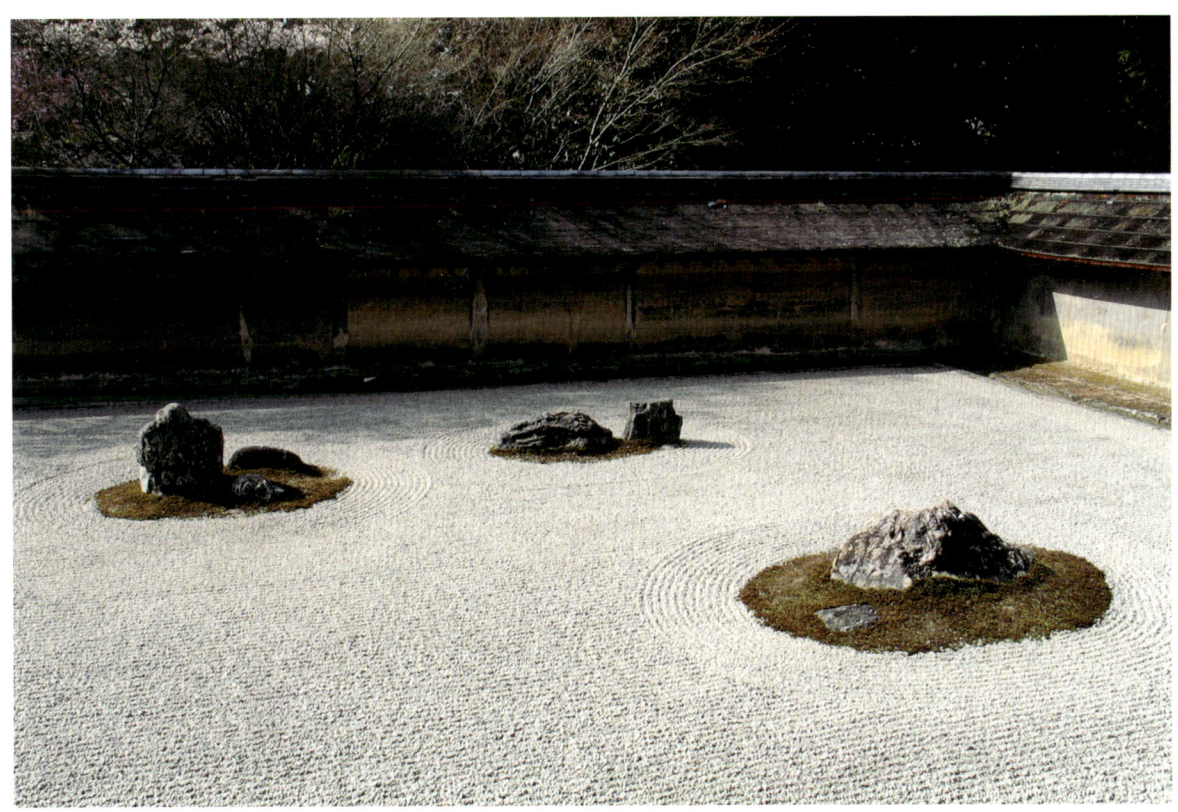

Dry Garden in RyoanJi © Stephane D'Alu / Wikimedia Commons / CC BY-SA 3.0

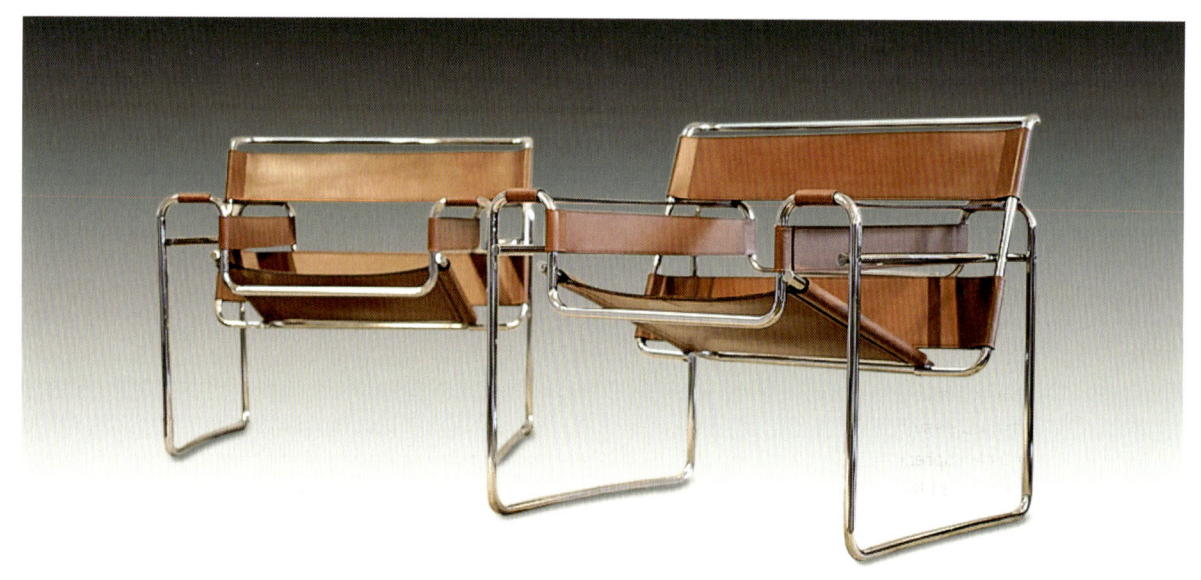

Oxblood Wassily Chairs © David Costa, Flickr / CC BY 2.0

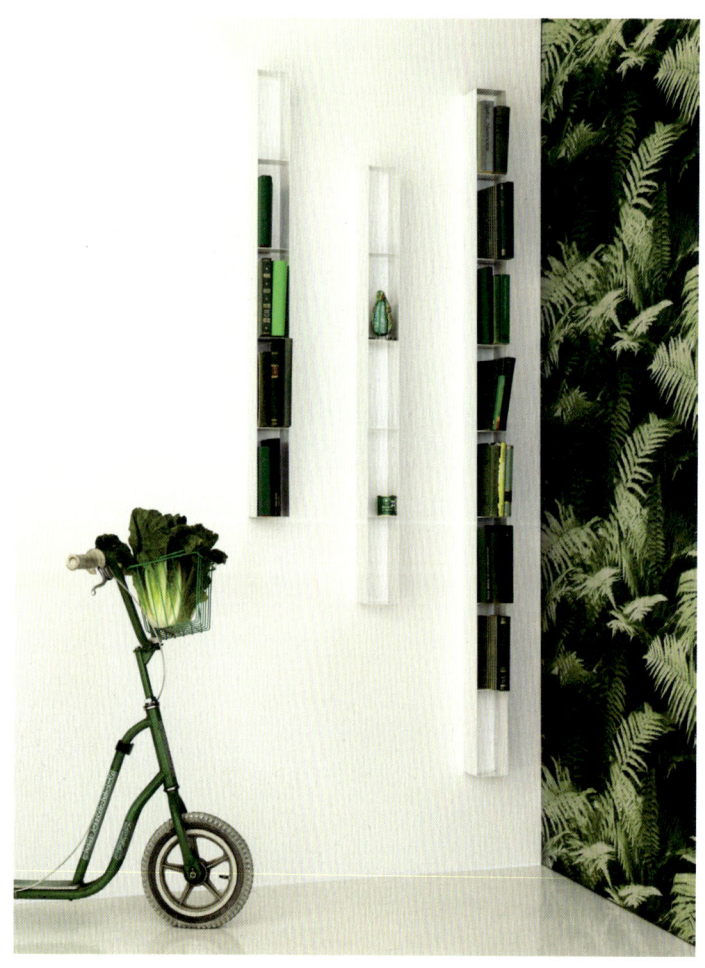

Luft Bookshelf © MottoWASABI Design Office

Development of Minimalism

Minimalist design is rooted in the reductive aspects of Modernism; it had gradually become a movement in response to the highly ornate design prevalent in previous eras. It quickly spread all over the world. The development of Minimalist design is a by-product of social, cultural, scientific and technological development.

Minimalist design first started in the early 20th century in architecture, roughly around the 1920s. Post-World War I architect Van der Rohe was one of the first prominent architects who used principles in his designs that came to exemplify Minimalist design. The reason Minimalist architecture started taking off was the availability of modern materials: glass, concrete and steel. Also, standardized ways of building were forming, which helped create more effective design and build Minimalist buildings. The trend continued through the mid-20th century, with the appearance of lots of notable designers and architects. Buckminster Fuller designed domes by using simple geometric shapes that still stand out and look modern today. The focus on simplicity spilled over into painting, interior design, fashion and music. Painter Frank Stella was quoted as saying, "What you see is what you see". Minimal art, in particular, grew in the 1960s in America. Similar to De Stijl, painters used only rudimentary geometric shapes in their works without decorations or any other elements.

Simplicity also spilled over into consumer products, with designer Dieter Rams using Minimalist style in designing products for Braun. IKEA, the Swedish furniture company, is another example of Minimalist designed products. Its furniture products are so simple and self-explanatory that people are able to assemble them by themselves without instructions.

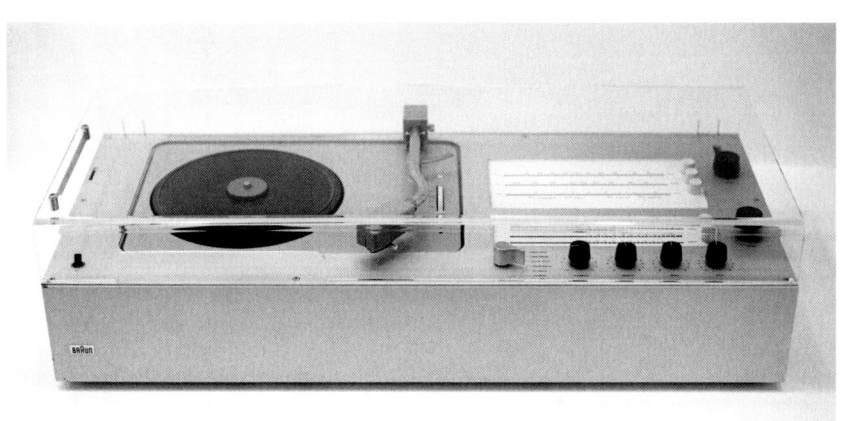

Record player and radio, Designed by Dieter Rams, © René Spitz

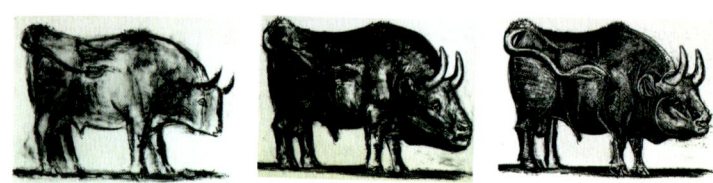

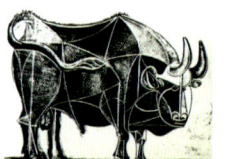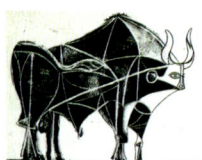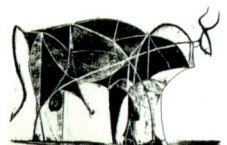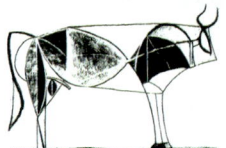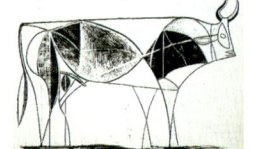

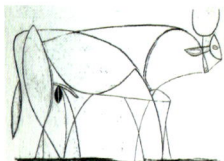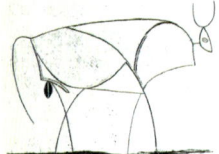

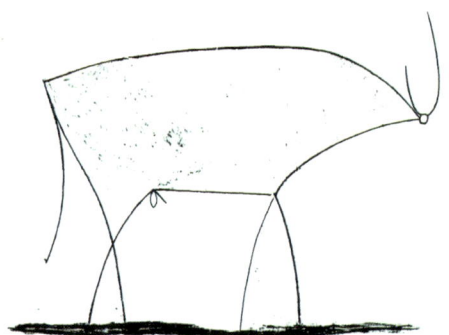

Minimalism in "Less is More"

Considering the reductive approach in Minimalist design, is it true that "less is more" could be attained simply by using less elements? Quite the contrary, the philosophy proposed by Mies van der Rohe is based on a high degree of abstraction of an object which follows extremely complex argumentation. This means that only when you learn about the subject comprehensively and meticulously while taking into account the different needs of the audience, based on which the simplification and abstraction develop, can your final work embody the the idea of "creating the greatest function with the least elements". Otherwise there would be just inane "less" which hardly sustains the details of "more". We can therefore consider "less is more" a dauntingly difficult design aesthetic. The bull, a series of lithographs, by Picasso turns out to be a clear exposition of such an aesthetic; he had made 11 of them to come to a bull constructed from only a few strokes. The creation process disclosed how the painter had been abstracting over and over again from a real bull.

The Minimalism, epitomized by the phrase "less is more", had also been influenced by a number of design trends. Today, Minimalism has become a mainstream design style, but designers' ideas about "less is more" is becoming increasingly diversified.

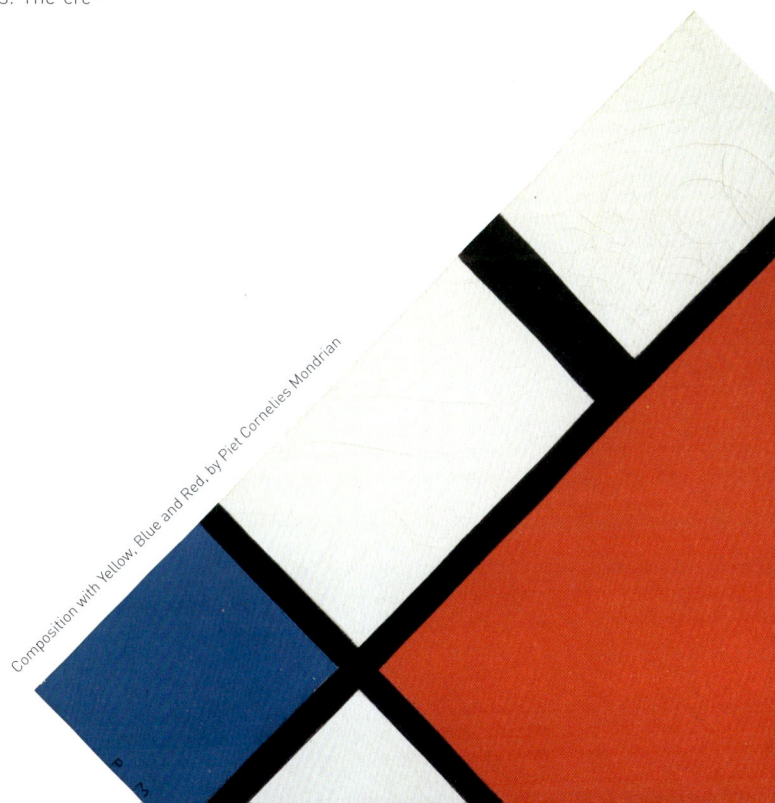

Composition with Yellow, Blue and Red, by Piet Cornelies Mondrian

Minimalist design uses the minimal design elements to express creative simplicity and ingenuity. Minimal colors, effective layout, clean and simple fonts, empty space, strong contrast, etc. help create more readable and effective designs. With fewer elements, Minimalist design receives wider acknowledgment.

Be aware that the more refined it gets, the more Minimalist your design will be. Take into consideration what your design wants to stress, what you want to present to the audiences, then keep and leave the only and right details.

To create a good and successful Minimalist design is not as simple. What it presents is always achieved through a difficult and complicated process. To strip down, there are some basic principles for a Minimalist design.

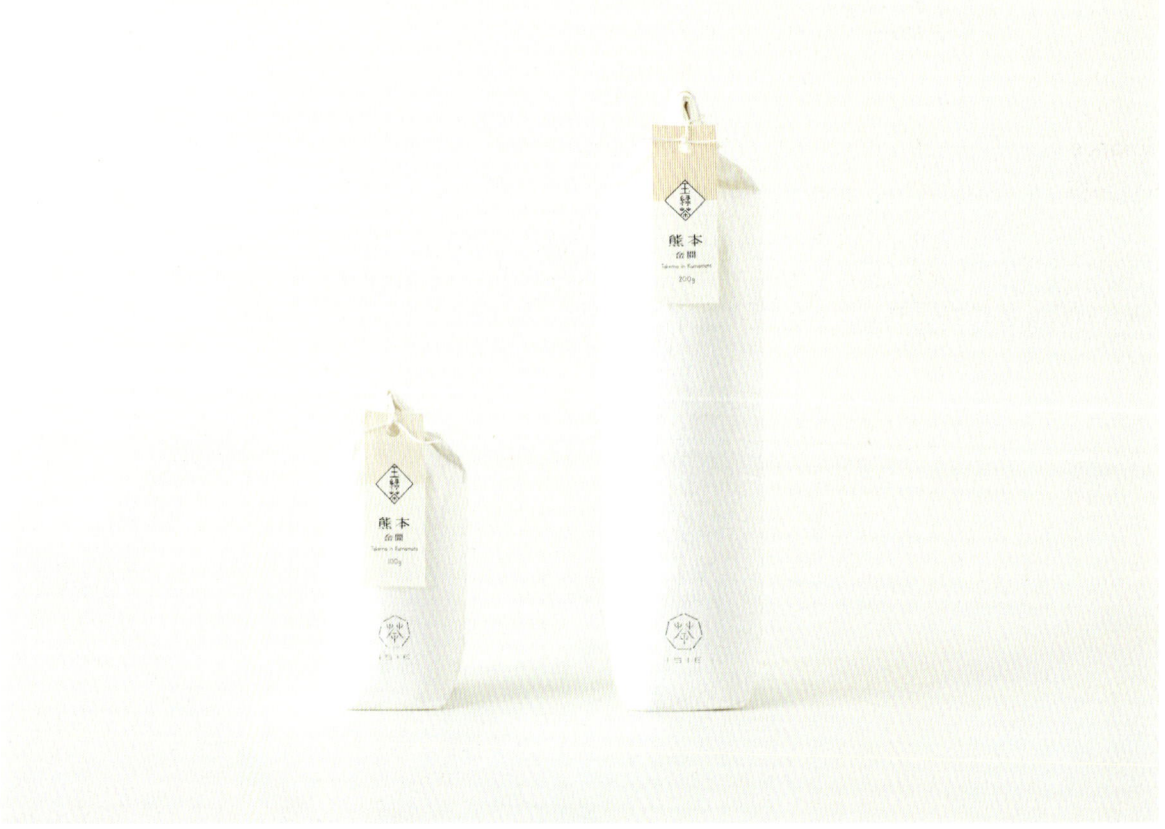

Photo: planning ES

Color

Most Minimalist designs apply white and black. These two colors are considered non-colors. When put together, they can form the strongest contrast, producing a powerful effect. Many fashion and interior companies always employ these two colors to embody elegant and classic texture. In fact, all colors can be used to make a good Minimalist design. It is most important to choose colors which are perfect for the brand and also speak with the audience.

Typography

Typography is a commonly used element in Minimalist design, which helps the brand to be special and direct. In web design, it is one of the most important elements because a website should be most readable and precise for the readers. Choosing Minimalist fonts and only applying a particular font could help avoid confusion and minimalize a design. At the same time, being absolutely clear is what typography must be in a Minimalist design.

Layout

Layout should be effective and clean in Minimalist designs. Putting the main element in focus and eliminating unnecessary information to let the viewers find the main information without consideration is the main mission. This requires an efficient arrangement and repeated exercises for designers. The more direct, the better.

White space

White space is also a very important element in Minimalist design, but it is very difficult to handle. In fact, white space has very strong power. It supports and balances the other elements in the design, although it seems to have the least information, even empty. Don't try to fill every space, instead, keep white space to emphasize certain elements over others.

Balance & Contrast

A Minimalist design applies the minimal elements. But it does not mean if one chooses the least elements or information, the better the design is. Moreover, if the designer strips the elements to the bare essentials as he or she thinks should be, the audience may have different opinions; it may lead to the result that the audience can't understand because of too little elements. So how to balance the elements used, neither too Minimalistic nor cluttered, is crucial. Besides, contrast is indispensable in a design. Minimalist design must take advantage of efficient contrast to make the design outstanding and readable.

MINIMALIST DESIGN IN GERMANY

Under Bauhaus's influence, the Germans lay particular emphasis on functionality and practicality which can be traced to the nation's philosophizing tradition. Bauhaus was a school which operated from 1919 to 1933 in Germany.

Combined crafts and fine arts, it was famous for the approach to design that it publicized and taught. The school stressed theory and practicum in foundation courses. The pupils were brainwashed through a series of rational straightforward visual training and re-established their new perspectives on perceiving the world. They were encouraged to have hands on experience in workshops, cultivating their practical skills. Even though this teaching method was considered odd at that time, it soon prevailed and became the singular pedagogical mode for modern art and design throughout the world.

After the school closed, the founders of the Bauhaus school migrated to America. Through teaching, they disseminated the ideology of Bauhaus which had revolutionary impacts on the architecture and industrial art pedagogy of the mid-20th century; it became a source of creative inspiration among students. It also had a tremendous impact on the architecture and industrial design sectors worldwide. Bauhaus style and genres are characterized by practicality and functionality. With values such as taking advantage of advanced technology and pursuing economic efficiency, it meets the needs of modern industrial production and people's lives.

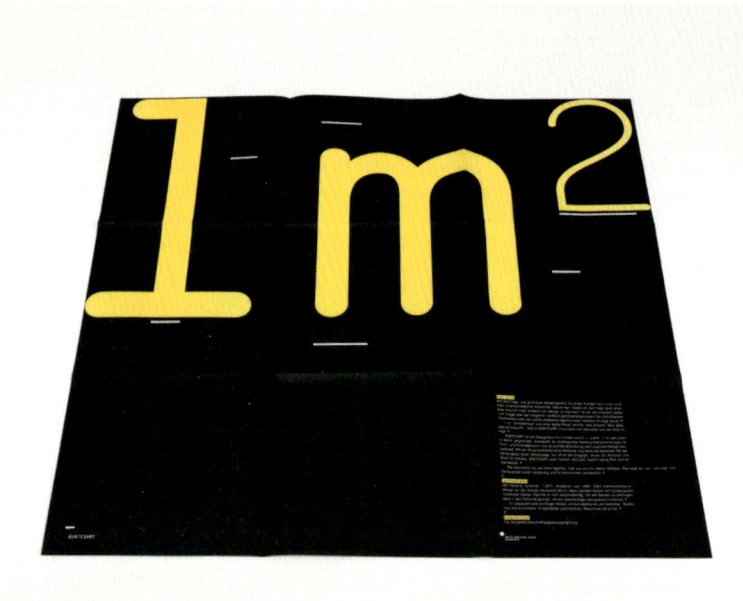

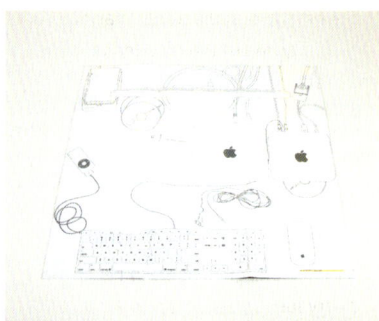

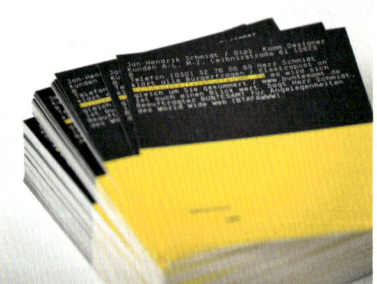

Client: BUNTESAMT
Studio: BUNTESAMT
Designer: Jan-Hendrik Schmidt

Berlin-based BUNTESAMT, a one-man graphic design office, consists of no more than a desk, 1m2 in size, and some utensils. As an alternative to large design agencies, BUNTESAMT appeals to mid-size companies and organizations alike by brushing aside its small size with high spirits and a bit of self-mockery.
Yellow and dark gray as the corporate colors and a strict grid system for the stationery are the basic ingredients of this branding. The typographical simplicity of the typewriter font and the government agency-like codes are broken up by humorous prose and the partially handwritten communication elements in the letter. The characteristics of BUNTESAMT are its personal style and its focus on what's essential for a great design. Small is sufficient.

Jan-Hendrik Schmidt   Designer of Buntesamt

Do you think your design of this project is Minimalistic ? How do you interpret the statement "Less is more" ?

The design of "BUNTESAMT" is Minimalistic. No pictures, no patterns. It mainly consists of two colors, some typewriter typography and a consistent paper stock. To be honest, this corporate design does not really need a logo to be understood as a brand. To me, good design is as little as possible and as much as needed. Design helps explain and visualize a product's function and gives information. So if you focus on that function, you should ask yourself which graphical ingredients are really essential and useful. That way you can figure out the needless freight and mere decoration.

How do you perceive Minimalist design ? Is it merely a fashion ?

I would not call it a fashion. I think Minimalist design is ageless because it is very functional. And it is nothing new. If you look at Otl Aicher's design for the 1972 Munich Olympic Games, you will see Minimalism at its best. That does not mean that everything has to be just white space without any colors or graphics. I am sure the look of Minimalistic design has changed. But the idea is still the same. For example, if you call icons a part of Minimalism, then, they have been used for more than 40 years. But their design has changed because everything has to have this glossy look and mirror effect nowadays. The purpose itself is still the same: how to depict a story or action by one pictogram.

As a global trend, how do people in your country react to Minimalist design ?

They react in two different ways. Some of them see brilliancy in the simplicity, while some say it is not worth the money. Even if Minimalistic design has a tradition in Germany, people do not deal with that fact naturally like in Switzerland or Denmark. Maybe it is a matter of self-confidence and part of the "German Angst". Some clients think that if they pay for design services, they have the right to expect as much design and decoration as possible.

I recently looked at the package design of a Danish organic flour company. They decided for a Minimalistic and clean graphical design composed of O-shapes to represent their product line. In Germany, it would be hard to find a company with such an attitude. I am sure that it needs some courage to decide for Minimalistic design in branding since your statement is very clear and to the point. If this is your corporate identity, then you have to stand by it with a self-confidence that shows "this is all we are and it is enough". In previous projects, I often heard deciders say "this is too risky for us" when it came to Minimalistic design. They were afraid that such a design might lower their chances of being successful in the markets. They did not think of the possibility to stand out, just like the Danish flour brand.

How do you see the effect of Minimalist design in a globalized world and different cultures ?

Minimalistic design has the ability to connect people in a faster way since it is easy to understand and brings information into focus. Some people feel that the lack of emotion makes it replaceable. But it has also a chance to work effectively for different cultures because of that simplicity.

Minimalist designs of different countries reflect different lifestyles or thinking of the people. How do these different lifestyles or thinking influence the Minimalist design in different countries ?

To me, the tradition of a Minimalist style depends on the culture and historic background of a country. For European people, everything in Japanese culture seems to be very subtle and calm. Scandinavian design seems to be very laid-back and open-minded. To me, it looks like there is no limitation and everything is possible. Sometimes I look at Danish design and I literally hear the designer say "Come on. Relax. It is just design." So this kind of Minimalism might be an analogy to their liberal thinking.

As I said I am not an expert in design history. When I think of German Minimalist style, Otl Aicher and the Hochschule für Gestaltung Ulm come to my mind. In the 1950s and 60s, his design was some kind of a re-start for German branding after the Second World War. Maybe his way of realistic thinking was part of the fact that everything had to be very functional for people to go on and start over.

MINIMALIST DESIGN IN JAPAN

The Japanese worship Zen, as a process of revelation, where nature is understood as the state of being of life prior to enlightenment. It means transcending common cognitive level and breaks away from common thinking mode in understanding world. The Japanese design is not a symbol. Neither does it pursue visual effects. It places a focus on harmony, serenity and low profile, being oneness with nature.

The similarity of Zen and Minimalist design is that both involve complex thinking and accurate calculation in order to realize the balance between form and function, design and raw material, material and spirit. Traditional Japanese design emphasizes economy and a great sensitivity to the natural environment. Due to the scarce natural resources of the country and dependence on massive imports of raw materials, the Japanese developed a long tradition in practicing simple living based on the reduction in natural resource usage and environmental impact. Their awareness of environment protection is highly influential on their aesthetic ideology and all areas of design, especially architecture design.

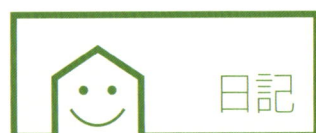 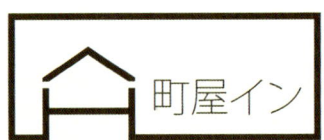 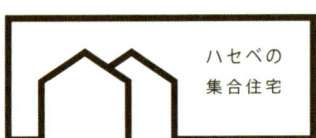

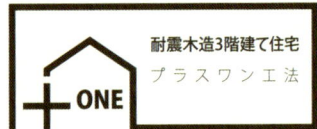 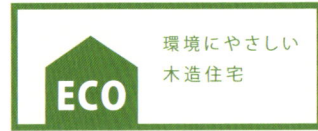 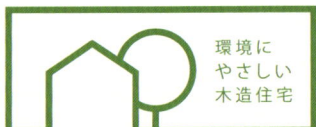

Client: HASEBE Co.,Ltd.
Studio: BCOME
Designer: Benigna Iwasaki

This is a corporate identity and website re-design proposal for HASEBE Co.,Ltd., a house maker in Tokyo, Japan. The challenge of this project was to give the company a new and modern appearance, so that it would differ from the style of average Japanese building company, appealing to a broader range of customers. Based on a fresh logo and icon design, BCOME provided the CI design and website proposal. The visual concept of the icon in the form of a simple house was to give the viewer an immediate idea of the company field. Thus, the logo can be easily incorporated in other parts of the corporate identity as a central theme. The uniform house icon, altering from section to section, is always recognizable and follows the idea of "simple is best" to give the company a steady identity base.

Benigna Iwasaki founder of BCOME

How do you interpret the statement "Less is more" in this project?

In one sentence: minimalize the design language in order to get the statement onto the point without any "accessory parts" to distract from the basic idea of the logo design.

As a logo is a very small creation, it is vital to have a clear message you want to transport with it. The shown sample, an abstracted house, is an approach combining the company / brand name with a visual form of what the company stands for: building houses. Our requirements for this project were universality (internationally acceptable), simplicity and differentiation (also from the older existing logo design).

How do you perceive Minimalist design? Is it merely a fashion?

Straight forward, simple and honest, and thus internationally comprehensible, that is what I love about Minimalist design and these are the standards I also try keep.

In my opinion, it is definitely more difficult to create something coherent with just a few lines, colors, items, whatever you create, may it be graphic, products, interior, architecture and so on. But if you manage to get to the essence of an idea and bring it into a simple and easily understandable form, then you have created something really good. I do not think that Minimalist design is merely a fashion; it has existed for too long and has proven to be quite sustainable. On the contrary, I think it already has quite deep roots, so I am very positive that even though there are many outgrowths in the world of design, Minimalist design will never disappear but stay as a constant base of "good design".

As a global trend, how do people in your country react to Minimalist design?

Due to the fact that I live and work as a German designer in Japan, I can probably say more about Japan than Germany. Traditionally, Japanese design is very Minimalistic, but many actual designs nowadays are quite overloaded. Still and maybe due to the tradition, there is a basic understanding and maybe even aspiration of Minimalist design. Here in Japan, I got the feeling that there are a growing number of (young) people, not only from the creative branch, who are very much interested in fresh and Minimalistic design, especially in product design. People often like to look at a finished Minimalist brand design, but if it comes to the development of their own brand, maybe they fear that Minimalism might limit the ability to carry the messages they want to be transported by the logo. In Minimalism, you have to trust a simple logo to present your brand universally, but some people need some courage to engage with the concept of it.

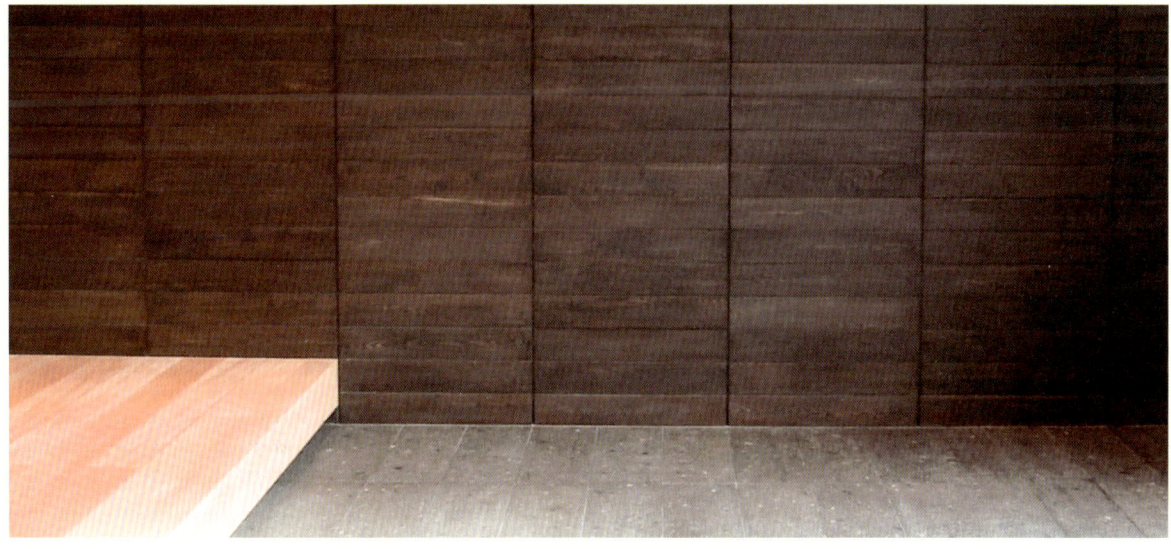

MINIMALIST DESIGN IN SWITZERLAND

The modern Minimalist design was first booming in the Netherlands. With its simple and practical forms, natural materials, it has become the main stream design style among north European countries. What's amazing is that its back to the basic style has become a standard for the design world. Not only has it crept into the everyday life of the north Europeans, it also has spread and made great impacts on designers worldwide.

The Swiss are known for their efficiency. They are highly efficient at work because they are enthusiastic about creation. They strive to improve technology so that they can leave the laborious work to machines. The term "frugal" has multiple meanings to the Swiss. First of all, it means practicality. It can be interpreted as the national characteristics. It is also a reflection of the moral virtue valued by the people. Northern Europe in 19th century was way behind developing countries like the United States and others. Poverty and scarce natural resource had shaped their life values. Harsh living condition had taught them how to make the best out of life.

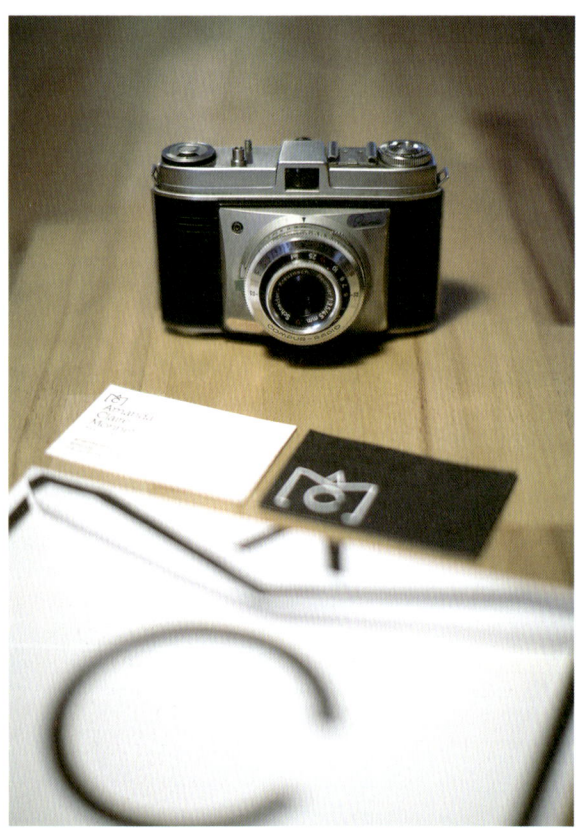 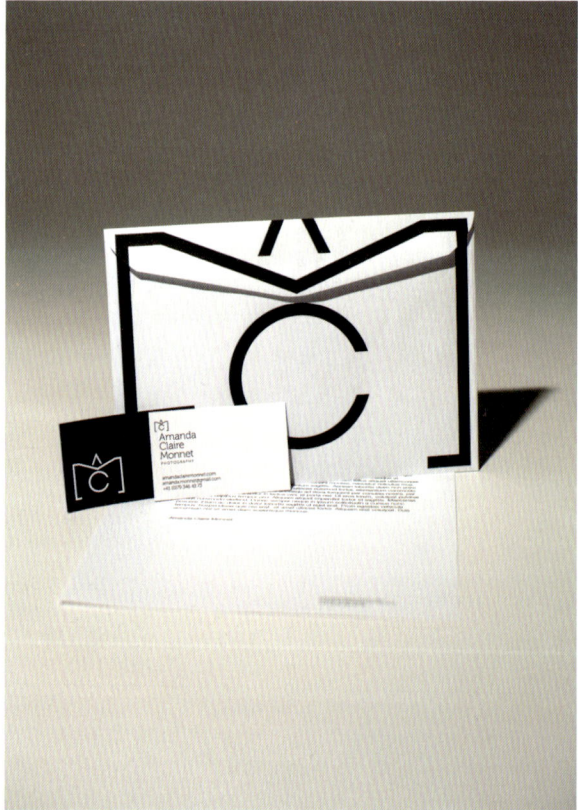

Client: AMANDA CLAIRE MONNET
Designer: Alessio Rattazzi

Amanda Claire Monnet is a Swiss photographer who asked Alessio Rattazzi to realize a new logotype for her activity. In the initial brief, Amanda gave Alessio complete liberty to decide which was the best way to represent at its best her work. She just said that she loved her full name to be involved, so Alessio started working with the three words and their initials. One of the things Alessio loves most to do is playing with letters, to find a way to transform letters into images that anyone who looks at the work can receive the message in the shortest possible time, and that's what Alessio tried to do with this logotype; it represents in a clean and direct way the art of the photographer, using as few elements as possible.

Alessio Rattazzi

What were your considerations when you chose Minimalist branding ?

I think a brand should always be clear. I'm not saying that has always to be black and white, but Minimalistic in a clever way. It keeps just a few important elements that allow the viewer to perceive what the designer wants to broadcast in the quickest possible time and let the logo remain in the viewers' mind. So I think a brand has always to be minimal.

As a global trend, how do people in your country react to Minimalist design ?

The Swiss design is recognized worldwide as Minimalist. There's a French writer's quote that I think describes perfectly the Swiss Minimalist style: "Perfection is achieved, not when there is nothing more to add, but when there is nothing left to take away."
   Many Swiss designers were the pioneers of Minimalism that we find in many of today's artworks, so I think the Swiss people are more accustomed than others to face with this kind of design. The Helvetica, for example, was designed in Switzerland by Max Miedinger in the 1957, but it's still the most widely used font for disparate purposes; this success is due to its simple, clean and Minimalist design.

How do you see the role of globalization or cultural clashes play in Minimalist design ?

The globalization is flattening and merging the different cultures and in the future, unfortunately, the world will be more and more globalized. This will bring to two main consequences in branding world: the first is positive after all because every person will have the same fruition of design, simplifying our work because a European will perceive the same message to an Asian or an American. The second is, in my opinion, very sad because it will forget the national cultures, making it difficult, if not impossible, to differentiate a European product to an Asian one. Can you imagine a Swiss cheese being advertised in the same way as a Japanese one?

30 Designers
// Less is More

1. My view to "less is more" thinking is related to world full of communication, looking at bigger frame of everything, not just my work in progress isolated from everything. Simplicity is needed wherever you look, spaces, design, branding, advertising. It forces us to keep our focus when we solve problems. "Less is more" is not always the most minimalistic solution. Actually it might not look minimal, but it works well. Good design is sometimes almost invisible. "Less is more" is powerful when it is relevant, but not an answer to every brief.

- *Marko Salonen* (Finland)

2. It is very easy to overdo a project. One unnecessary detail can spoil the entire design and the final project. Hence, designers should bear in mind that refrain themselves from garnished details and elements during the process of creating a project while following the rules of simplicity and functionality.

- *Beza Projekt s.c* (Poland)

3. The idea "Less is more" is similar to a Zen painting. It takes a lot of time to become a master, but then even a trait brings to perfection. What we are discussing is not about quantity but about quality. And the main is the internal content.

- *ONY Studio* (Russia)

4. A pure identity is not only sustainable, but also fashionable. Less is more also communicates the environmental part—less ink, less plastic.

- *Heydays* (Norway)

5. Less is not more. Less is less. Less is the objective. Refinement is the product of informed, reductionist contemplation. When superfluous triviality is removed, a thing's essence is what remains.

- *Berger & Föhr* (U.S.)

6. We always aim to give our design room to breathe within the space it occupies, by doing this it allows a clear hierarchy to be created. The concept "Less is more" can be carefully achieved using necessary graphic elements in a balanced and harmonious way.

- *Motherbird* (Australia)

7. The less is more concept, responds to the idea of knowledge of the product or brand. If you know what you want to communicate, your design ends up being more simple and direct. It is not about saying less, but saying the necessary.

- *Atipus* (Spain)

8. We believe that voidness is an essential element in graphic design because it serves to focus on subjects, words and images. It also serves to give order and hierarchy.

- *makethatstudio* (Italy)

9. It doesn't mean that less time was invested to build up the concept, to the contrary, sometimes it´s harder. It´s just that each element is there with a purpose and this purpose at the end is to transmit a feeling or communicate something in an appealing way to the eye.

- *M.CANTU* (Mexico)

10. "less is more" keeps me honest as a designer because I must focus on and communicate only the fundamental values and qualities of my client's product or service.

- *Be Friendly* (Australia)

11. Less is only more when you start with a strong idea or concept for the development of the design process.

- *Pete Rossi* (UK)

12. A perfectly executed and constructed minimal design should stem from an aesthetic decision supported by solid grounds.

- *Anagrama* (Mexico)

13. "Less is more" is a great idea or goal to work towards that's easier said than done. It requires a discipline and intention to strike a balance between austere and interesting.

- *Ghost* (Australia)

14. The minimalist design should be clear and easily understood one in order to humorously convey the message and incorporate element of playfulness as it compels the viewers to interact and have fun with it.

- *Chris Trivizas* (Greece)

15. Every project demands its own vocabulary. Its own balance, its boldness and its own space.It is the essence of the details that define it. Not more, Not less.

- *Blok Design* (Canada)

16. Less is more is the golden rule in design. Any design element should help convey that essence, otherwise it is abundant.

- *Lesley Moore* (the Netherlands)

17. Whether to simplify the design is not important to me. An effective design itself would eventually eliminate the excessive. So i suspect the idea that equates simplicity with impressiveness.

- *6D-K* (Japan)

18. The simplicity of style allows past and future artwork to breathe with clarity and an assured elegance.

- *Root* ((UK)

19. It is not just about being eco-friendly. As a graphic designer, we should think of our planet and take care of it.

- *Futura* (Mexico)

20. Every day, the world produces so many designs. Because of this, it gets harder and harder to produce relatively original design especially if one decides to use minimalist design language.

- *Mirko Ilic Corp.* ((USA)

21. As Philippe Starck puts it: "The designer today should not help to produce more- he has to help produce fewer and better things. There is a beauty, an aesthetic, and a philosophy of less."

- *Dennis Müller* (Denmark)

22. It is to empty a space in design to let viewers feel and think.

- *Masaomi Fujita* (Japan)

23. To talk with the inner self, you need to keep the things in front of you at a distance for a while.

- *Yuta Takahashi* (Japan)

24. Typography and the "white space" are essentials to create clever and elegant designs.

- *Isusko* (Spain)

25. By removing all unnecessary decoration and displaying only one large pasta ,you cant misunderstand the content.

- *Stellan Rexmark* (Sweden)

26. "Less in more" means less design, more ideas.

- *Interbrand* (Australia)

27. It is the best way to define a brand in simple and economical style.

- *Graphical House* (UK)

28. "Less is more" is to eliminate all unnecessary elements.

- *Ajda Bevc & Petra Bukovinski* (Slovenia)

29. Less expression is More imagination.

- *sekiura design* (Japan)

30. A simple design engages viewer's curiosity.

- *Bailey Lauerman* (USA)

武蔵野美術大学

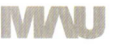 Musashino Art University

JAPANESE PAINTING, PAINTING, PRINTMAKING, SCULPTURE, VISUAL COMMUNICATION DESIGN, INDUSTRIAL, INTERIOR AND CRAFT DESIGN, SCENOGRAPHY, DISPLAY AND FASHION DESIGN, ARCHITECTURE, SCIENCE OF DESIGN, IMAGING ARTS AND SCIENCES, ARTS POLICY AND MANAGEMENT, DESIGN INFORMATICS

The Hidden World

Daigo Daikoku

Art Director at Daikoku Design Institute
Awardee of JAGDA New Designer Award 2011

◀ With the aim of emphasizing the role of the art university as a venue for creative activity, the message was condensed into the beauty of color. The diverse potential of art's expressive activity was captured in ovals with soft gradations.

I believe design has been endowed with the ability to convey the meaning that words fail to describe. Design plays various and diversified roles in today's society. As a designer myself, I am involved in different fields such as graphic design, video and space design, yet, I constantly remind myself to be conscious of the universality in my design. One can display as many as 100 truths about something. But if they are not well communicated, there a shadow will cast on them, which makes it even more difficult to get to the clear images of the truths.

In a world full of different values, to identify the essence among them and to hold tight to it, I believe, is of the greatest importance. Being not a mere superficial visual communication technique, minimalist design is in fact an act to pinpoint such an essence. In other words, minimalist design asks designers, relying on their own aesthetic sense, to boldly discard the excessive and secondary elements, and get to the really important elements.

A good minimalist design has many things hidden under its effortless surface. Exactly because of the minimal expression, the viewers' imagination space is widened, which leads them to freely explore deeper in the hidden world.

Noh, a classical Japanese musical drama which is similar to Kabuki, is a stage performance that removes all redundant elements and focuses on the true aesthetics. Even in Japan, few people watch Noh performance. But once you watch it, you will find it interesting and mesmerizing. If you do not see through the surface and try to understand those continuous subtle moves, you might find it tedious. But just watch calmly for about 30 minutes, you will notice and experience its mystery and profound meaning in its tranquility. From the delicate expression changes on the faces of the Noh performers, you can feel all the human emotions. At this point, the Noh stage becomes dynamic and interesting. Viewers will make every effort to use their five senses to experience the subtle yet exciting changes in the air and then can realize how sensitive the five senses are. This is when the heart is touched and shocked.

When the smallest change or element reveals the most, people are touched the most and such experience is engraved in the memory. With the sensibility of a viewer, one tiny yet important element works magic, with few words needed in the description. To put it in another way, one's curiosity can be triggered by a very little element, which is the very base of the provocative nature of Noh performance. Minimalist design in itself is the output of an aggregation of various energy and thoughts that impress and touch a heart.

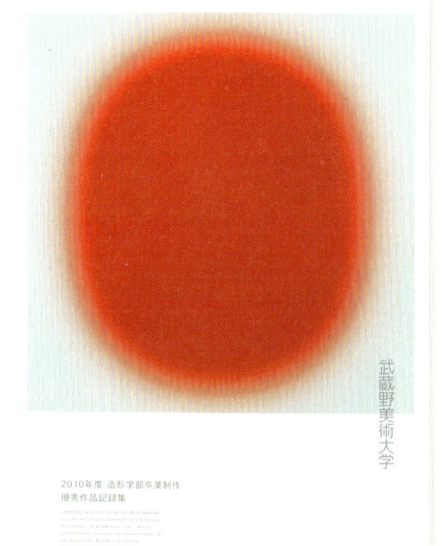

2012年度 入学試験ガイド

Musashino Art University

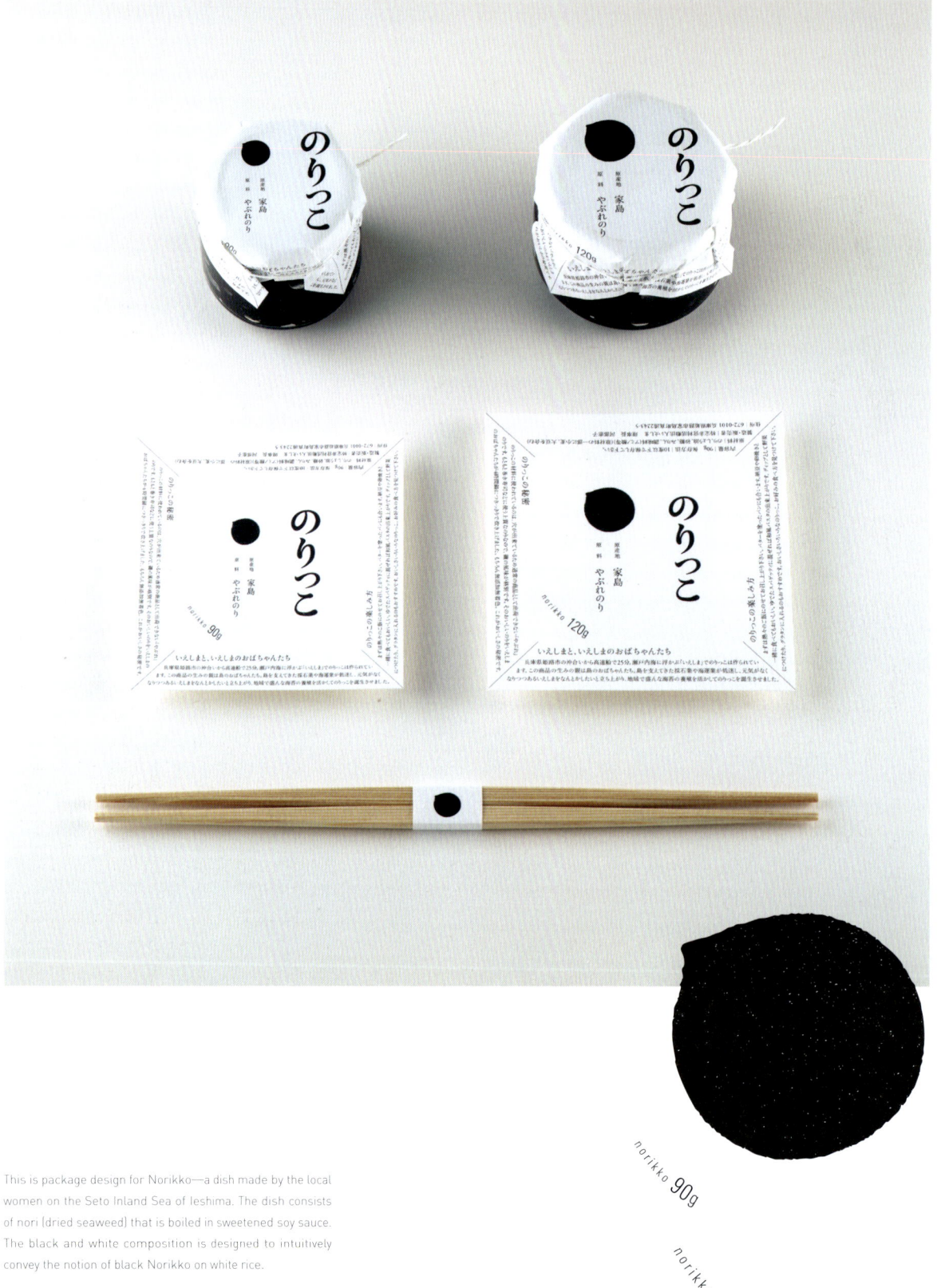

This is package design for Norikko—a dish made by the local women on the Seto Inland Sea of Ieshima. The dish consists of nori (dried seaweed) that is boiled in sweetened soy sauce. The black and white composition is designed to intuitively convey the notion of black Norikko on white rice.

norikko 90g

norikko 120g

海と島と
のりっこ

When it comes to the concept of intelligibility and clarity in design, there is often doubt in my heart. Minimalist art has long been established as an expression technique in art. In the design world, however, minimalist design is often seen as a mere superficial outside. It doesn't mean intelligible or simple design. Under its simple and clear surface lies a much deeper and very mysterious world. We tend to lose interest to know something further once we are too familiar with it. Take my own experience as an example, since I was a child, I have been in contact with various drawings, films or photos, products or constructions, or even raw materials or characters, etc. The reason that they can hold my attention and attract me for long is the mystery and the unknown in them which keep inspiring me to learn more and to know further.

Modern society is filled with easily accessible information. In contrast, simple representation may not be able to provide sufficient information, which could create concern or uneasiness to people who have gotten used to large amount of information. But at the same time, it grabs the essence and charm to win your heart in the blink of an eye.

Japanese design is often regarded as the embodiment of minimalist design. Japanese designers may not be aware of a work 's minimalistic nature, yet the world has put it into the minimalist category. Not all Japanese designers agree on that thought though, which is probably because the Japanese look at design as an "expression" rather than a "solution". I agree with this. What really matters is not the thought or the idea but whether a pleasant and fresh scene can come to life after the work is done. I often remind myself to experiment and innovate, which, I think, is a duty entrusted to designers. To add dynamic design in the graphic, three-dimensional, video and space fields is, to me, a lifelong mission.

To know new things, of course, is crucial but we need to believe in the sense of the human body that is based on where one was brought up, the air and sunshine he or she has felt, and many things more. This sense brings up resonance, regardless of the change of eras or cultural background differences. A minimum stimulation can lead people to dig deeper of what's behind and to spontaneously capture the spirit and mystique of certain things, hence bringing happiness into daily life.

Minimalist design enables the viewers to be proactive, which is a spirit that will have long lasting influence on human lives and behaviors.

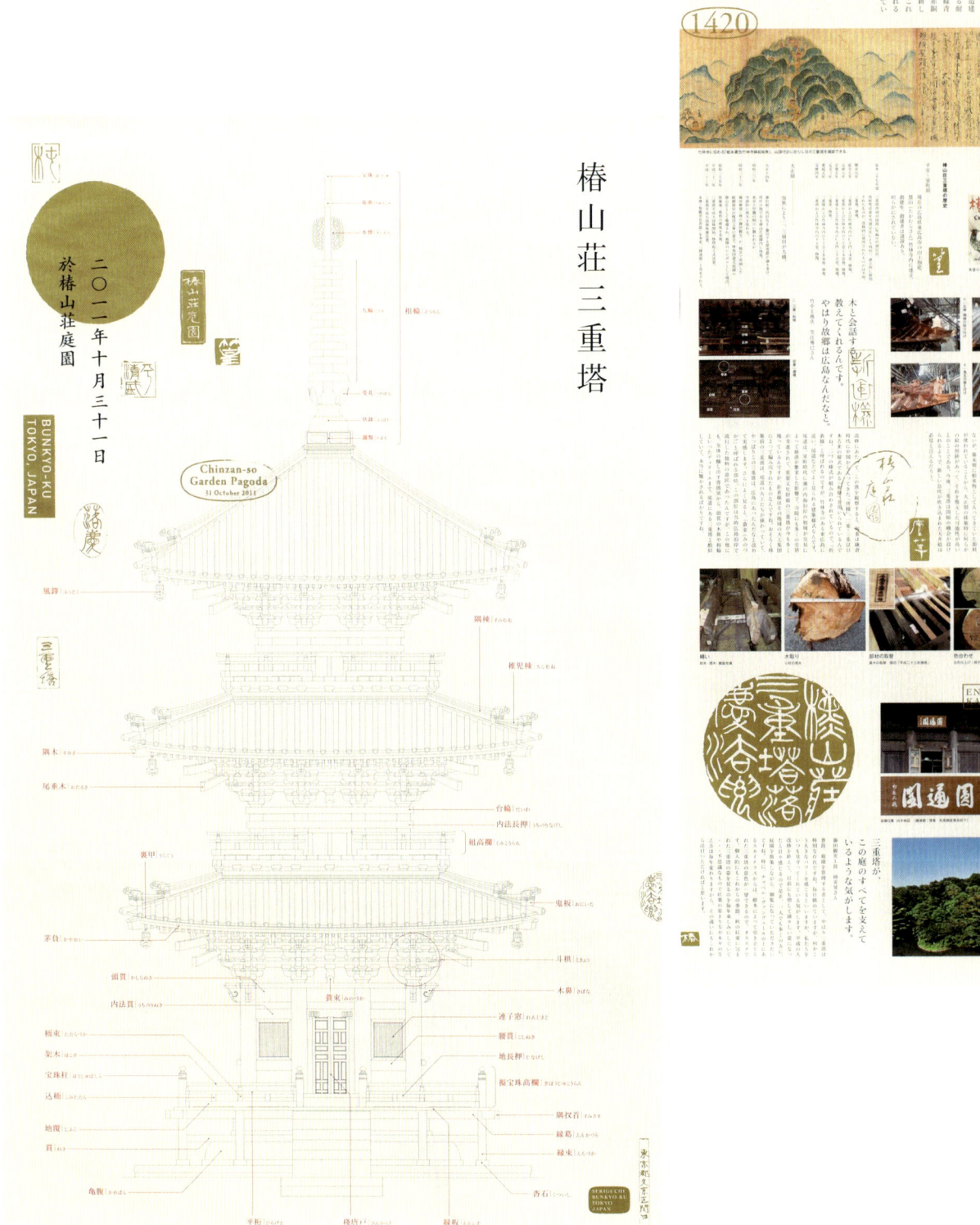

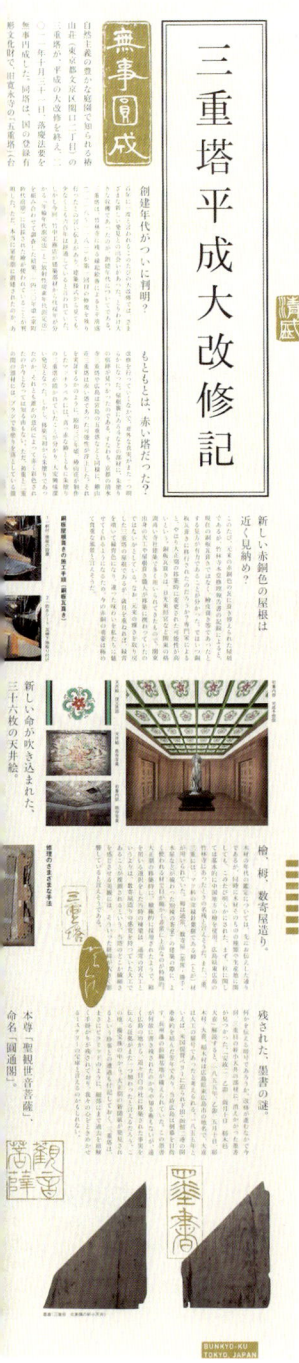

◀ These were communication tools for the Buddhist ceremony on the occasion of the completion of the Heisei repairs to the historical three-story pagoda at Chinzan-so Garden, made to be consistent with the three-pagoda motif used for the ground-breaking ceremony from the previous year. The "History" and "Camellia" volumes from the Chinzan-so Sensho (The Chinzan-so Library) book series were combined into a commemorative package along with an old-fashioned Japanese billboard-style poster that described the process and behind-the scenes episodes from the renovation of the pagoda.

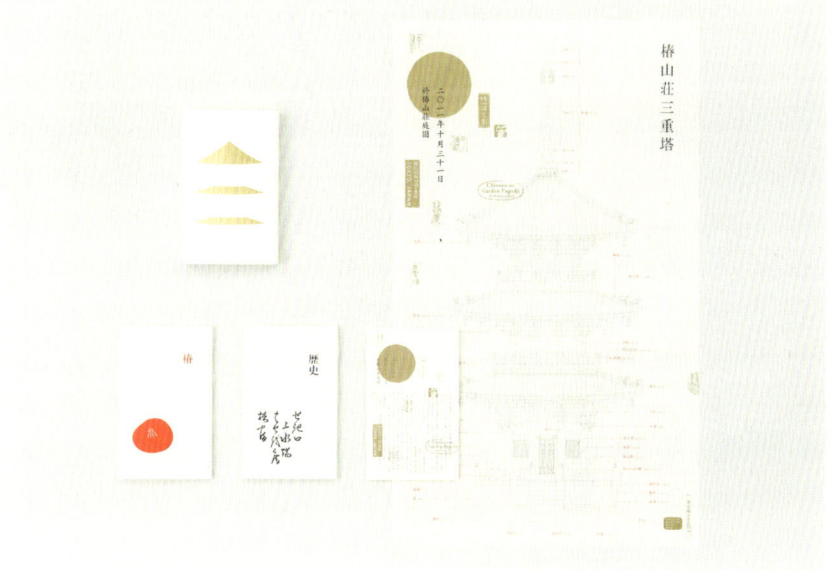

Anorak er et ... kun består av ... vi utvikler strate... løsninger til ... mekampanjer.

The Power of Limitations

Lars Kjelsnes

Co-founder of Heydays

◀ Anorak is a creative agency developing strategies and solutions for ad campaigns. They pride themselves on being creative first, working close with their clients throughout their projects. Heydays wanted to visualize the cut through attitude that represents their approach towards their clients. An energetic green line divides every surface, creating two equal surfaces—Anorak and the client they're working with. This green line appears in numerous ways, making each surface a new representation of this relationship.

* Milton Glaser
Born in June 1929, Milton Glaser is an American graphic designer, whose prominent designs include the "I♥NY" logo, Bob Dylan poster, and the logos for DC Comics from 1977 to 2005, etc.

The term "Less is more" can first be found in a poem written in 1855 by Robert Browning. It became known as the dictum of renowned German-American minimal architect Ludwig Mies van der Rohe. Often cited or re-phrased as "Less is more, more or less", "Just enough is more" (as American design legend Milton Glaser put it), and "More is more". But of course, in keeping with the saying itself, I believe, the original is clearly the best. An important aspect in dealing with simplicity and minimalism is to know what the essence is. The phrase implies that simplicity, clarity and peeling of layers help to get down to the original message, while adding layers on top is likely to cause confusion or mixed messages.

I wouldn't say we are minimalists. But our work embraces simplicity, purity and a minimal approach, which is to convey the idea and concept in the most essential way. Cutting down on unnecessary elements can lead to great things in the aspects of communication and sustainability.

In a society that is constantly filled up with more messages, ads, and choices each and every day, there come various attempts by creatives to

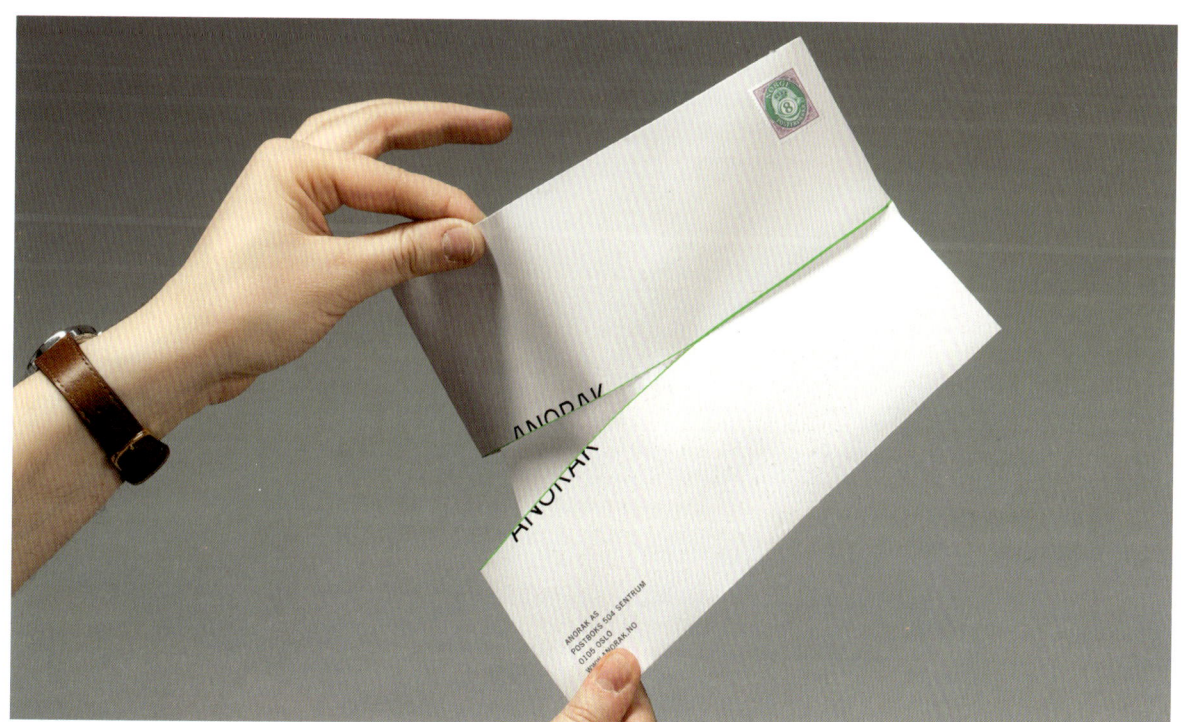

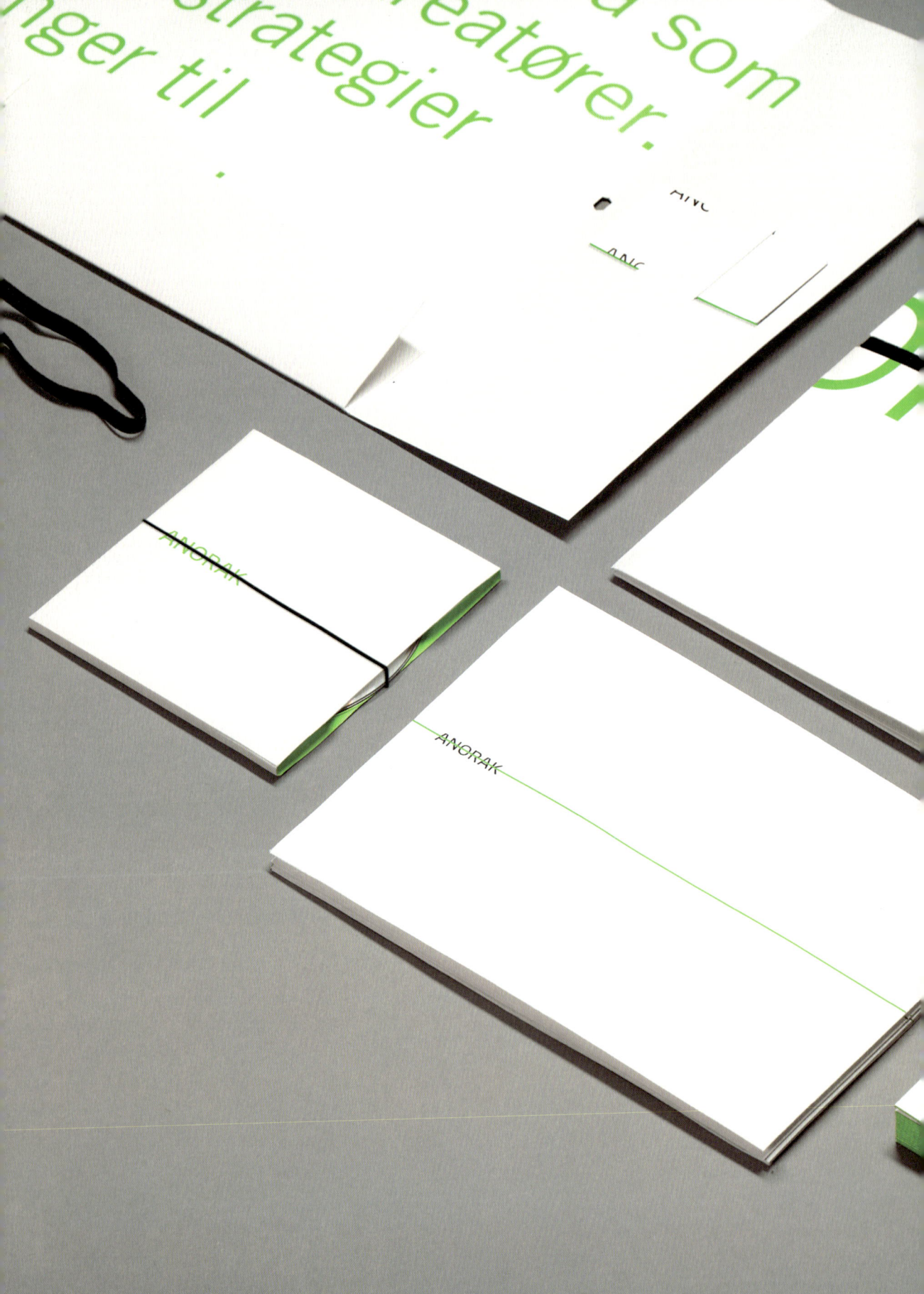

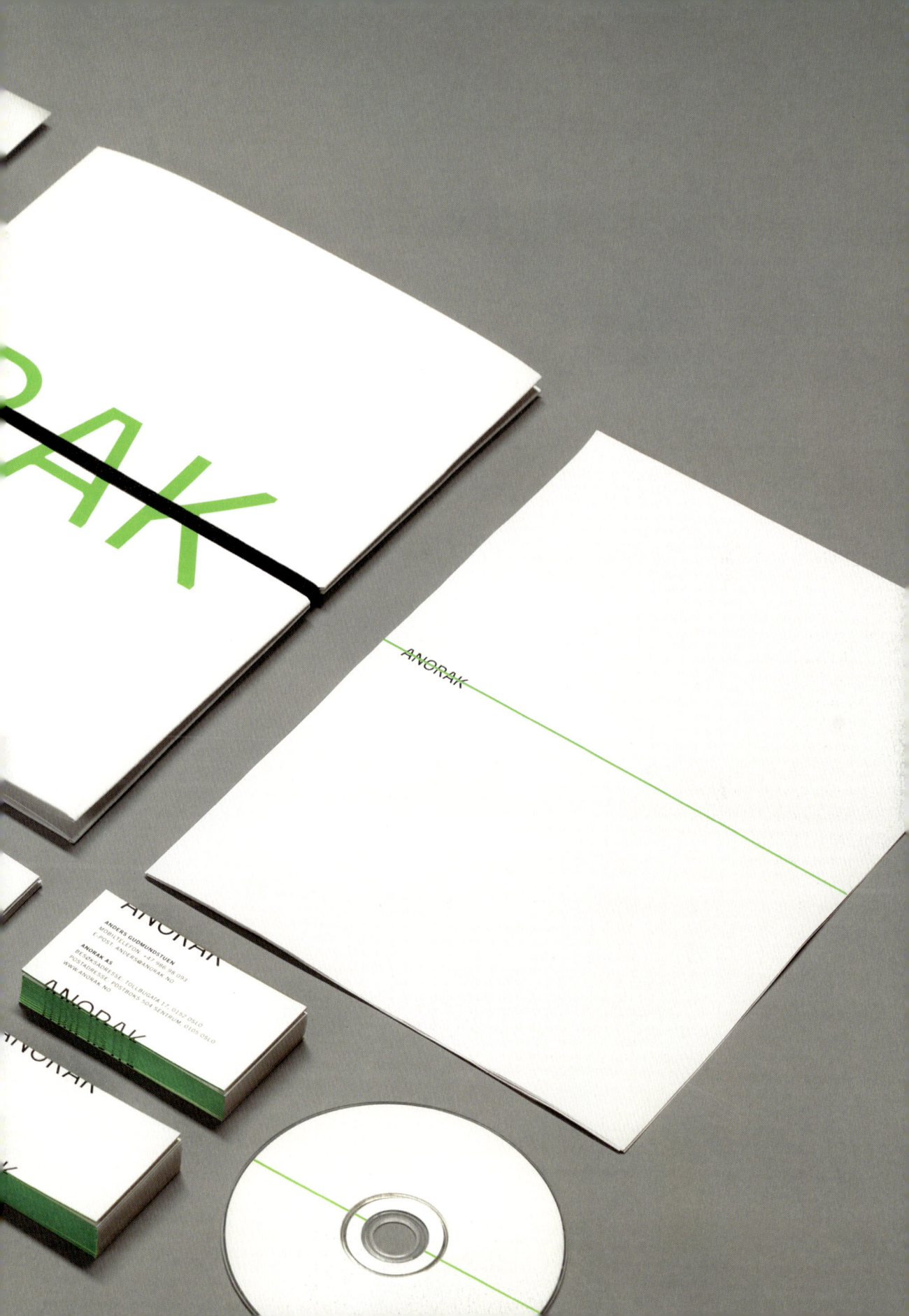

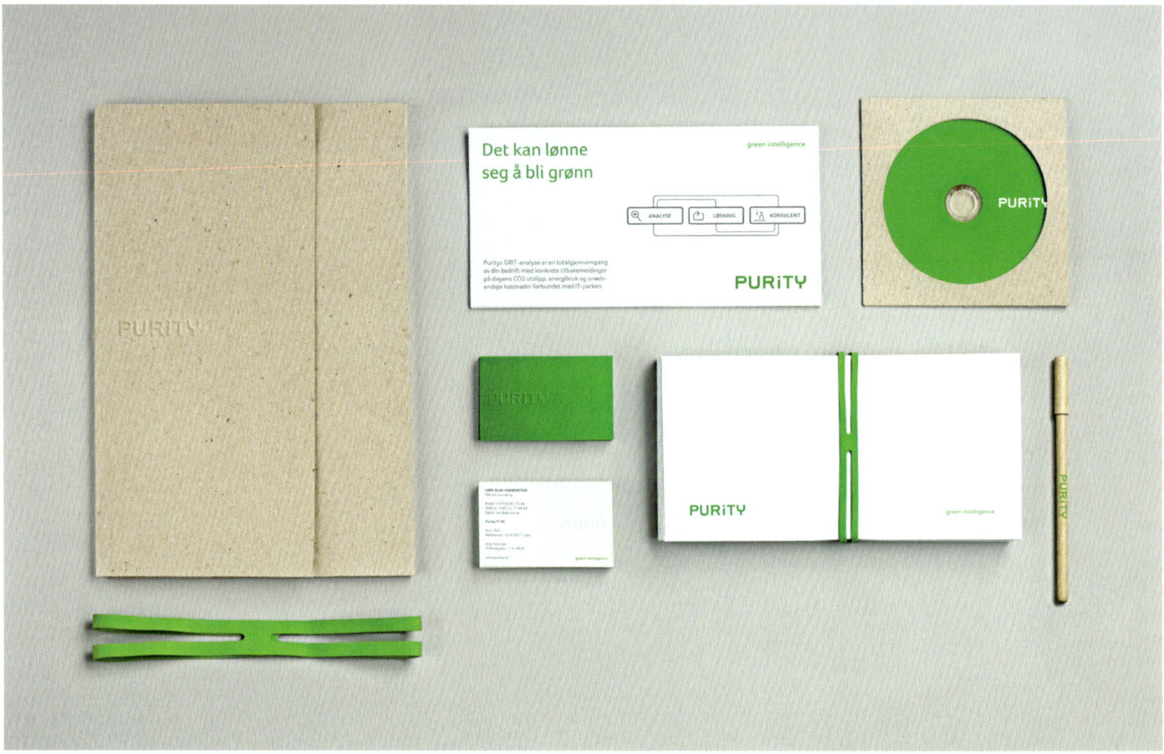

remove the redundant while retaining the essence. But it is not easy. Adding layers upon layers to what you're working on is, for a professional, the easy part. To be serious about simplicity and bold enough to make choices on what to cut is the tricky part.

In where we're from, Scandinavia, simplicity has been with us all along. We live right at the edge of nature, and when not working, we hike and ski in nature. Because of our close connection to nature, we've always been close to raw natural materials. Relying on the power of sturdy and natural materials is one of the reasons why we approach graphics with minimalism. Living with nature is an embodiment of a simple way of living, considering that in Norway our idea of a vacation often involves living and sleeping in the simplest conditions. We strive to design identities, stationery, brochures, posters and magazines that are sustainable and something you want to hang on to instead of

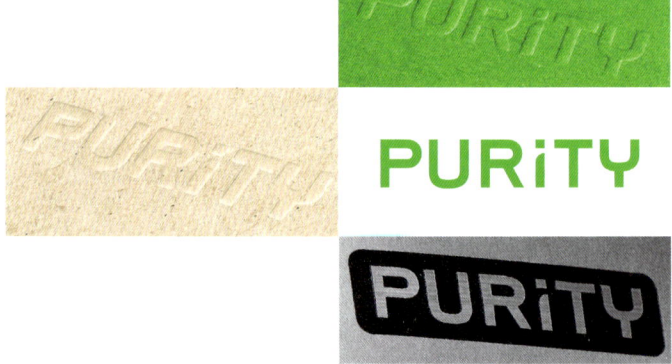

Purity is an IT-consultancy focusing on green IT, building energy efficient and powerful server solutions for larger companies. This helps on lower environmental impact, improved performance and reduced costs due to lower energy consumption. Heydays wanted to mirror their green philosophy in the identity with a strong symbol in a green landscape, using few print colors and recycled paper stock.

something you want to throw into the closest garbage bin. In this day and age, standing out might be more important than ever. But in the end you don't want to be the one who is obviously and desperately crying out for attention in a crowd. It's about coming up with the small surprises and nifty details that carry the message of the concept — be it a surprising choice of material or a completely new way of doing a stationery item.

For me, simplicity is a guideline in the many choices we are faced with nowadays. I have thousands of font files on my computer, among which about 20 to 30 will be used in my professional life. Although there are a lot of reasons for the choices I make every day, I think part of it has to do with "less is more". Choosing the path of simplicity, while good for conveying the core of a message, it works out great in terms of eliminating the bewildering amount of choices we have, without compromising.

When we work on certain projects, we use constrains, which can be seen as a branch of minimalism. Having total freedom can be the hardest. On some of our most open projects we work with constrains, dogma-like rules like using one typeface in black at size 12 points or using no color. For example, in a poster we did, one of these restrictions we set was that the one typeface should be set in 2 columns of 25 points and 250 pt. With such rules as a ground, we have been able to do some of our best works. As designer and writer Frank Chimero puts it in his book *The Shape of Design*: "Limitations are the fuel for improvisation, becoming the barriers that hold the sand in the sandbox so that we can play".

If I were to look at how minimalism influences my daily life, I need only look at the way I'm writing this article. I'm using an Apple iMac and iPad —two super simple products from a company that has achieved their success almost exclusively through simplicity. Both are basically just designed as black frames containing the screen, using highly durable, and quality materials. The keyboard and iPad aluminum are cut directly out of the hole in the iMac, screen—a simple, but clever production method. I'm writing in an app called iA Writer which is connected to iCloud, allowing me to continue writing on my iPad when riding the bus to and from work. This app is a breakthrough in that its features are deliberately cut down to focus on the app, sessence—writing. It feels like a true notepad for the computer, there are no possibilities for font management, colors or other configurations. While this app has been criticized for its lack of features, which I think is its true genius. With today's screens, computers, graphic tools and programming languages, you can basically add as much features and graphics as you would like. In the competitions in megapixels, screen sizes, new features and so forth, many forget to look at the essence to do one thing well.

There is an artwork by the Swiss duo Peter Fischli and David Weiss (who just passed away) from 1991 called "How to Work Better". Although it was painted on an office building in Zürich, and thus might carry a message aimed at the clichés of office work, I think it really integrates working with simplicity and minimalism in design. I really like the simple message and how it's directly aimed at work routines.

HOW TO WORK BETTER:
1. Do one thing at a time
2. Know the problem
3. Learn to listen
4. Learn to ask questions
5. Distinguish sense from nonsense
6. Accept change as inevitable
7. Admit mistakes
8. Say it simple
9. Be calm
10. Smile

Working in the spirit of "Less is more" and cutting down the unnecessary can lead to some of the best work this earth has seen.

How to work better

1.
Do one thing at a time

2.
Know the problem

3.
Learn to listen

4.
Learn to ask questions

5.
Distinguish sense from nonsense

6.
Accept change as inevitable

7.
Admit mistakes

8.
Say it simple

9.
Be calm

10.
Smile

Photo: Yuta Takahashi

Design Projects

Three

Studio: Nakajima Design | Designer: Hideki Nakajima

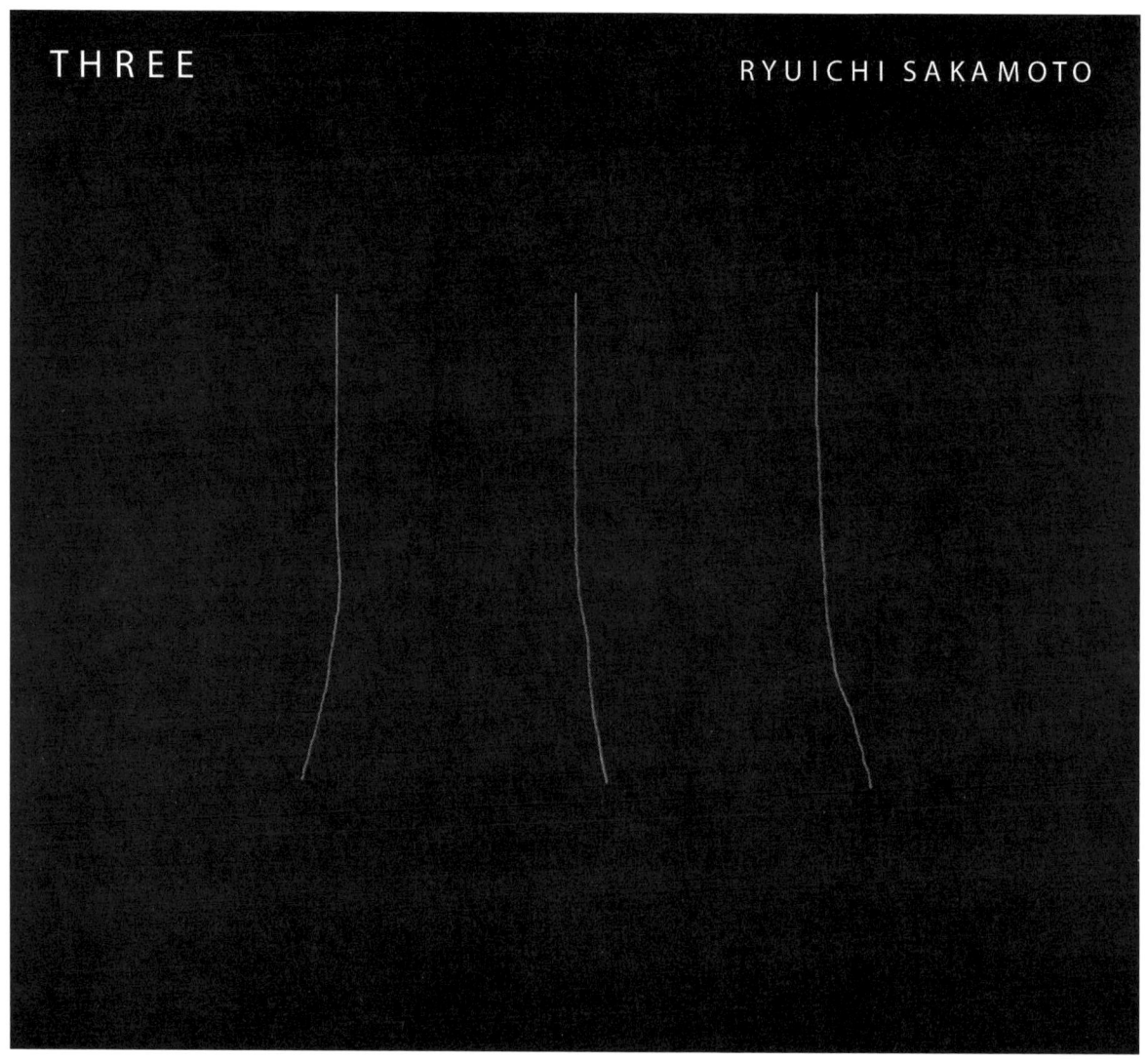

This album cover was created for Ryuichi Sakamoto's album Three, which featured the then new arrangements of Ryuichi's trio works in 2011. In the design, a combination of three lines were created to serve as an analogy to the trio performance by three artists. Since the word "three" is similar to "tree", the visual also resembles a tree growing from the ground.

Playing The Orchestra 2013

Studio: Nakajima Design | Designer: Hideki Nakajima

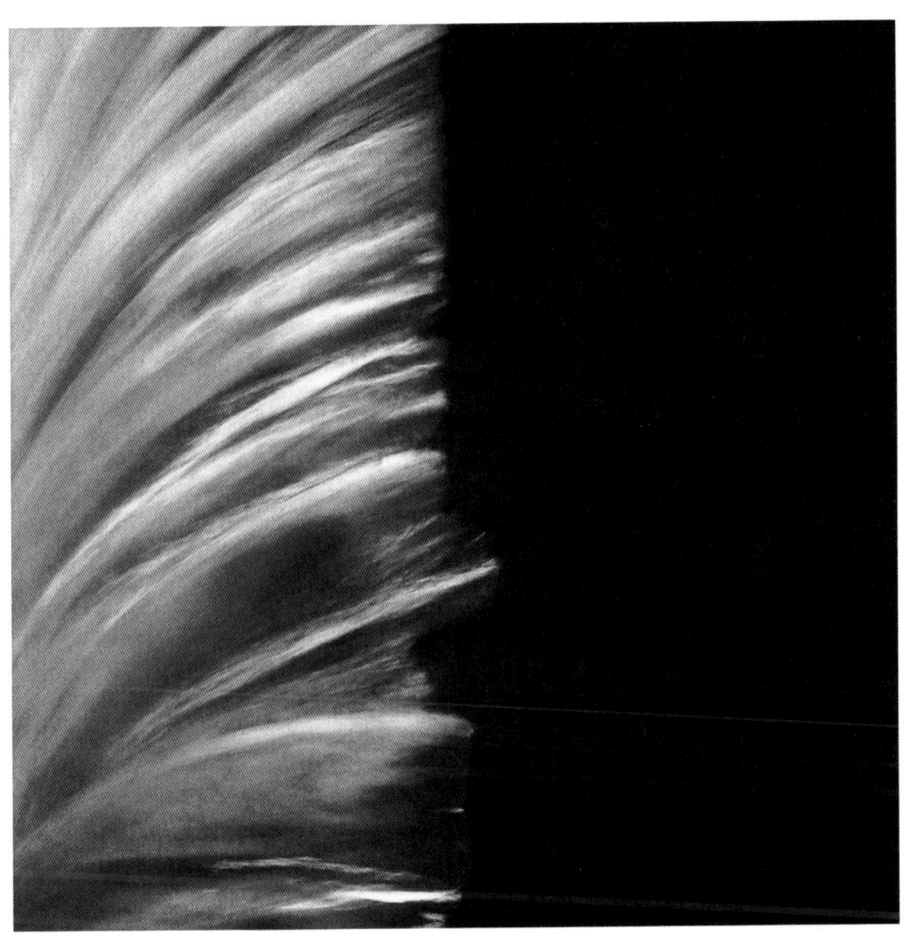

This work is a CD cover designed for Ryuichi Sakamoto's album Playing the Orchestra 2013, which contained the best tracks selected from Ryuichi's performances of full orchestra. A view of looking down on a waterfall from the top was adopted, upon which the image of the orchestra was overlapped in a way that it produced music that also flow linearly just as water running down.

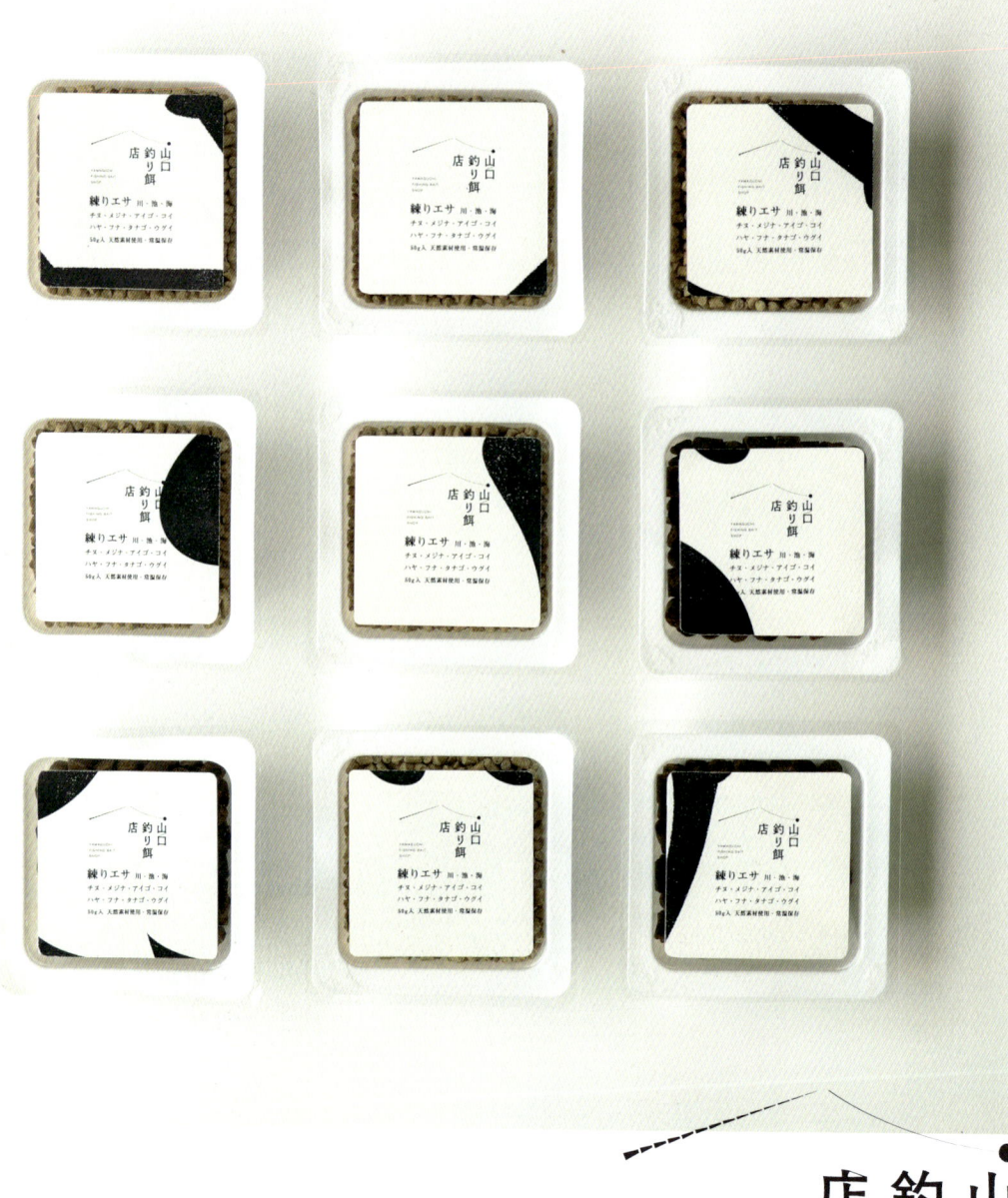

The Yamaguchi Bait Shop

Designer: Agata Yamaguchi

Brand Identity for this fishing baits shop was inspired by the silhouette of the kanji "魚" (pronounced "sakana", meaning "fish". By using only black and white, the designer intended to emphasize the outline of this character. In the poster, the designer also tried to break the original structure of the kanji and make its broken pieces collapse while maintaining its recognizability.

YAMAGUCHI
FISHING BAIT
SHOP

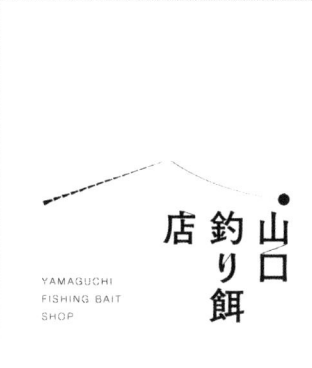

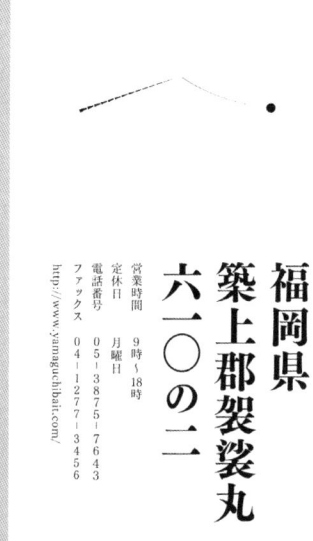

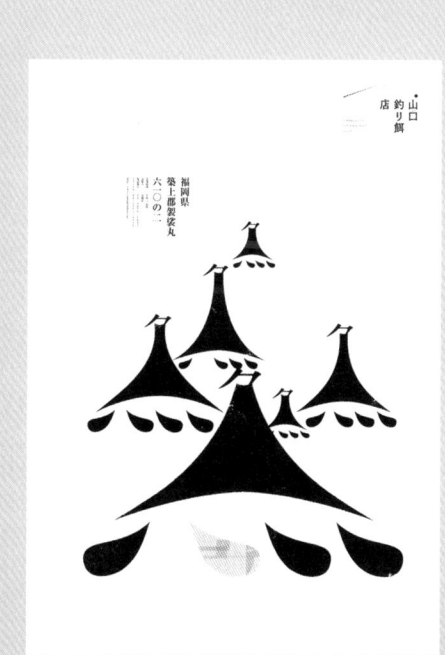

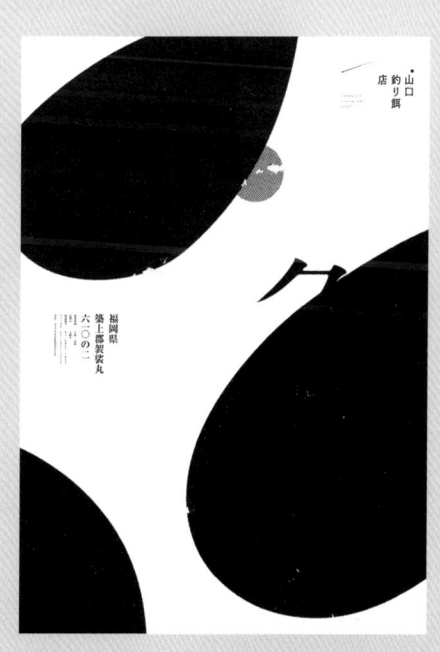

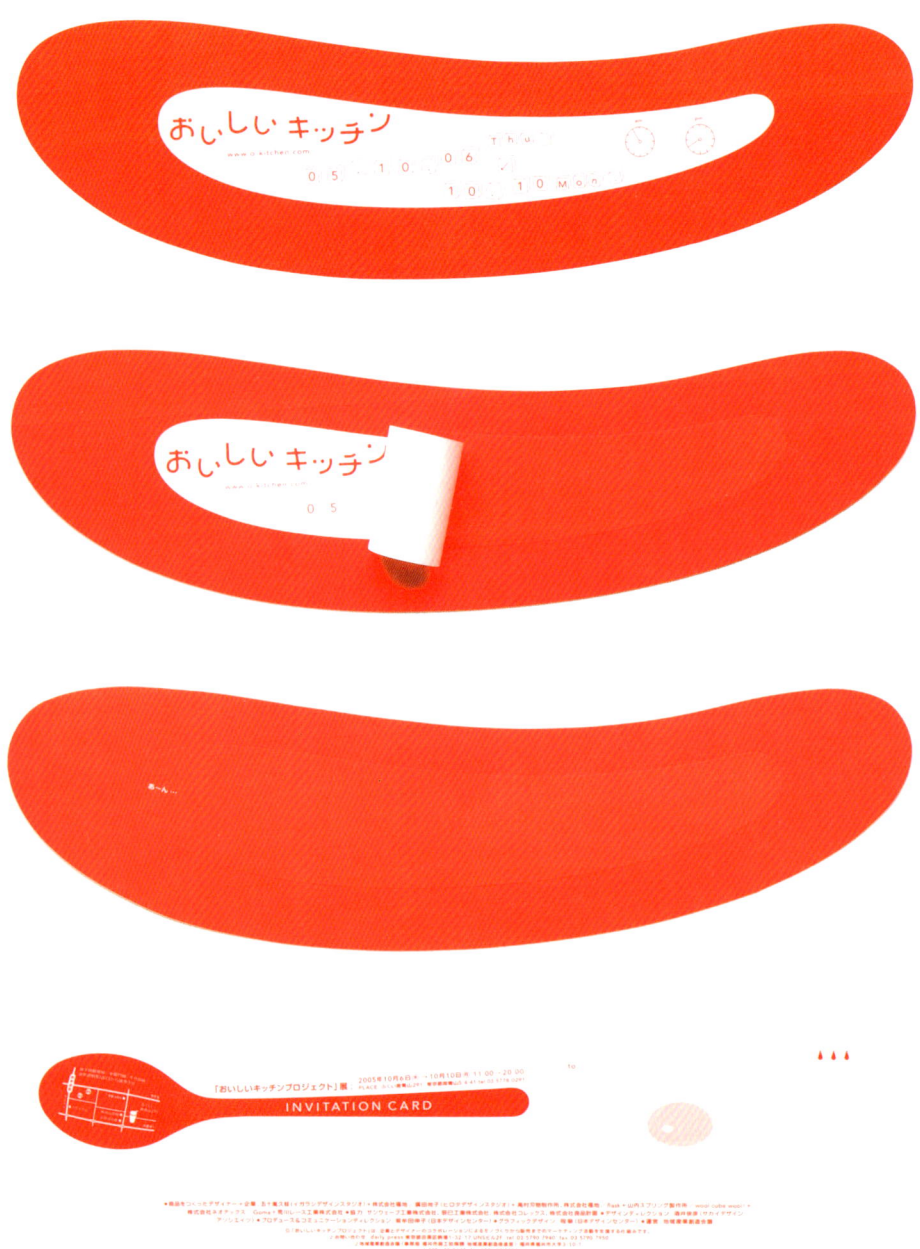

Oishii Kitchen

Studio: NIPPON DESIGN CENTER | Designer: Cheng Li

Oishii Kitchen Project is a brand of kitchen appliances brand developed by Fukui City´s local businesses and designers. It combines local traditional well-done technology with modern design, aiming to revitalize the local industry. The annual plan invites new designers and companies to participate and release their new products in exhibition.
Inspired by the name of the project, the logo was designed to resemble the smile on people's face when they are tasting good food. From cream biscuits, napkins to invitations, the designer gave expression and function to this shape and the work, exploring its possibilities in different ways.

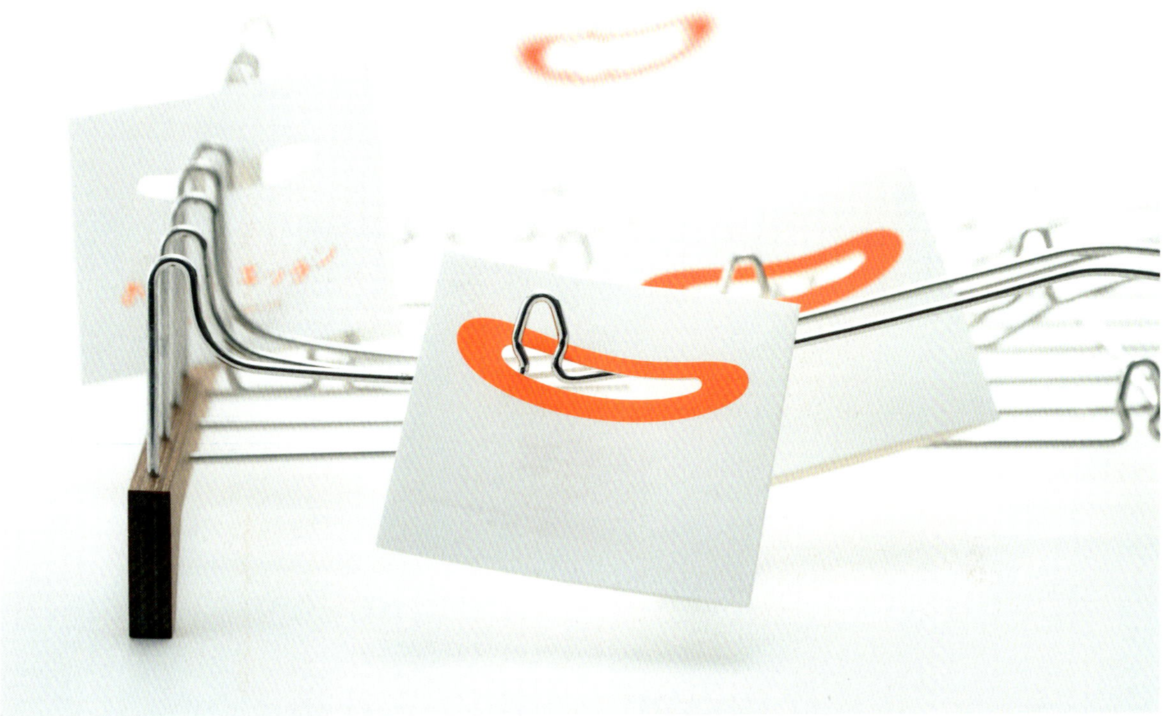

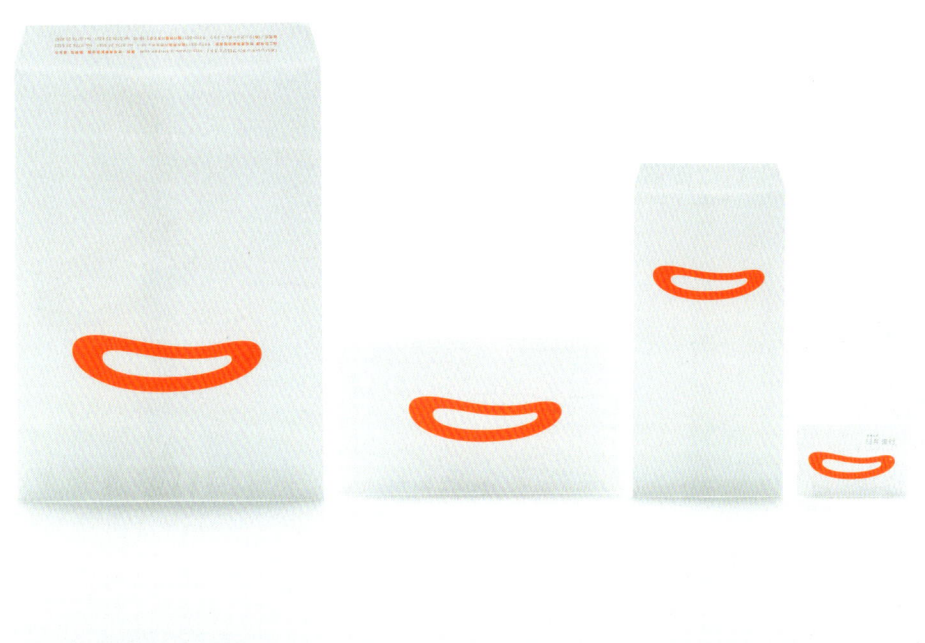

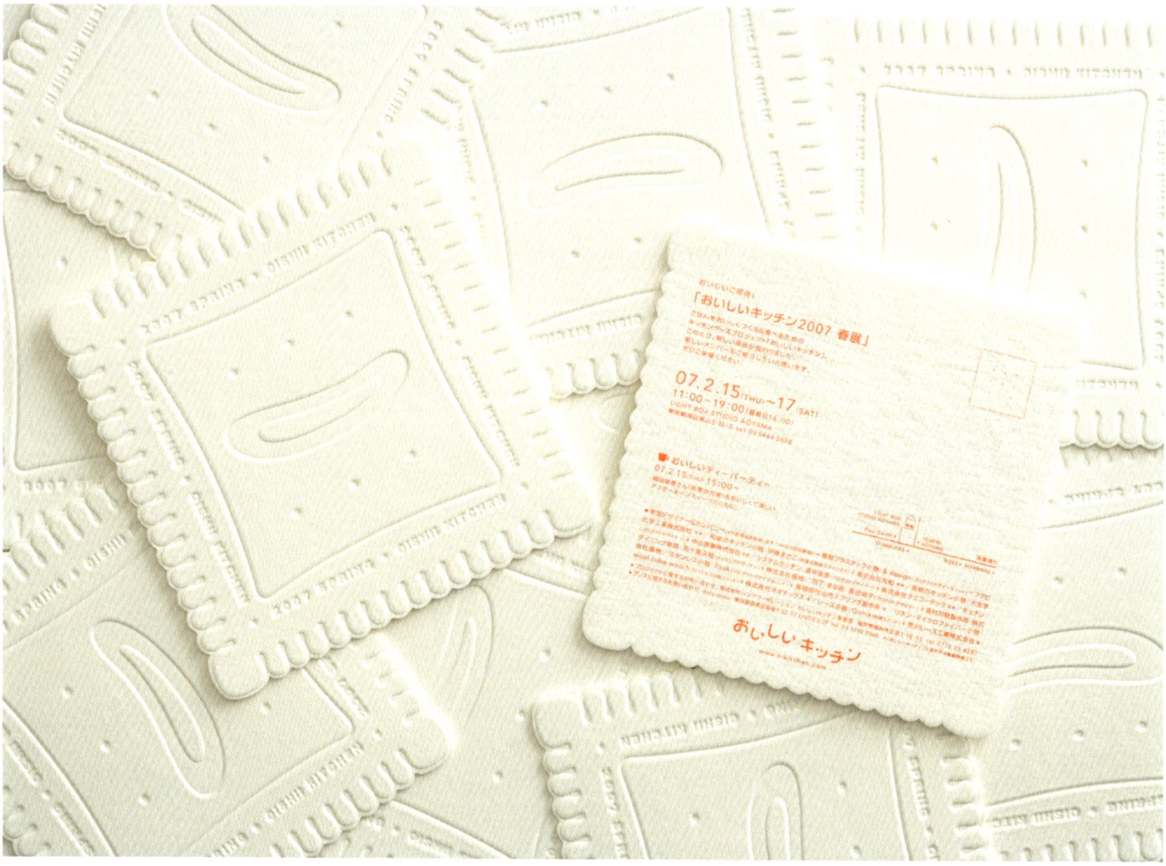

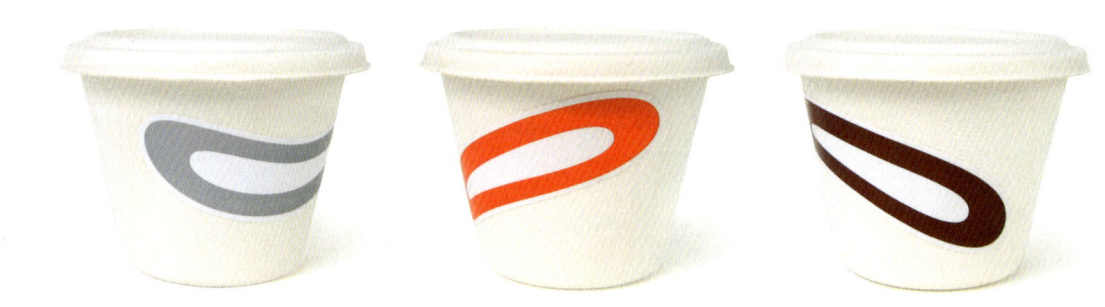

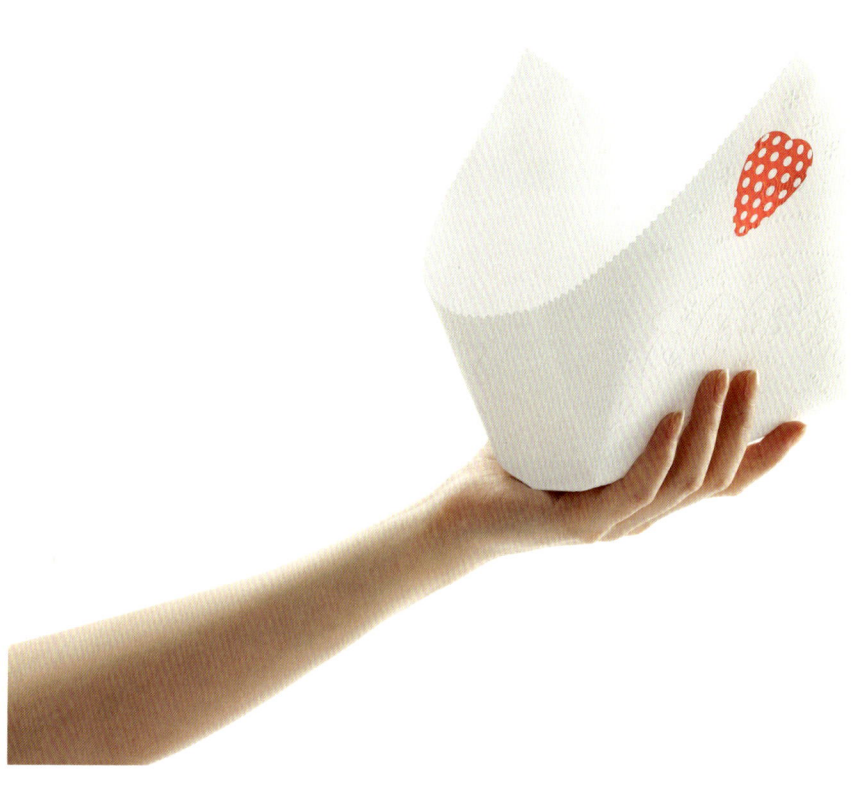

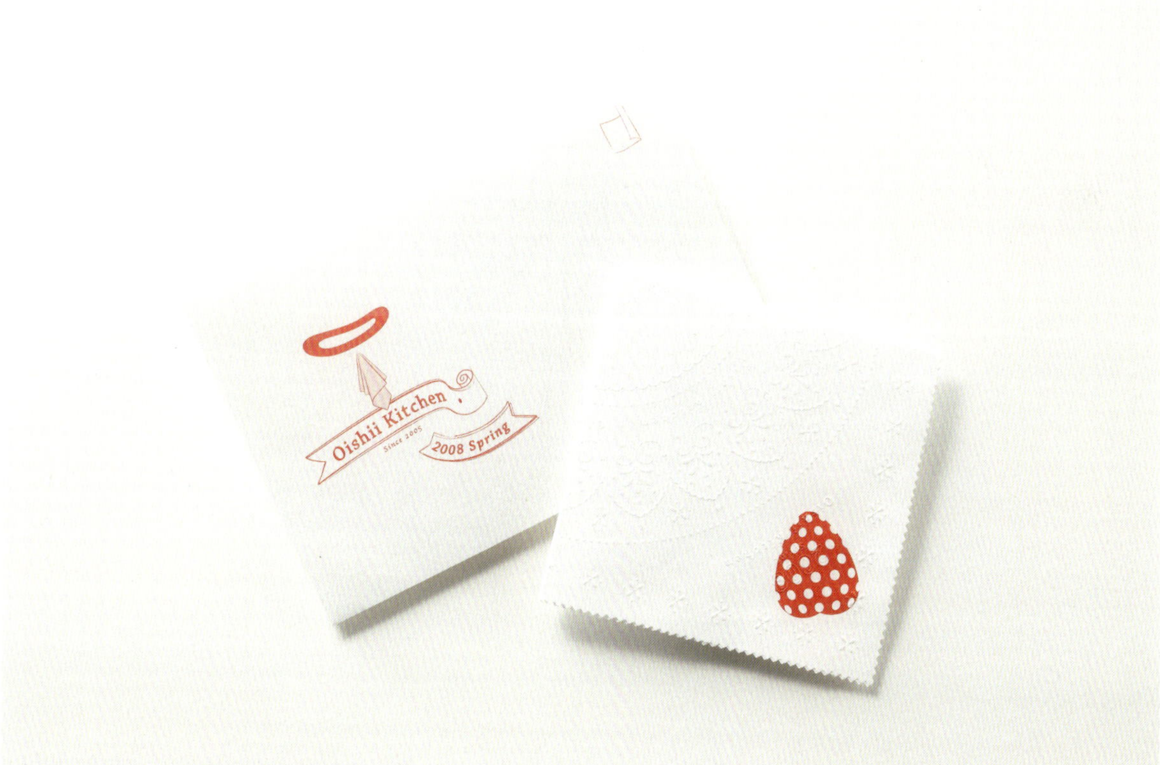

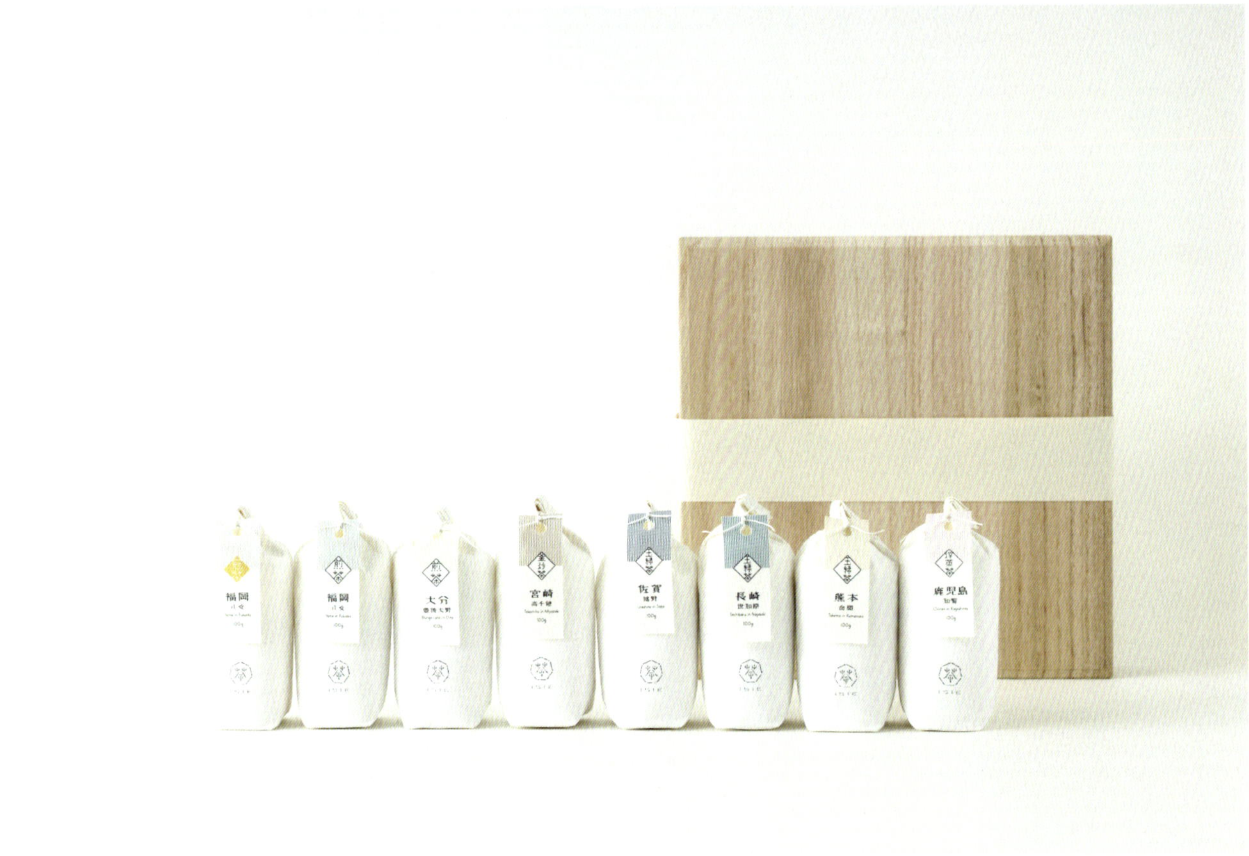

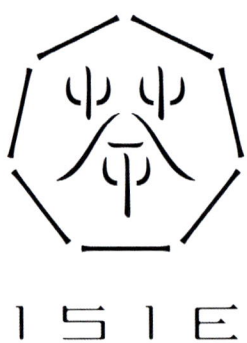

151E

Studio: Planning ES

The brand name is derived from the Japanese idiom "Ichi-go ichi-e", meaning that every meeting or every moment is once in a life time. The heptagonal shape of the logo represents the 7 prefectures in Kyushu, Japan. The colors of the packaging are drawn from the colors of 7 prefectural birds.

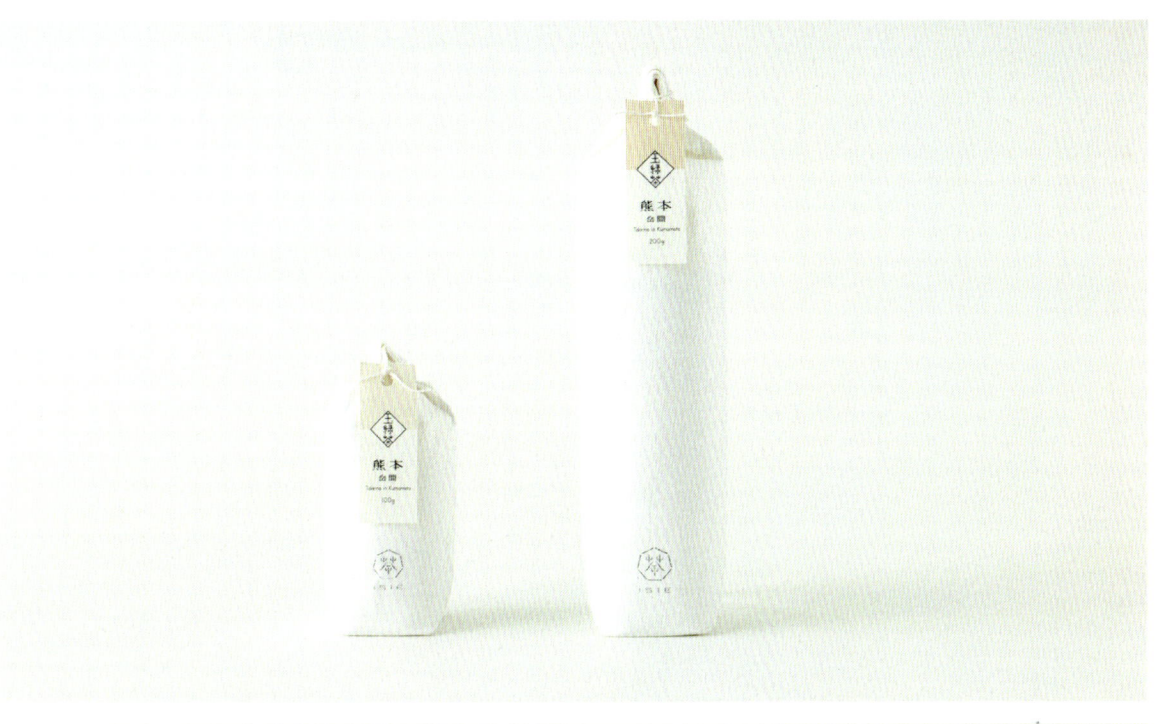

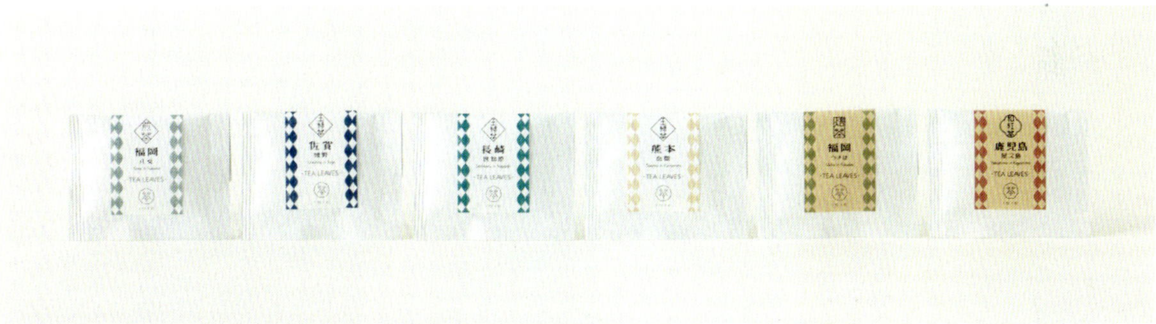

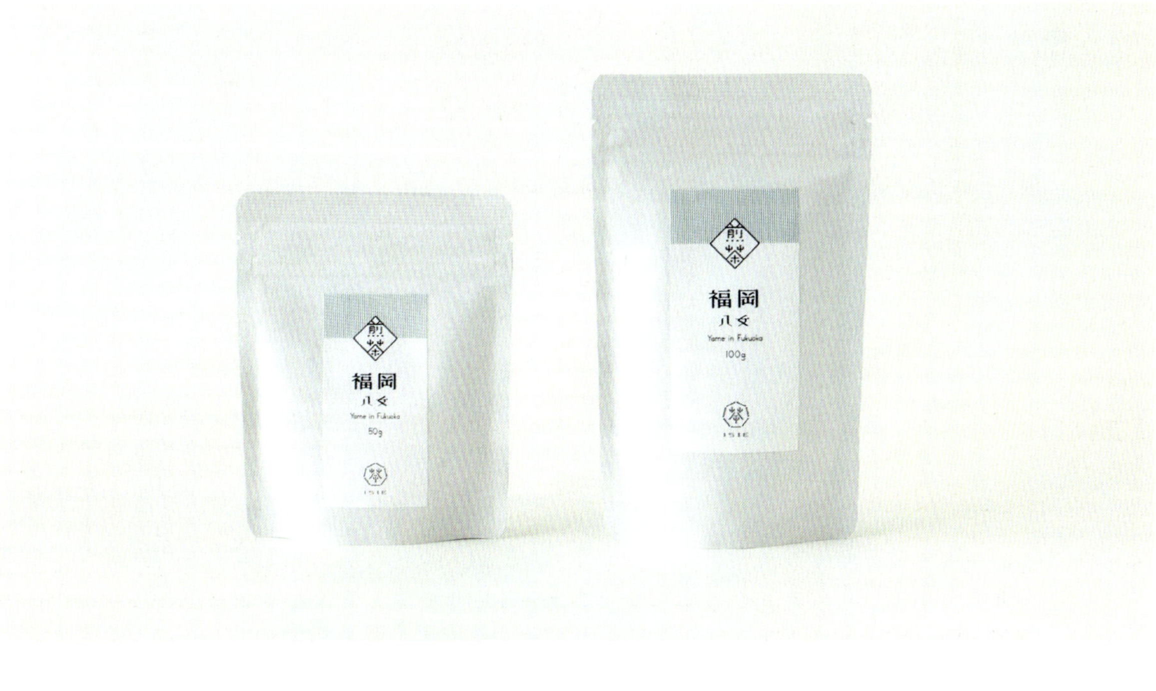

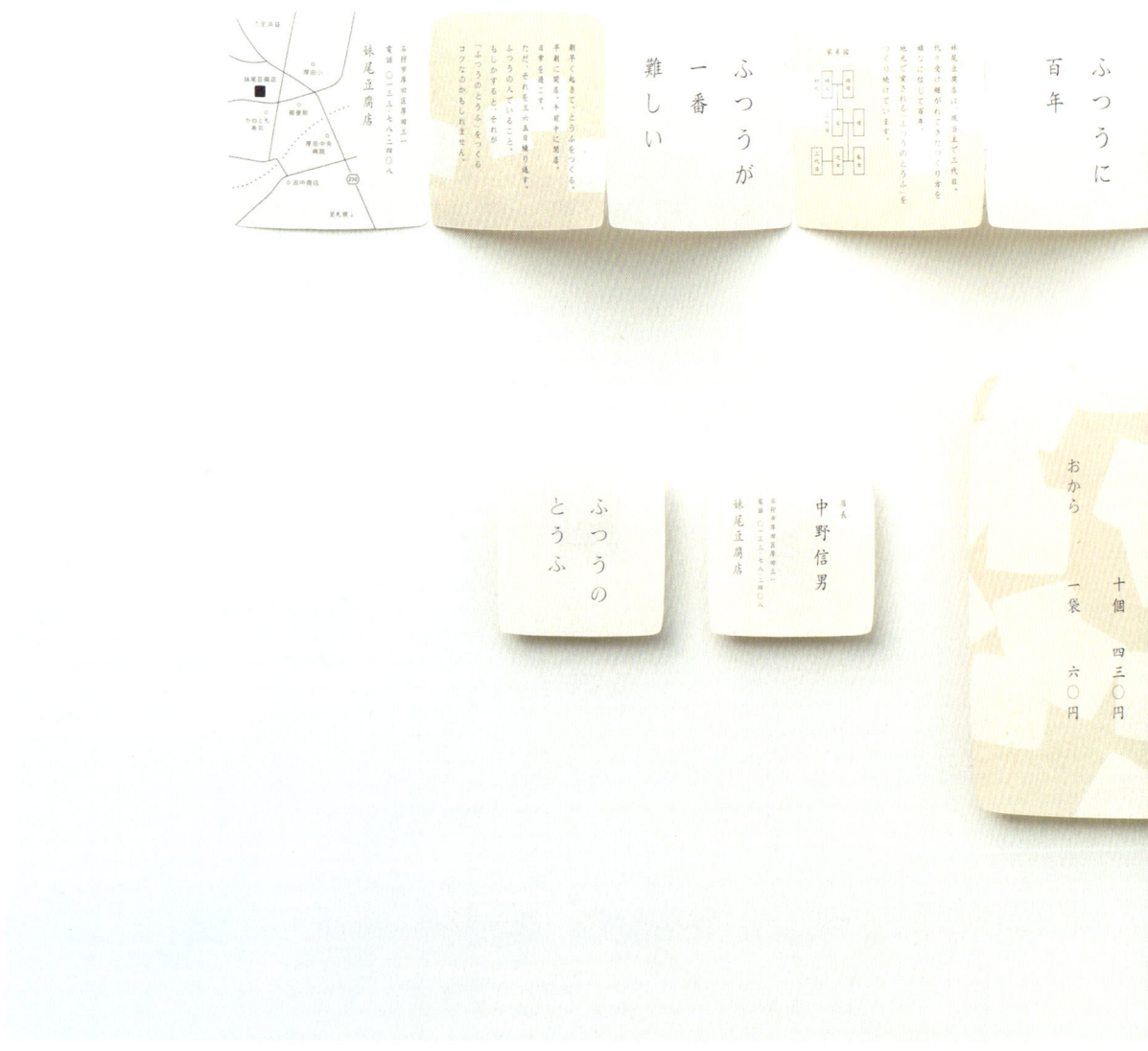

Super Normal

Studio: KD | Designer: Junya Kamada, Atsumi Saito

The packaging is characteristic of its use of traditional Japanese wrapping cloth, Furoshiki. The brochure as well as the graphics on it took the shape of tofu, while its colors were aimed at presenting the white and translucent tofu.

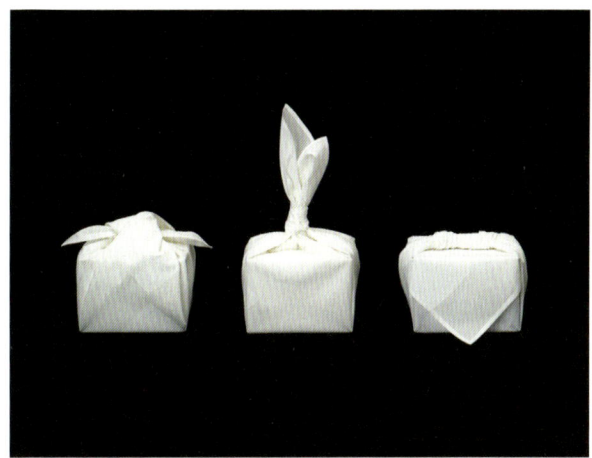
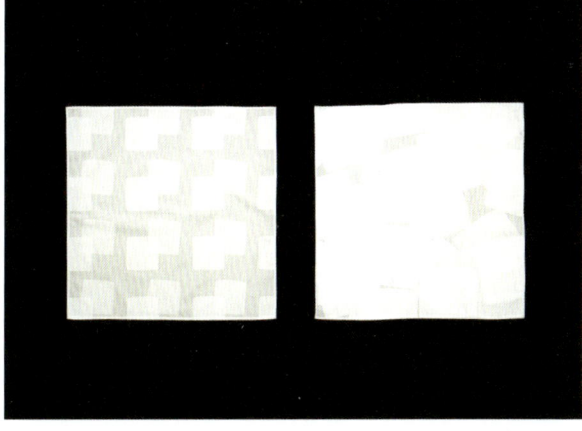

ふつうの
とうふ

とうふ　一丁　一五七円

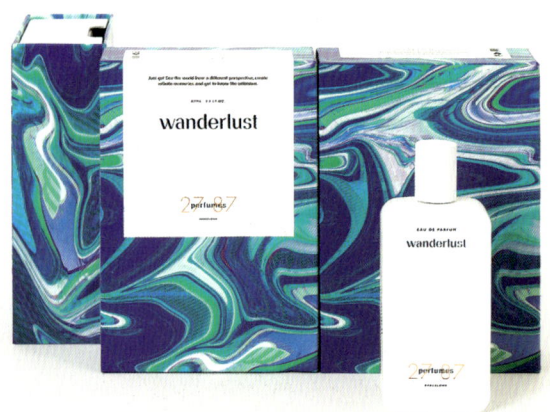
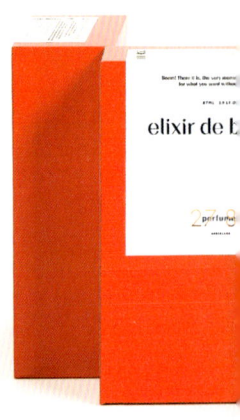
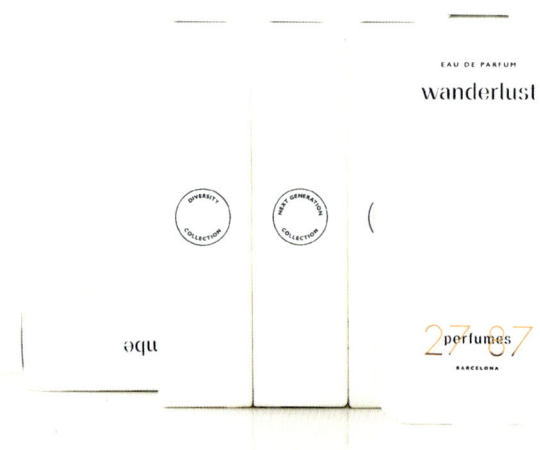

27-87 Perfumes

Studio: Ingrid Picanyol Studio | Designer: Ingrid Picanyol

Inspired by the present generation, a bottle with blunted rectangle shape that characterizes technological devices was created. Since a constantly changing generation needs naive design, the graphics for the entire collection featured blank canvas for projecting individual's unrestricted imagination while the packaging is based on concepts of each scent. The unconventional opaque bottle invites people to experience the scent with the most important sense: smell.

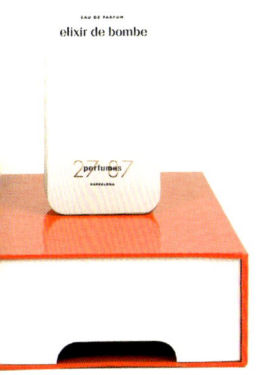
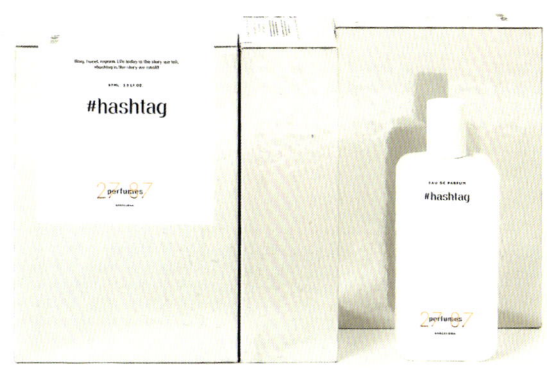
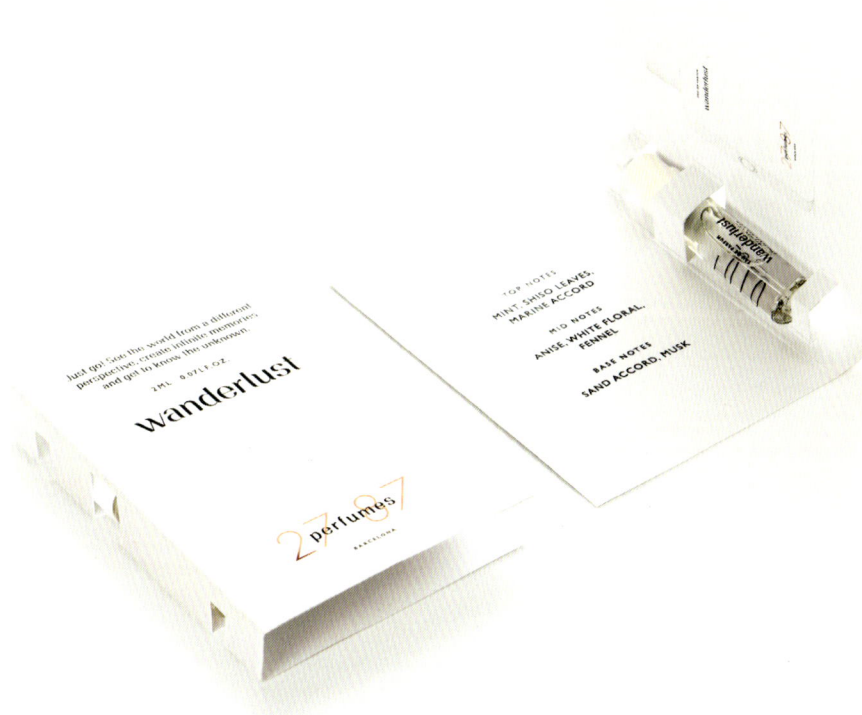

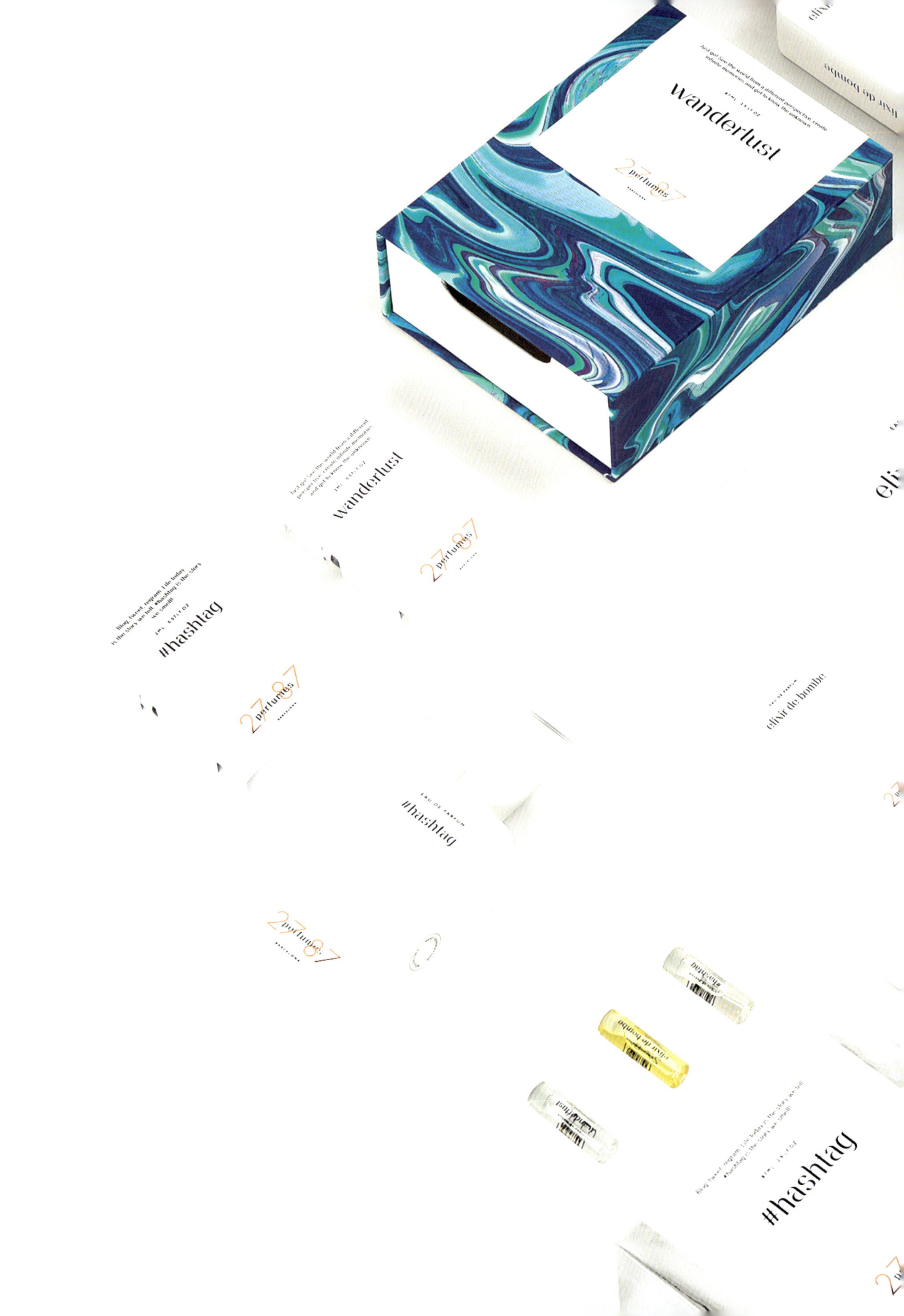

wanderlust

#hashtag

elixir de bombe

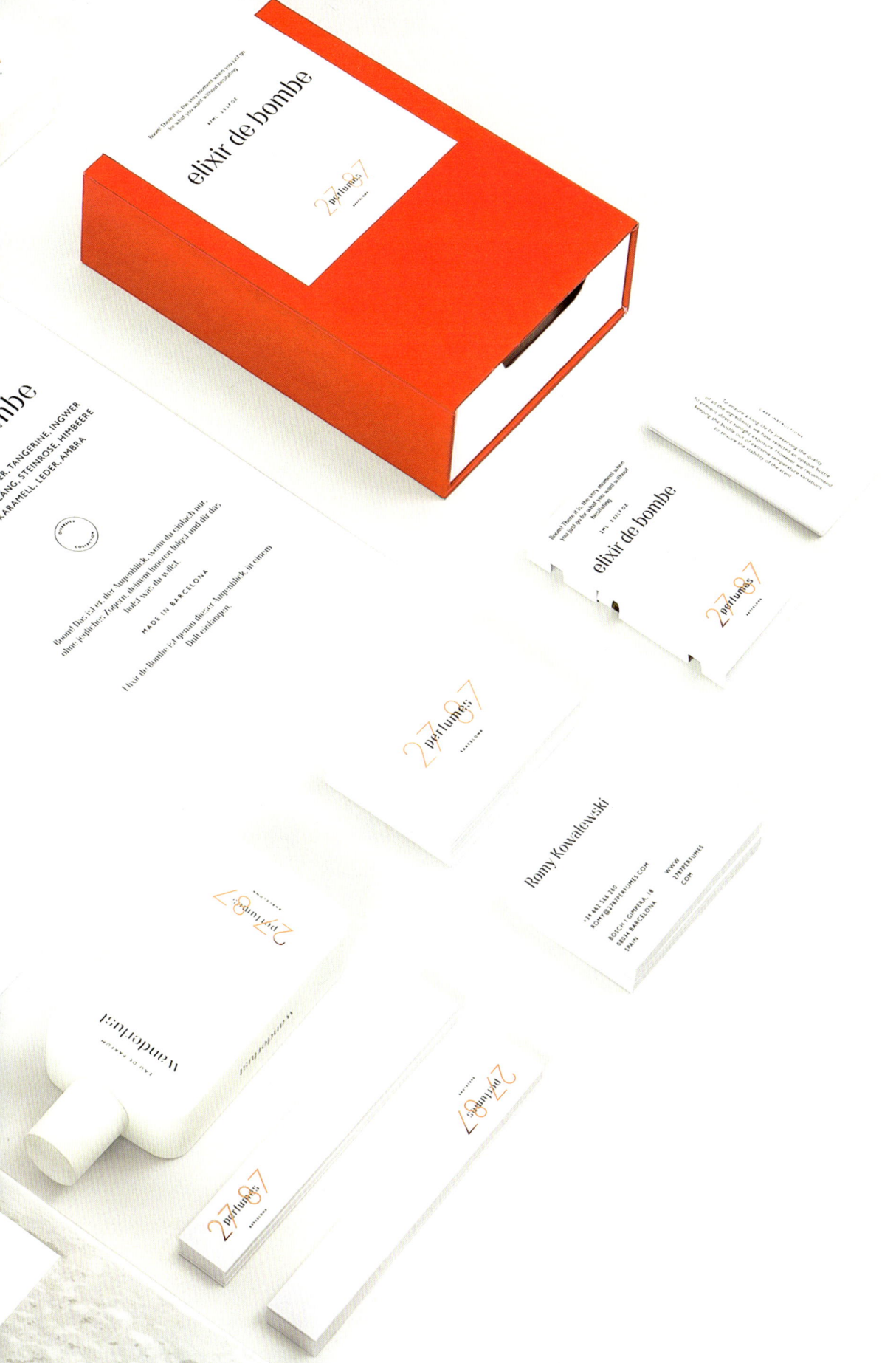

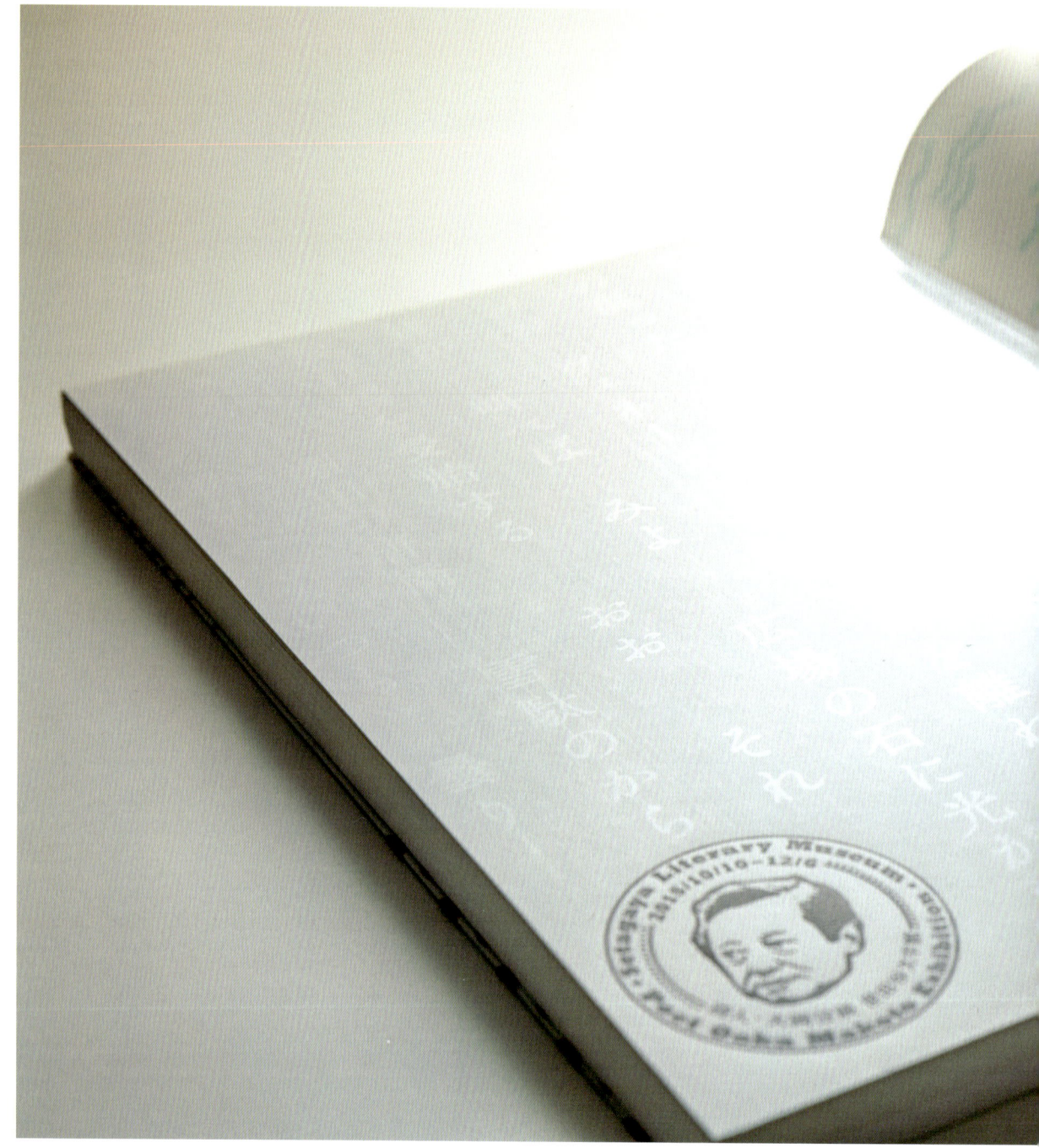

Poet Ooka Makoto Exhibition

Studio: ABEKINO DESIGN | Designer: Hirokazu Abeki | Photographer: Katsushi Takakura

The advertising materials were created for an exhibition held for the great Japanese poet Makoto Ooka. To accentuate Makoto Ooka's lyrical world, the posters and flyers were designed with minimum materials. A bold and fascinating typography was chosen for the advertising while the finishes resemble that of letterpress printing. On the cover of the book a poetry printed with varnish will reveal itself when being viewed with certain lighting.

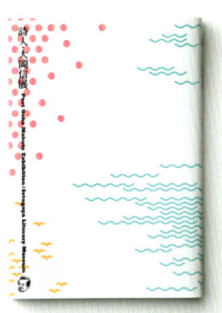
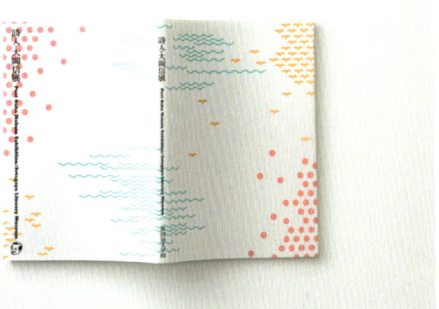
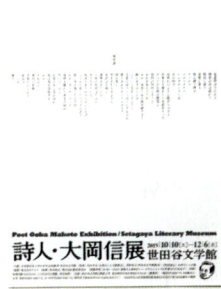
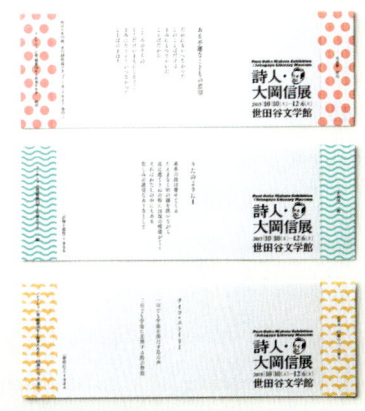

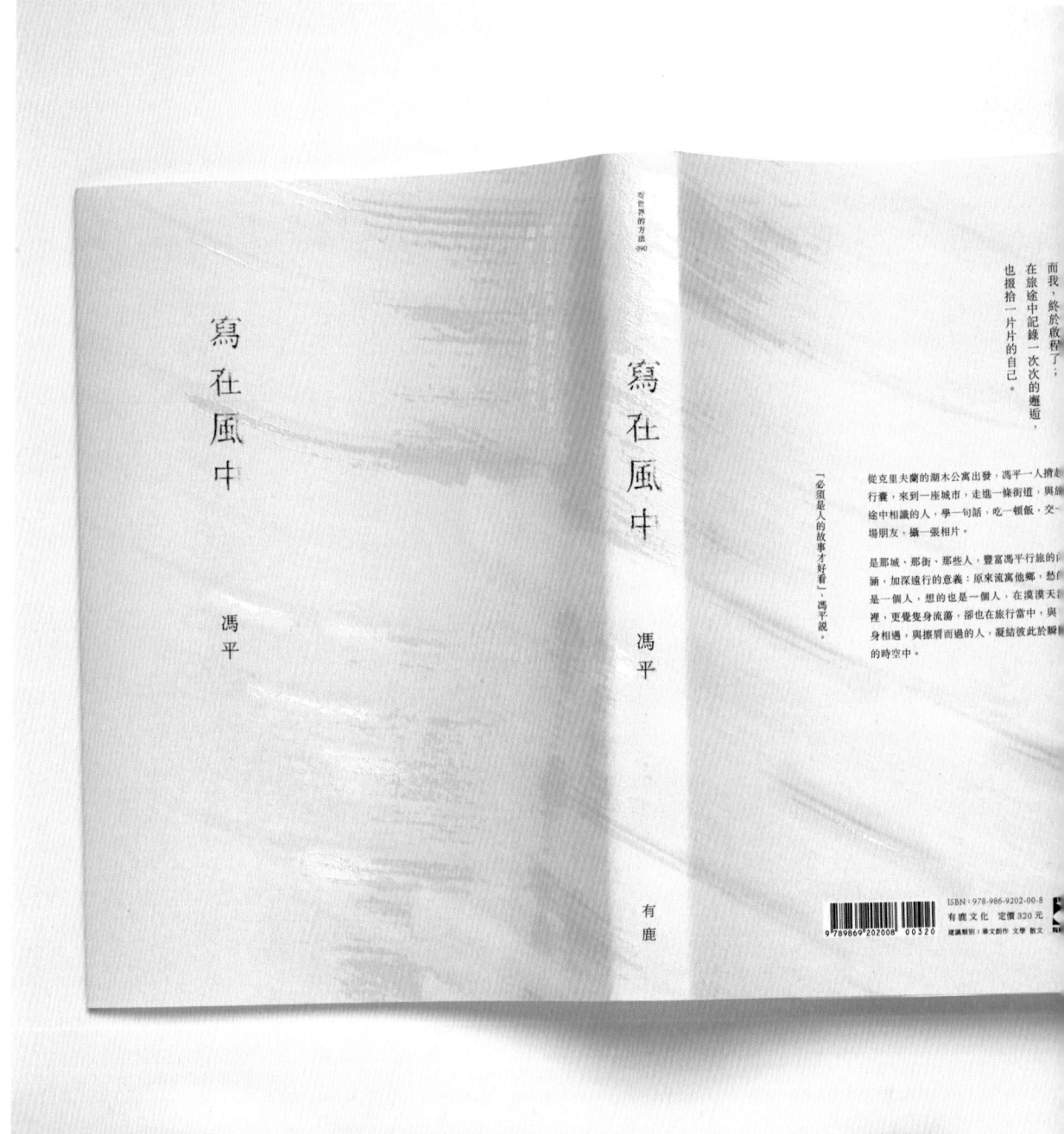

Xie Zai Feng Zhong

Studio: Shanba Design | Designer: Hung Yu-Kai

This is the book cover designed for *xie zai feng zhong* (writing in the wind), an anthology of travel writings, by writer Feng Ping. A special layer of reflective texture on the book jacket enriches both visual and tactile experience. Its tilting patterns mimic blowing wind, recalling those moments and memories captured in the writings. The typography of the book title incorporated the effect of wind erosion, as if it has been engraved on something or it is a mark left by time. The inside cover expresses one's smallness against the universe's vastness.

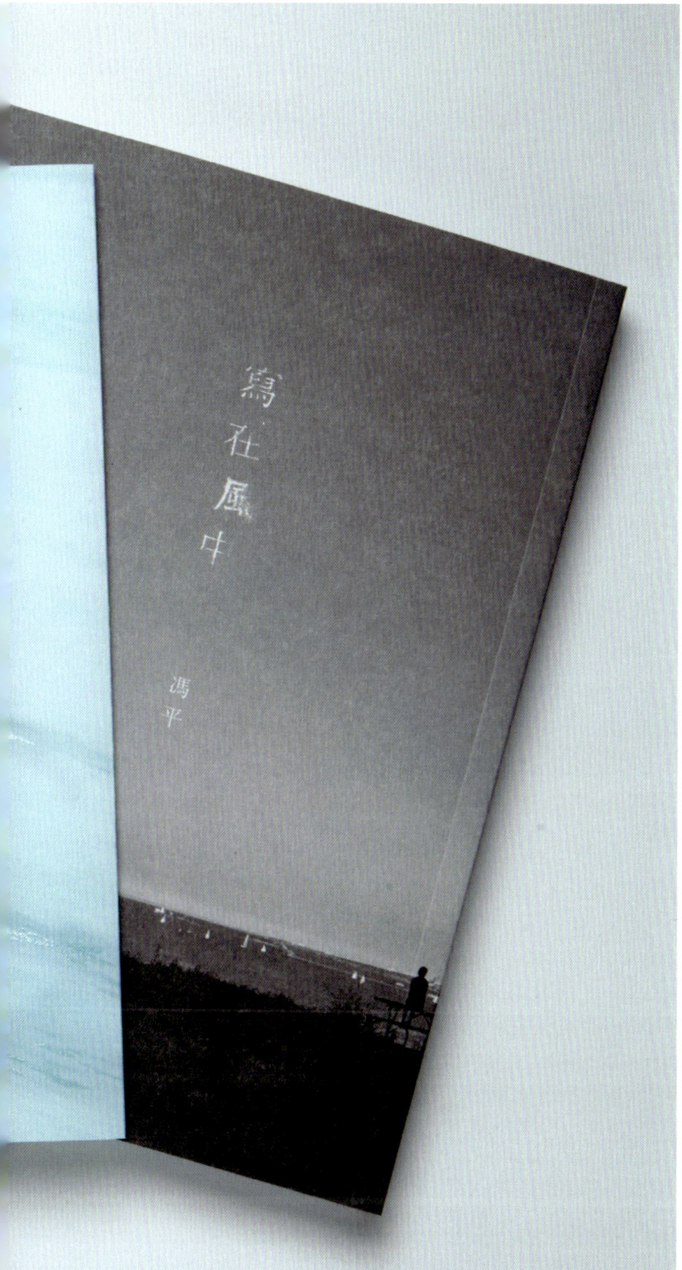

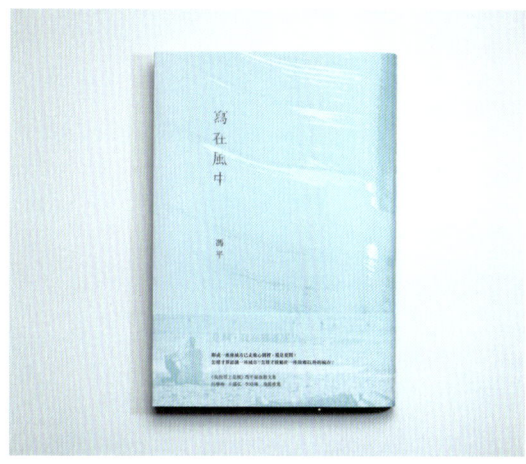
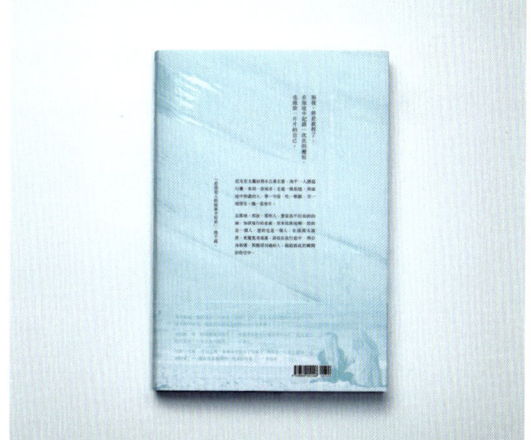

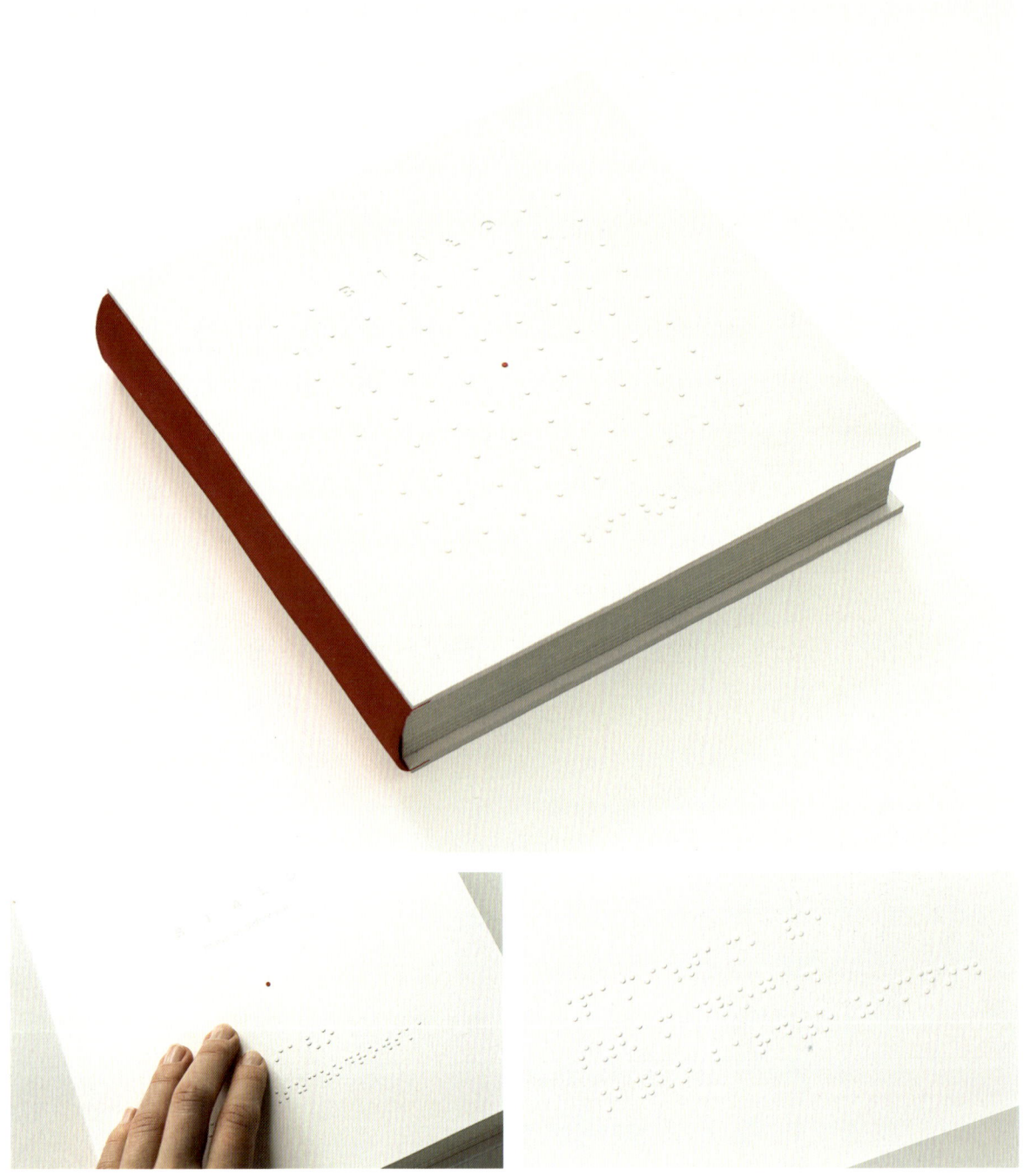

Biało

Designer: Maria Szczodrowska

Based on the idea that book has been made to appeal to the sighted and the unsighted alike, the designer created a book that incorporated tactile pictures and traditionally printed and embossed Braille texts to broaden the reading experience to multisensory perception. In the short text, the topic of vision loss has been subtly developed, providing rationale for all formal procedures applied in this work.

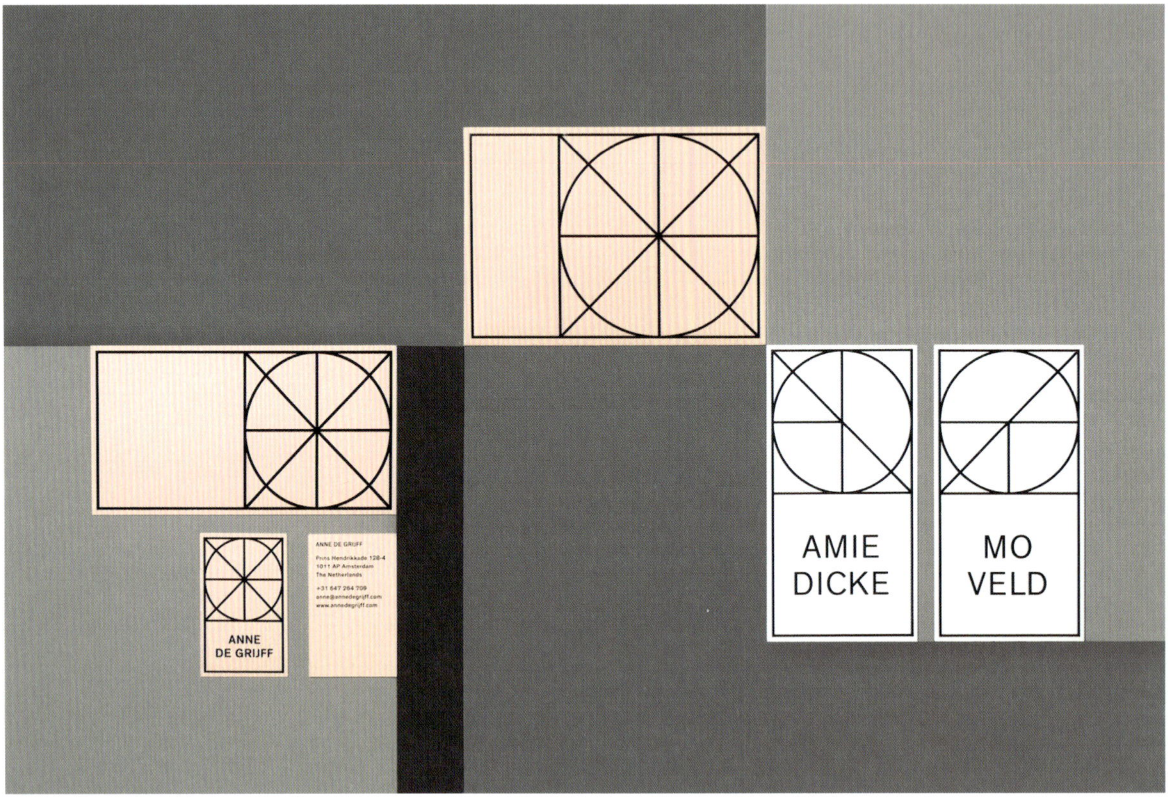

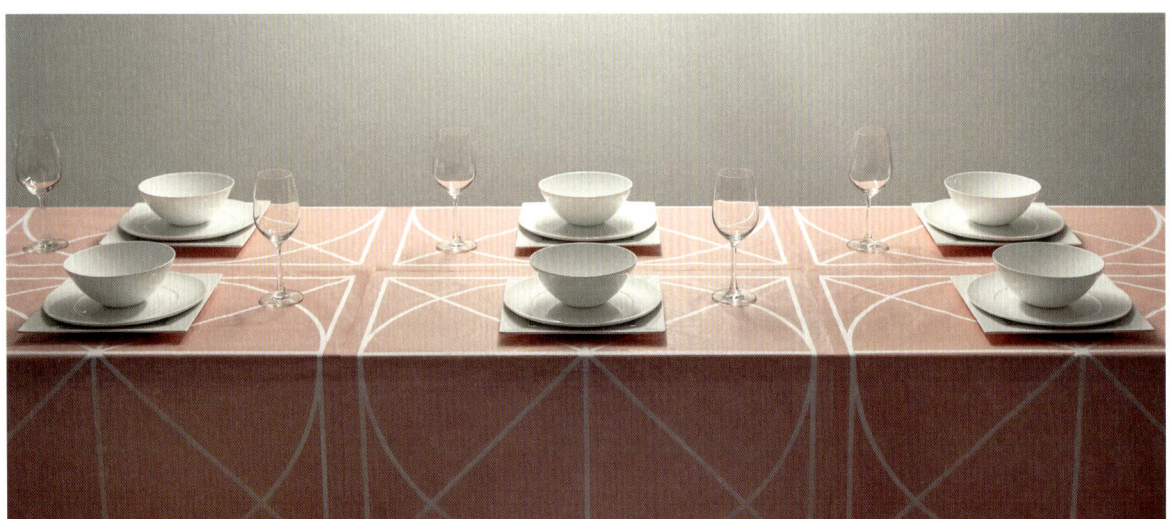

Anne de Grijff

Designer: Mainstudio

Anne de Grijff is a Dutch fashion designer. The design centered on the concept of "made to measure", and was created as a flexible grid incorporating the shapes of a square, circle, cross, and plus sign. The bold lines of the graphics can be deconstructed and reconfigured into countless compositions to create an infinite number of such shapes, which is a reflection of the variety of materials used by the fashion designer. The identity also functioned as a template for other designed items such as hang tags, bags and stationary.

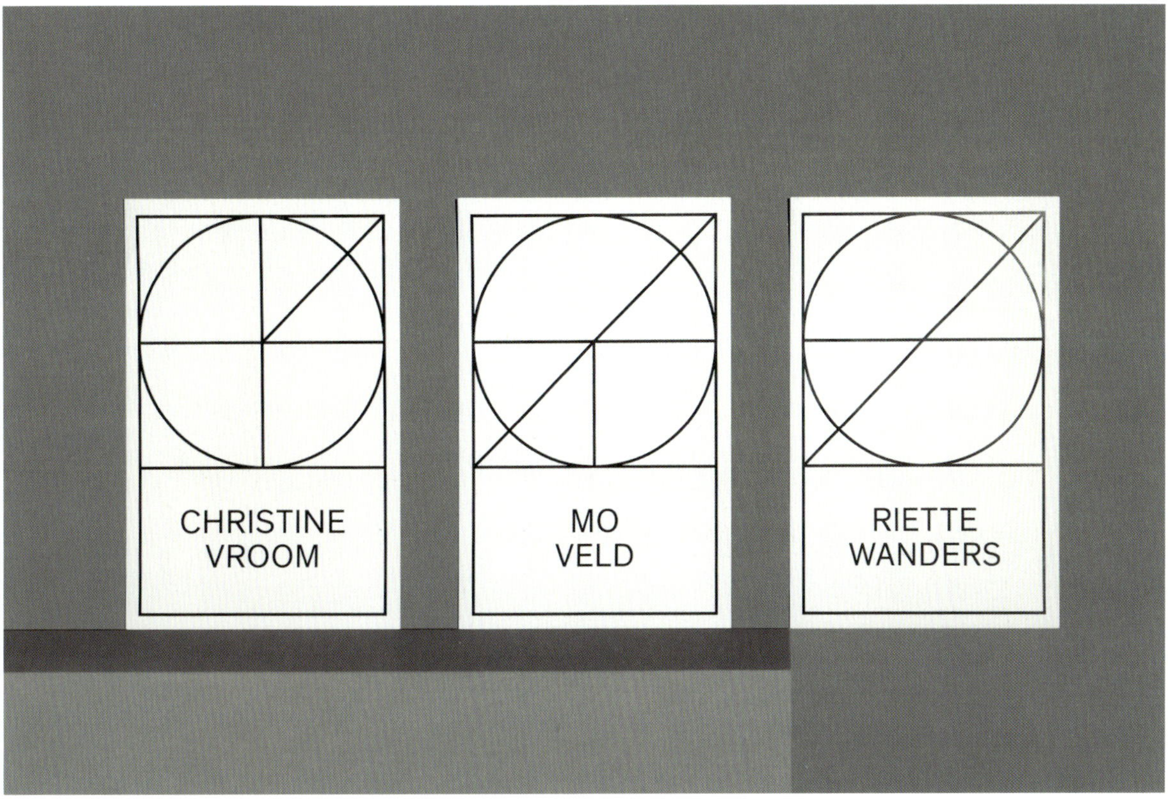

CHRISTINE VROOM

MO VELD

RIETTE WANDERS

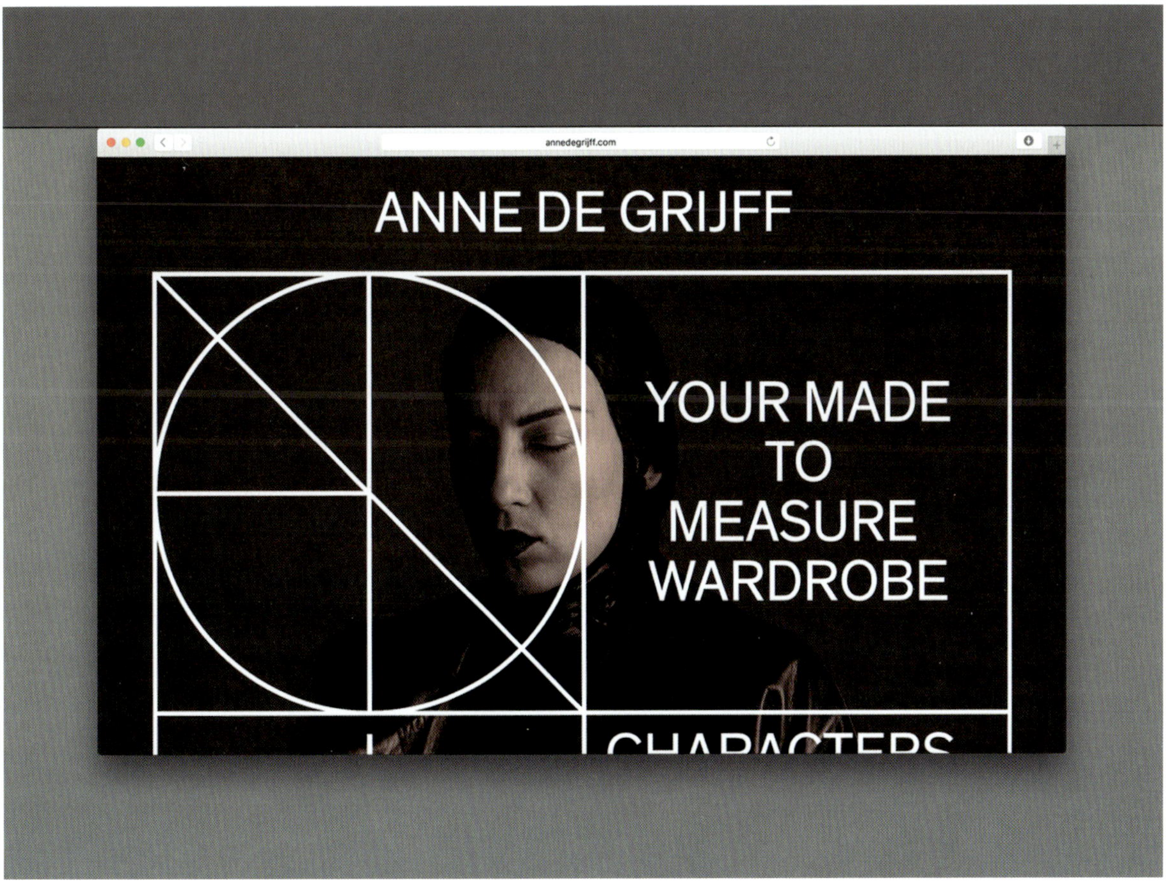

ANNE DE GRIJFF

YOUR MADE TO MEASURE WARDROBE

CHARACTERS

リンゴ酸の奏でる、爽やかな余韻

可愛くて飲みやすい、でも本格派。
"日本酒"の新しい可能性を広げていく
カジュアルスタイルの純米吟醸酒。
白ワインに多く含まれるリンゴ酸が奏でる
奥ゆかしい香り、甘みと酸味の調和、爽やかな余韻。
軽快な後味は、冷やすことでより一層
美味しくお飲みいただけます。
日本酒に馴染みのない方にも新しい味わいと喜びを
そんな想いから生まれたのが「きのえねアップル」です。

日本酒の世界は、もっと広がっていく

Junmai Ginjo
Kinoene Apple

Kinoene Apple

Studio: tegusu Inc | Designer: Masaomi Fujita

An amiable yet authentic image was created for Kinoene Apple, a seasonal premium sake with malic acid which brings forth a refreshing aroma. The apple-shaped bottle necker was devised to increase recognition. The brand name was written in Kanji to maintain its bond with traditional Japanese sake. The long and narrow label made up of Japanese paper arrived at a light expression soothing for summer, just like the sake.

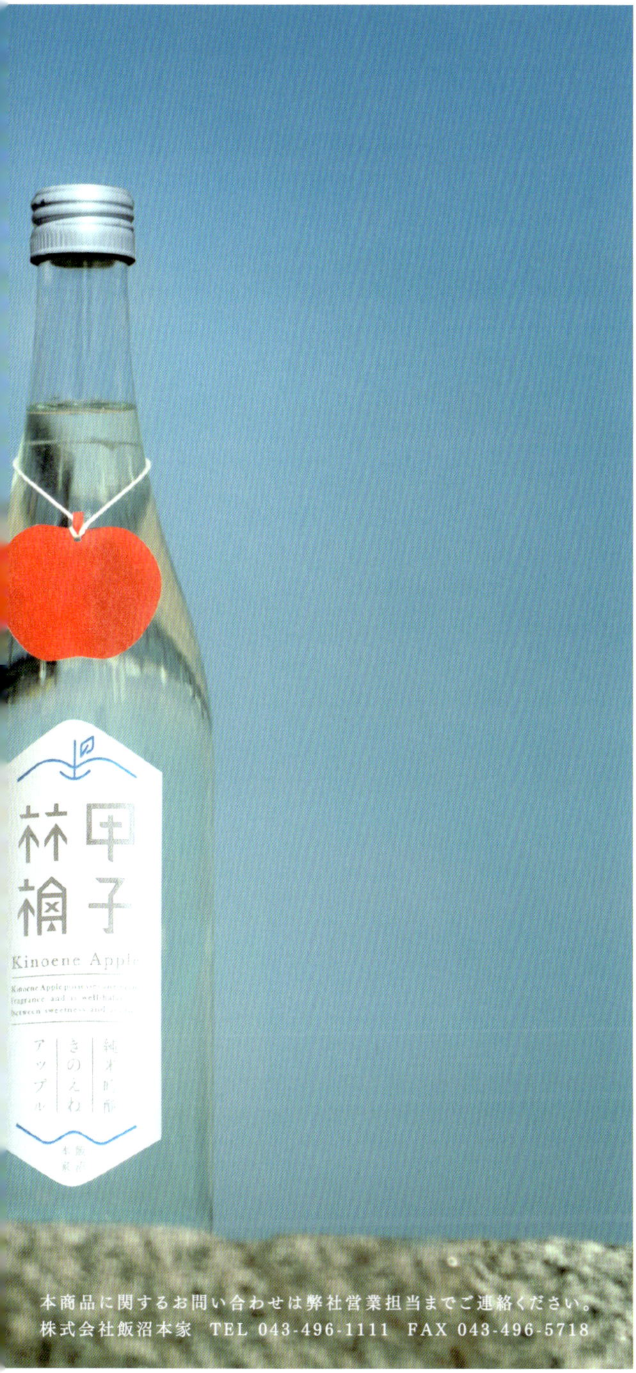

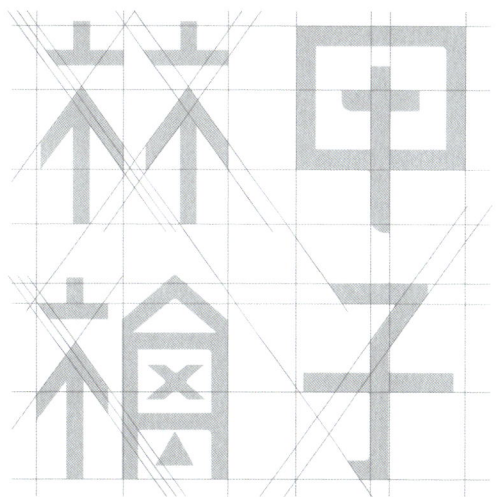

Kinoene Apple

Kinoene Apple possesses an elegant fragrance and is well-balanced between sweetness and acidity.

本商品に関するお問い合わせは弊社営業担当までご連絡ください。
株式会社飯沼本家　TEL 043-496-1111　FAX 043-496-5718

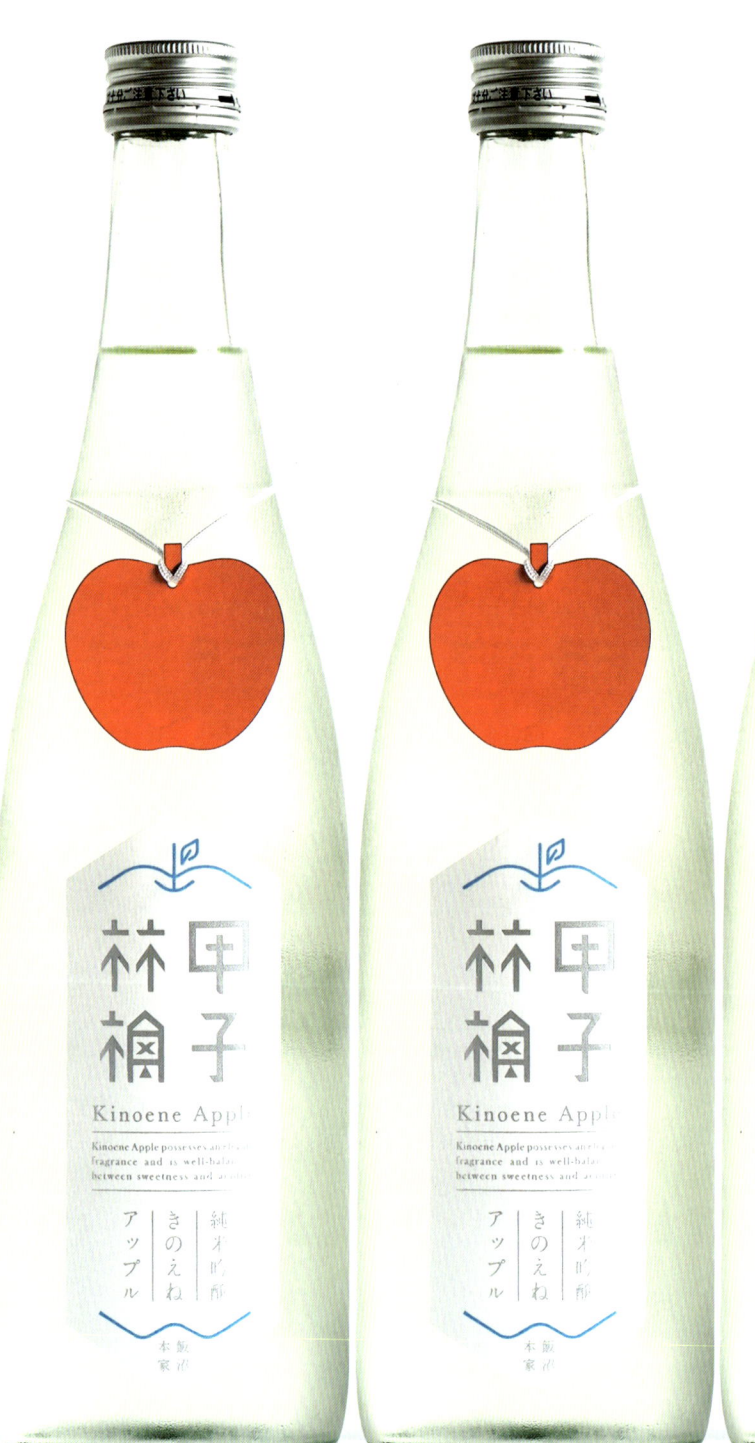

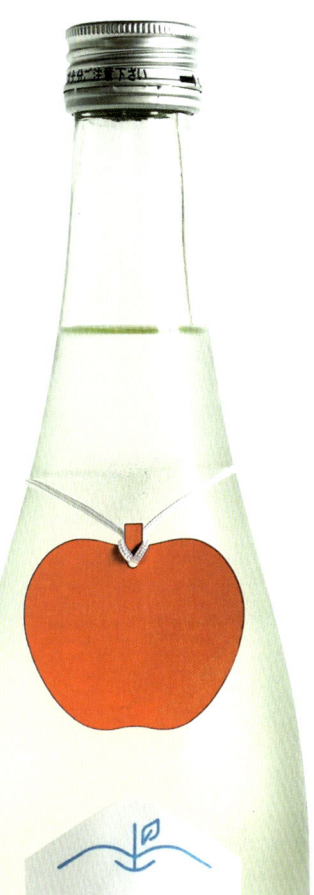

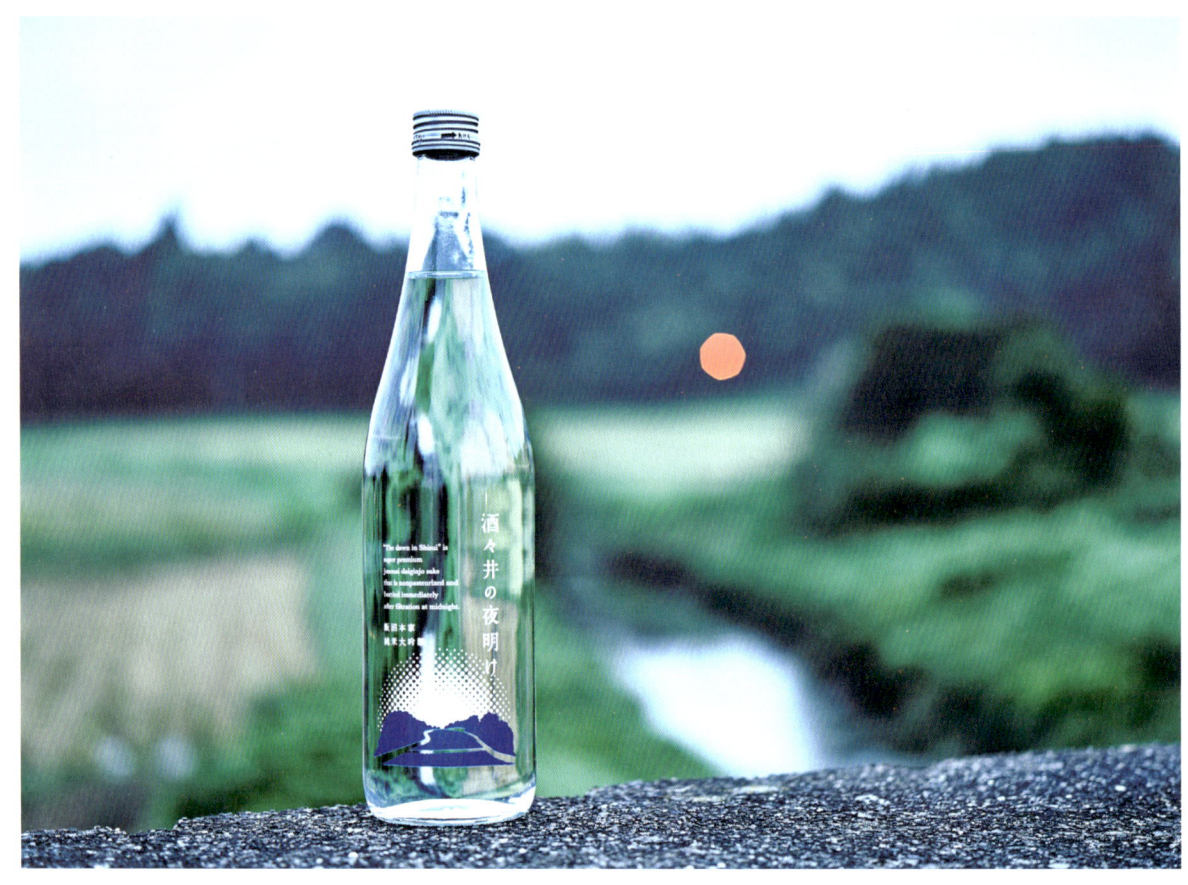

SAKE NOUVEAU

Studio: tegusu Inc

Designer: Masaomi Fujita

For the advertisement for Sake Nouveau, dark blue, a color of the sky before sunrise, and a combination of rural landscape's silhouette with gradation of dots were employed to capture the crack of dawn when the sake was bottled and delivered after filtration at midnight in Shisui Town, where the established sake brewery makes freshly pressed sake. Printed directly on the bottle, the design accentuated the transparency of the liquid, suggesting the refreshing and clear taste.

祝う、
味わう、
響き合う──。

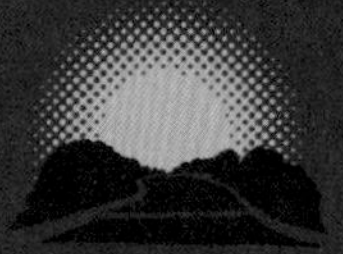

夜明け前にしぼり始め、
その日のうちにお届けする
一日限定製造の純米大吟醸。
初しぼりを祝い、生まれる人の輪。
自然と心が響き合う、ひと時。

酒井
夜明

Sake Nouveau

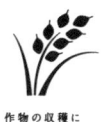
作物の収穫に
感謝し祝う

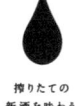
搾りたての
新酒を味わう

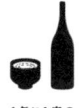
1年に1度の
贅沢を共有する

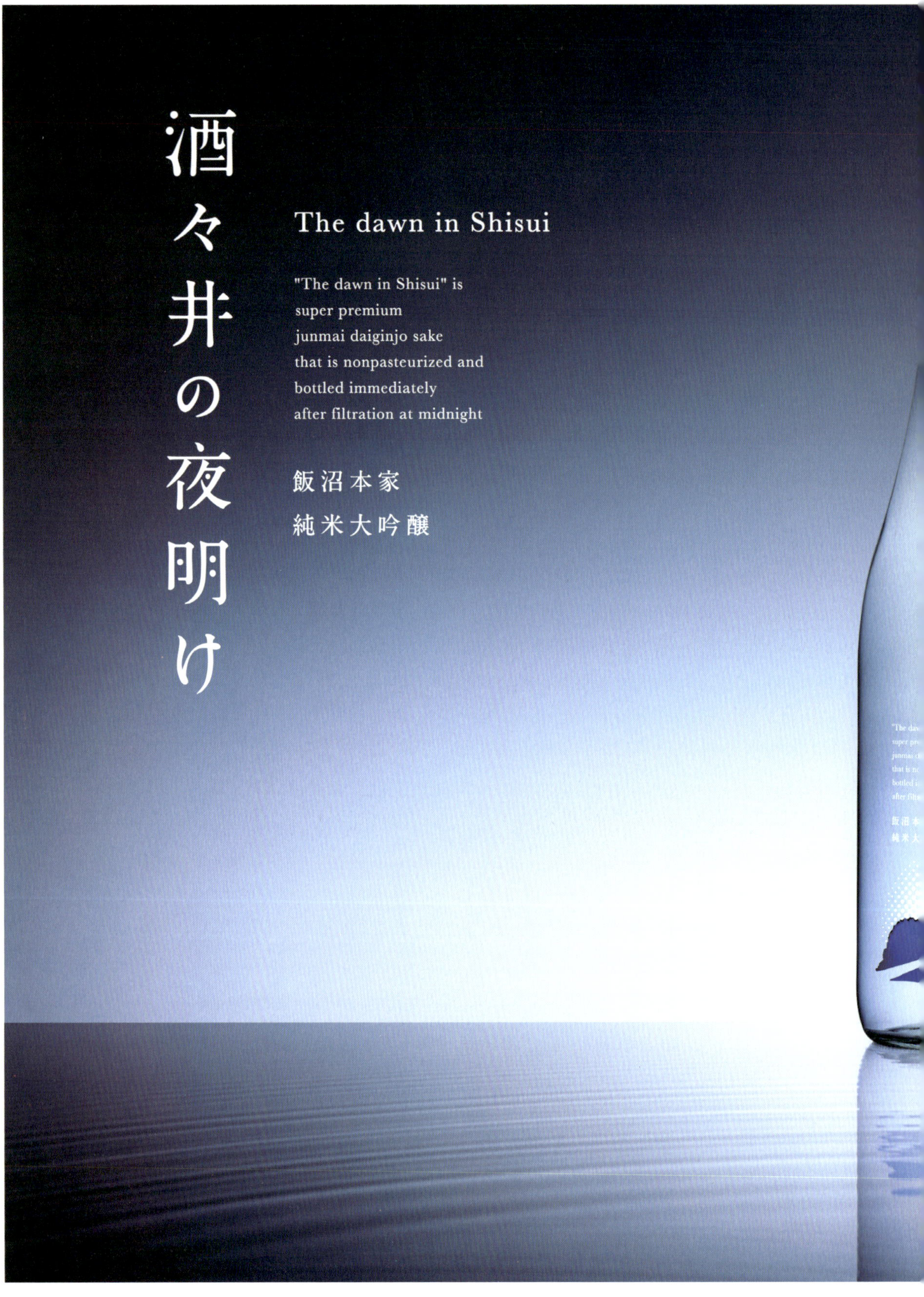

酒々井の夜明け

The dawn in Shisui

"The dawn in Shisui" is
super premium
junmai daiginjo sake
that is nonpasteurized and
bottled immediately
after filtration at midnight

飯沼本家
純米大吟醸

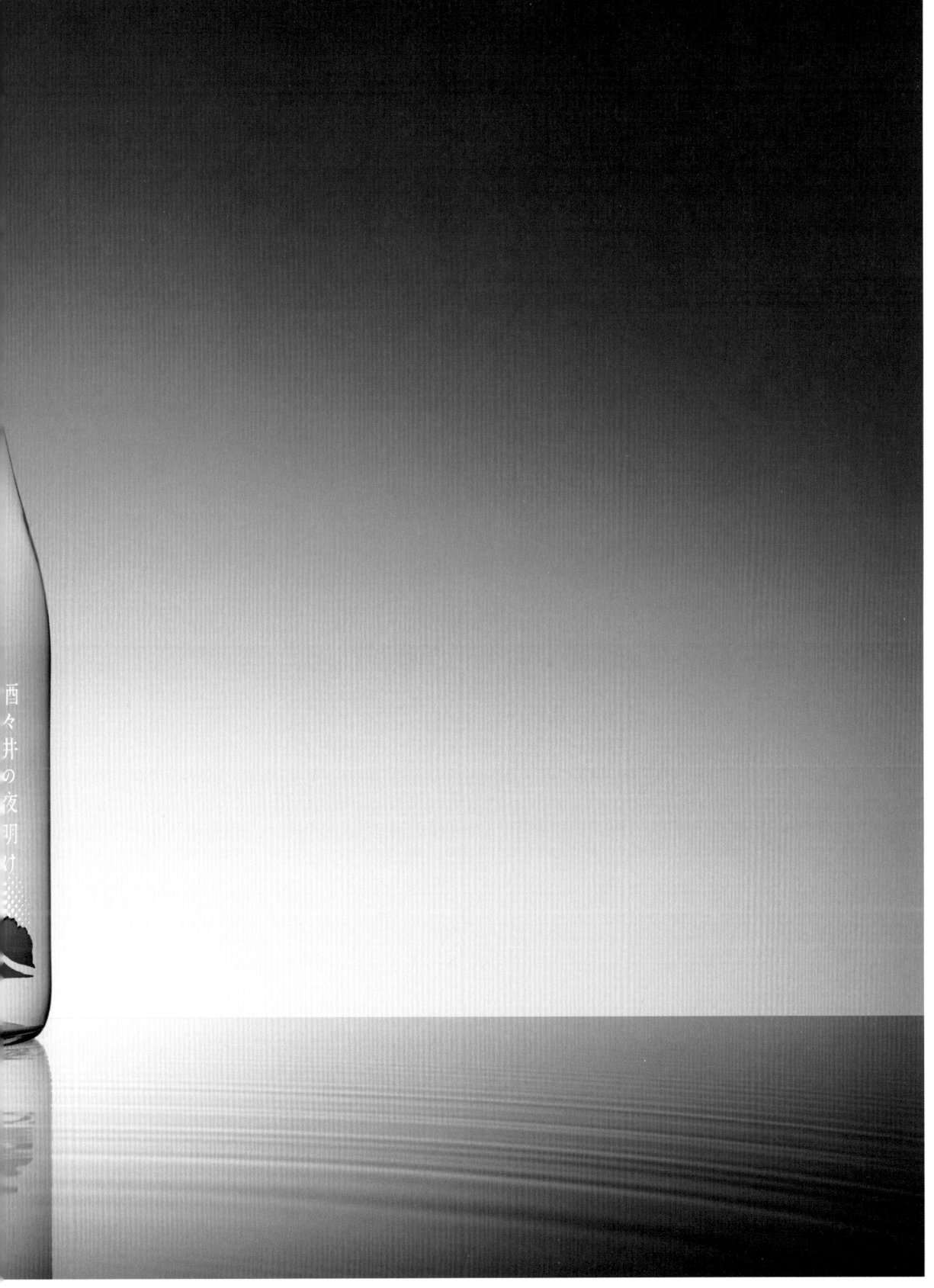

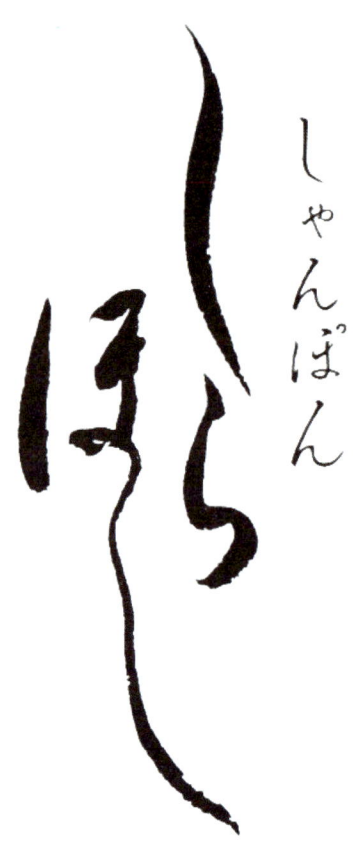

Shirahoshi

Studio: BULLET Inc. | Designer: Aya Codama

This is a packaging design for the sparkling Japanese sake Shirahoshi, a collaboration product of Imayotsukasa Sake Brewery and professional baseball team Yokohama DeNA BayStars. It exhibits a fusion of Japanese and Western features—a label suitable for champagne combined with Japanese calligraphy. Star motifs symbolizing the baseball team are scattered around the edge of the label, mimicking the dispersal of carbonation and evoking the impression of champagne.

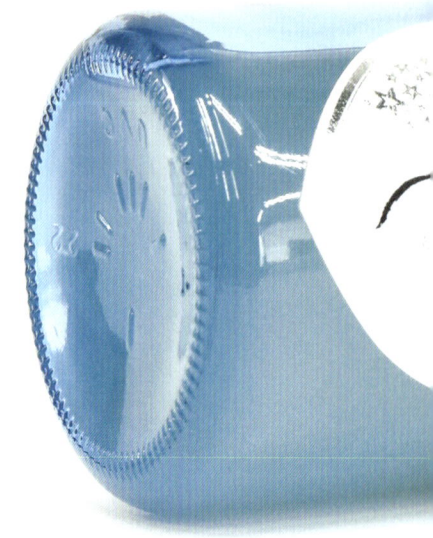

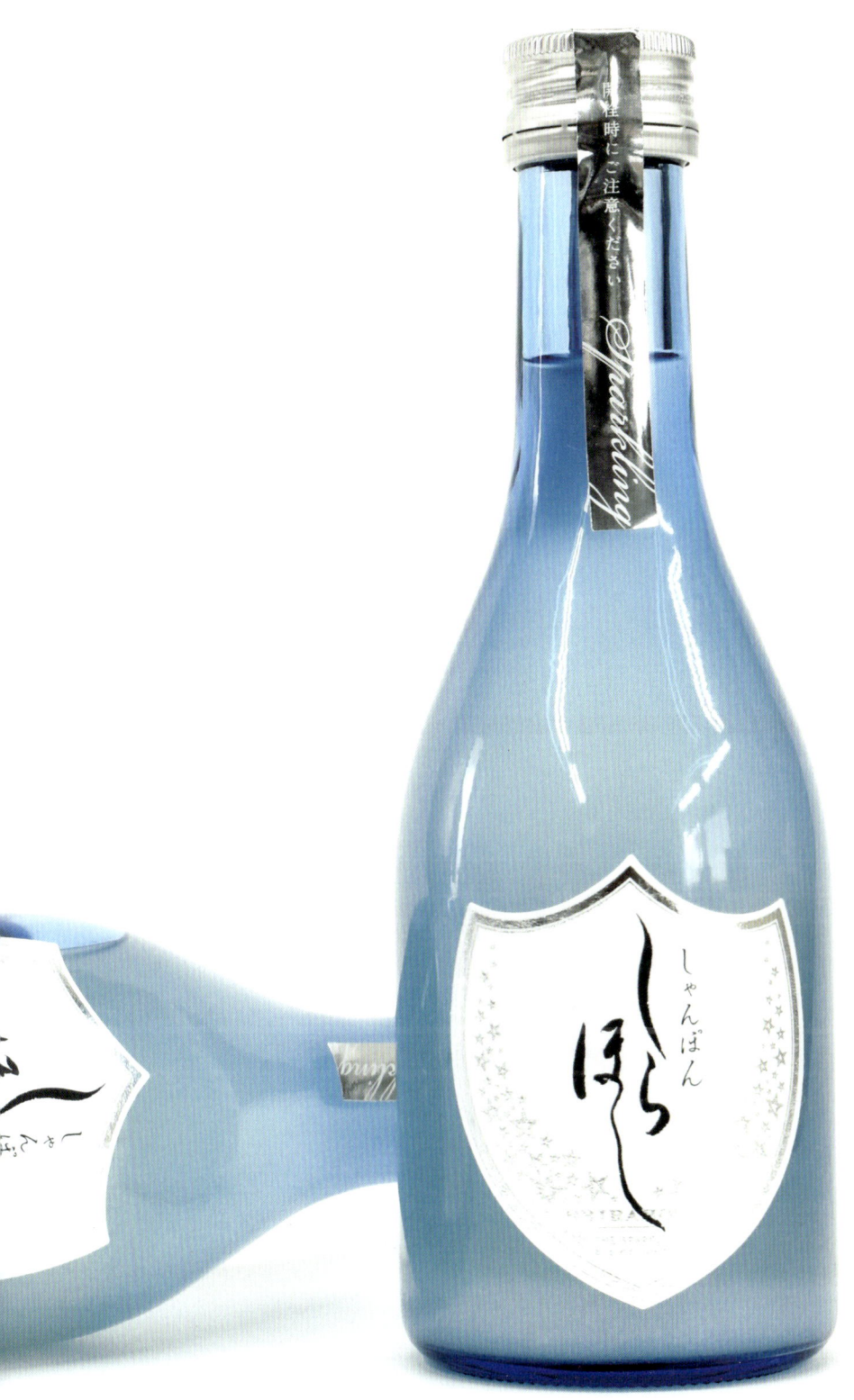

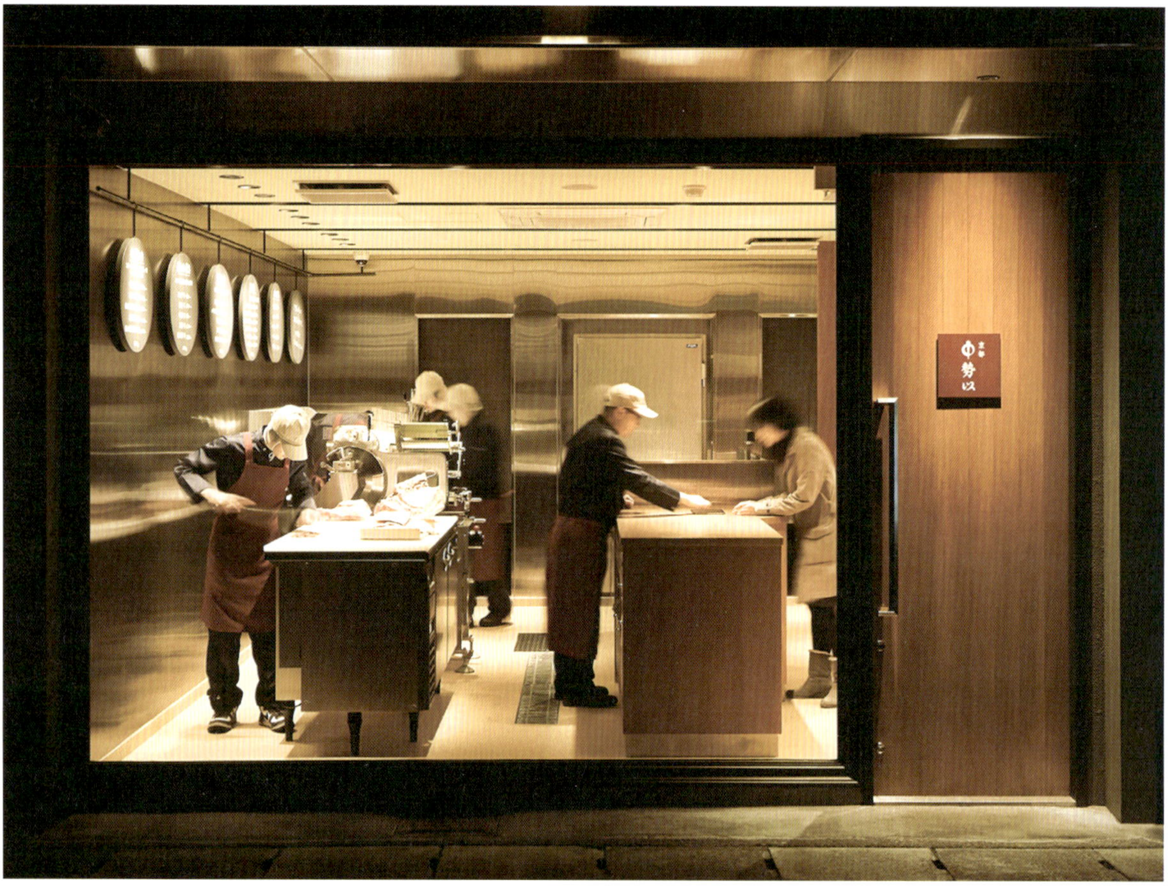

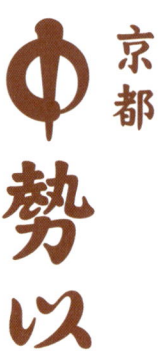

Kyoto Nakasei

Designer: canaria

Kyoto Nakasei is the pioneer of dry-aged beef in Japan. The shop's design and logo has been overhauled and features a circle with a single line through the center that emulates the character "中" used in the shop's name, expressing the owner's credo: "bringing cow, people and meat together". The wine-red of dry-aged beef is the brand color.

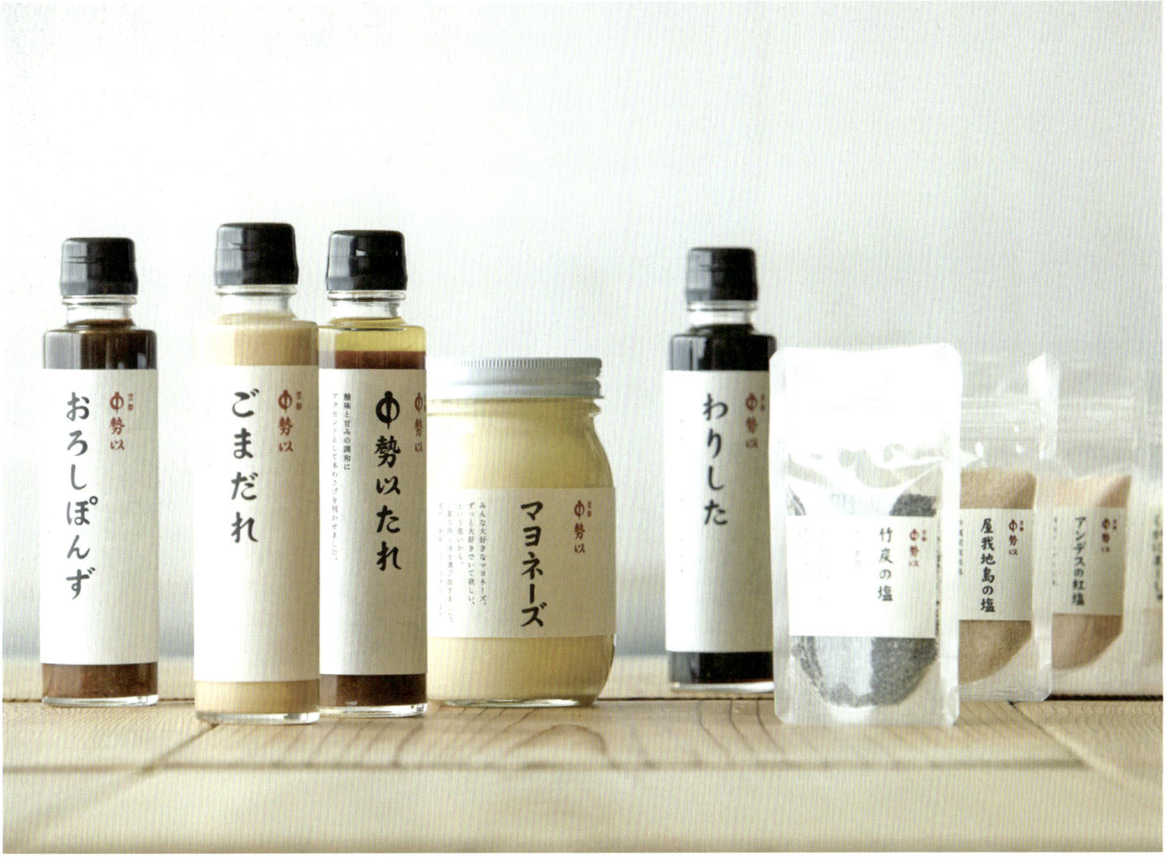

73

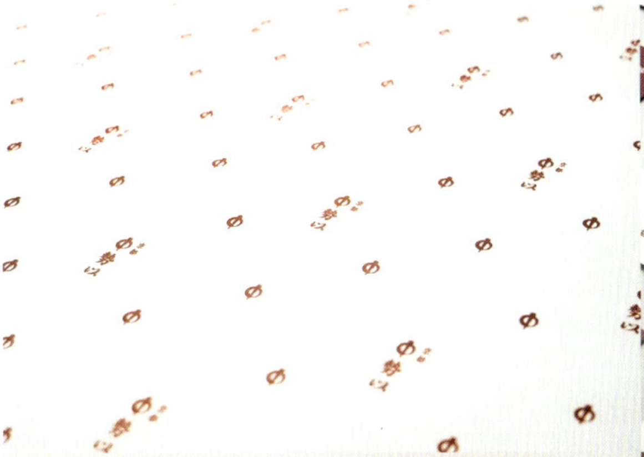

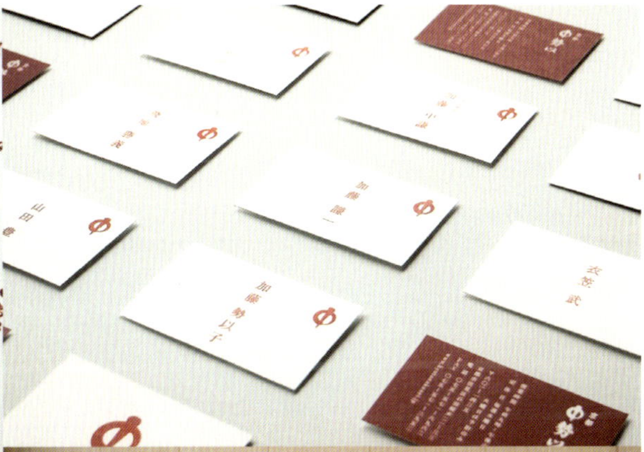

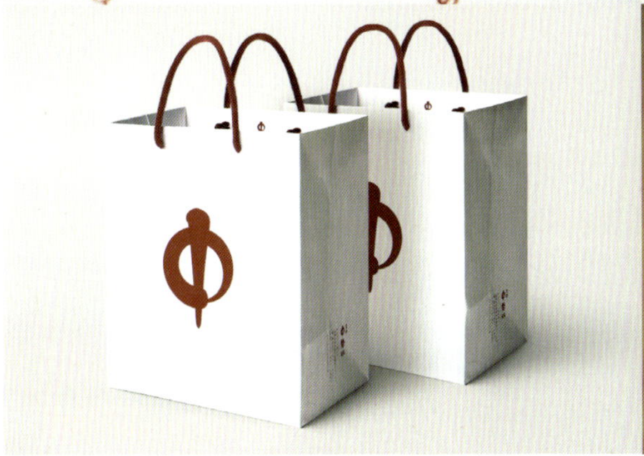

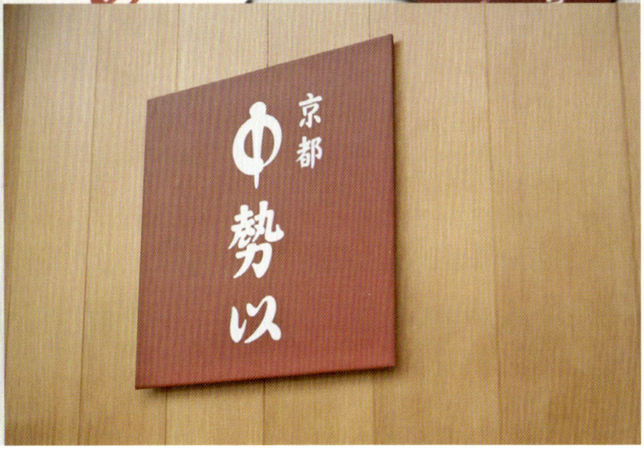

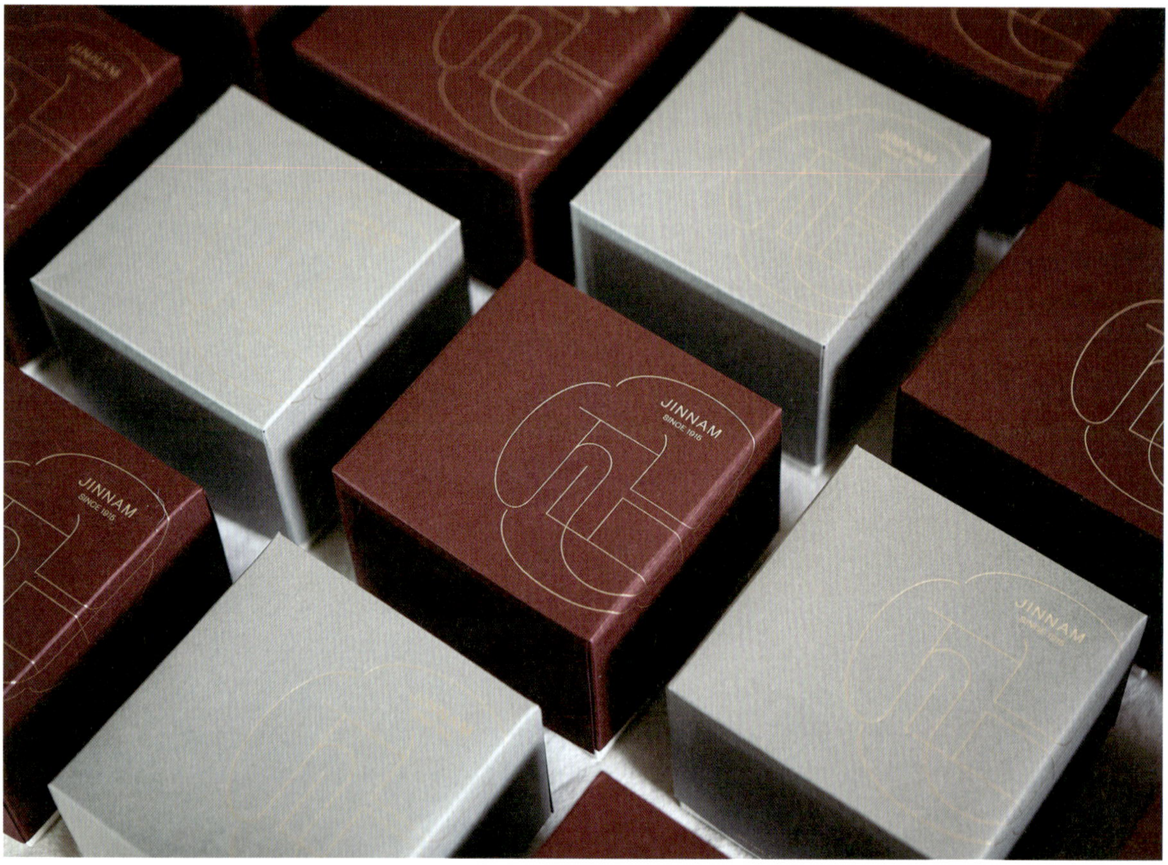

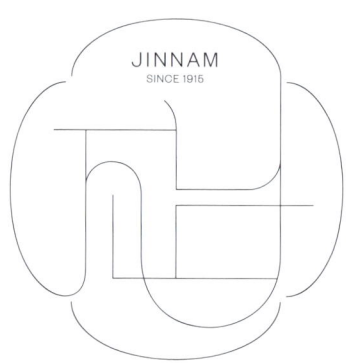

Jinnam

Studio: CFC Studio

This work is a branding for Jinnam Agricultural Corporation, which has been producing high-quality fermented food since 1915. Based on two Korean letters "Jin" and "Nam" and the local scenery, designers created different graphics to represent the Jinnam village where fresh ingredients were harvested, hoping to engage intimate communications between the brand and viewers.

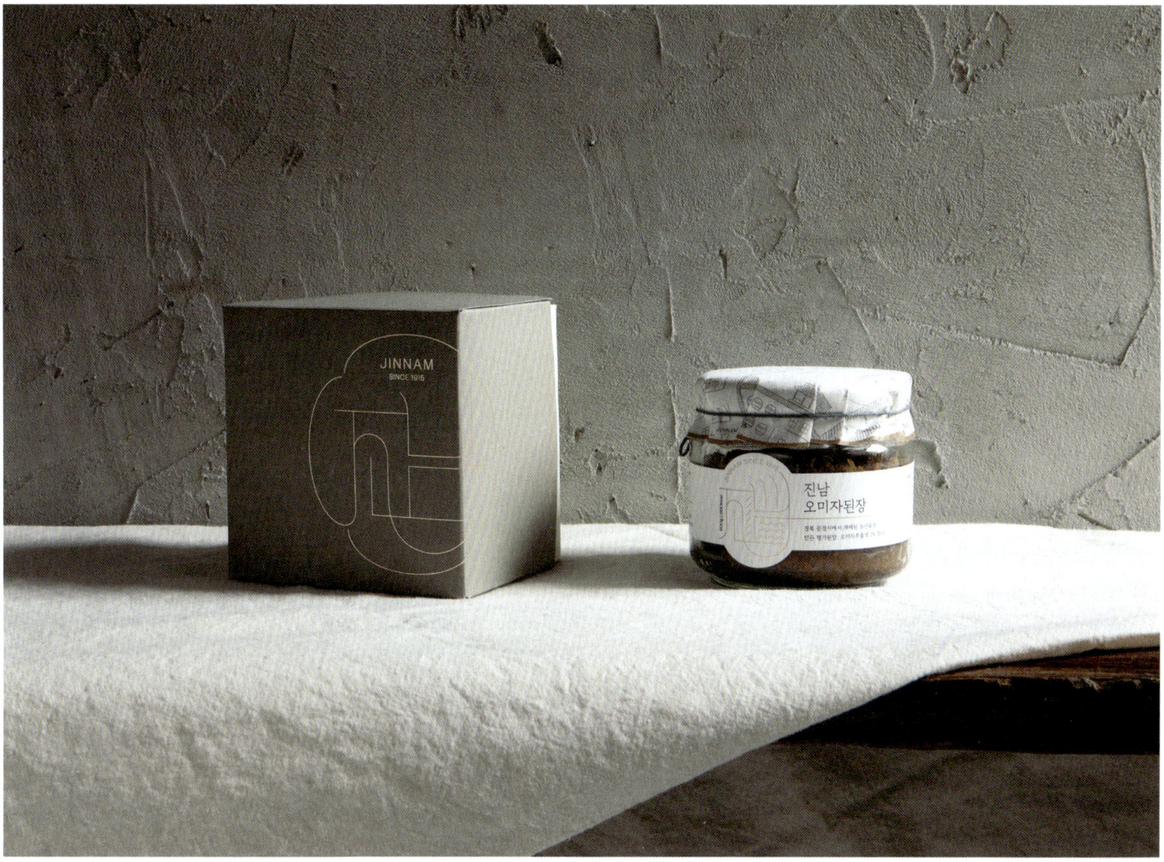

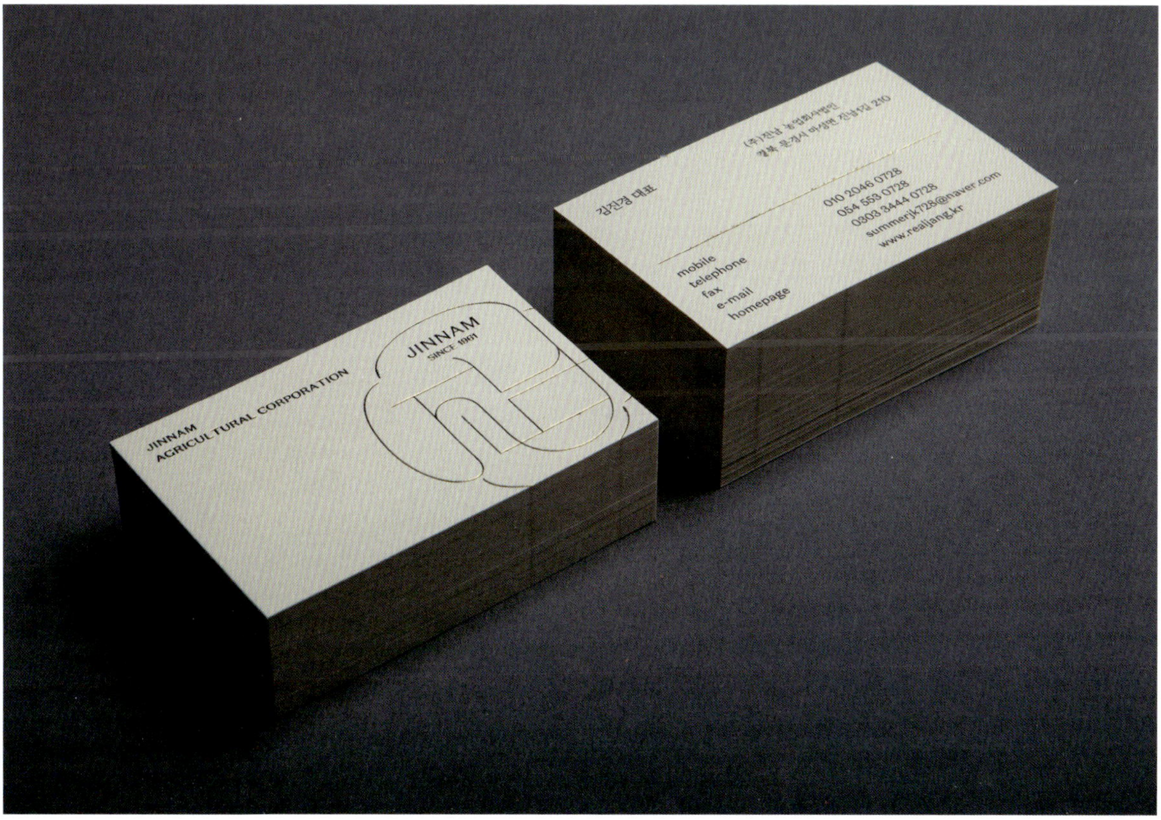

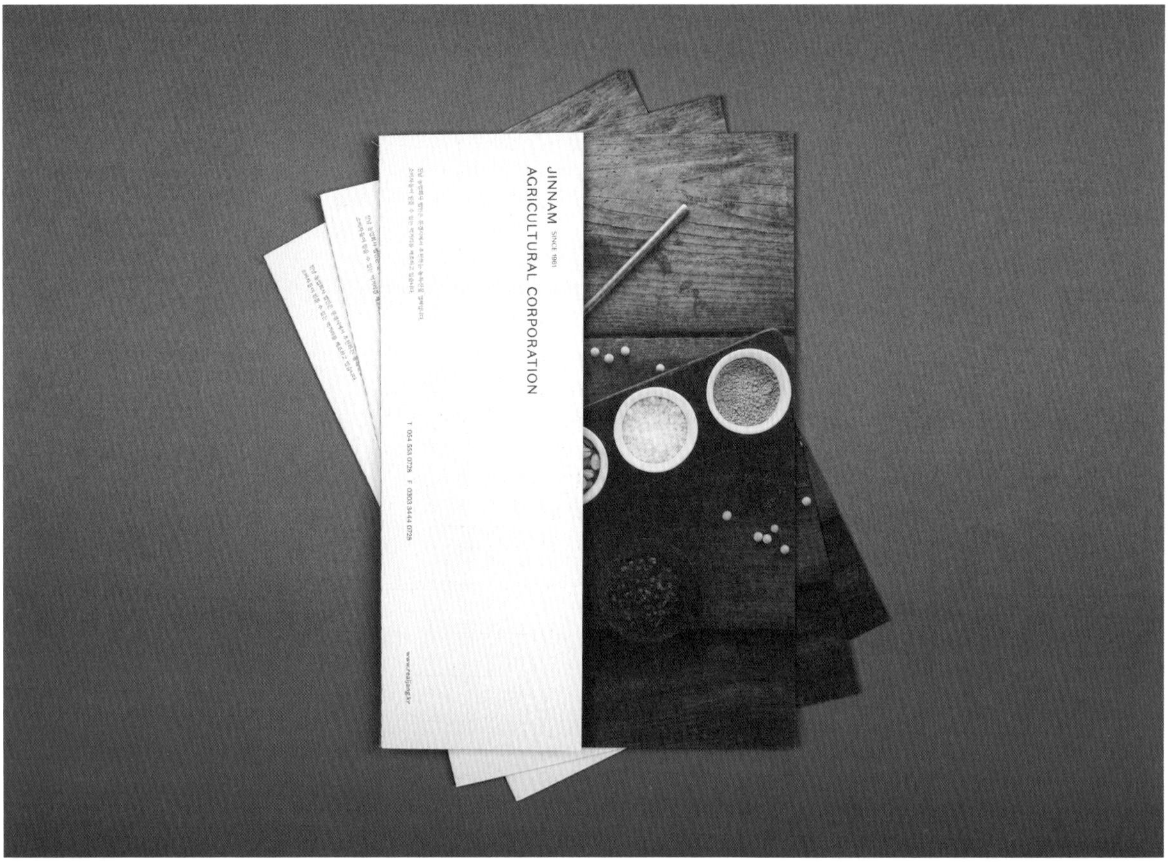

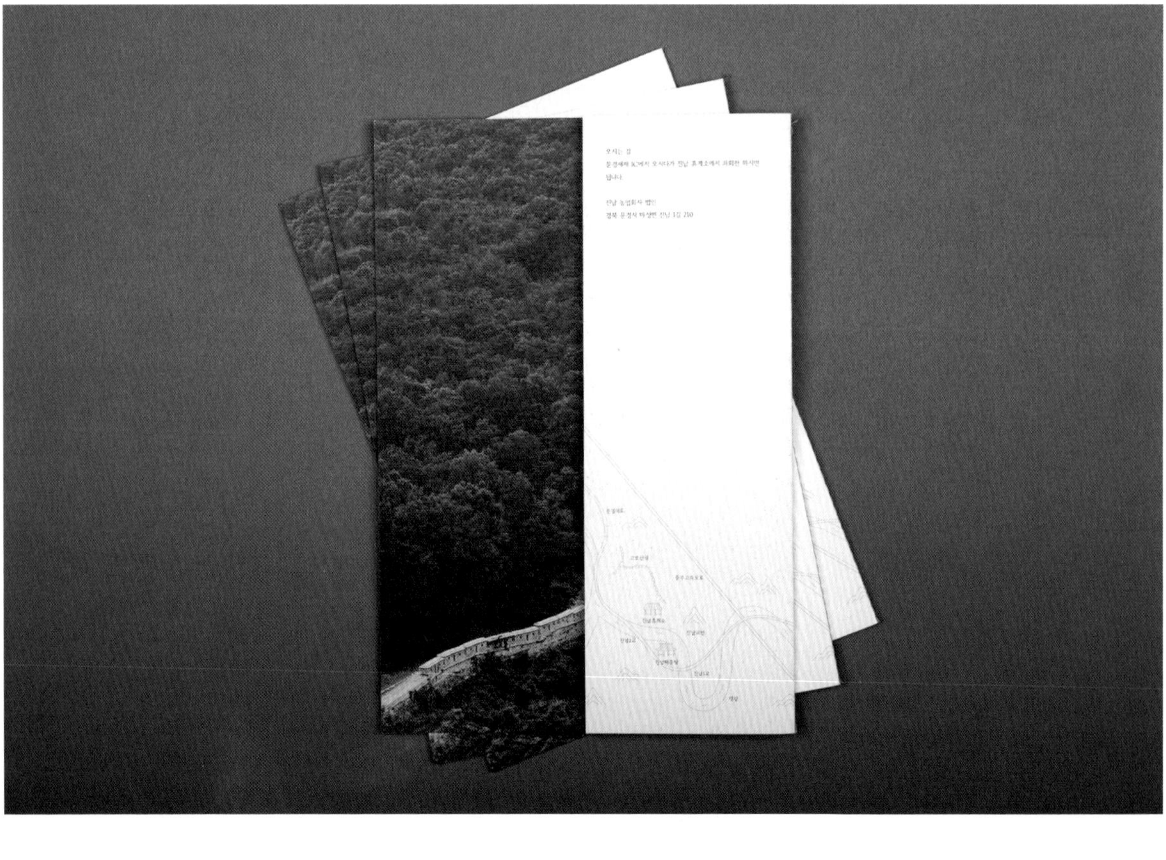

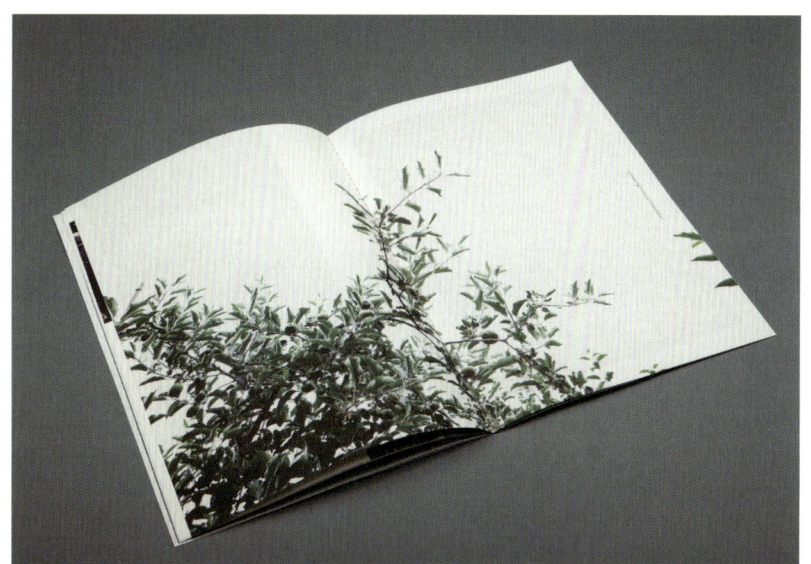
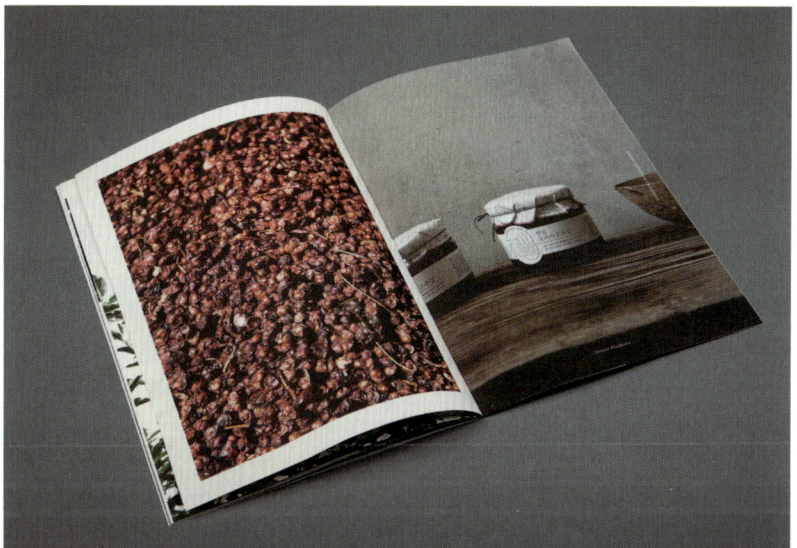
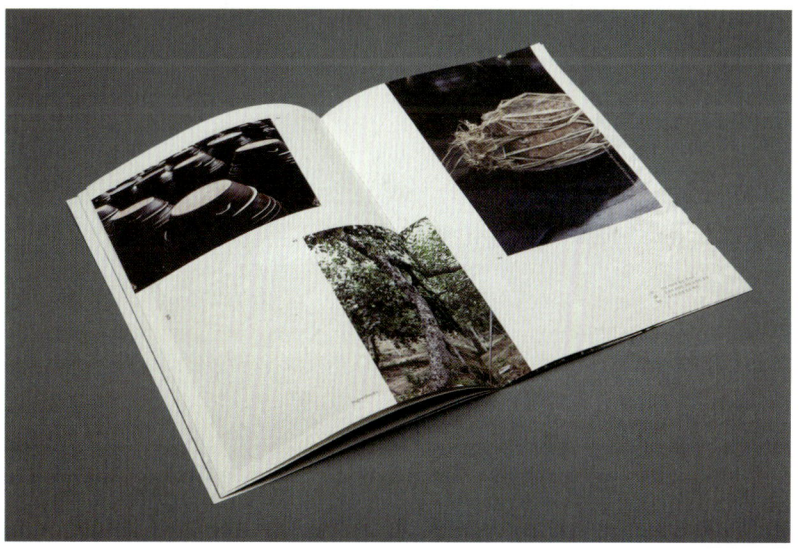

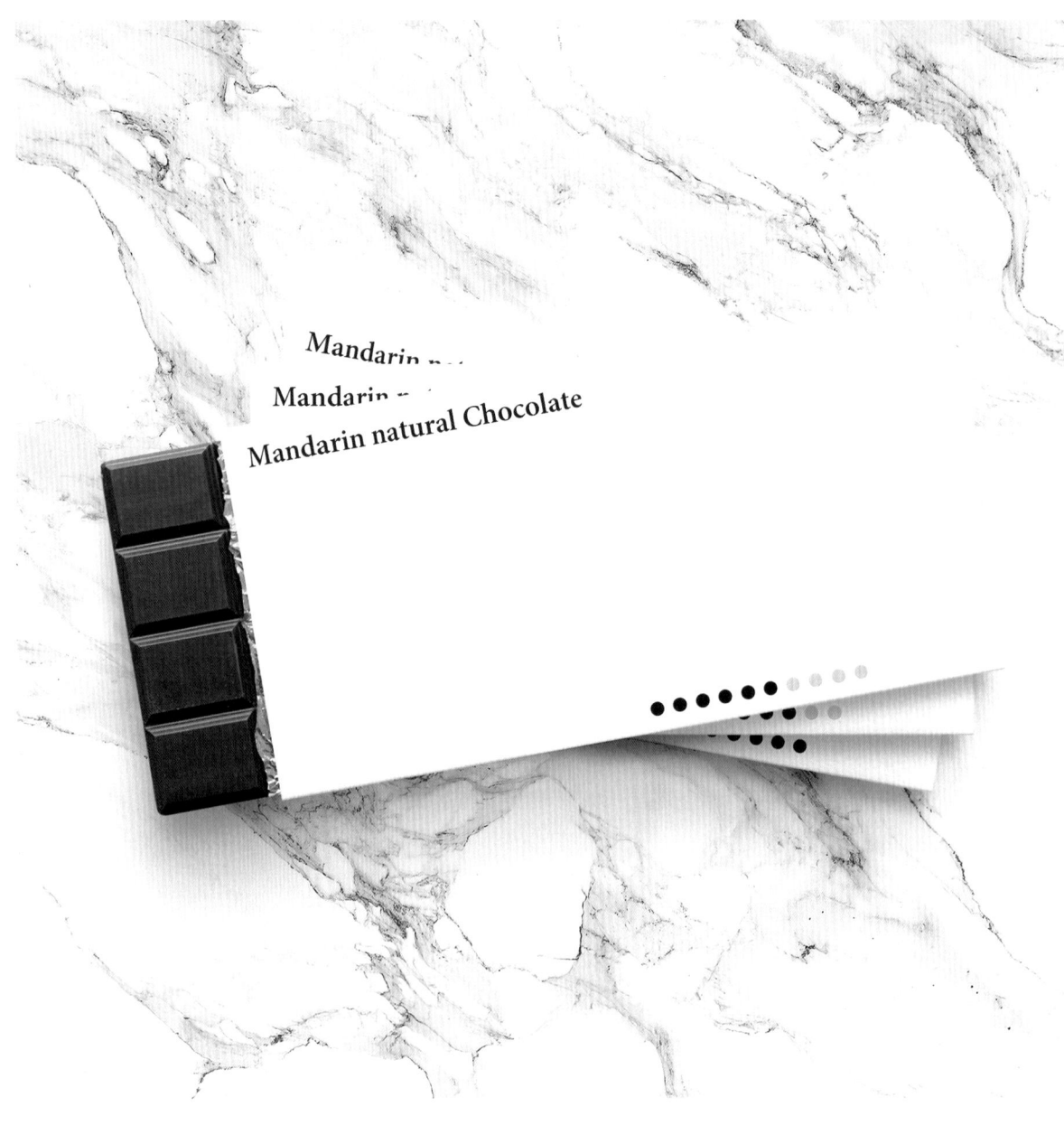

Mandarin Natural Chocolate

Designer: Yuta Takahashi

The quality chocolate brand who is dedicated to improving the quality of people's lives expresses itself through a modernistic graphic system characteristic by stunning white. The distinct identity integrates a minimalistic elegance with a contemporary impression, bringing out a lovely and novel image. An array of dots on the packaging subtly indicates the chocolate's intensity, ranging from 60%, 80% to 100%.

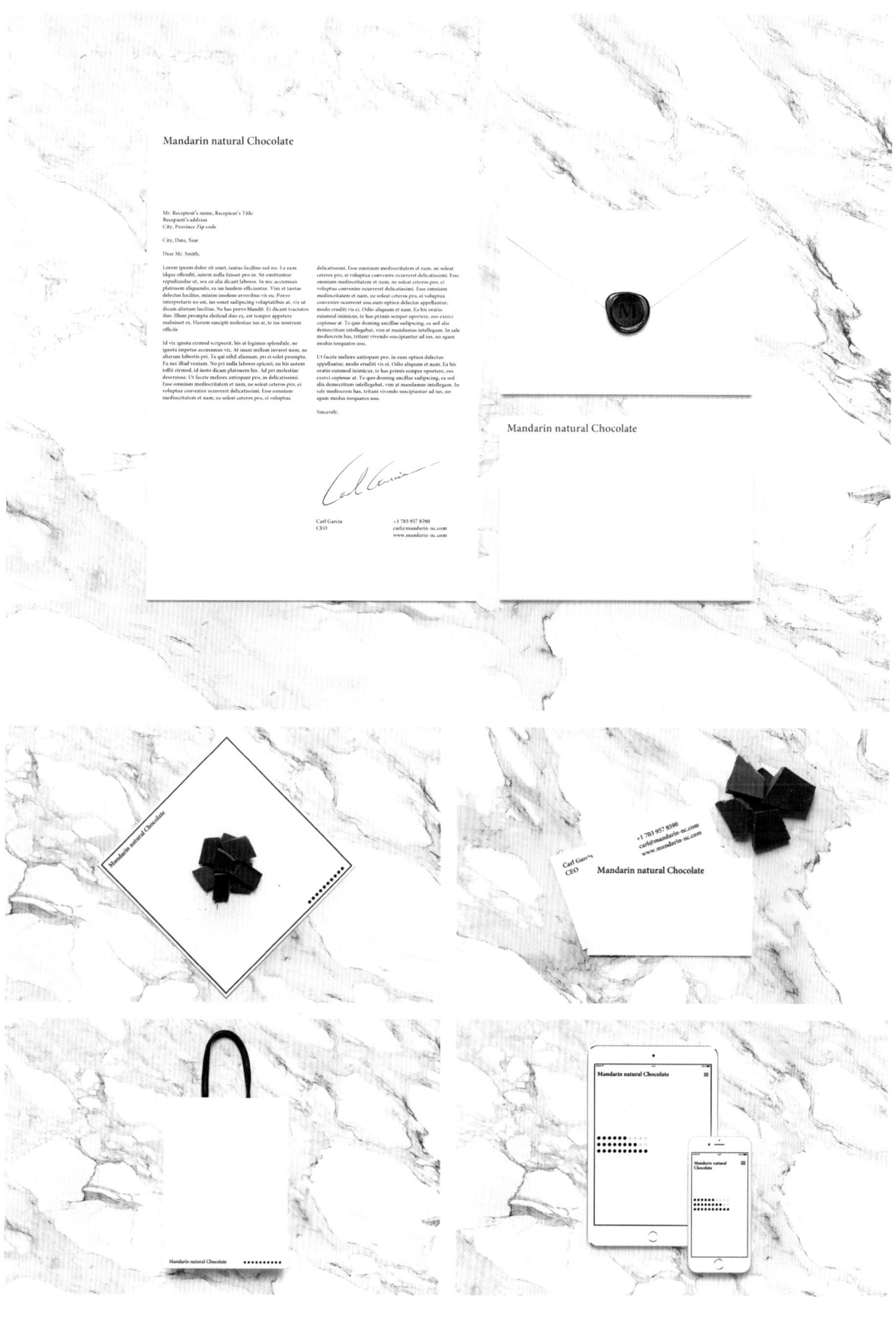

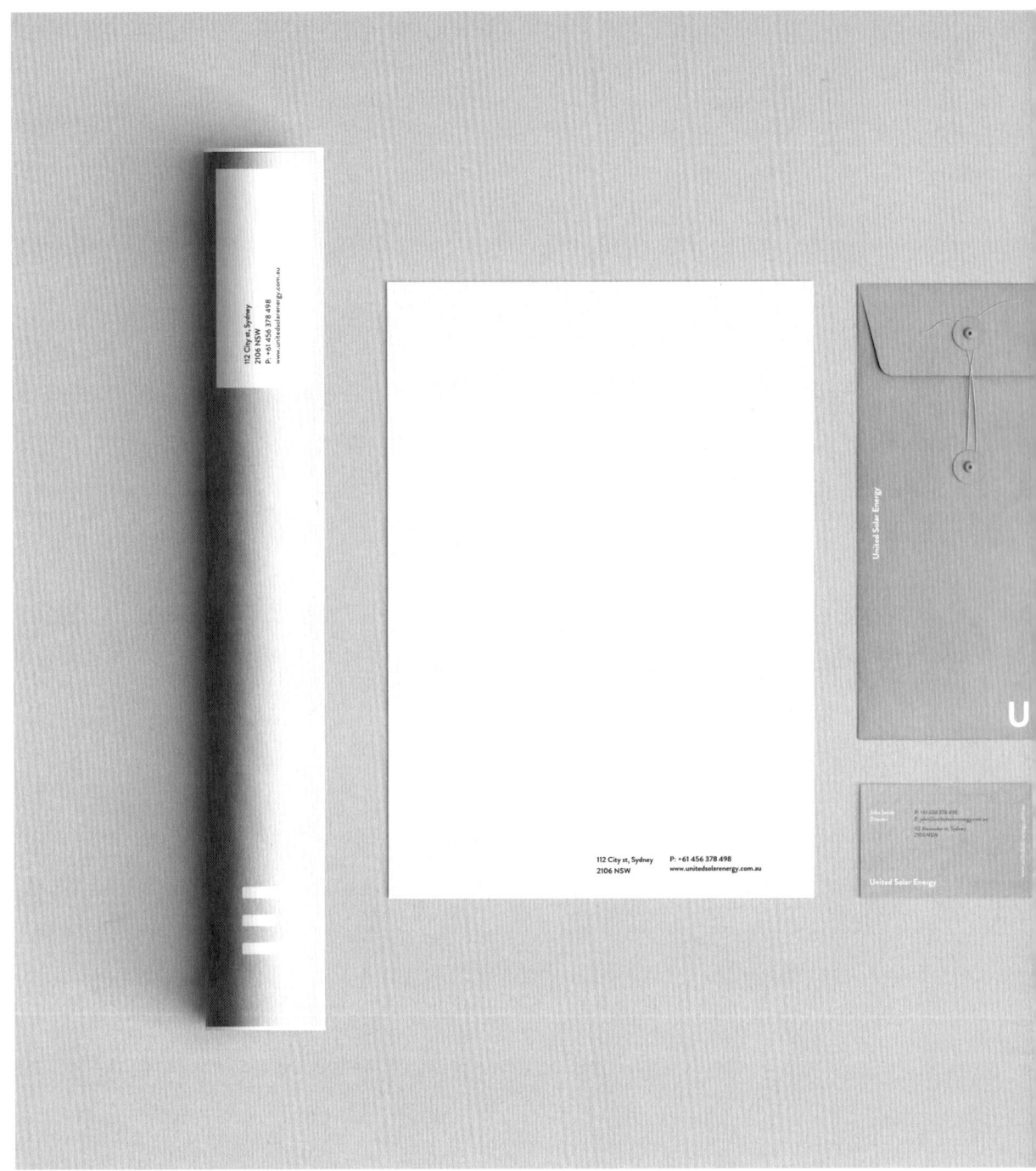

U-S-E

Designer: Madelyn Bilsborough

A new brand identity was created for United Solar Energy highlighting its beliefs in cost-effectiveness and its supply of solar panels and installation. The designer stuck to a minimal, grey toned color palette with hints of orange to bring vibrancy to the collaterals and to indicate the power generated. The "E" in "USE" acts as three panels, becoming a unique mark for the brand across all collateral items.

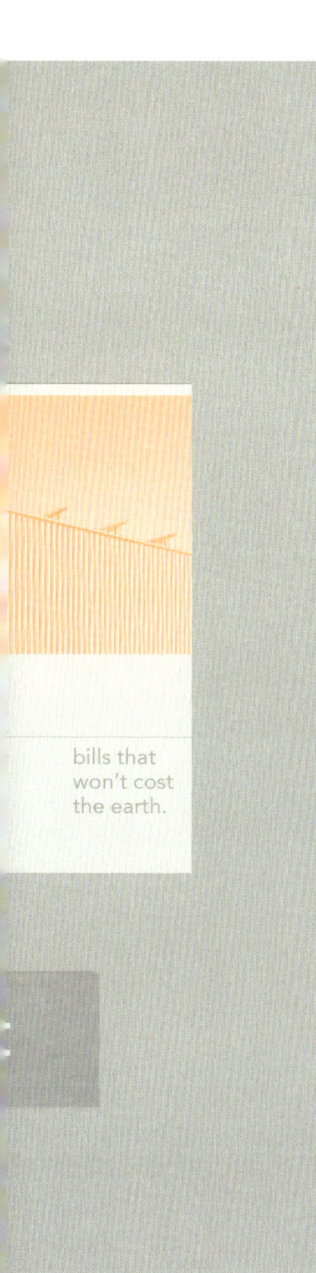
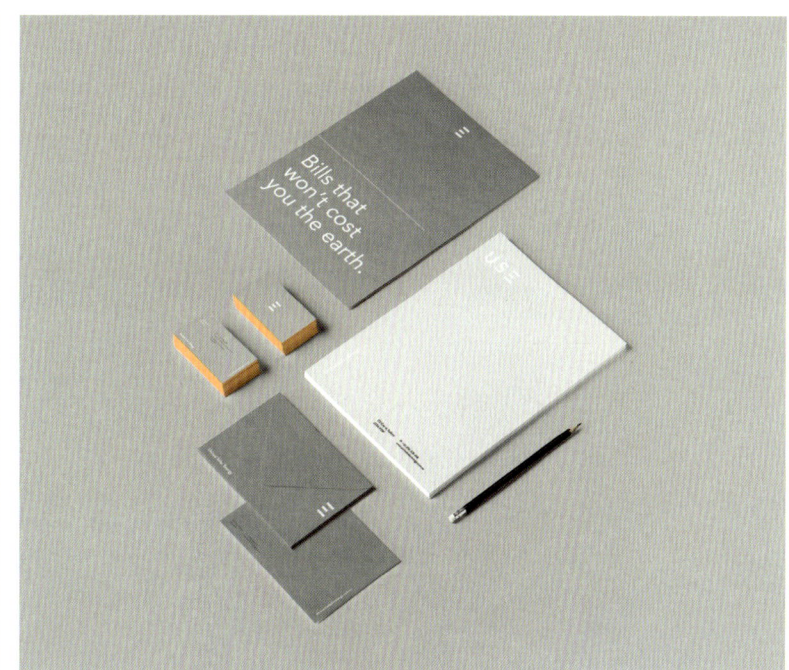
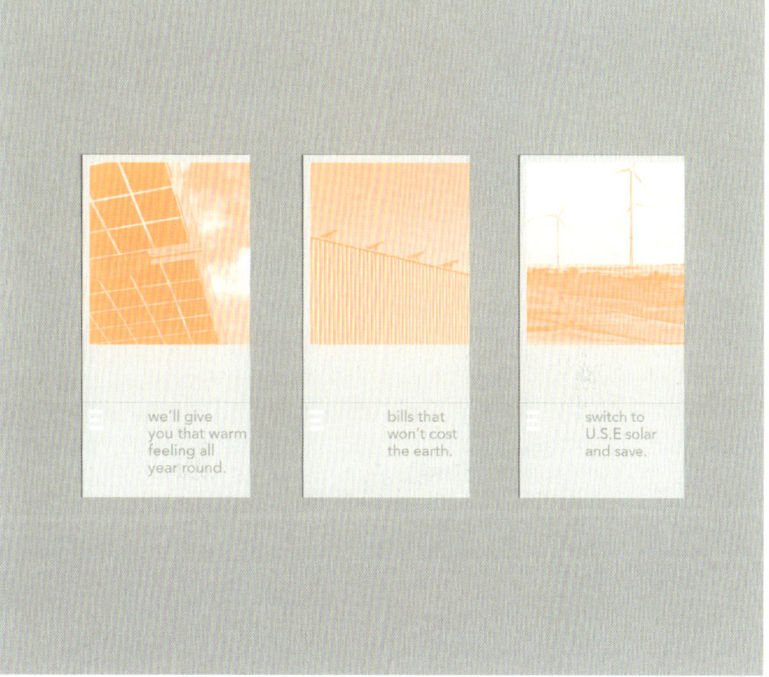

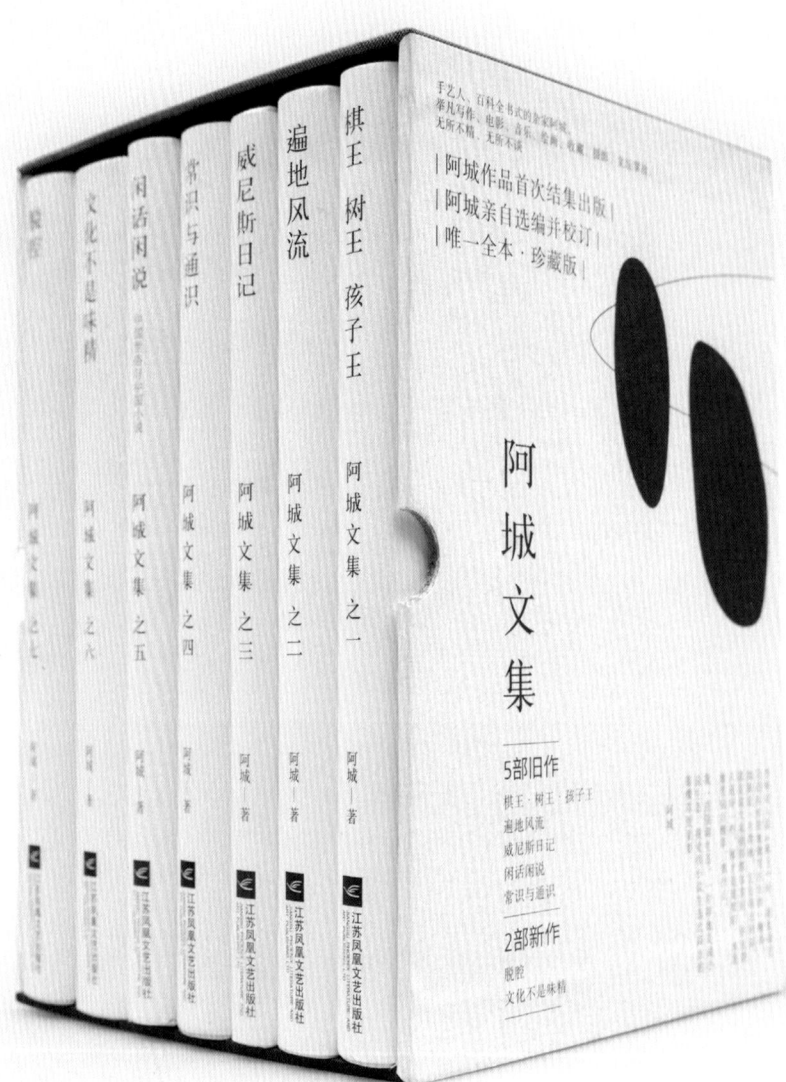

A Cheng

Studio: One Thousand Times | Designer: Zhu Sha

For the visual design for the new edition of *Collected Works of A Cheng*, the studio created a set of printing archaize font as the main visual element. The font helped maintain a consistency through the whole collection and highlighted the blankness in the composition. This seemingly effortless visual expression coincides with A Cheng´s literature style.

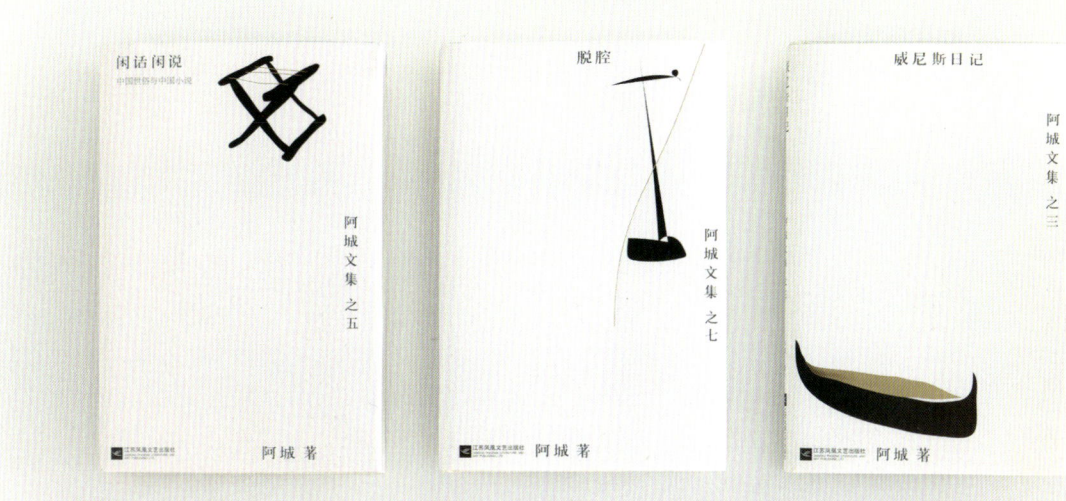

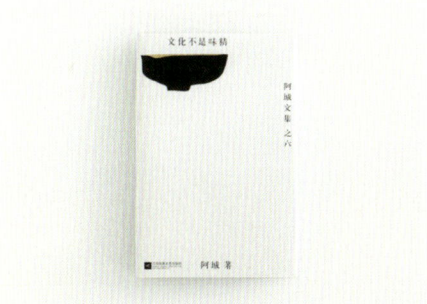

阿城文集

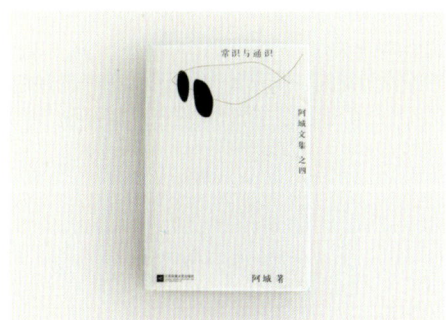

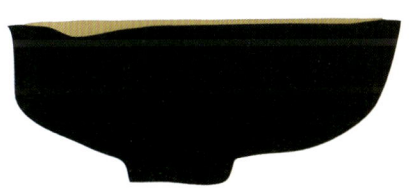

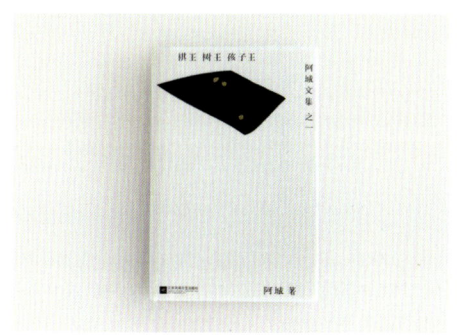

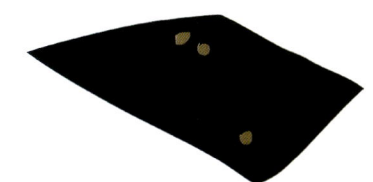

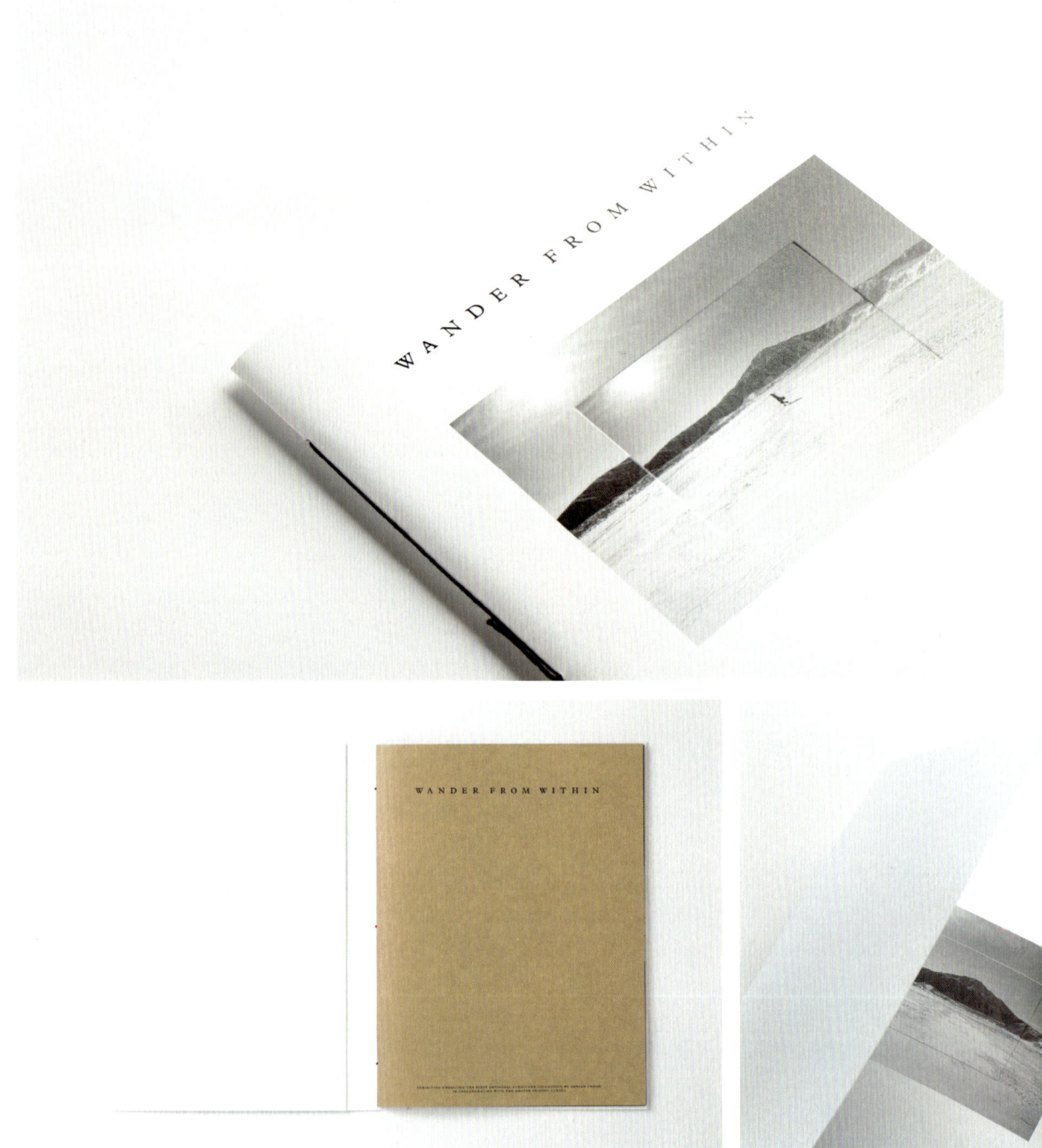

Wander from Within

Studio: Toby Ng Design | Designer: Toby Ng, Ronald Cheung

Event identity and catalogue created for an exhibition that unveiled Khora's artisanal furniture collection. To reflect the concept of Khora, a philosophical space between being and non-being, physical and non-physical, a resized key image was superimposed on the original to create a frame as a dimension to a metaphysical world that transcends the reality. Printed on the finest Japanese paper, the catalogue was hand sewn to resemble the artisanal craftsmanship.

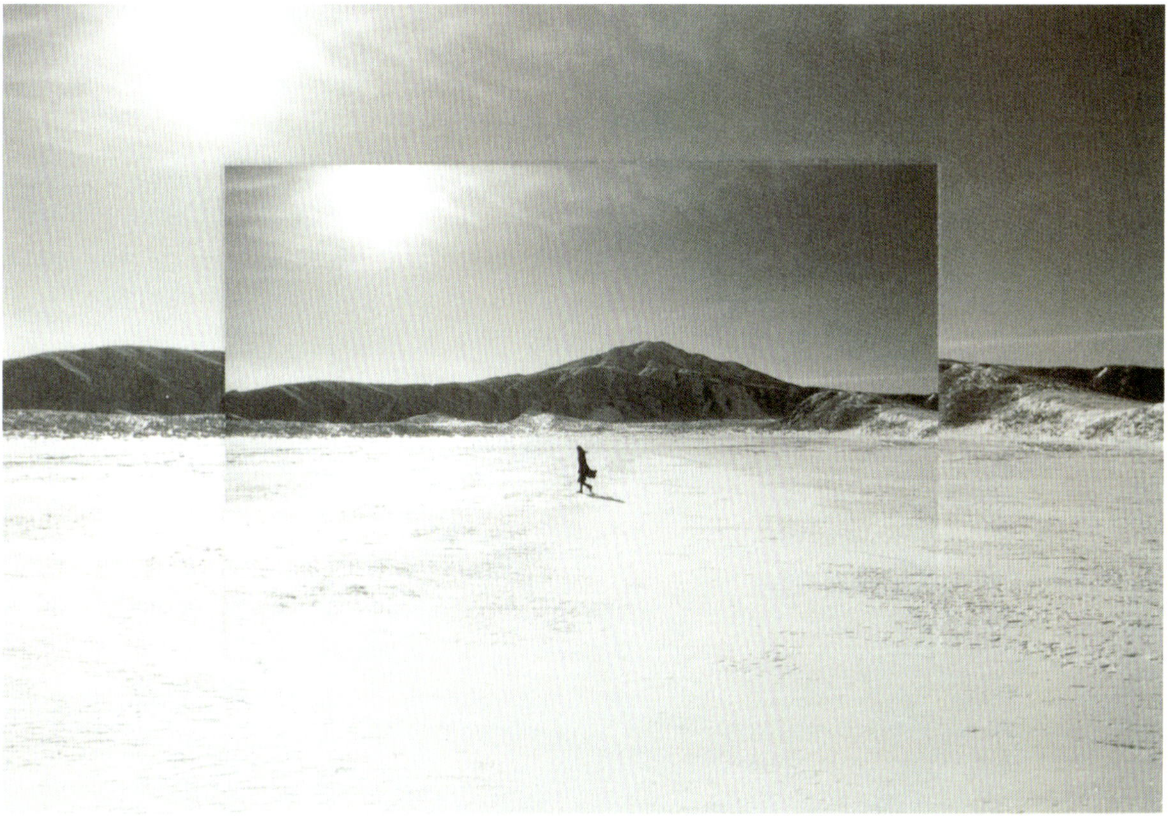

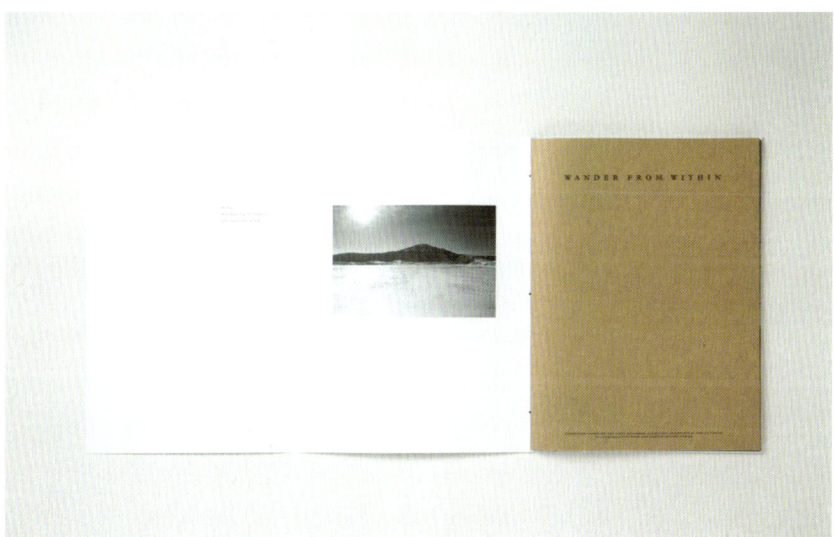

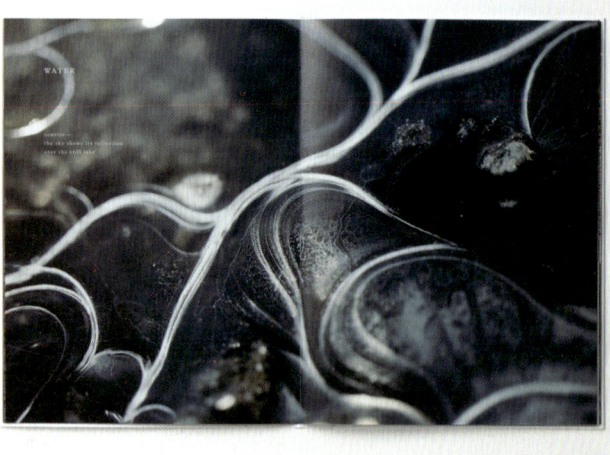
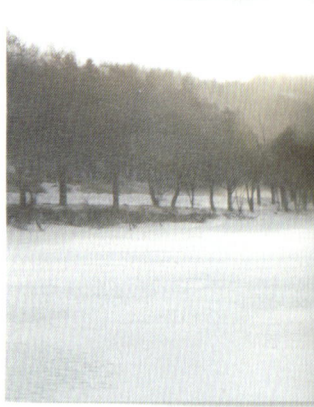
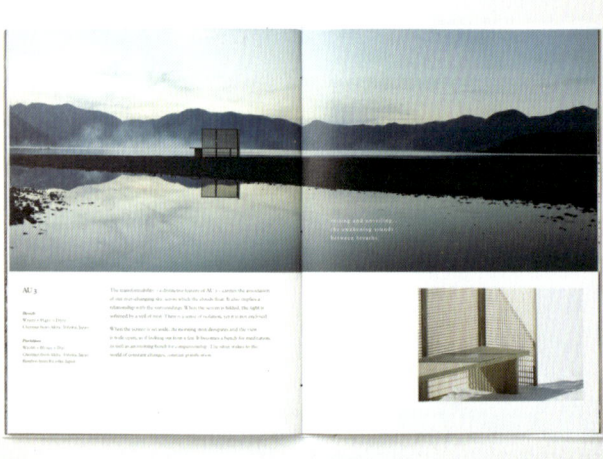
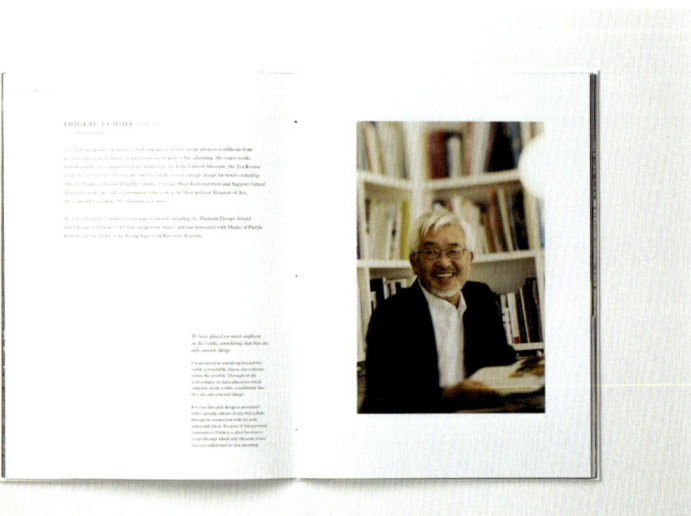

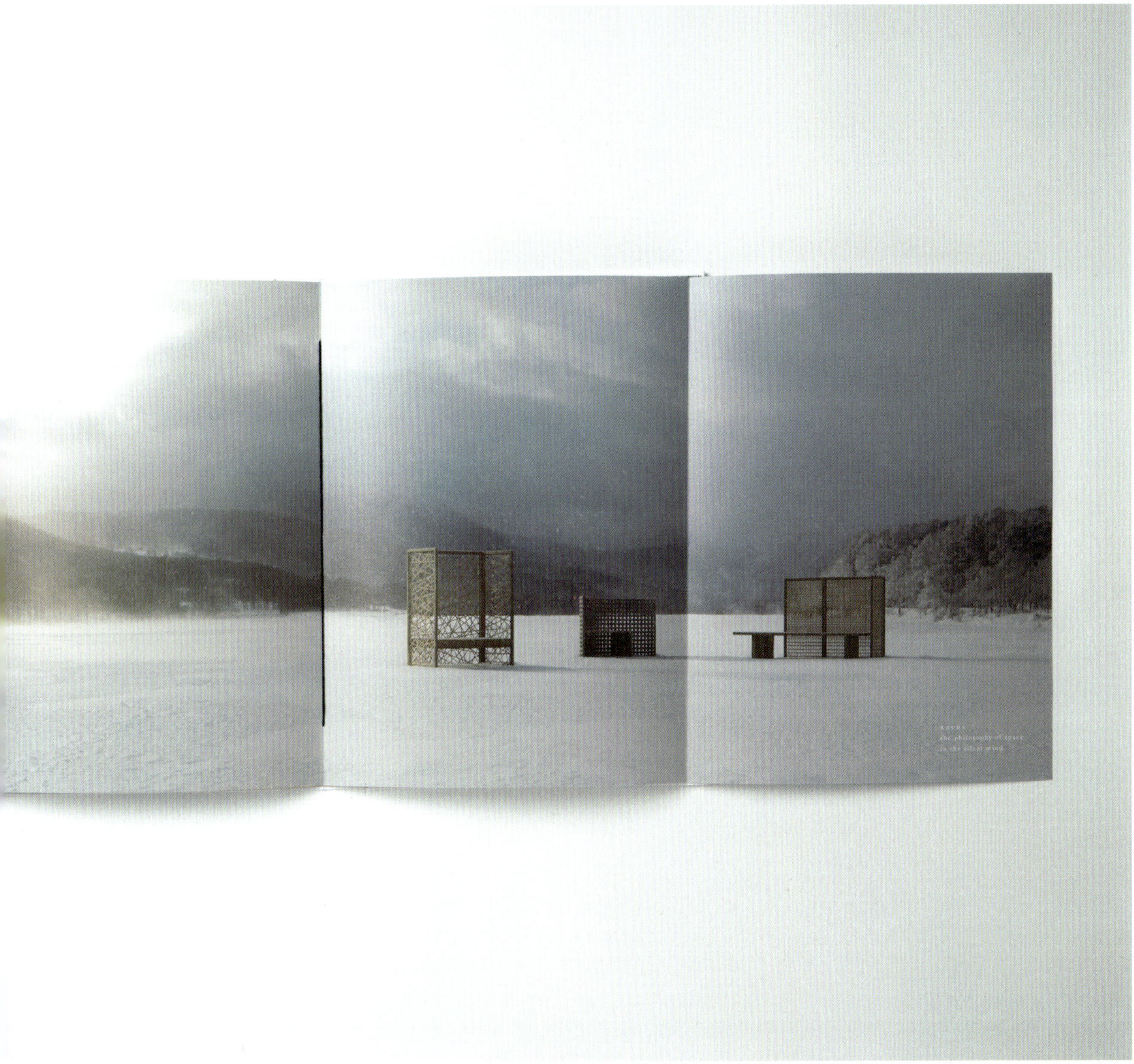

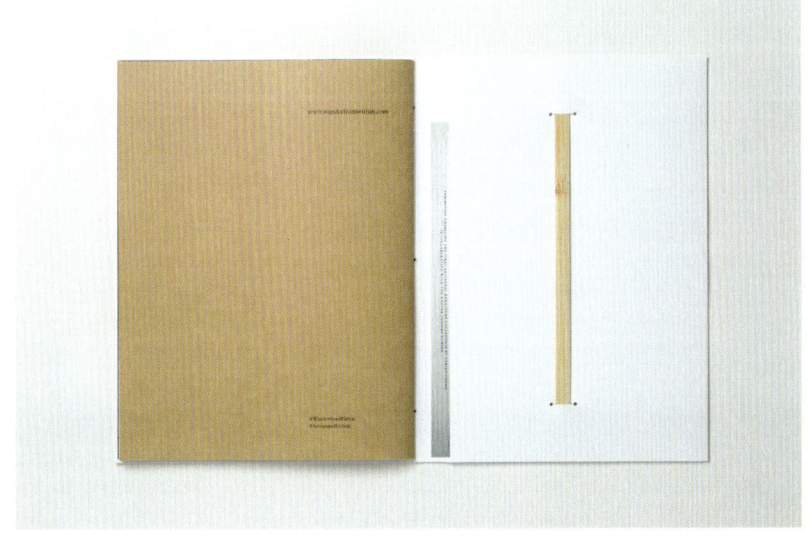

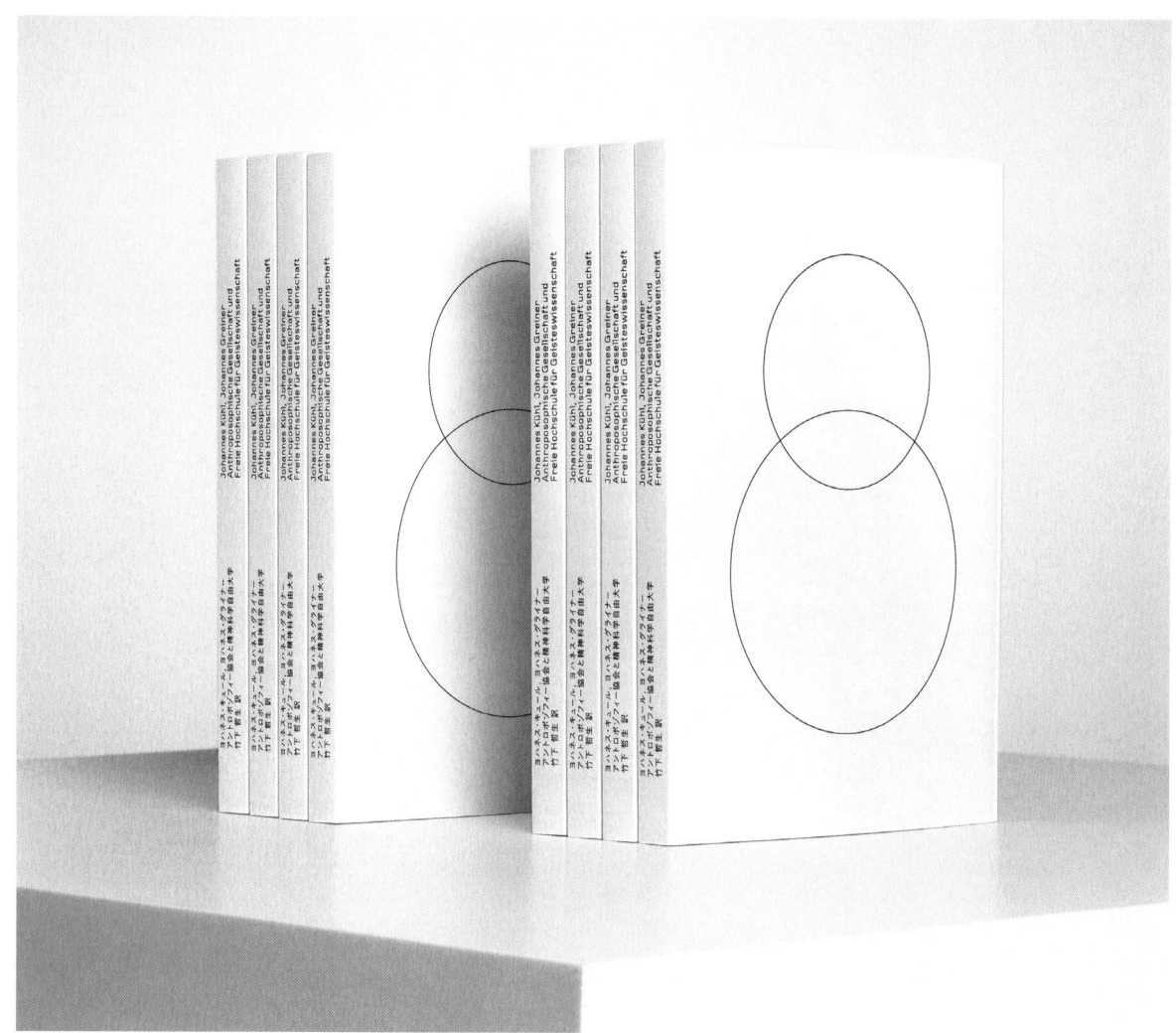

Anthroposophische Gesellschaft und Freie Hochschule für Geisteswissenschaft

Designer: Yuta Takahashi

This modern book design of minimalist and elegant beauty was constructed with simulation from art, interior design and lifestyle. The key visuals on the cover clearly depict the book's intention to explore the relationship between the society and school. Presenting the content of thought on a white background is uniform throughout this series. The artistic touch of attention to details can be traced from even the minute gimmicks.

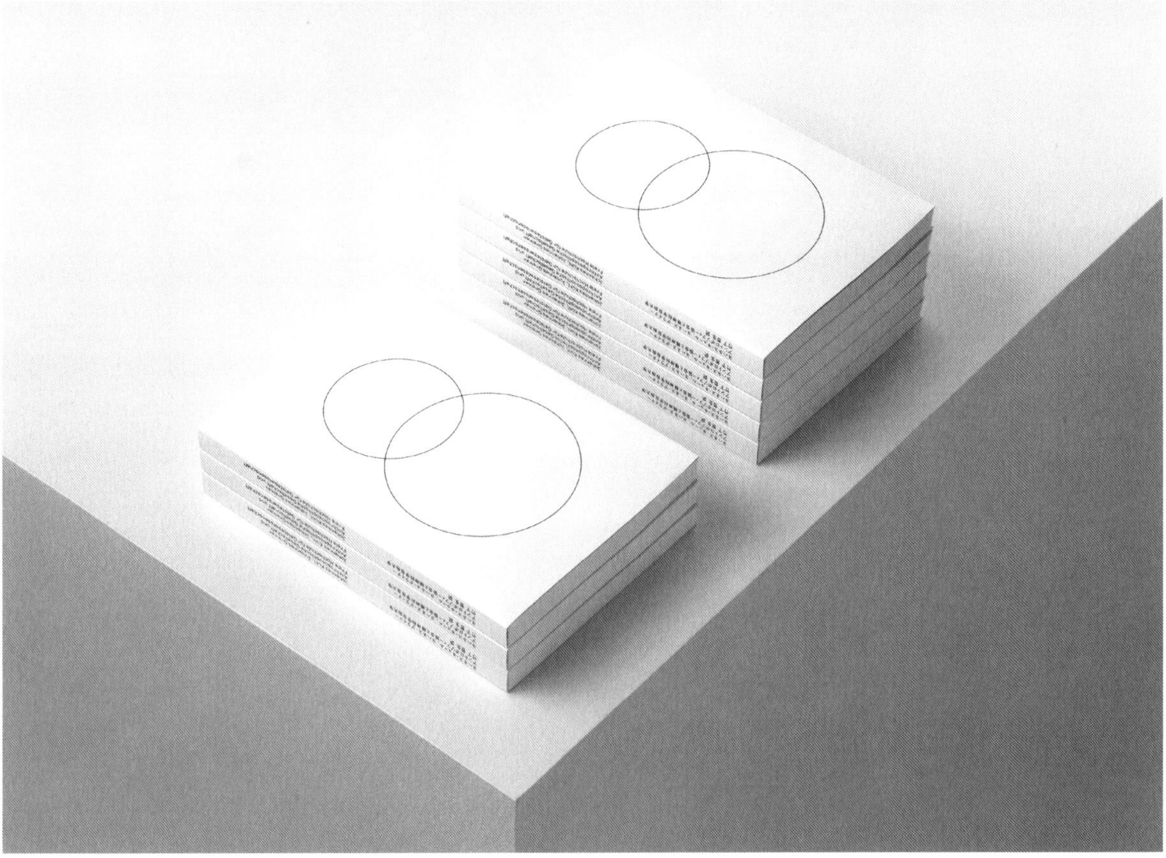

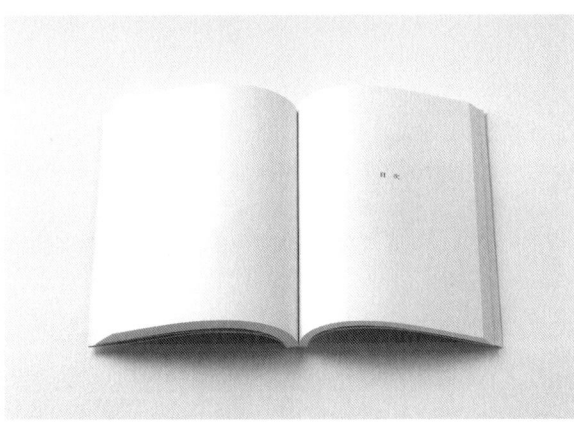
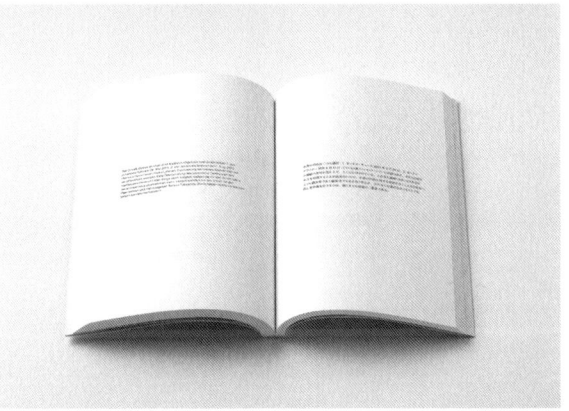
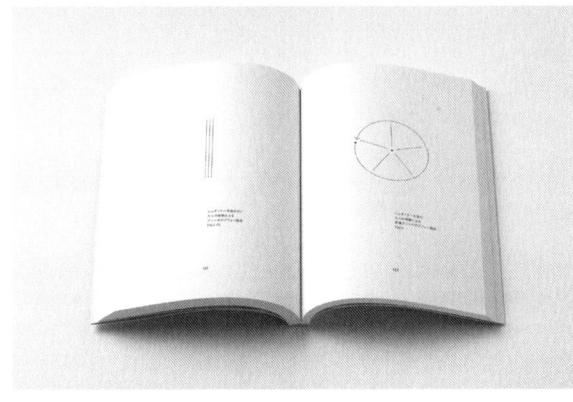
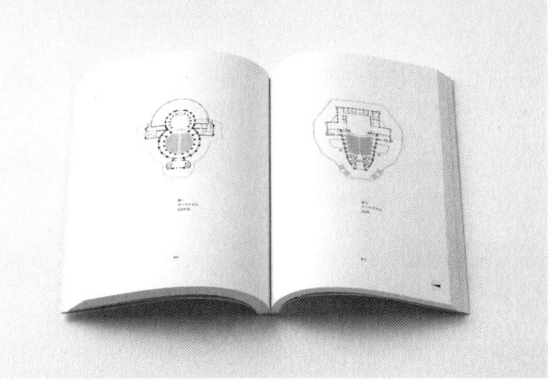

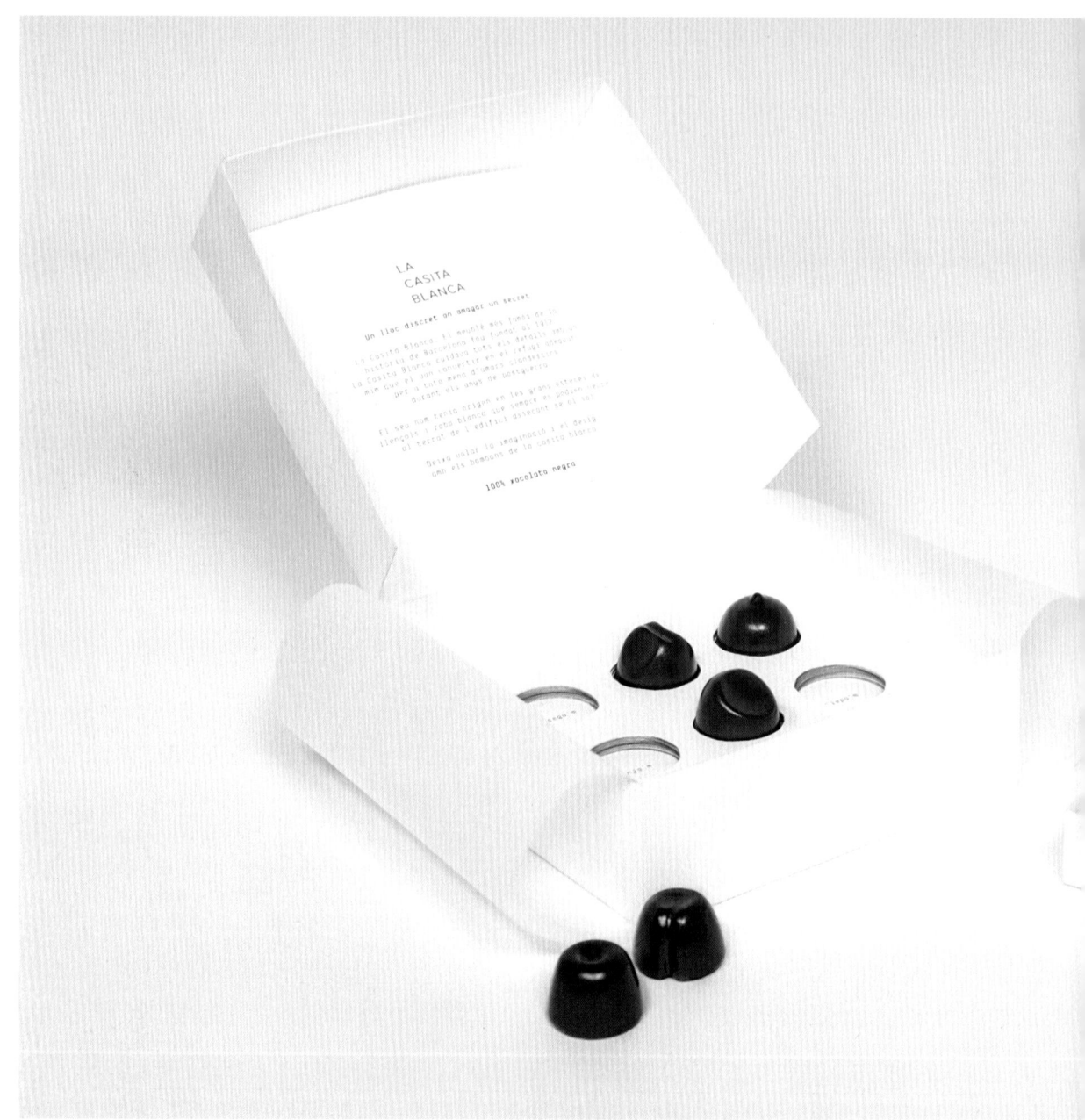

La Casita Blanca

Designer: Laura de Miguel, Cristian Varela, Maria Romero

The mysterious, elegant and impressive chocolate and its packaging were inspired by the famous Meublé in the history of Barcelona, a building with white linen stretches on the roof and whose attention to details once made it the perfect shelter for clandestine love. Against the white packaging, the rich brown chocolates stand out boldly. The brand name will be revealed by pulling the small tab attached.

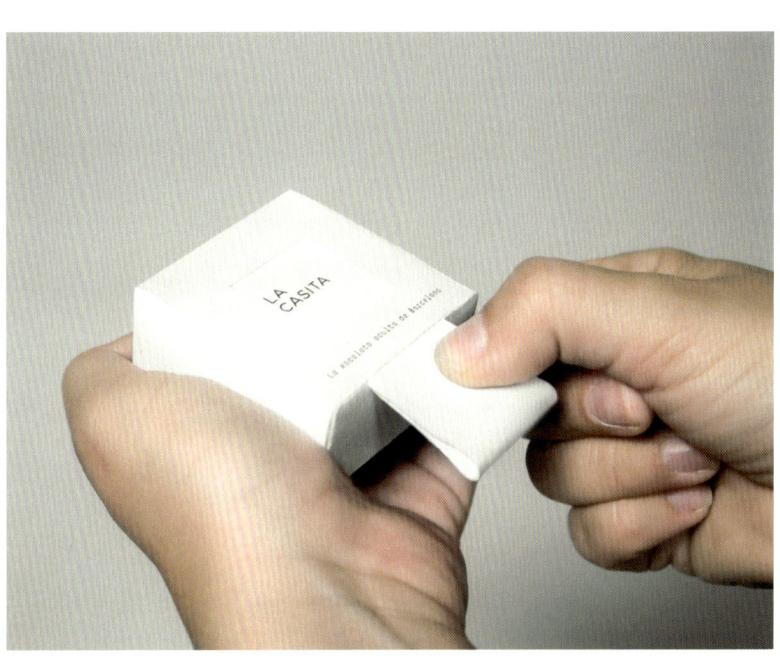
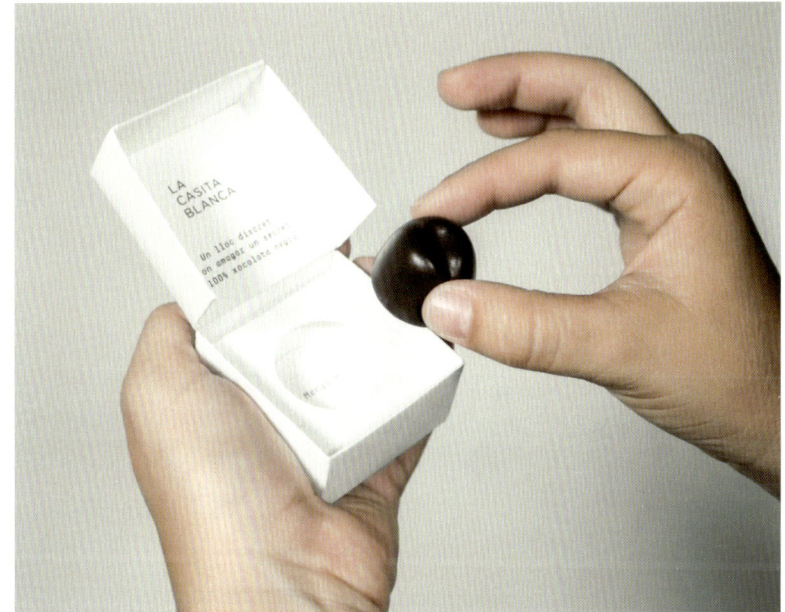
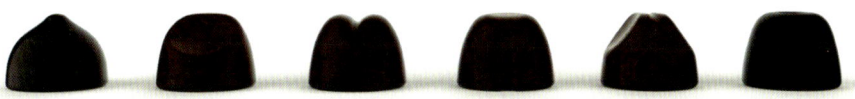

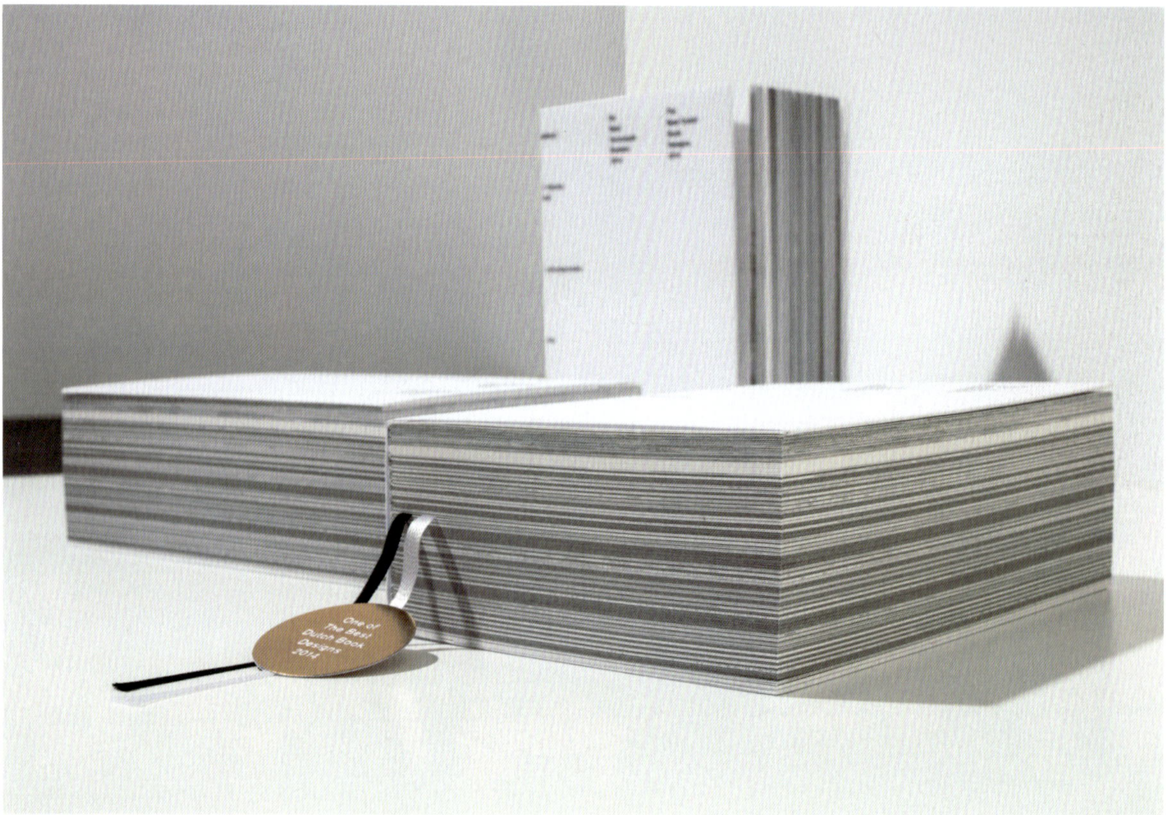

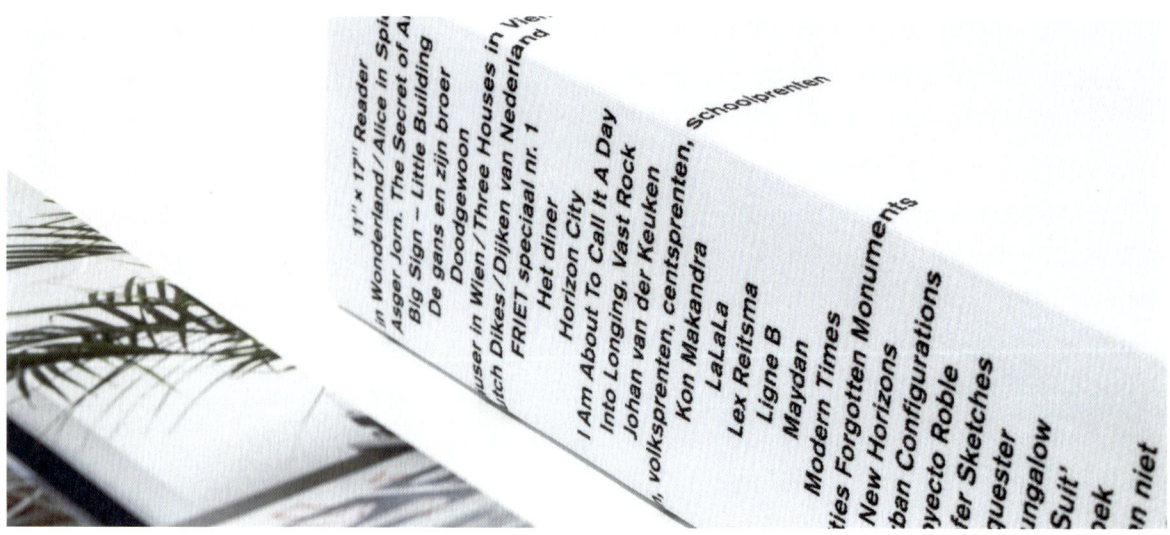

The Best Dutch Book Designs 2014

Designer: Haller Brun

This small, brick-like volume introduces the awarded books in the Best Dutch Book Designs 2014. Each awarded publication is presented in a thorough way, including a color photo of the designer's bookshelf with the book on it, all the interior layouts of each book in stamp size, the jury report in Dutch and English, and the technical information. The main part of the book is only printed in black and white to support the analytical character of the presentation of the books.

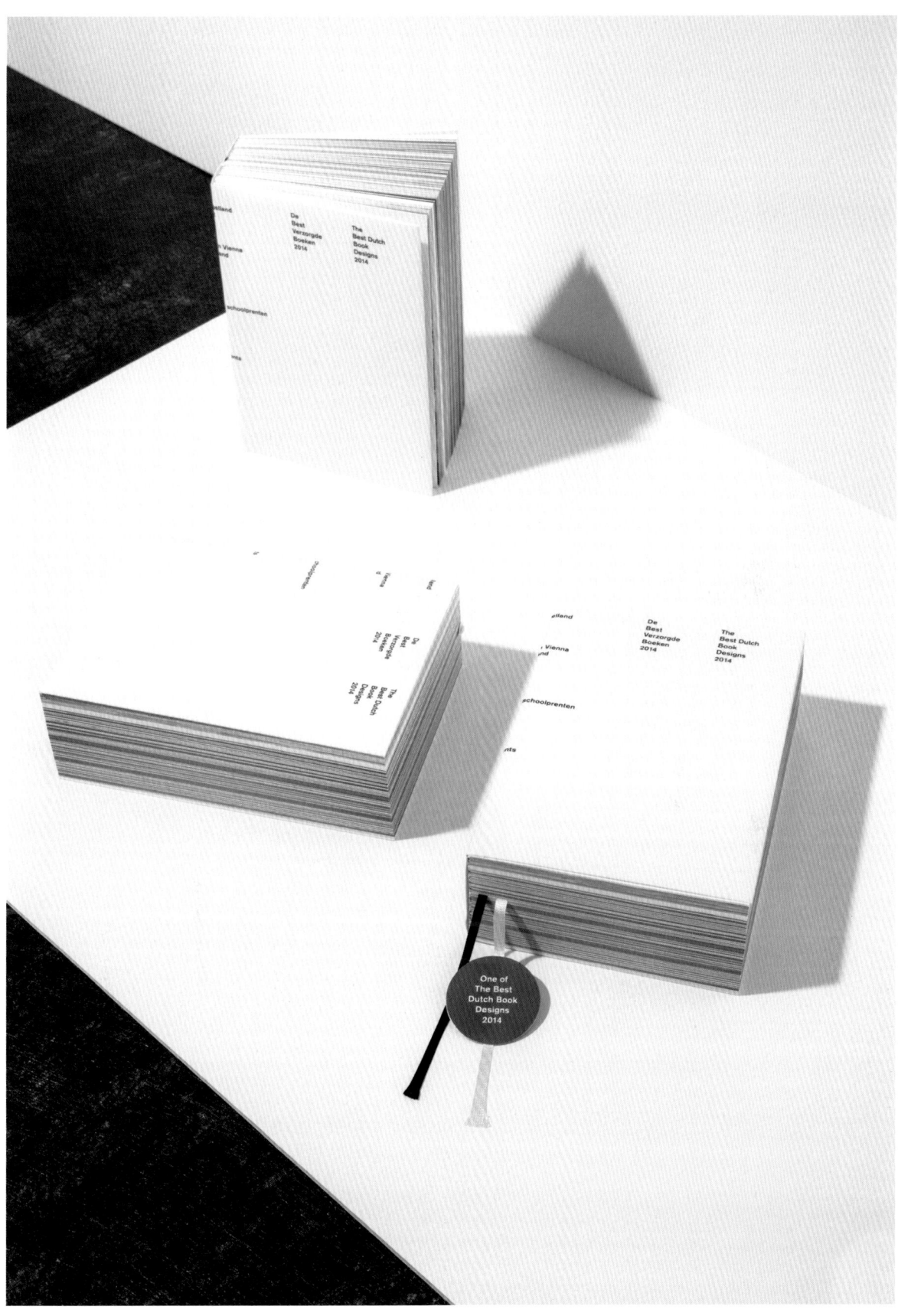

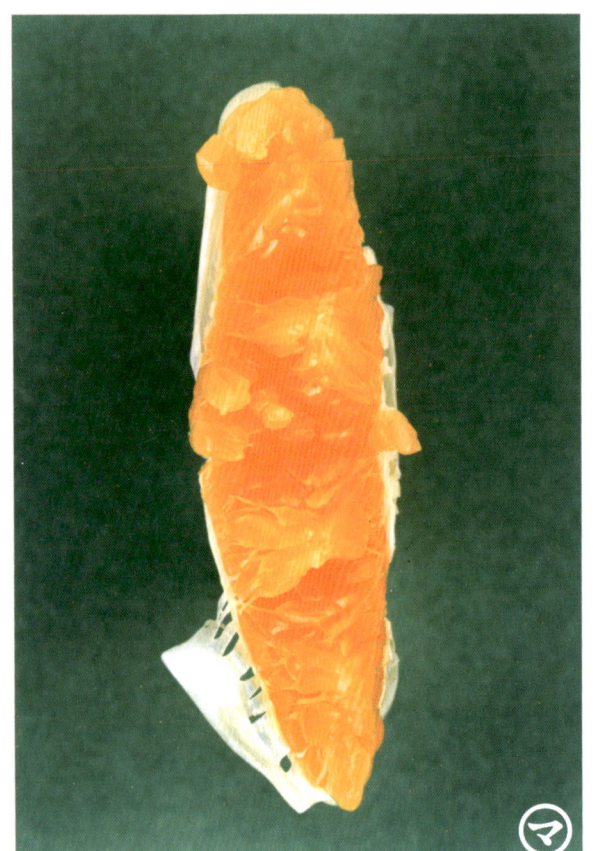 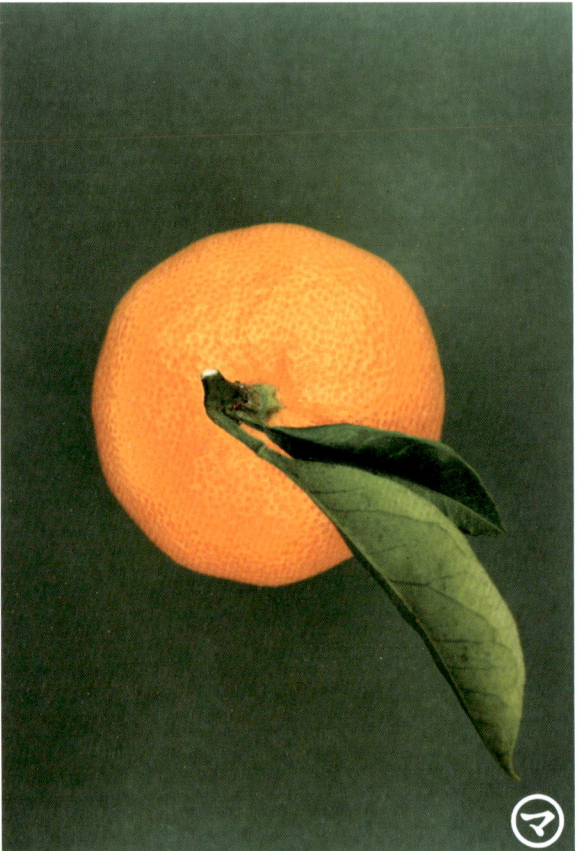

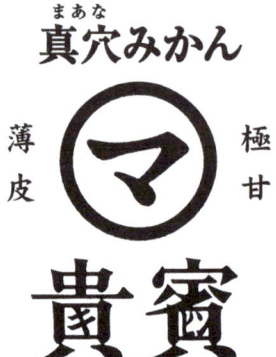

Maana Orange—KIHIN

Studio: Taku Satoh Design Office Inc. | Designer: Taku Satoh, Natsuko Fukuhara

Maana Oranges, produced at the Maana area in Ehime Prefecture, is one of the most delicious kinds of oranges in Japan. KIHIN brand is known as the best quality brand among Maana oranges. The small, thin-skin orange has a delicious sweet taste complimented with a bit of sourness that make the brand stand out. In addition to the highlight of the taste, designers want to accent the brand with an appealing regionality of the production area.
Because the Chinese characters of KIHIN(貴賓) is sometimes too difficult even for the Japanese to read, the designers replaced their core with their corresponding Japanese (katakana) alphabets "キヒン", to make it easier to pronounce. The design appears to be simple, yet a great amount of efforts were put in such details.

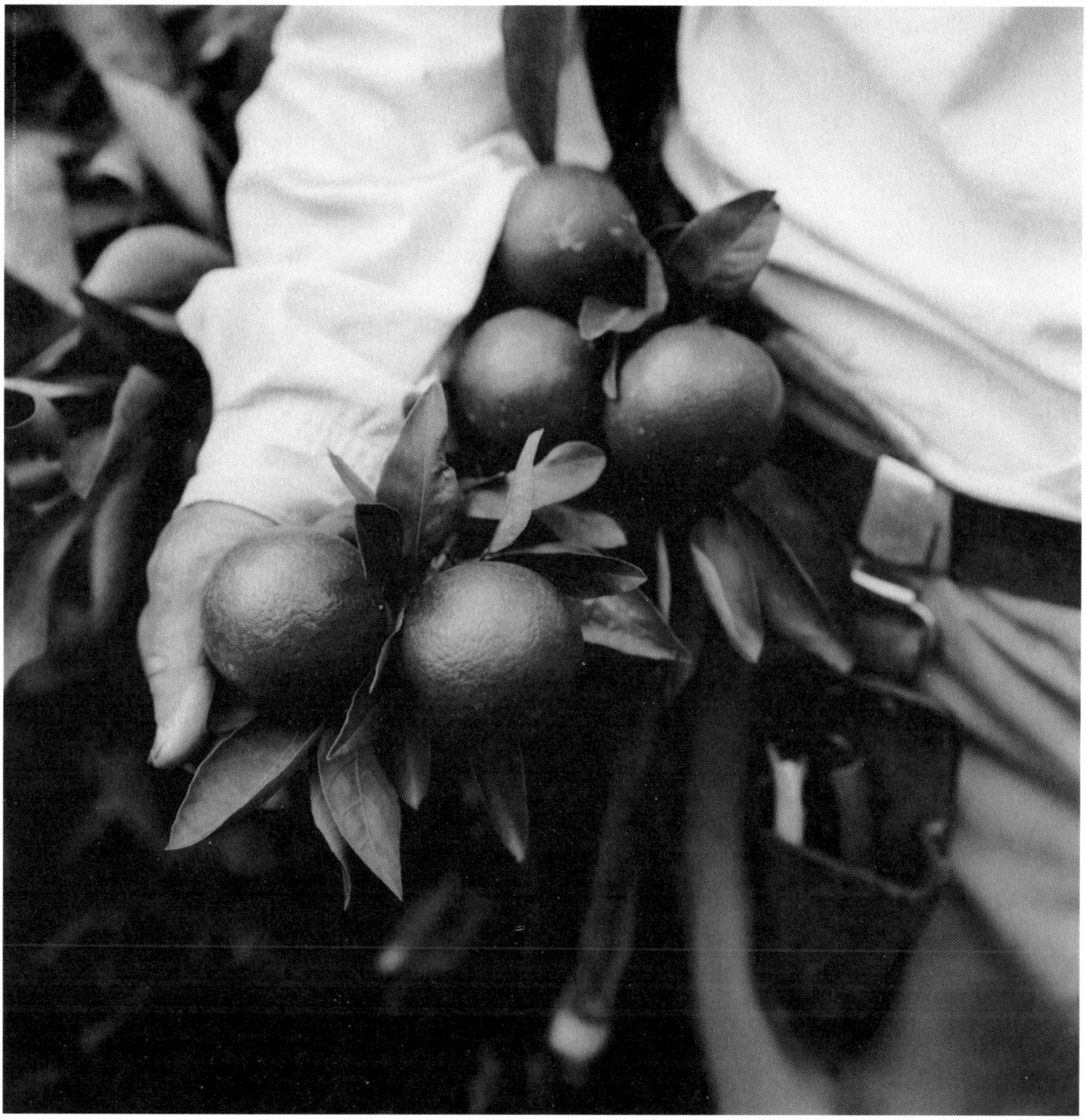

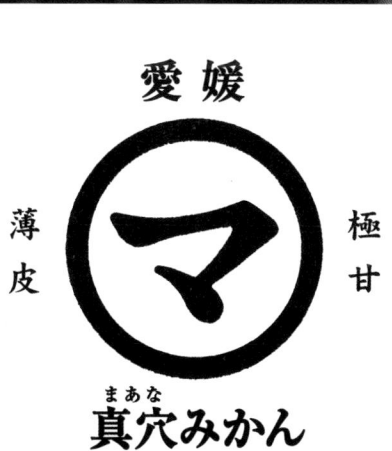

愛媛

薄皮　極甘

マ

真穴(まあな)みかん

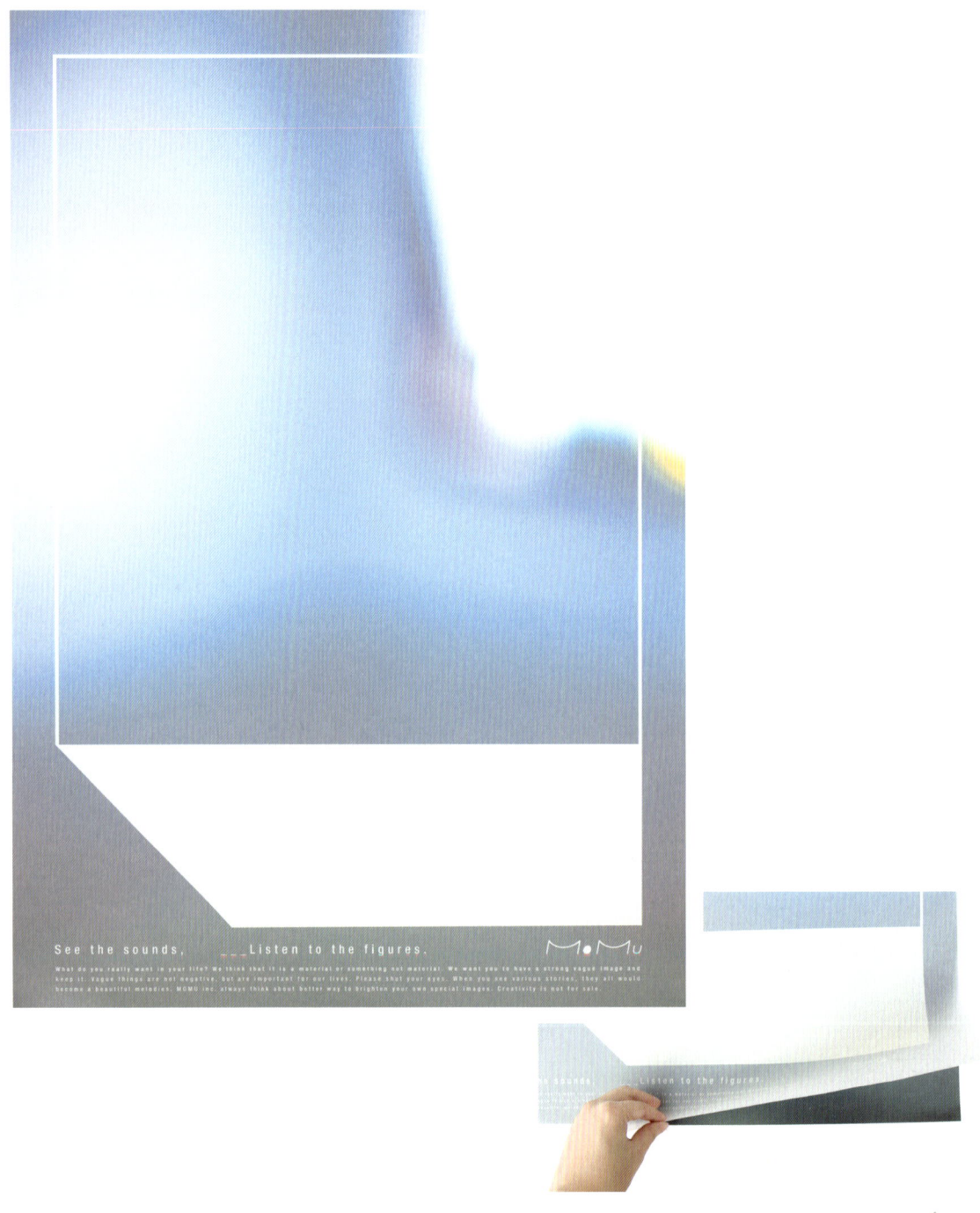

See the Sounds, ___ Listen to the Figures

Studio: room-composite | Designer: Tomoya Kaishi | photographer: Mina Imai

The designer placed transparent papers printed with typographic elements on highly chromatic photographs, the colors of which were tuned to a pale tone, to arrive at a vague impression desired by MO-MU. The abstract nature of sound and sight were expressed through the work.

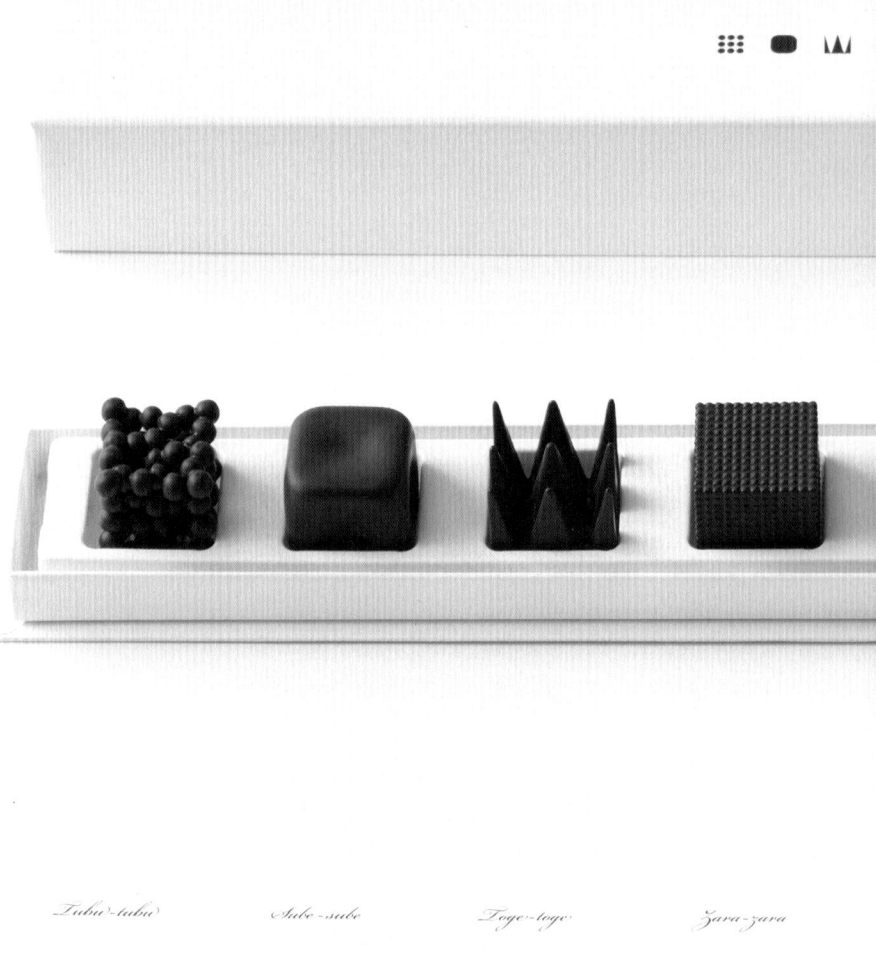

Tubu-tubu   Sube-sube   Toge-toge   Zara-zara

Chocolatexture

Studio: Nendo

Instead of paying attention to cocoa's country of origin, percentage content or technique of the chocolatier, the designer turned to the shape of chocolate for his creative concept. The 9 different types of chocolate are made within the same size, 26x26x-26mm, featuring pointed tips, hollow interior, smooth or rough surface textures. While the raw materials are identical, the distinctive textures create different tastes. Each chocolate is named after Japanese expressions used to describe texture.

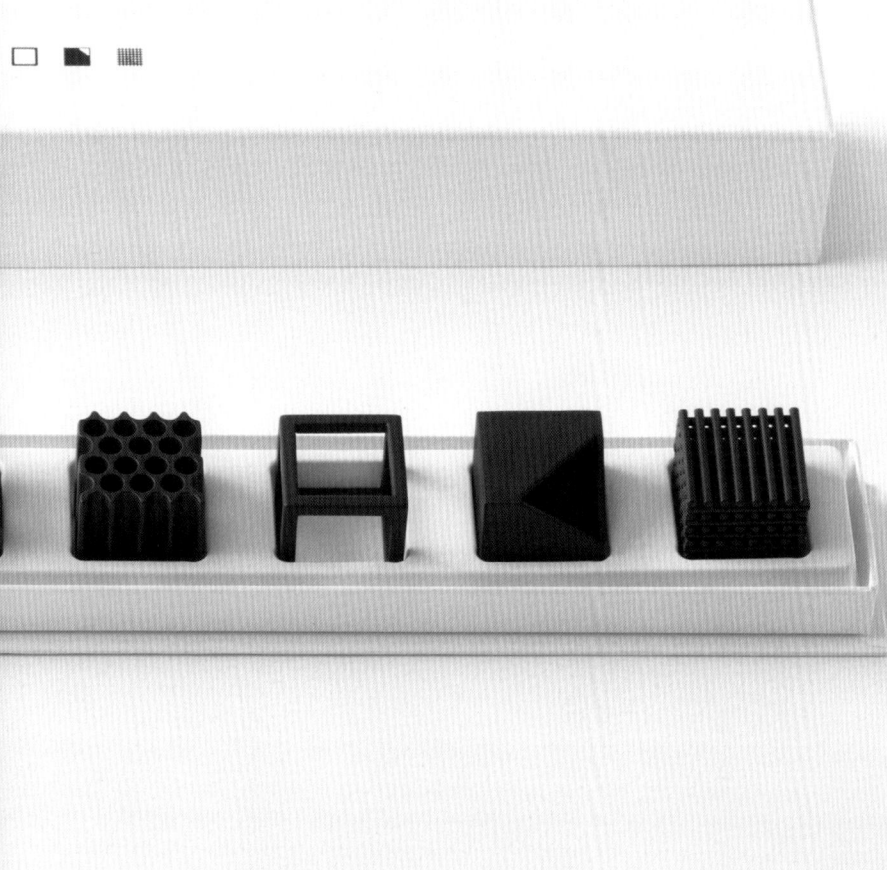

Fuwa-fuwa   Poki-poki   Suka-suka   Zaku-zaku

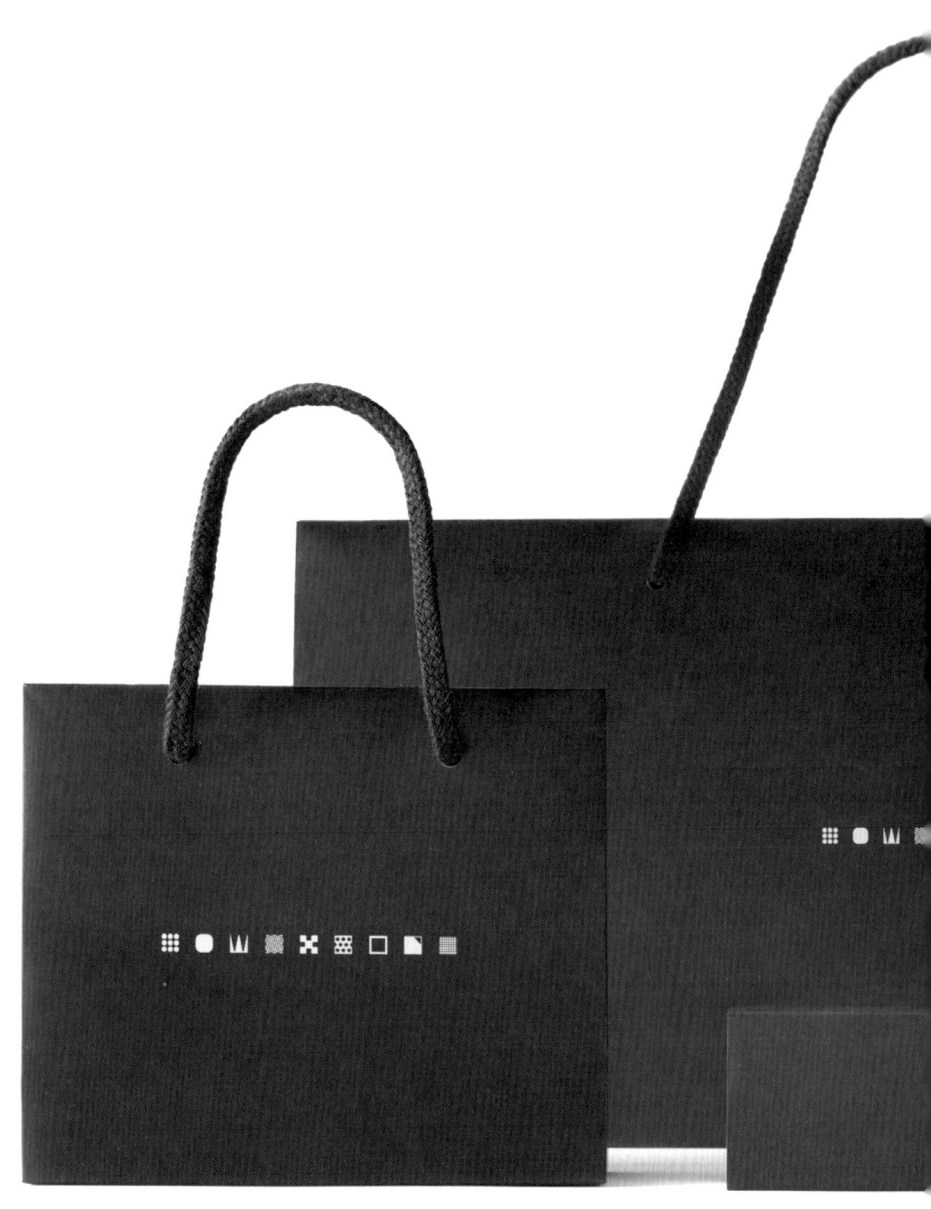

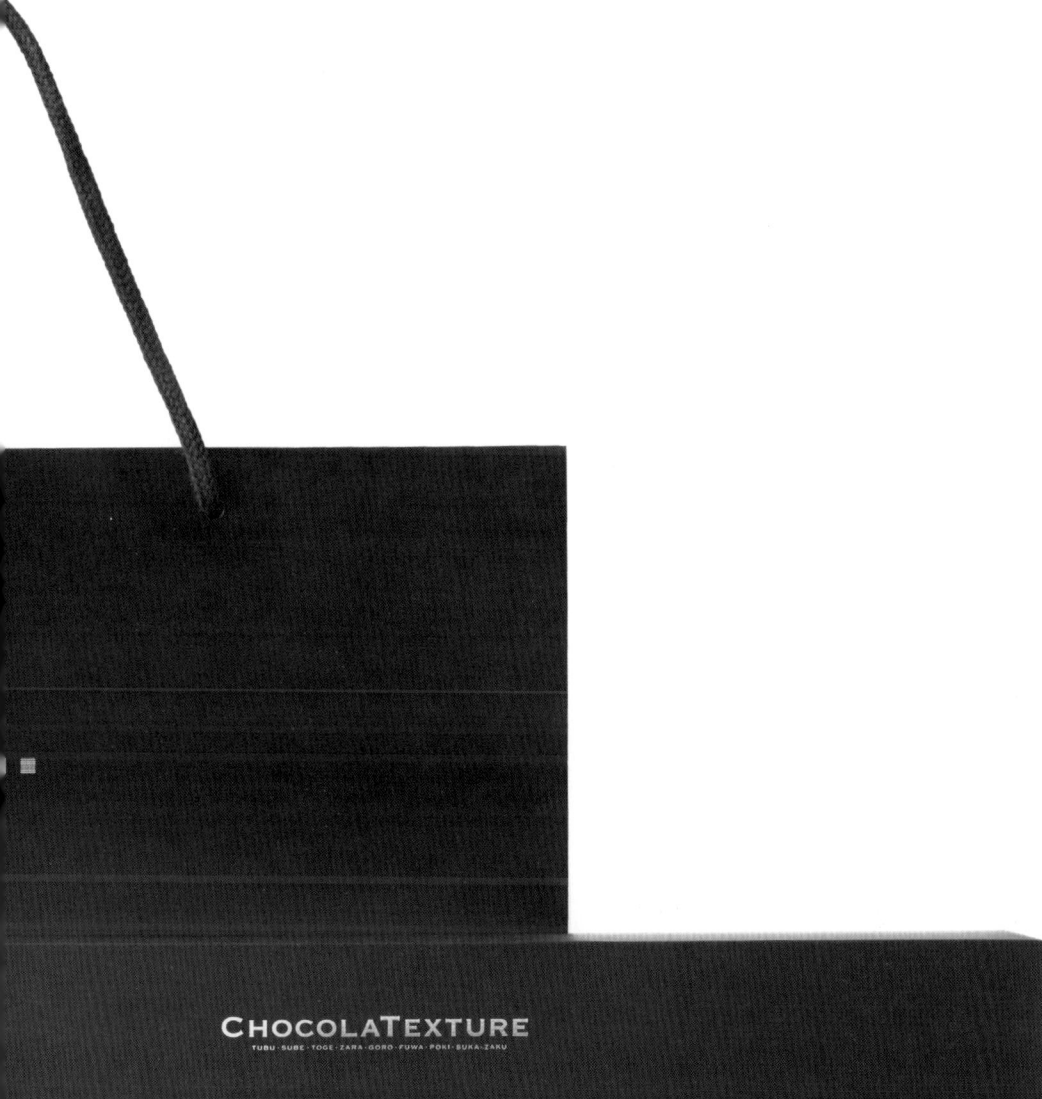

Midlight

Studio: Studio Naam

Using geometric shapes or those derived from dot, line and plane as design elements, the superfluous embellishments are taken away and the most essential form is retained. In such a way of abstracting the design image, more space for imagination is possible.

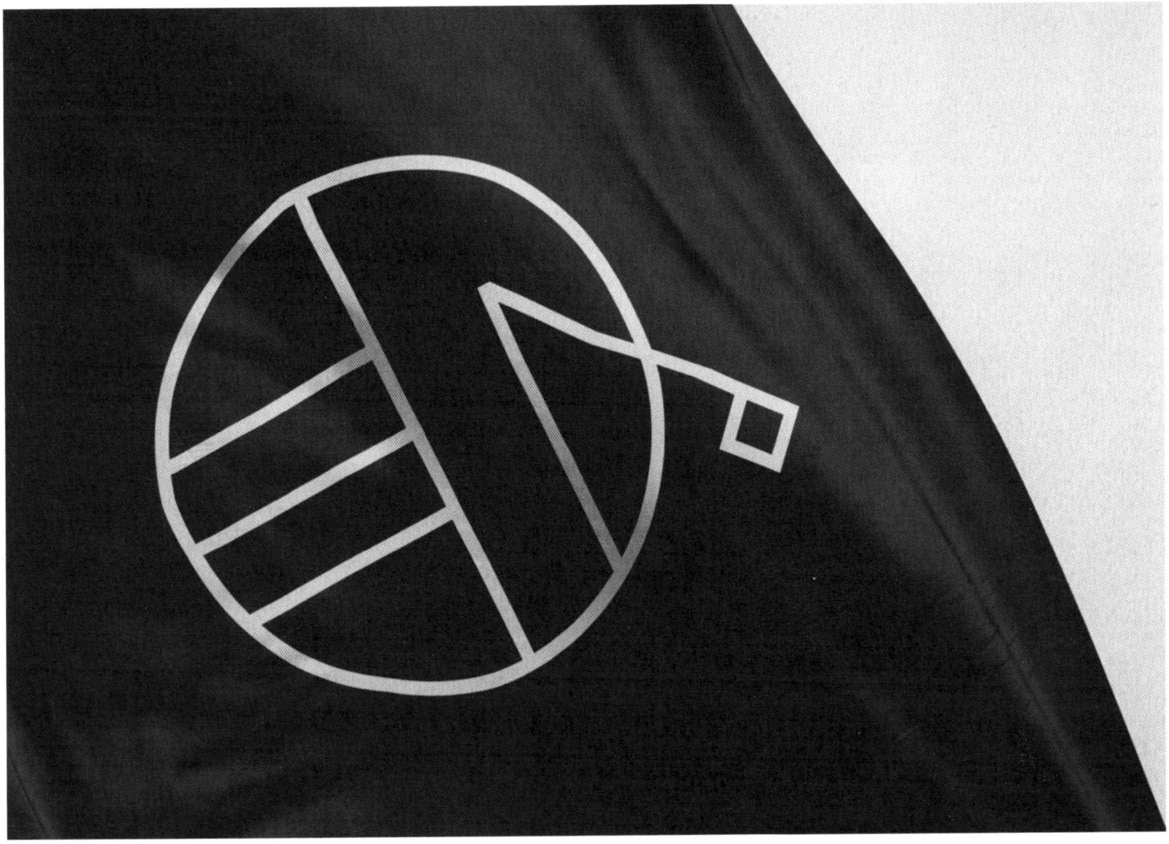

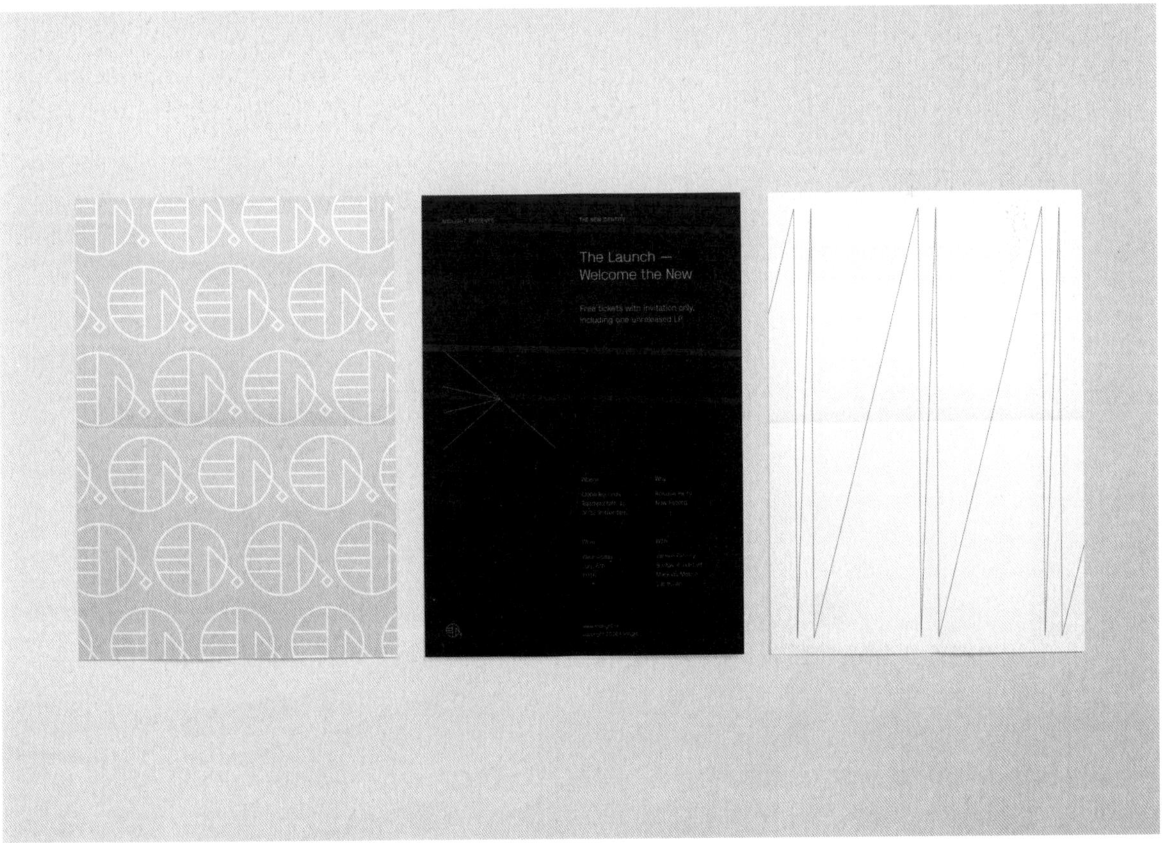

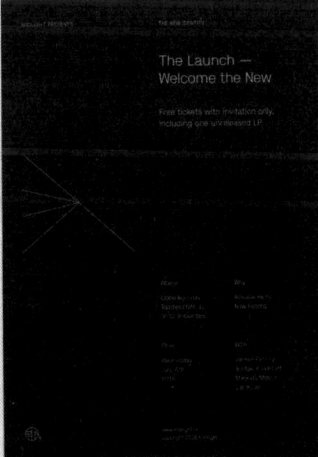

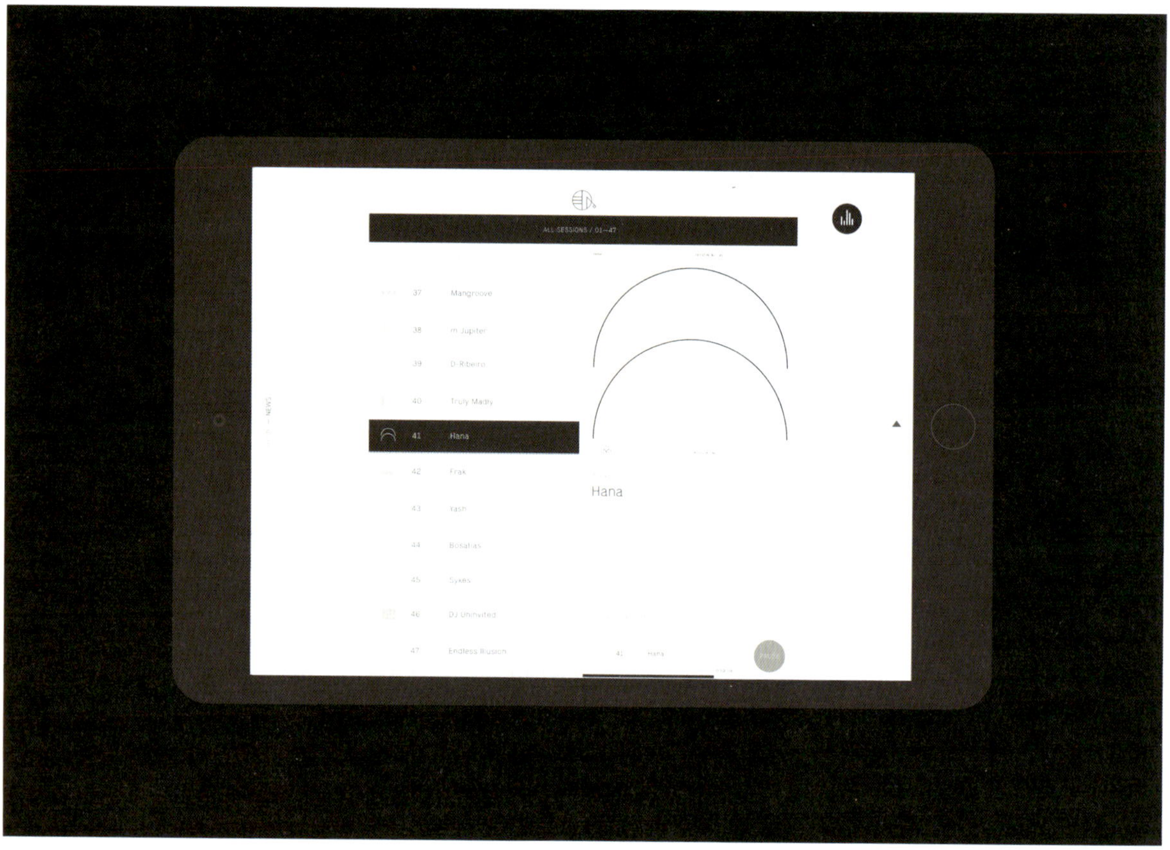

104

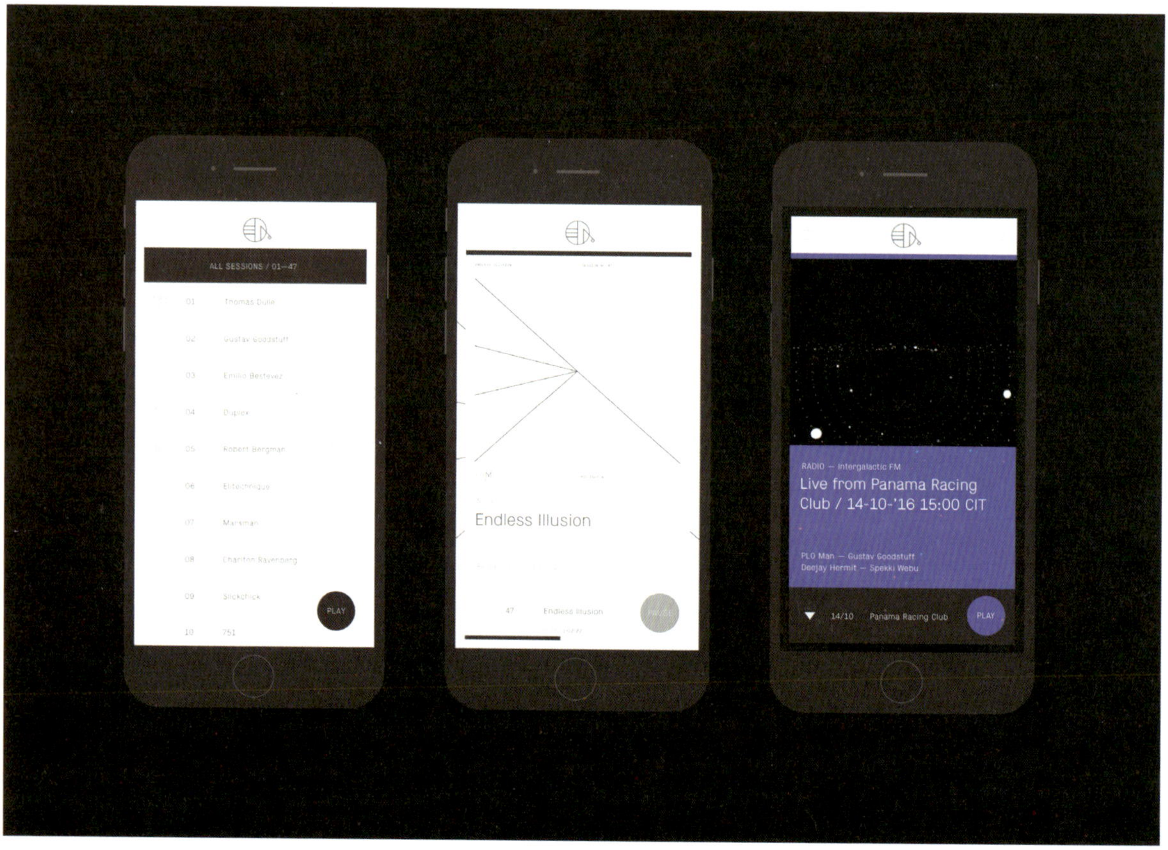

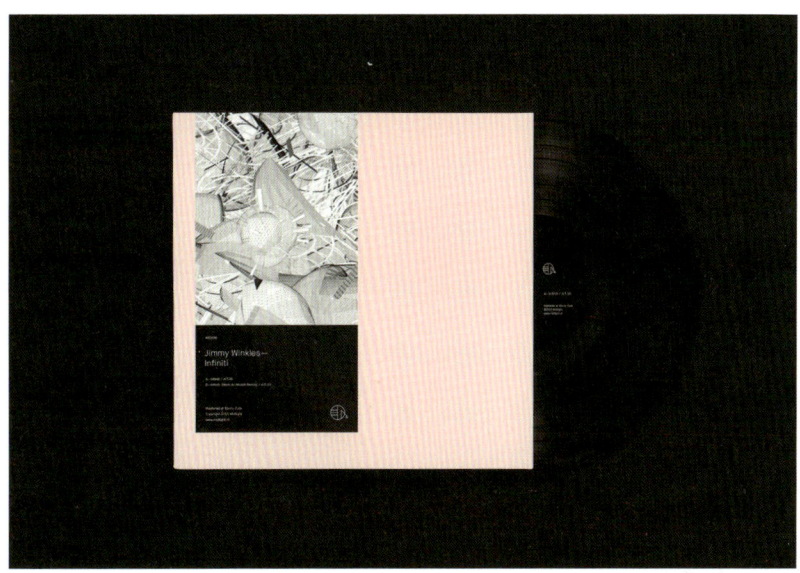
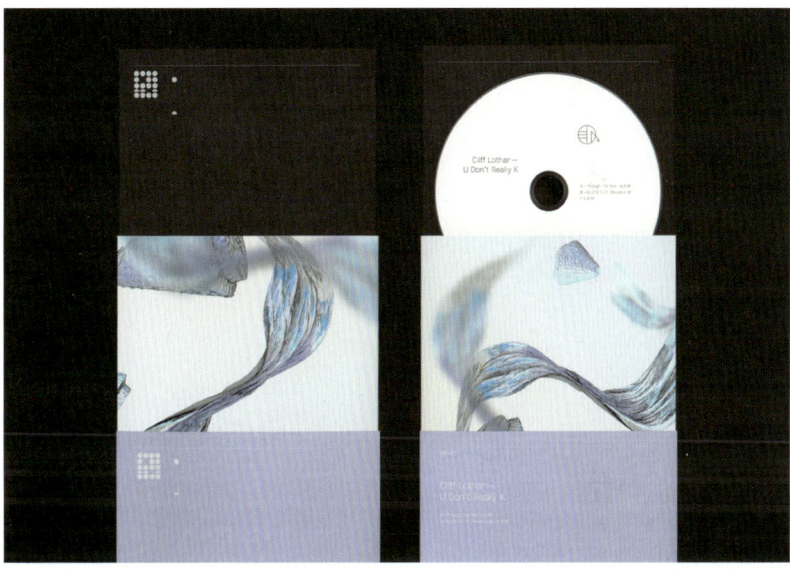
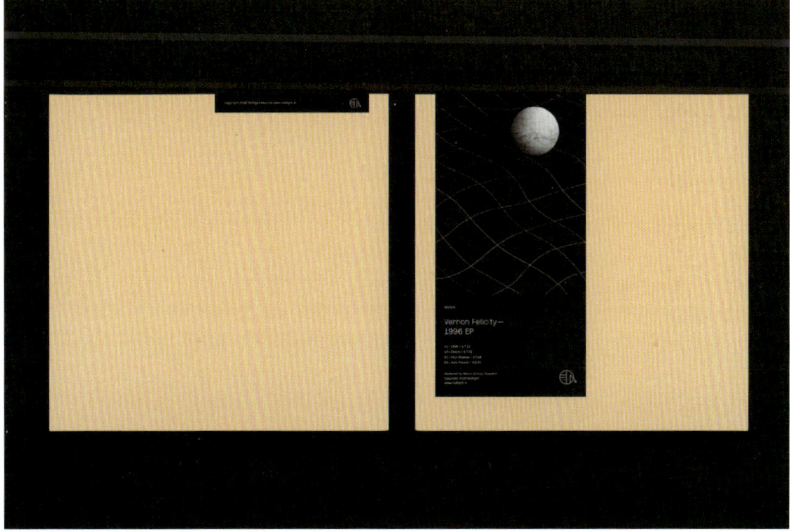

Tsurutama

Studio: nottuo Inc.　|　Designer: Kouhei Suzuki

Tsurutama is a new brand of Tsurunotamago Honpo, a time-honored Japanese shop which created the special Japanese marshmallow confectionery about 120 years ago by enveloping Anko (traditional Japanese red bean paste) with marshmallow from Western culture. This innovative Japanese sweet, with a round shape like eggs and a fluffy texture, became a confectionery representative of Okayama.

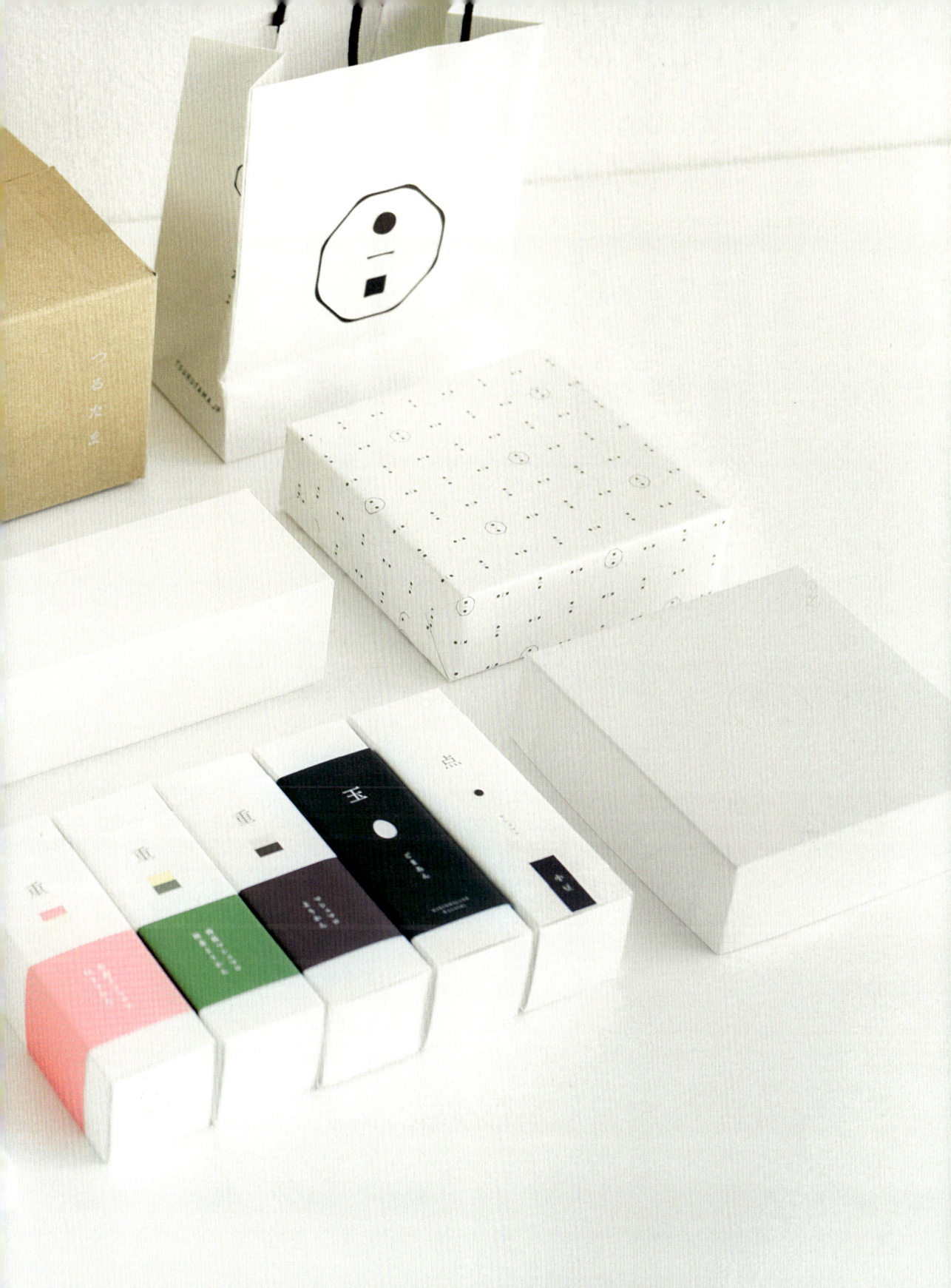

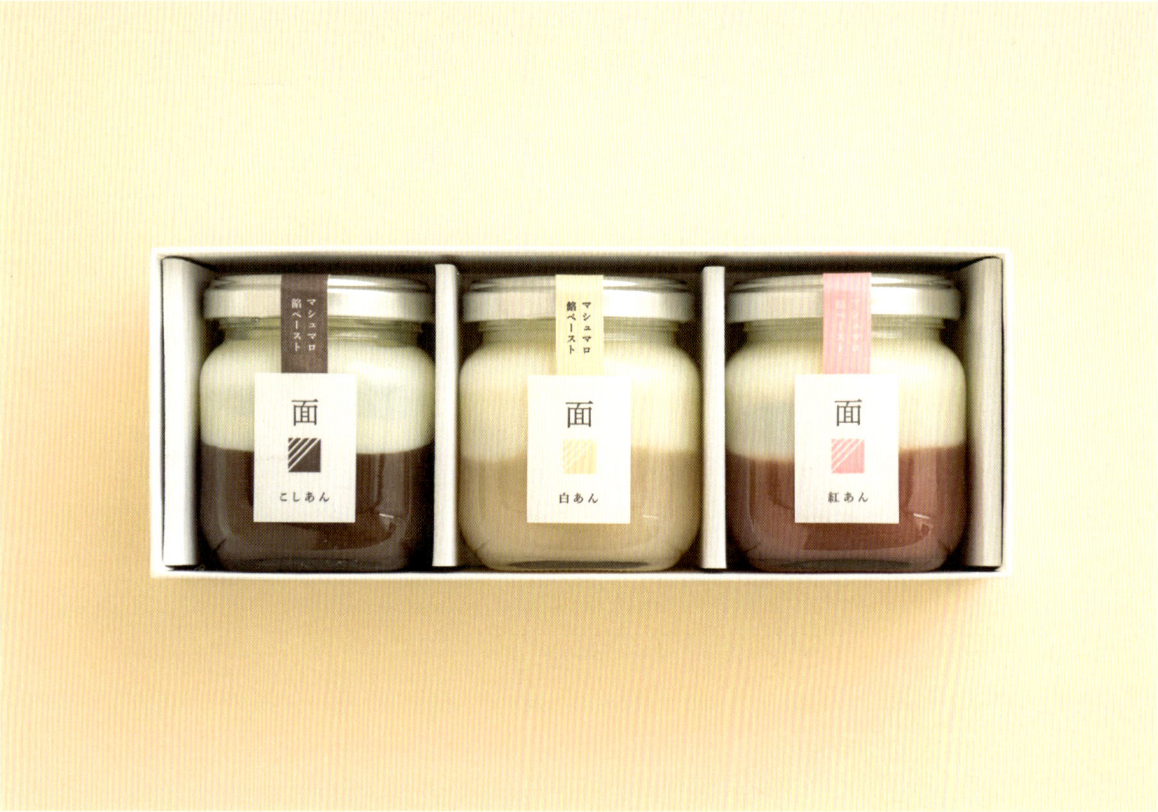

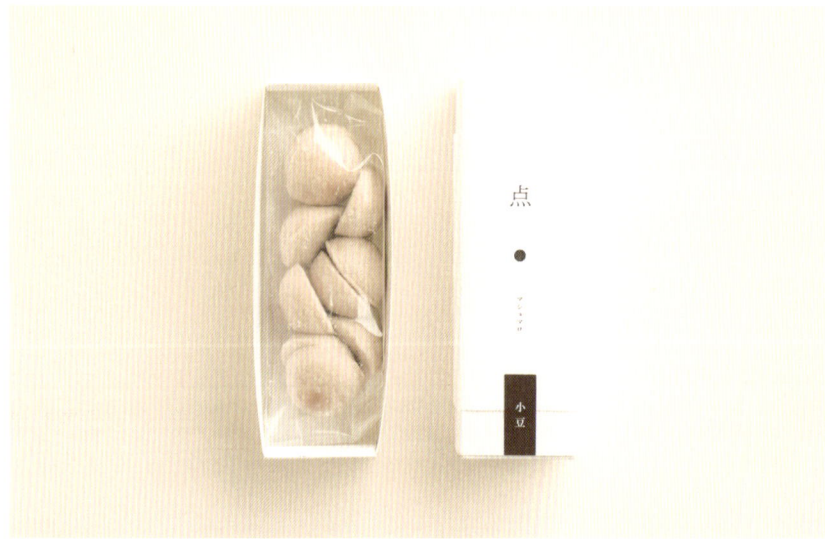
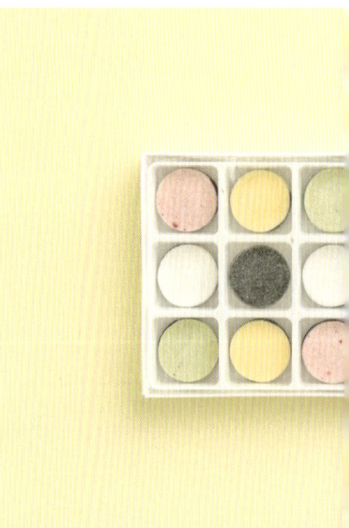
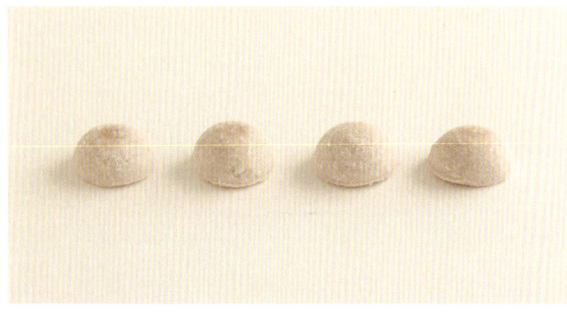
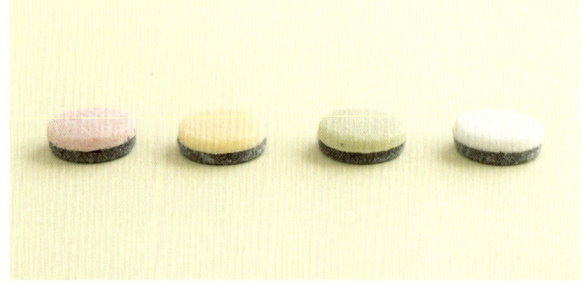

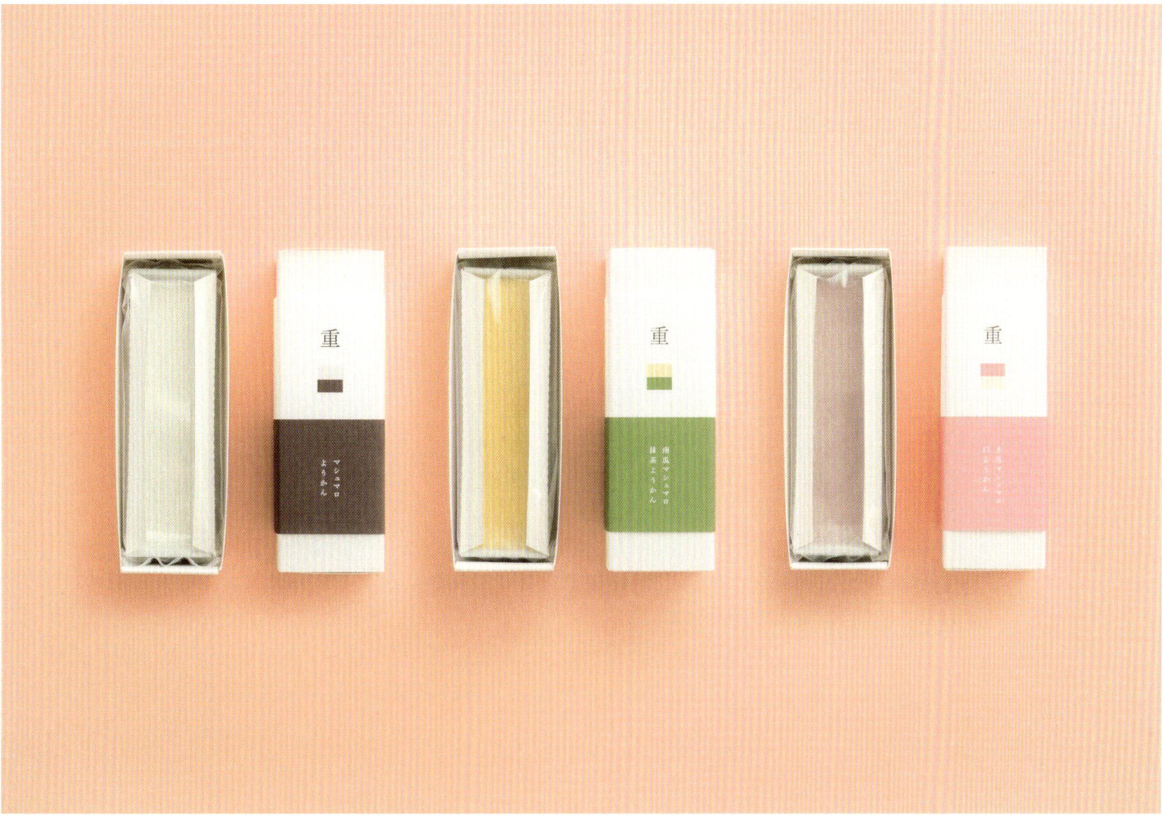

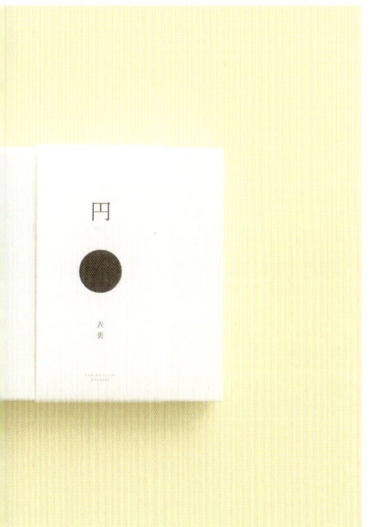
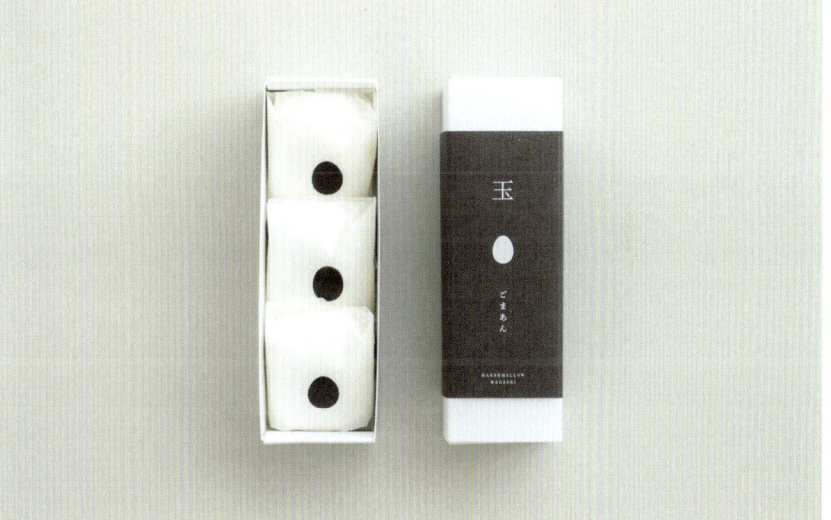
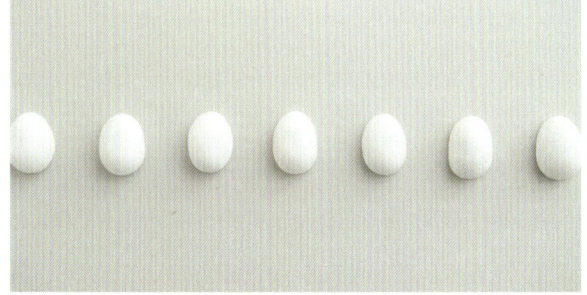
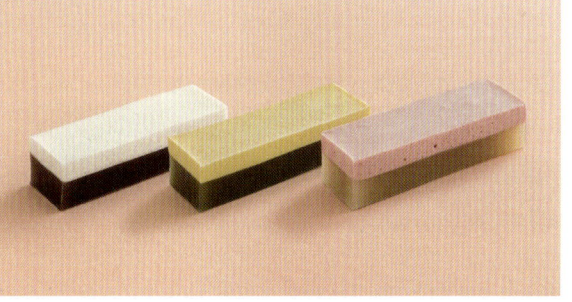

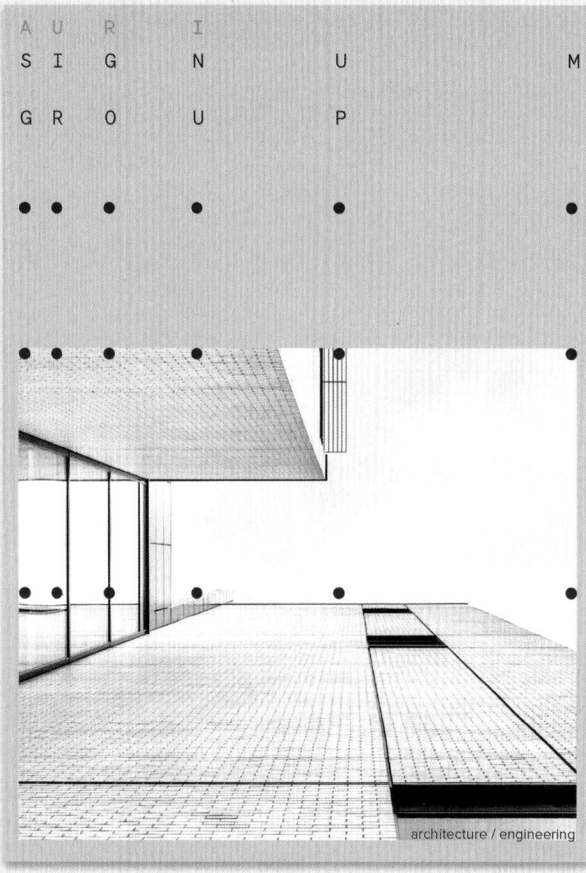

Auri Signum Group

Studio: omsky studio | Designer: Oksana Paley, Alice Retunsky

Auri Signum means "golden standard" in Latin, signifying the supreme quality, which, in the context of architecture, refers to golden ratio. In the branding for the architectural studio Auri Signum Group, both the horizontal and vertical distances between letters and words are designed in strict accordance with the proportions of the golden ratio.

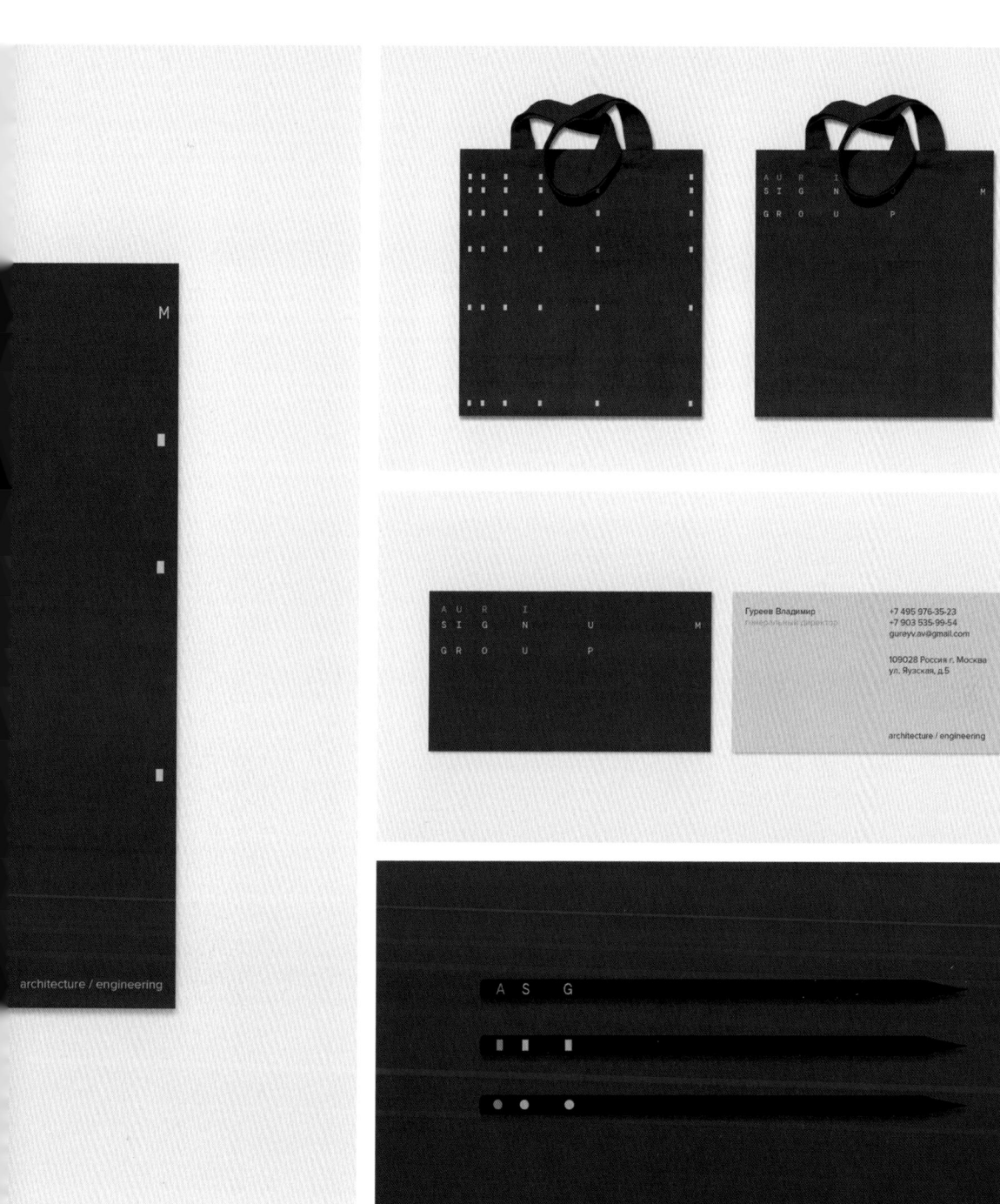

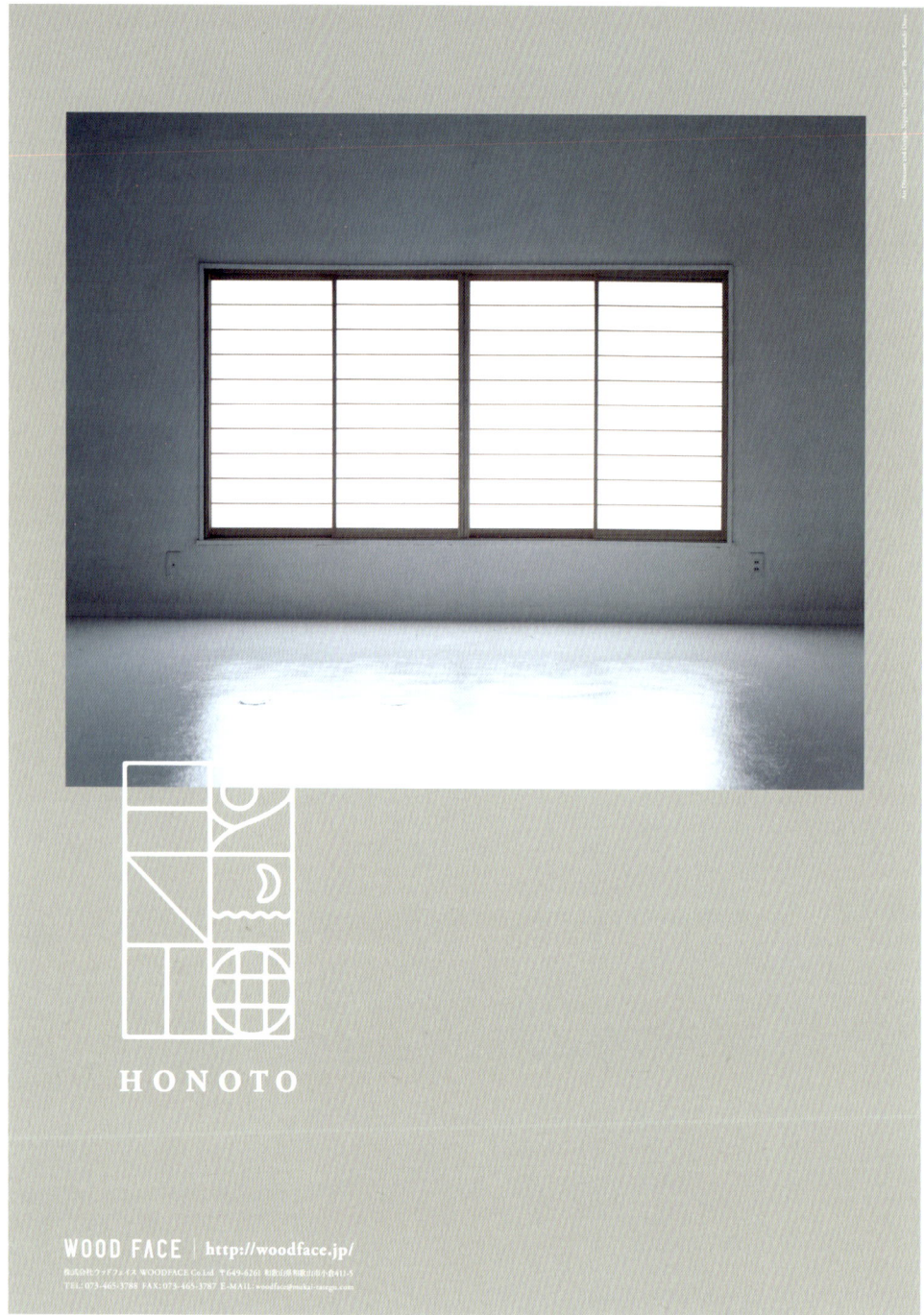

Honoto

Studio: Nippon Design Center, Inc. | Designer: Junya Maejima

This visual identity for shoji brand "Honoto" aimed at promoting shoji for a comfortable modern life. It consisted of a new logo and new communication and promotion materials such as the catalog and the website. The logo incorporated features of shoji and can be adjusted into different forms, just like sliding doors. Key visuals focused on the soft light provided by shoji.

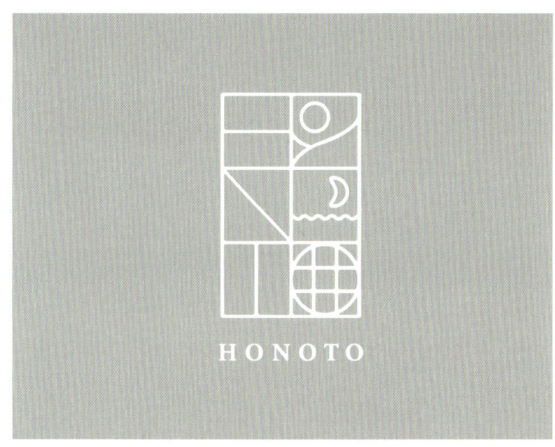
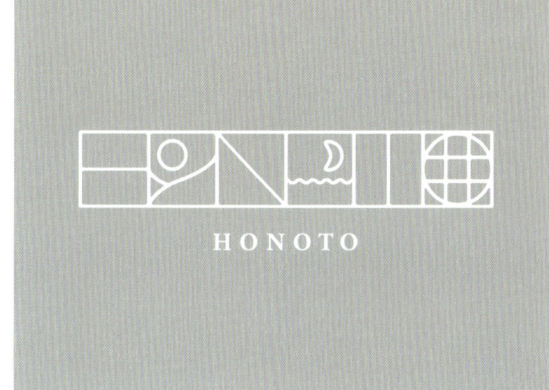
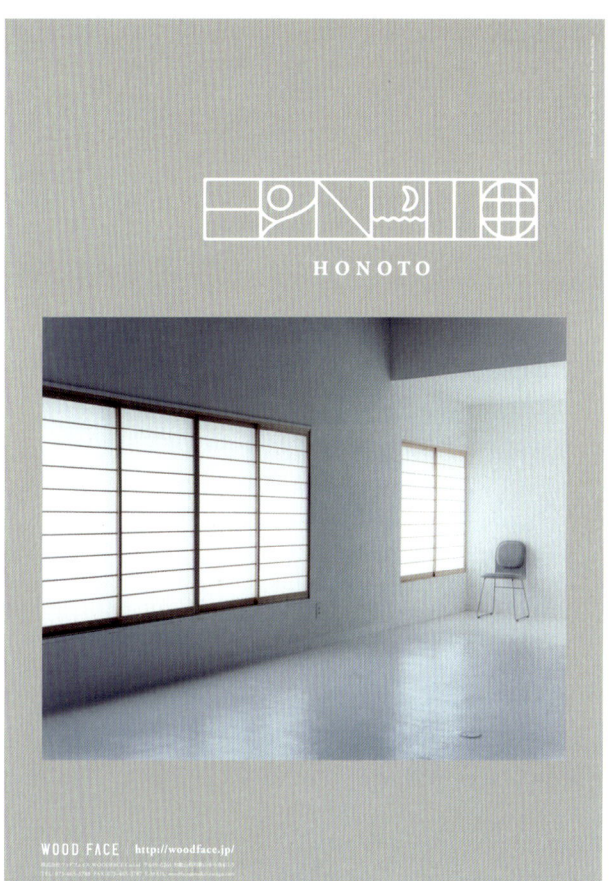
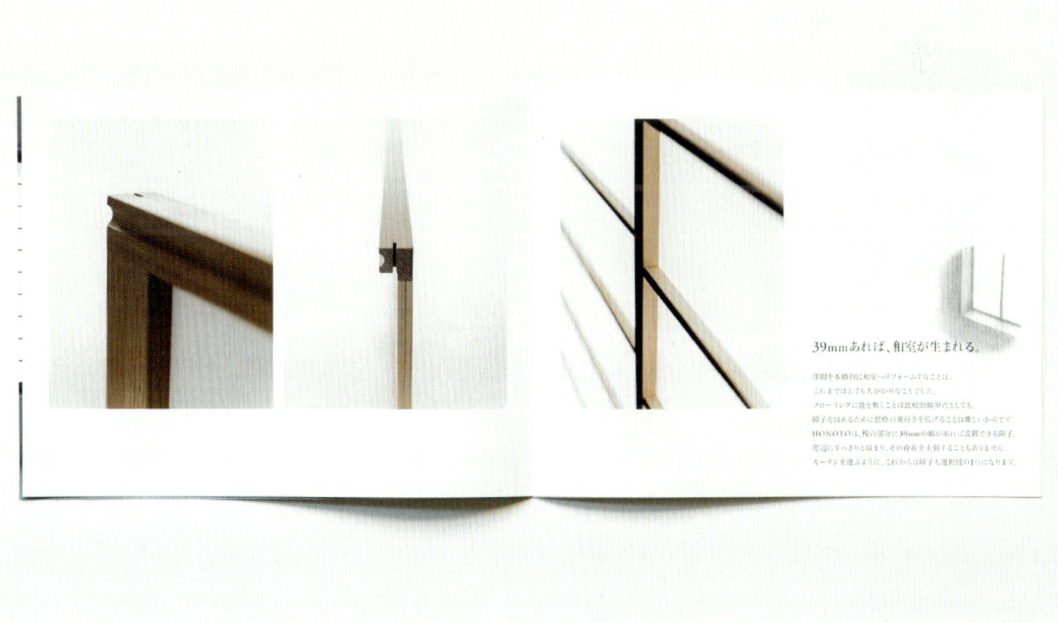

Nou-no-mai

Studio: E.Co.,Ltd. | Designer: Kenichi Matsumoto

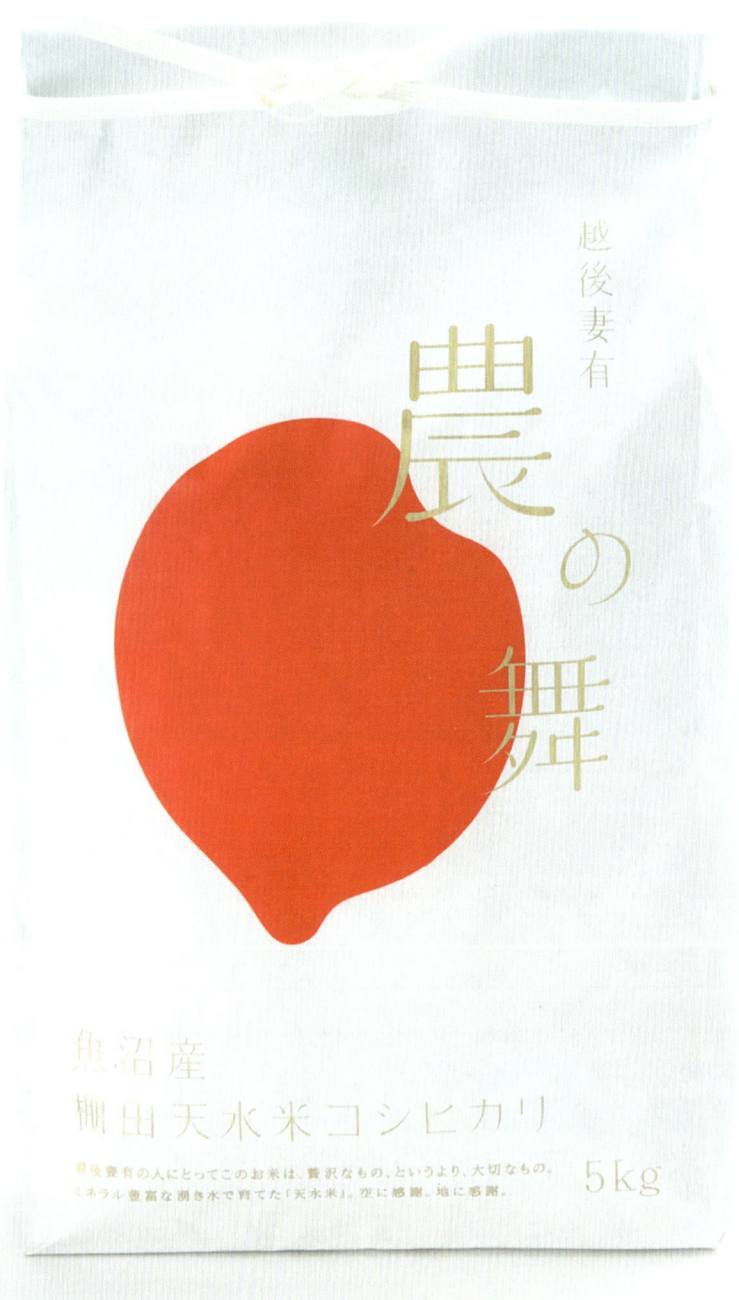

Rice is the main farm crop of Japan. The fresh water and the weather, along with the toil of the farmhouse workers culminate in this product, The mark on the packaging represents water, the sun, the Japanese flag and rice, which is also a tribute paid to the hard-working farmers. The silk-screen printing is an indication of perfection which is the pursuit of the product.

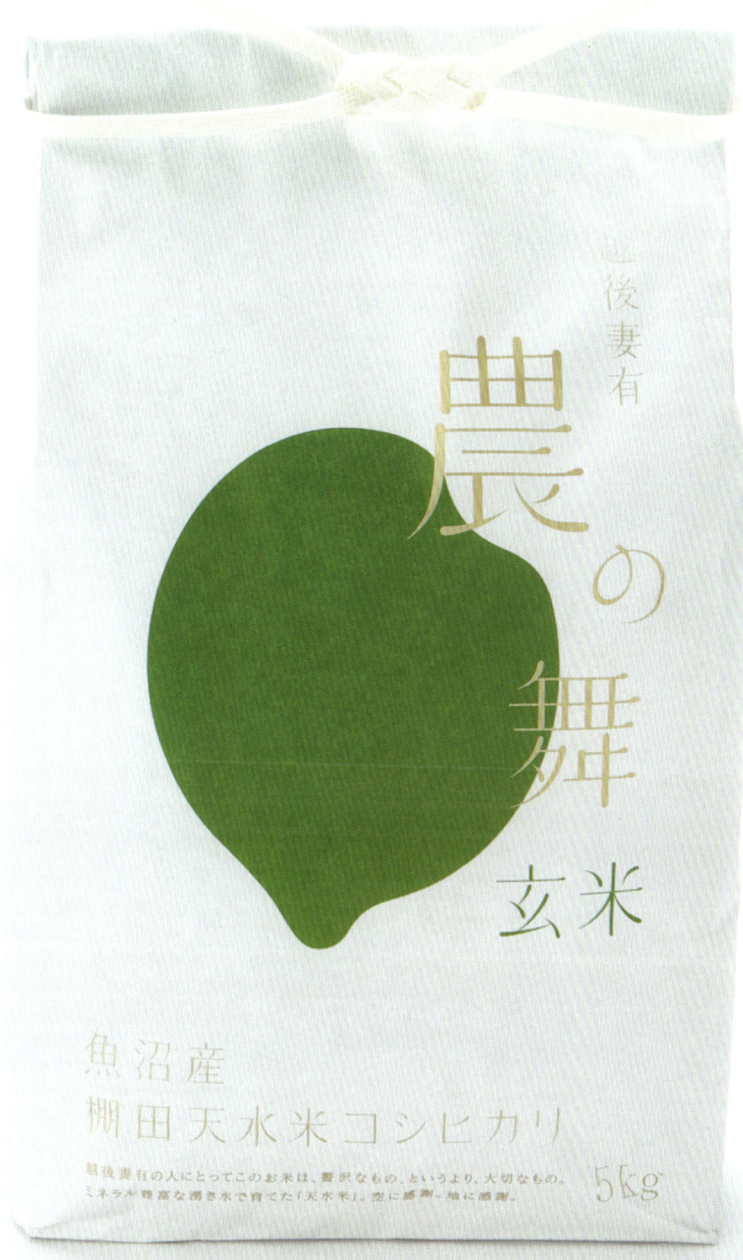

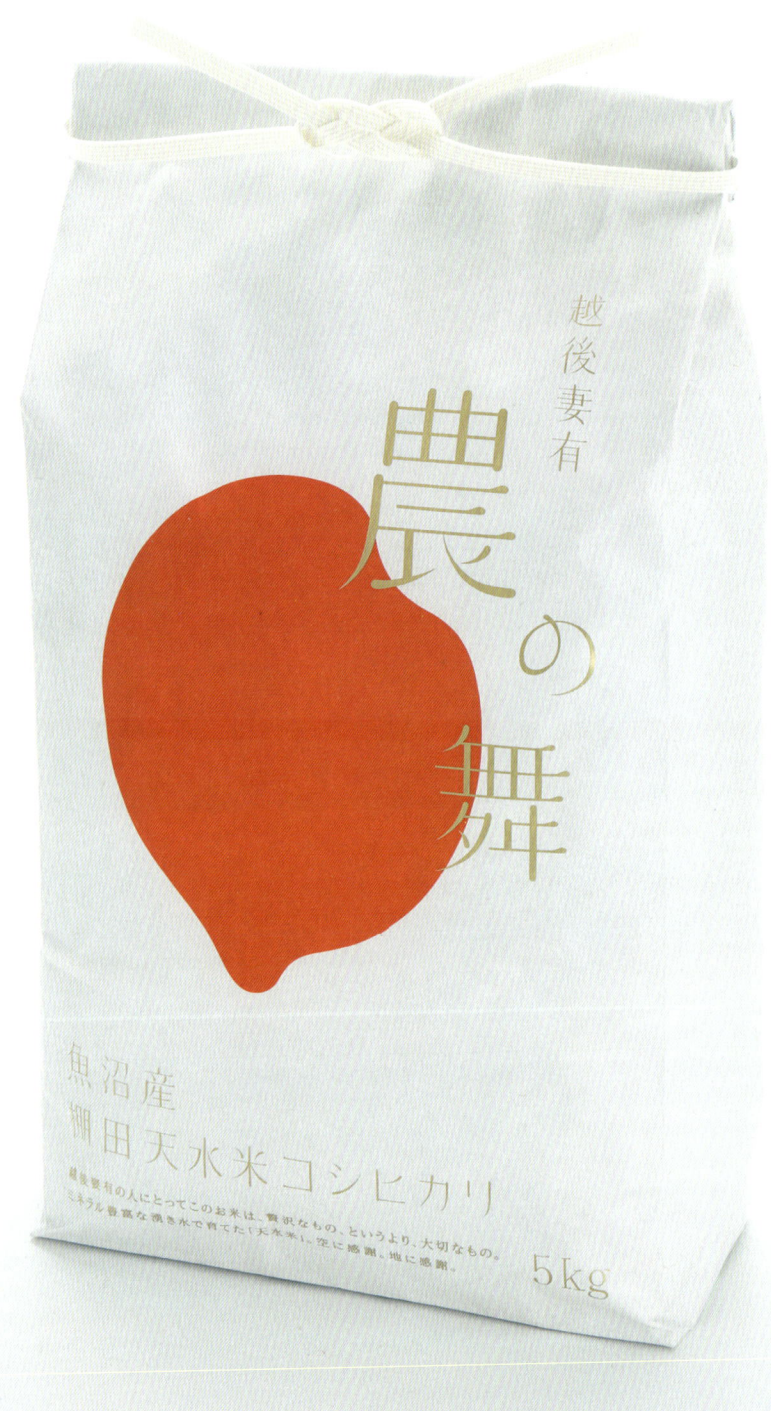

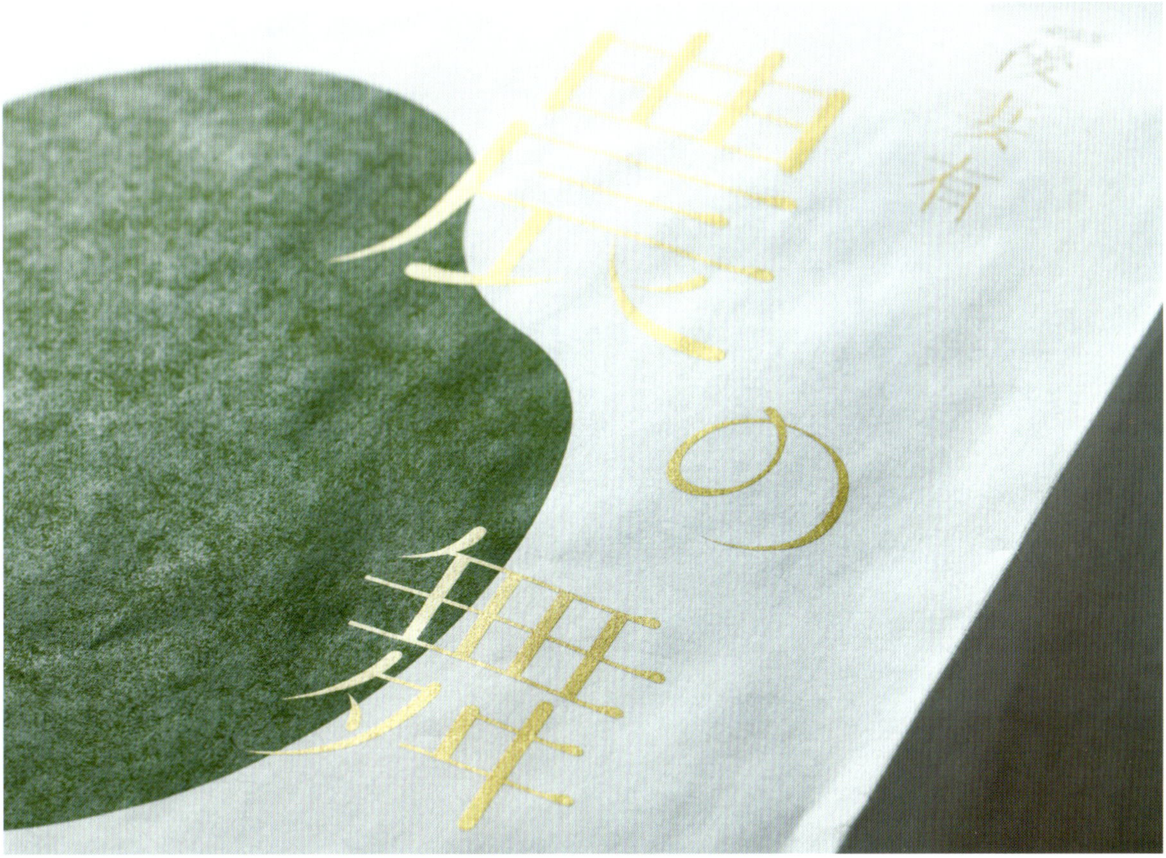

燕の舞

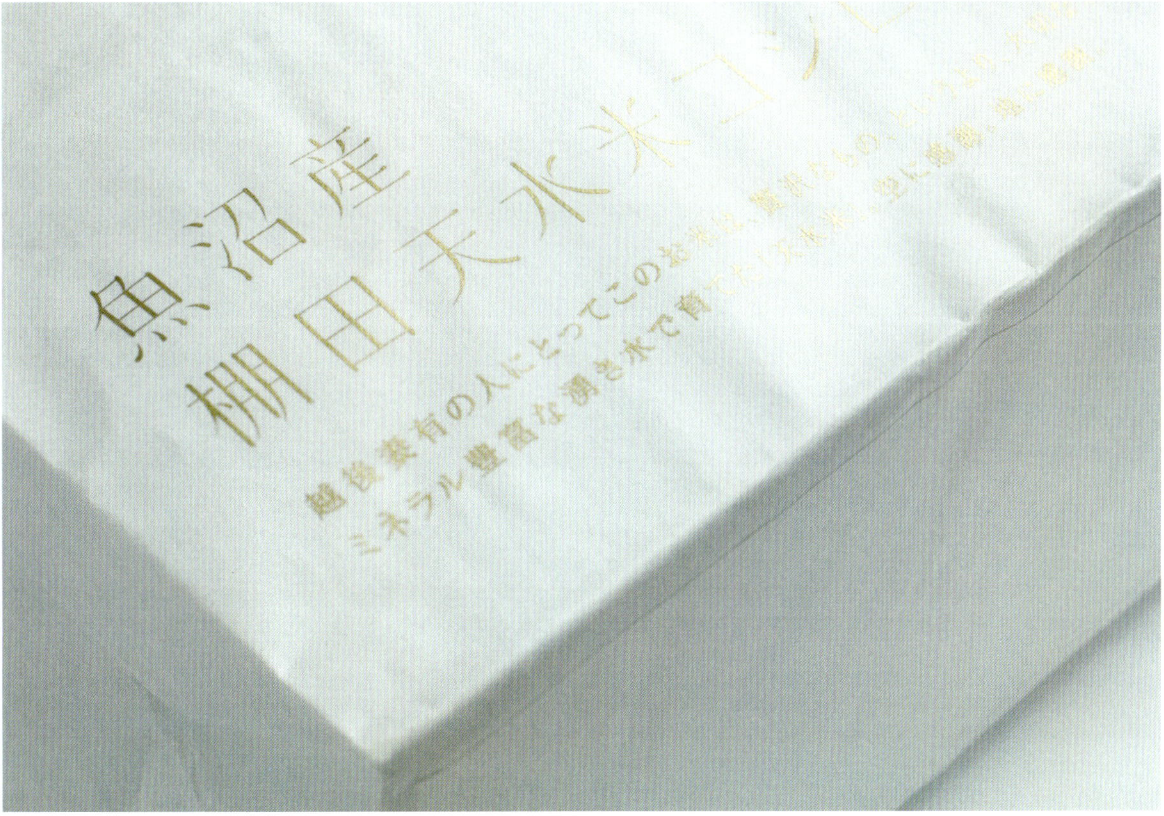

魚沼産 棚田天水米コシヒカリ

越後農有の人にとってこのお米は農業のトップにランクイン
ミネラル豊富な湧き水で育てられた米は、美しく香気、甘い香り

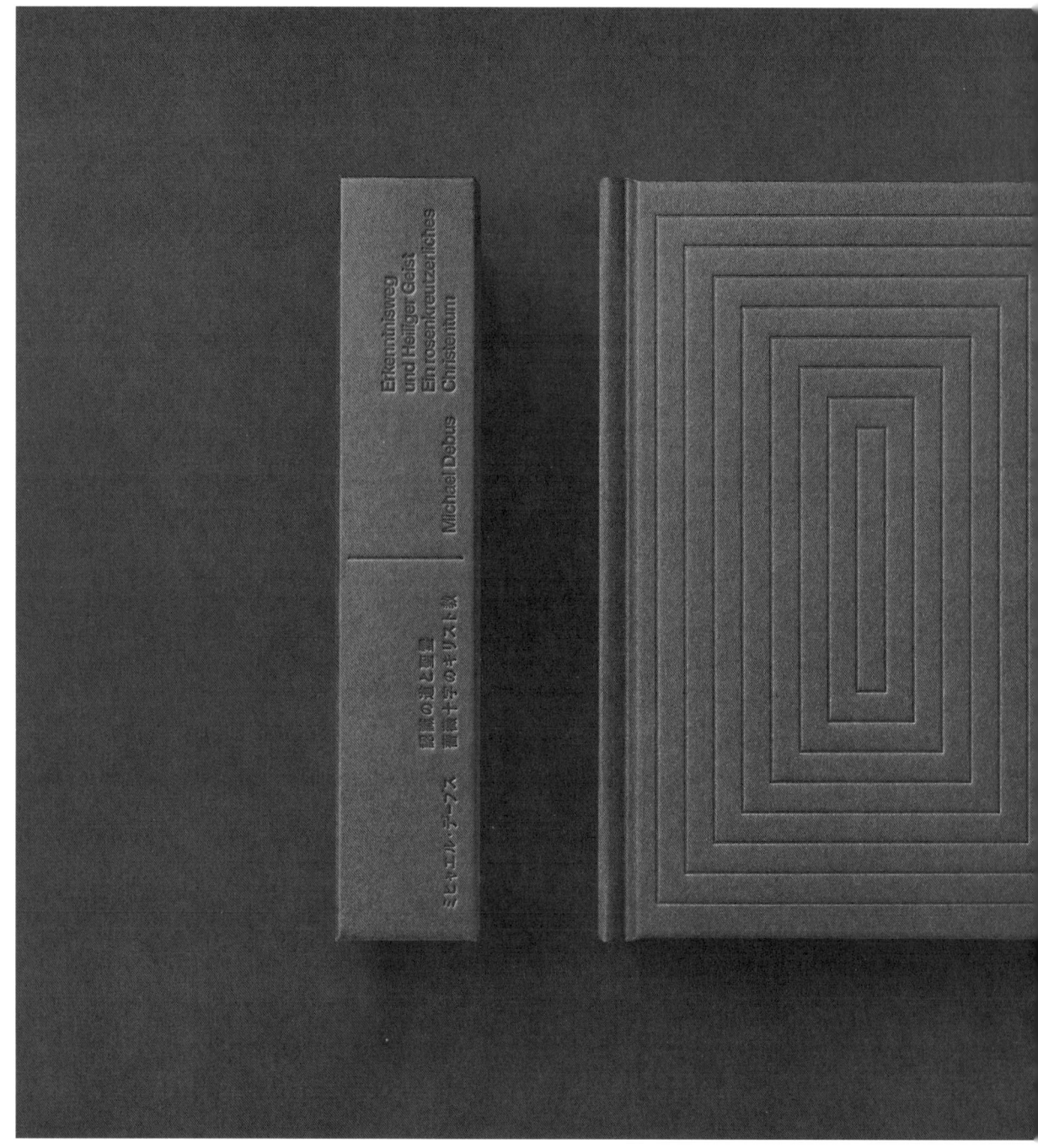

Erkenntnisweg und Heiliger Geist

Designer: Yuta Takahashi

The book unraveling wisdom under the veil of myths and legends featured a unique design that combined modernity and minimalism. The cover presented the idea of a corridor of doors of knowledge appearing and being opened by thought, at the end of which emerges the letter I. Through the use of neutral colors between light and shadow, the transition of reader´s awareness from darkness to daylight was captured. The entire system is a reminiscent of the cloister in church.

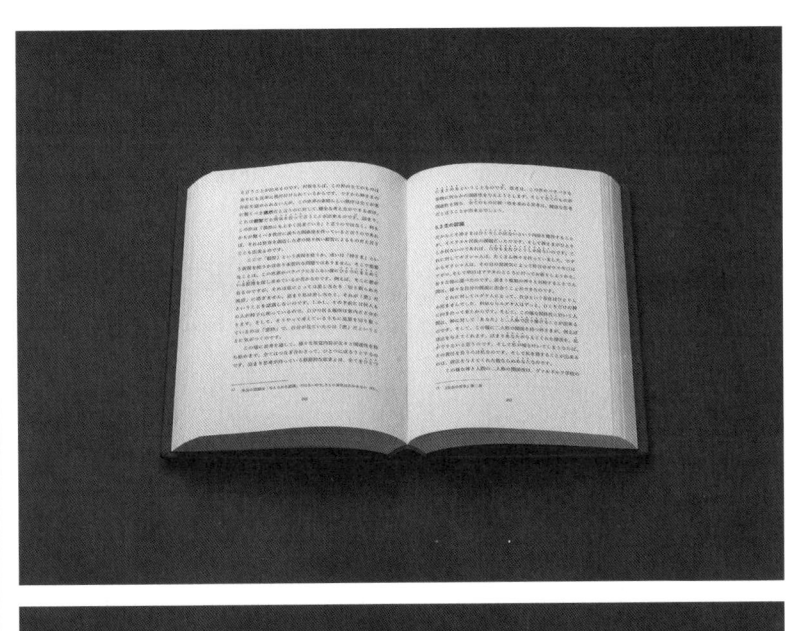

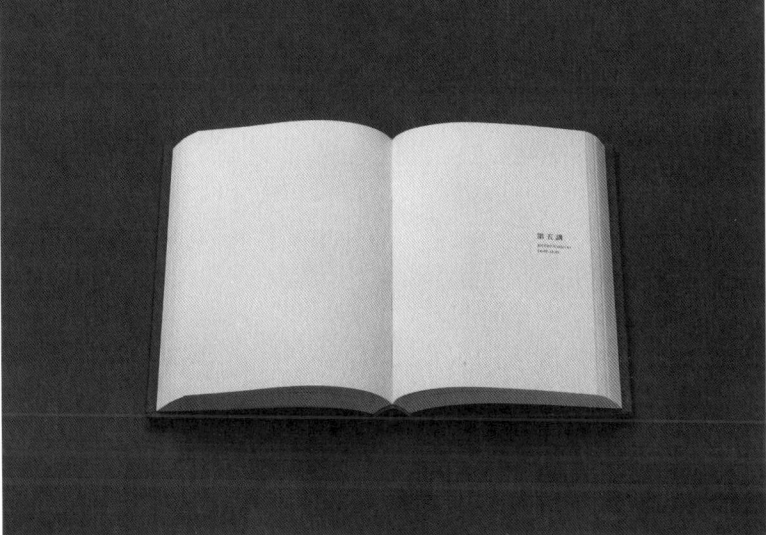

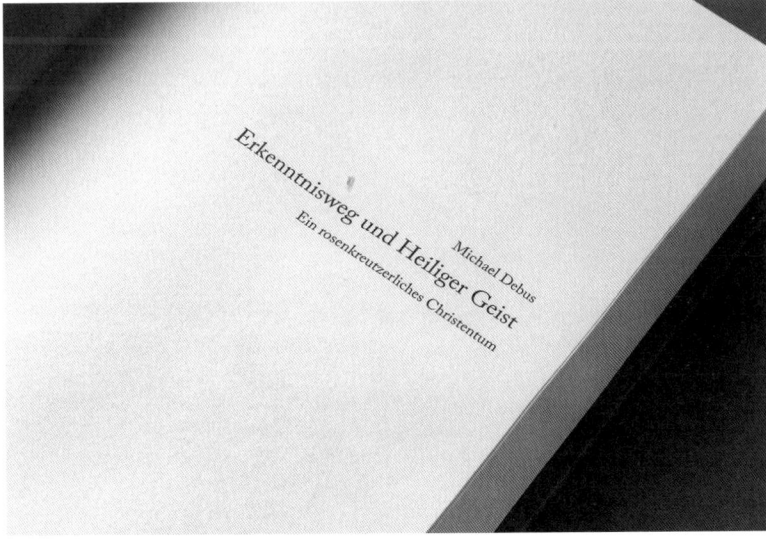

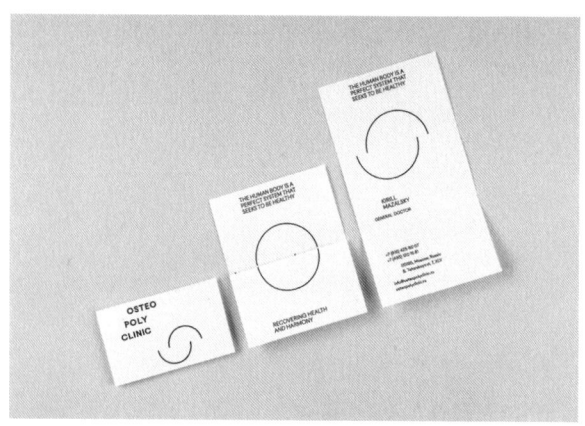
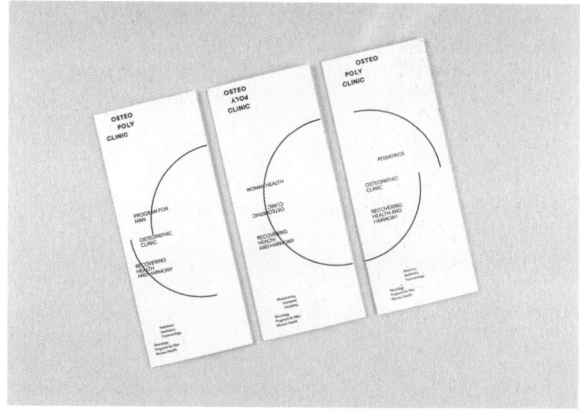
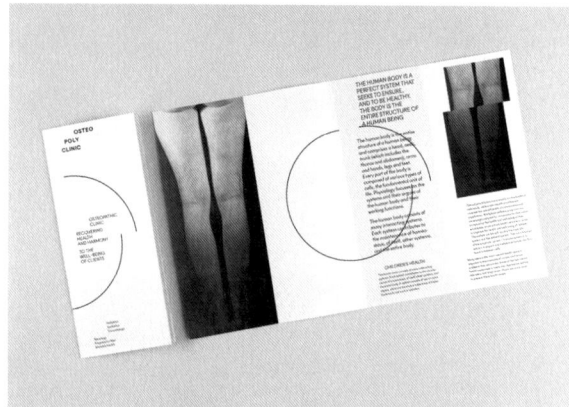
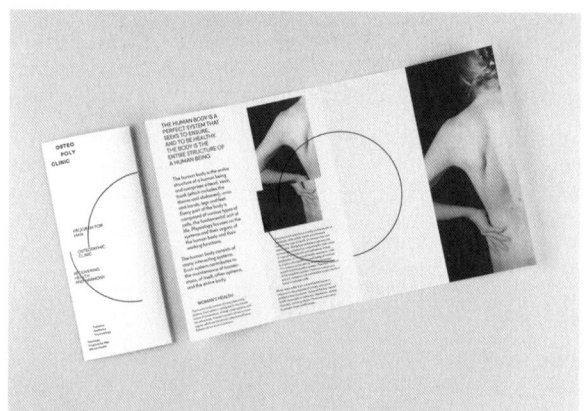
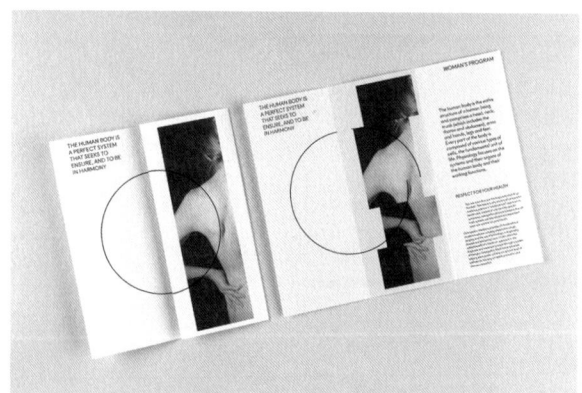

Osteo Poly Clinic

Studio : Ermolaev Bureau | Designer: Vlad Ermolaev, Eline Van Der Ploeg, Anastasia Tolstokorova

Based on osteopathy, this brand identity features a complete circle that symbolizes perfect health and a broken circle that indicates problematic health. All visual elements work in connection with the logo. If the circle deforms, other elements change accordingly, just like the mechanism of the human body.

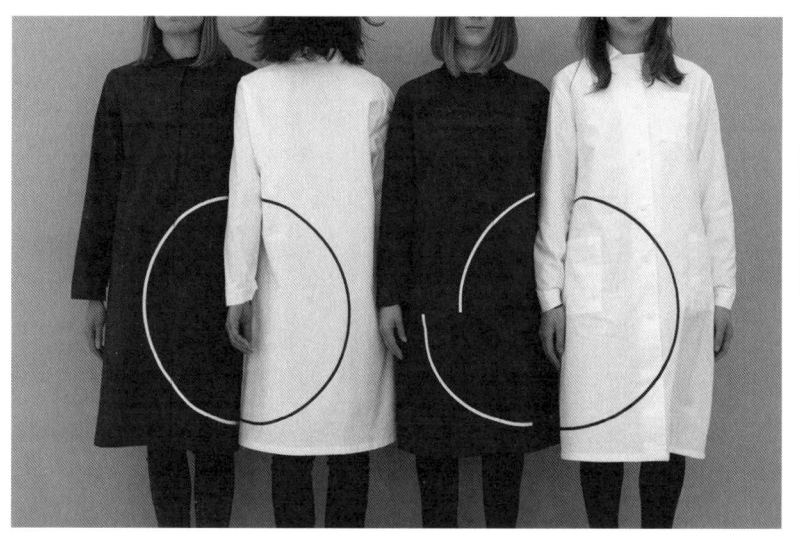
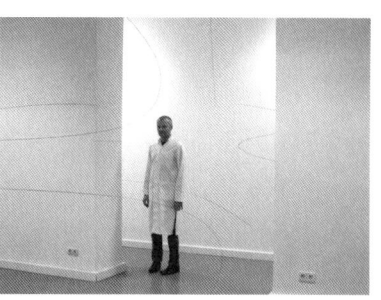
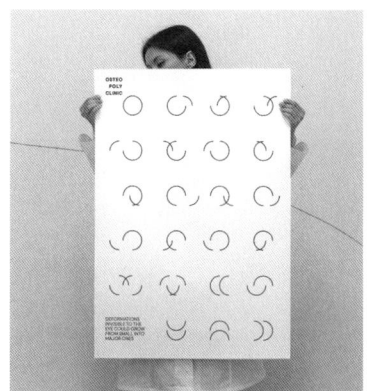
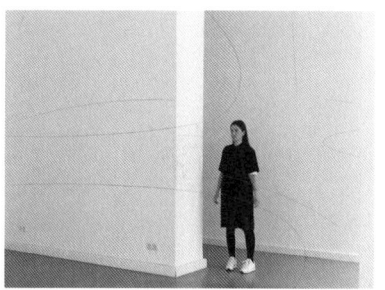
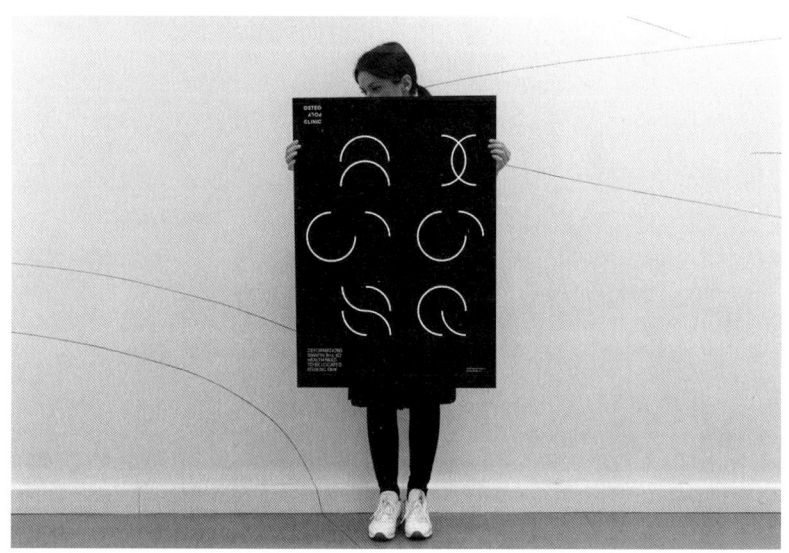

OSTEO POLY CLINIC

ONCE TREATED THE HUMAN HEALTH BECOMES A PERFECT SYSTEM AGAIN

Osteo Poly Clinic is a Moscow clinic specializing in osteopathic medicine. The clinic's approach is to restore natural beauty and harmony in the human body that was damaged by stress, injuries and diseases, to provide overall good health and wellbeing.

info@osteopolyclinic.ru
osteopolyclinic.ru

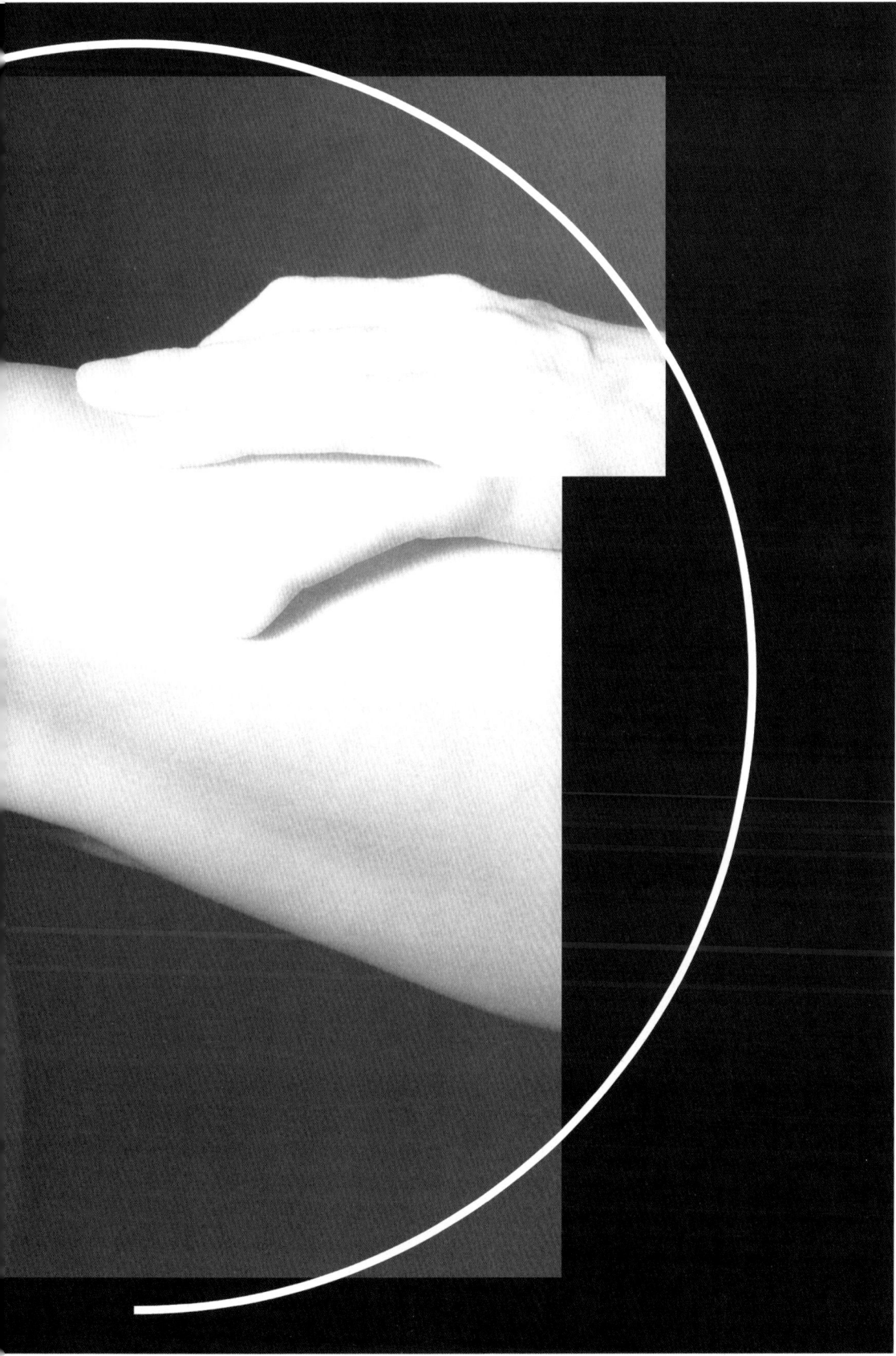

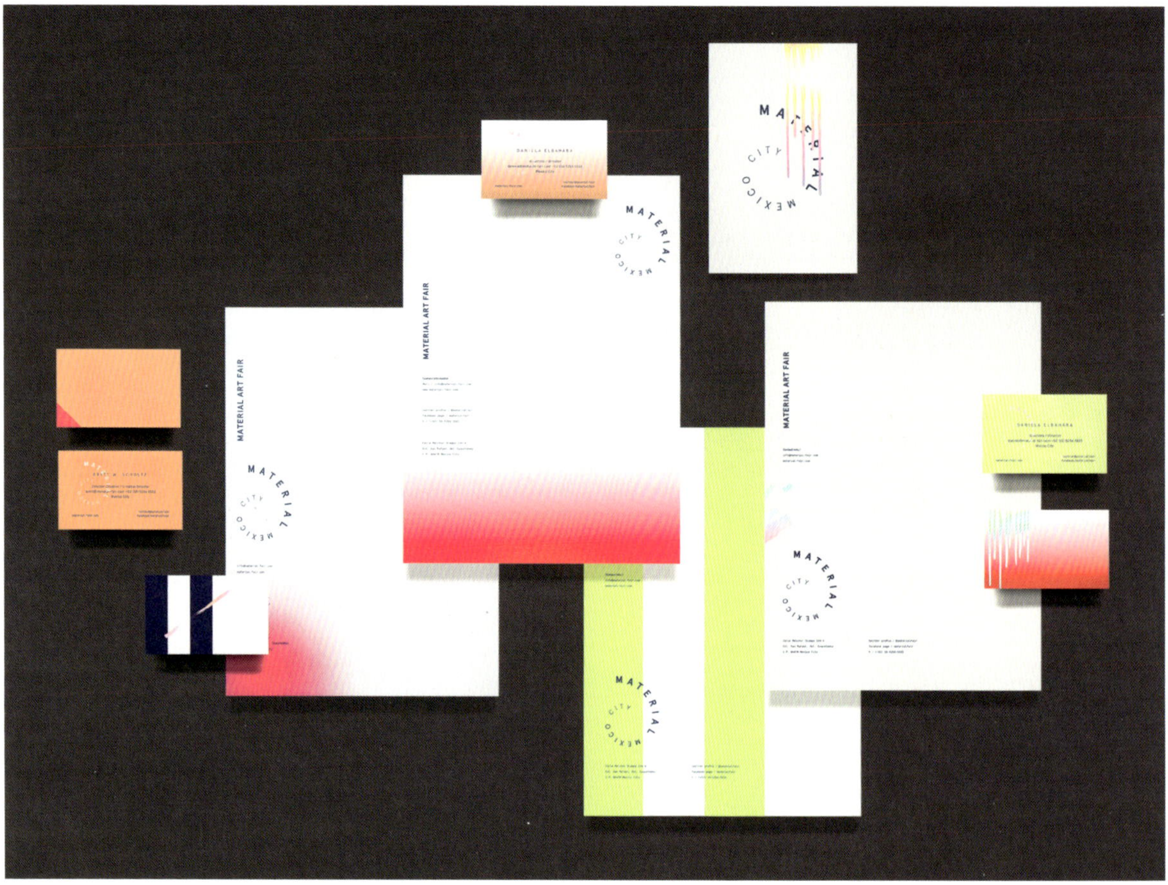

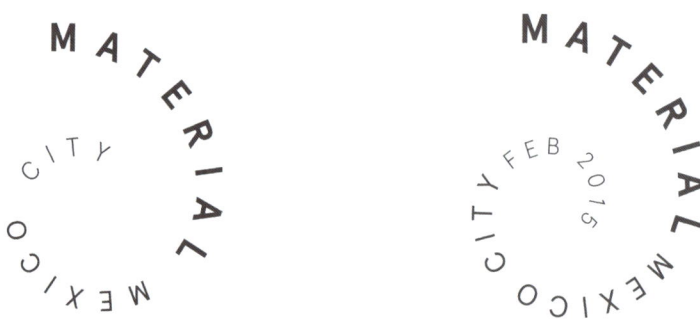

Material Art Fair

Designer: Anagrama

Material Art Fair is a contemporary art fair dedicated to emerging practices in Mexico City. The design proposal conveys the essence of this fair; each piece is unique and shows its own presence without neglecting the consistency of the brand. The color palette and the compositions of elements reflect the merging of street and modern art.

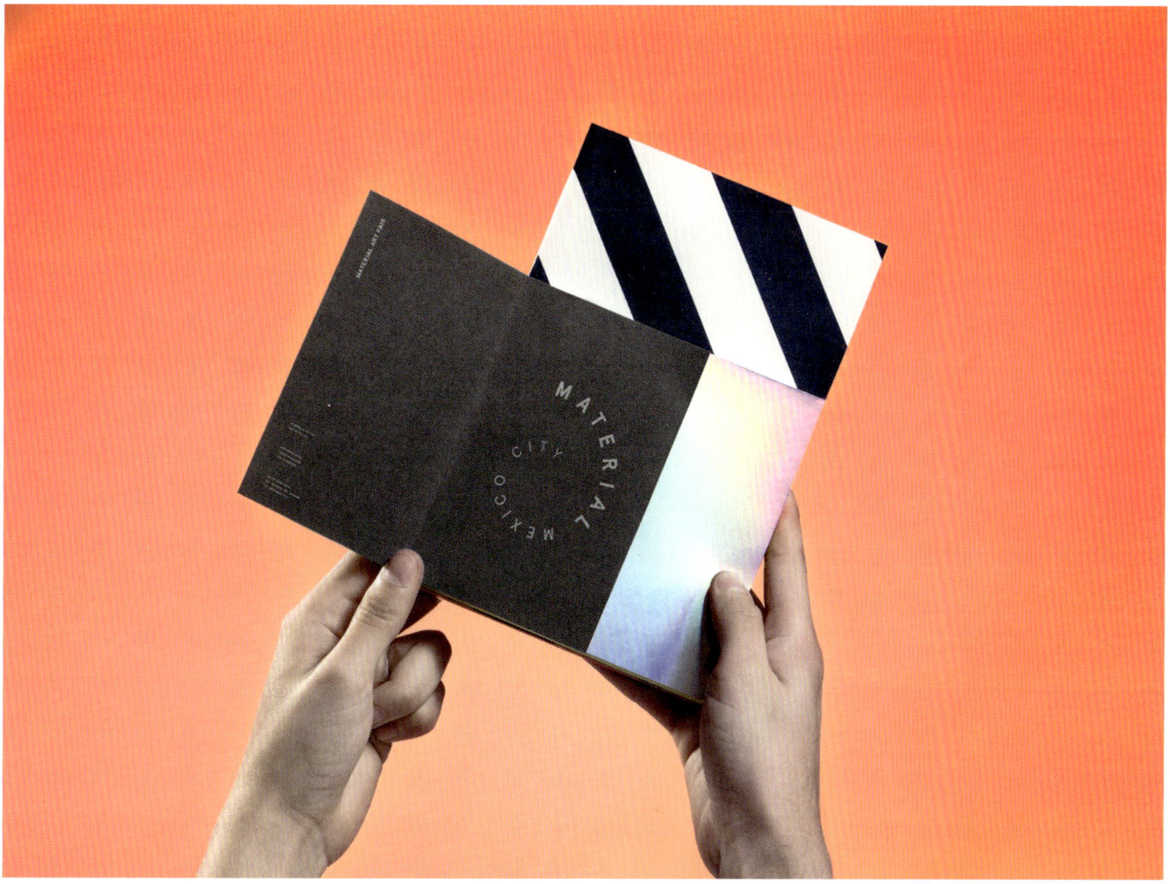

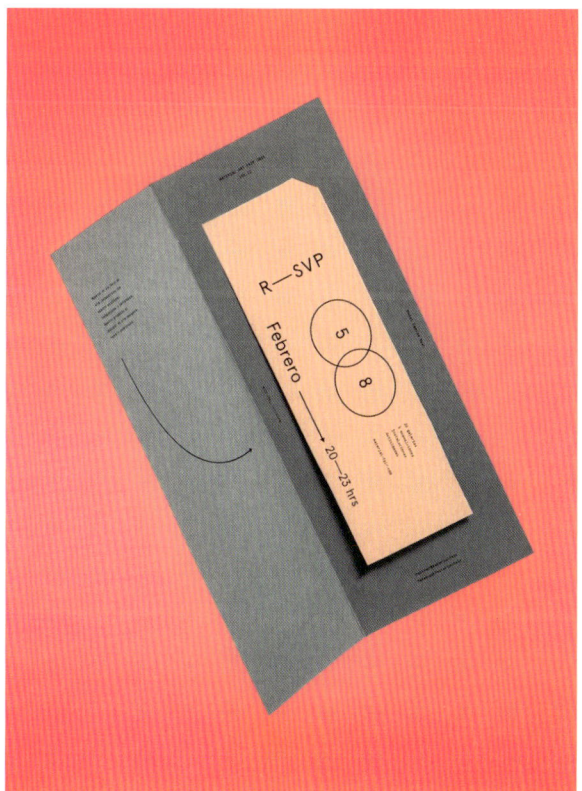
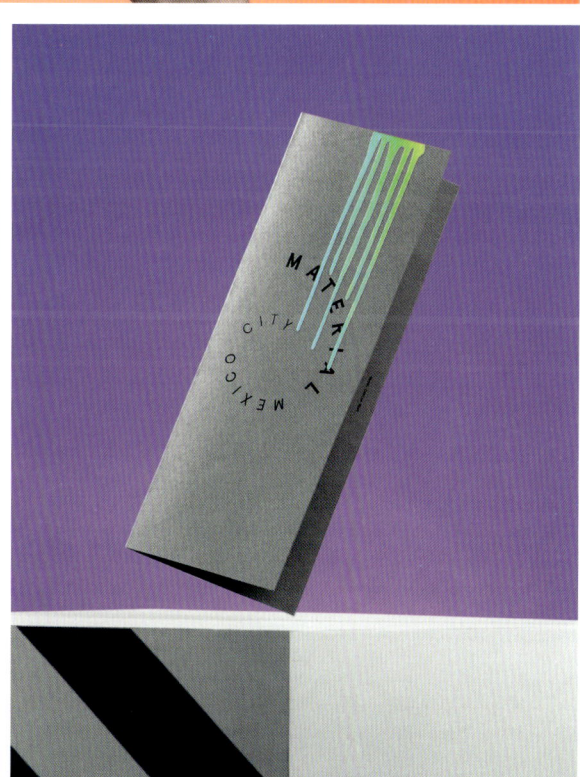

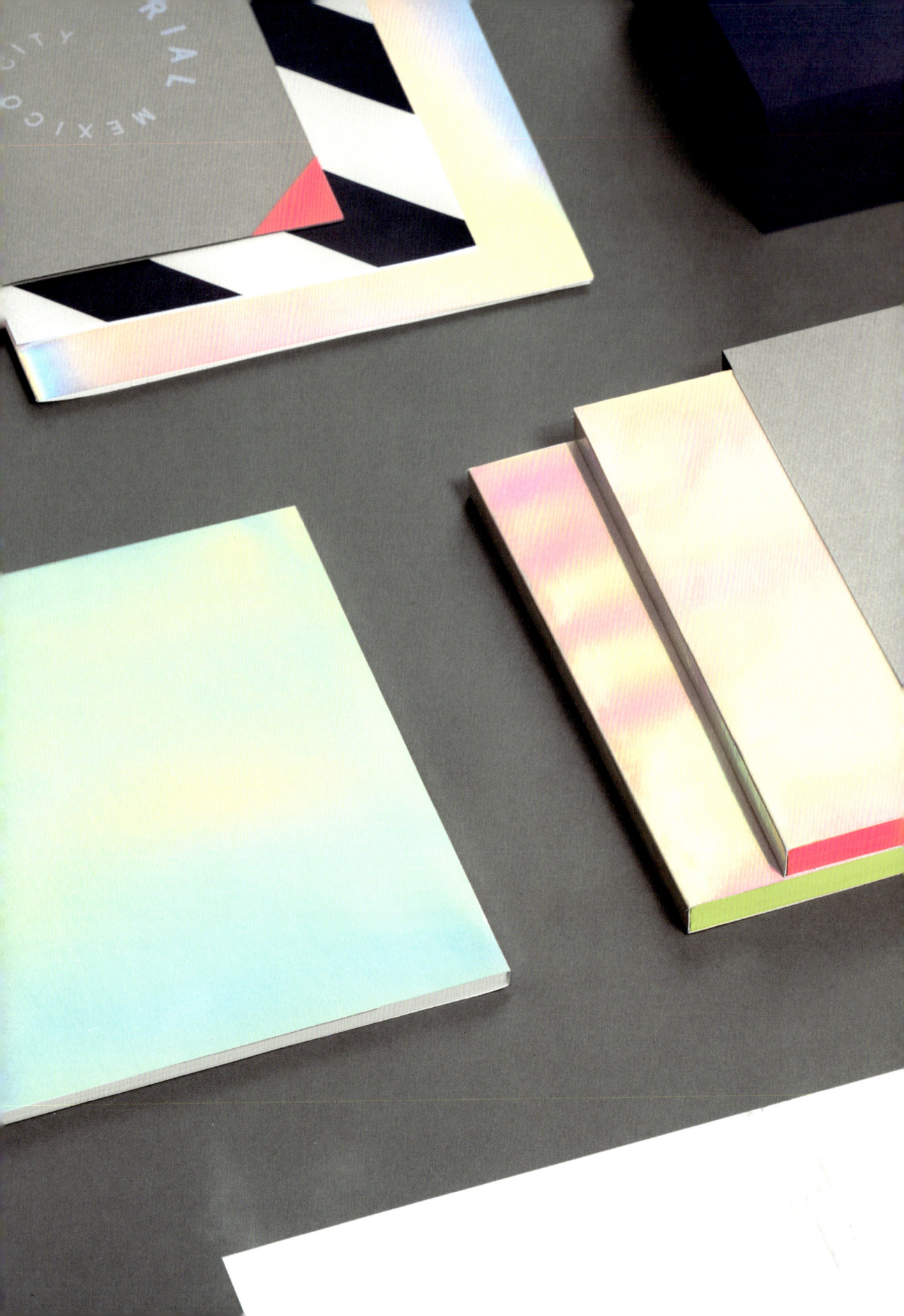

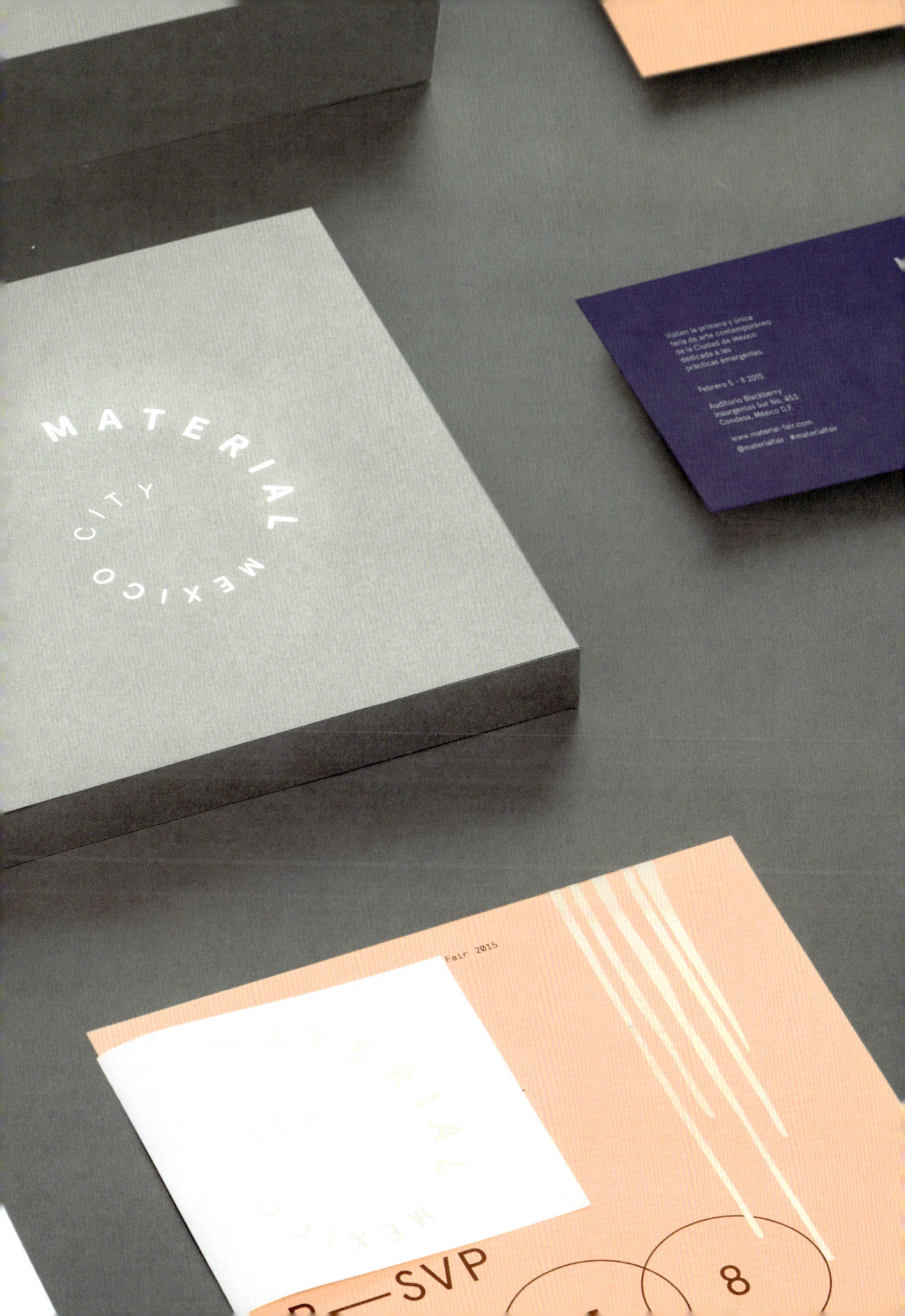

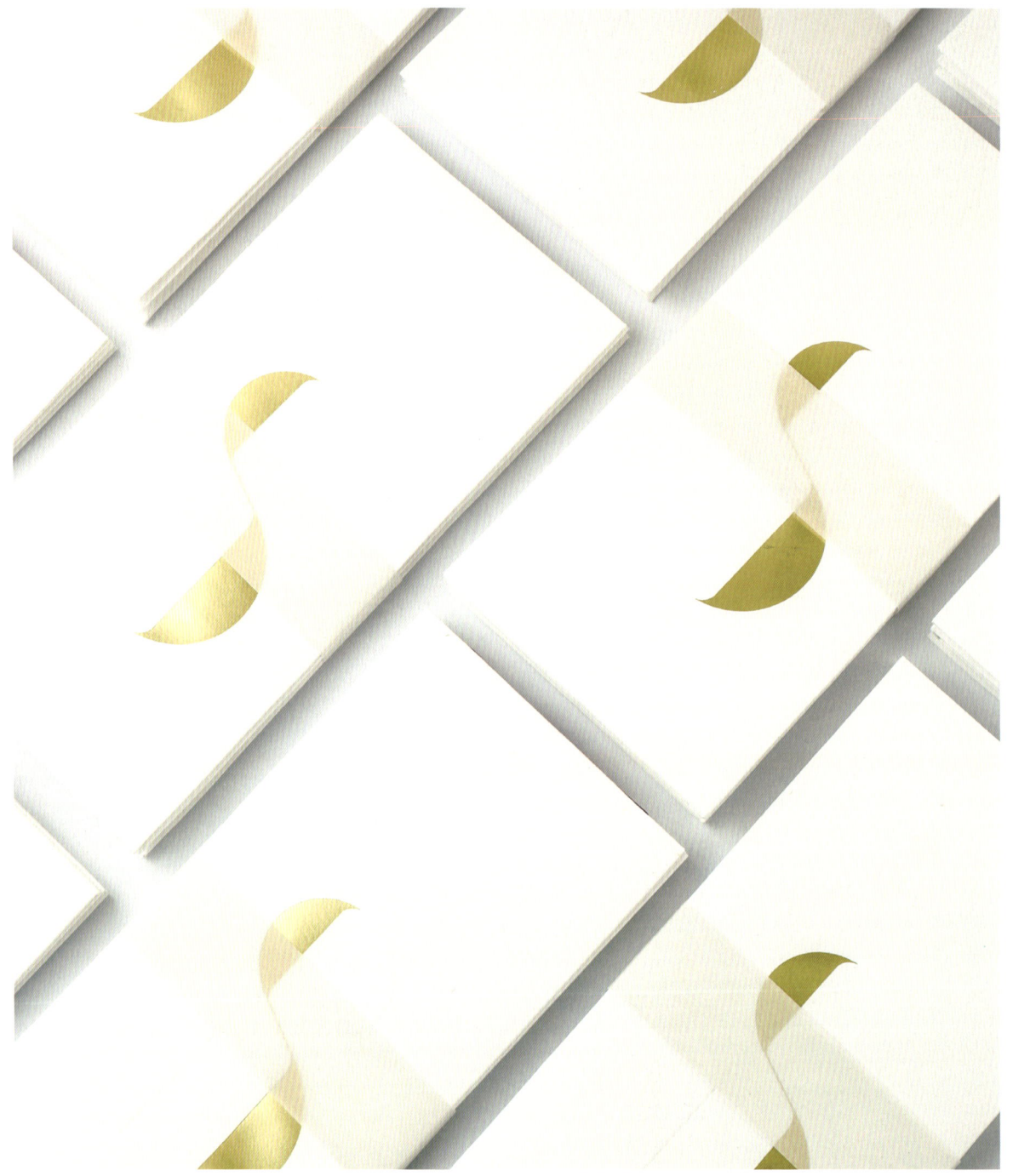

Minimalist Red Packets I

Studio: Kong Studio | Designer: Kevin He

Number 8 is believed to be auspicious in Chinese culture as it rhymes with the word "Fa" that means wealth, lending its frequent presence in festive greetings. The horizontal 8 is similar to the infinity symbol. This design marries the two concepts to signify a continuous cycle of fortune unfolding a year of longevity with prosperity.

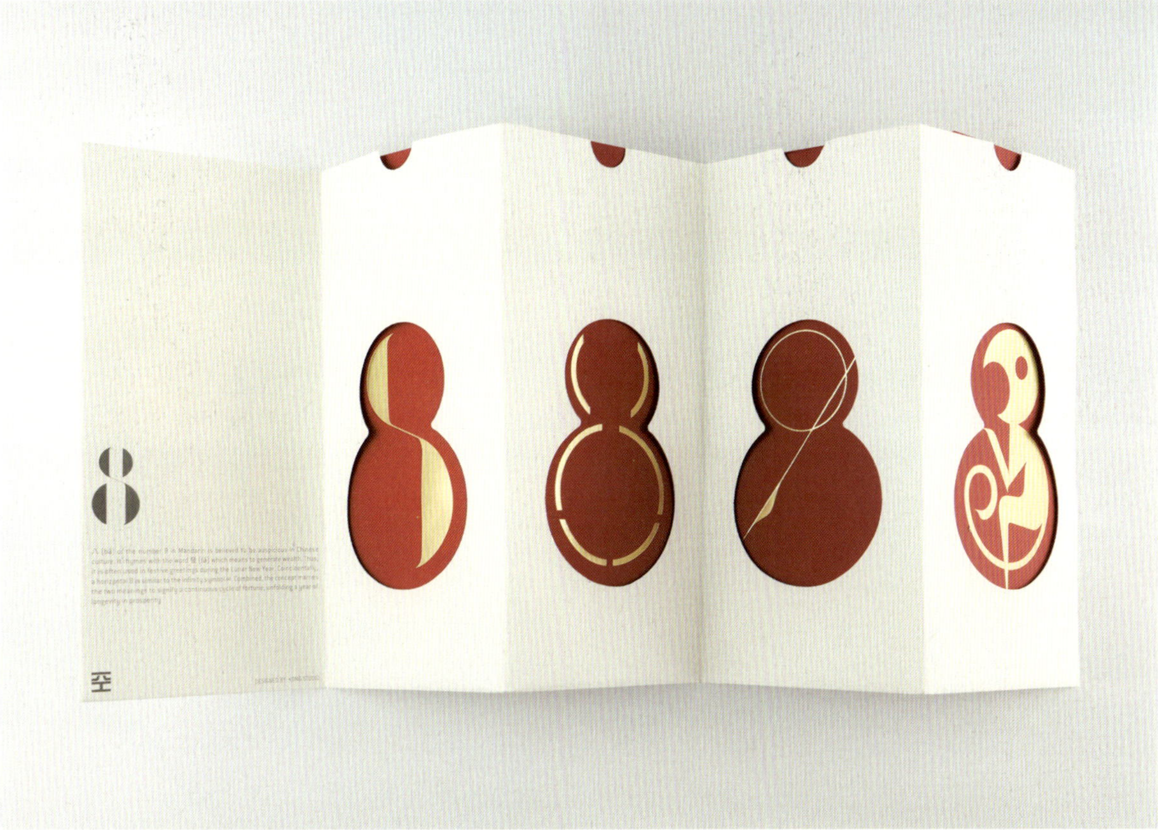

8

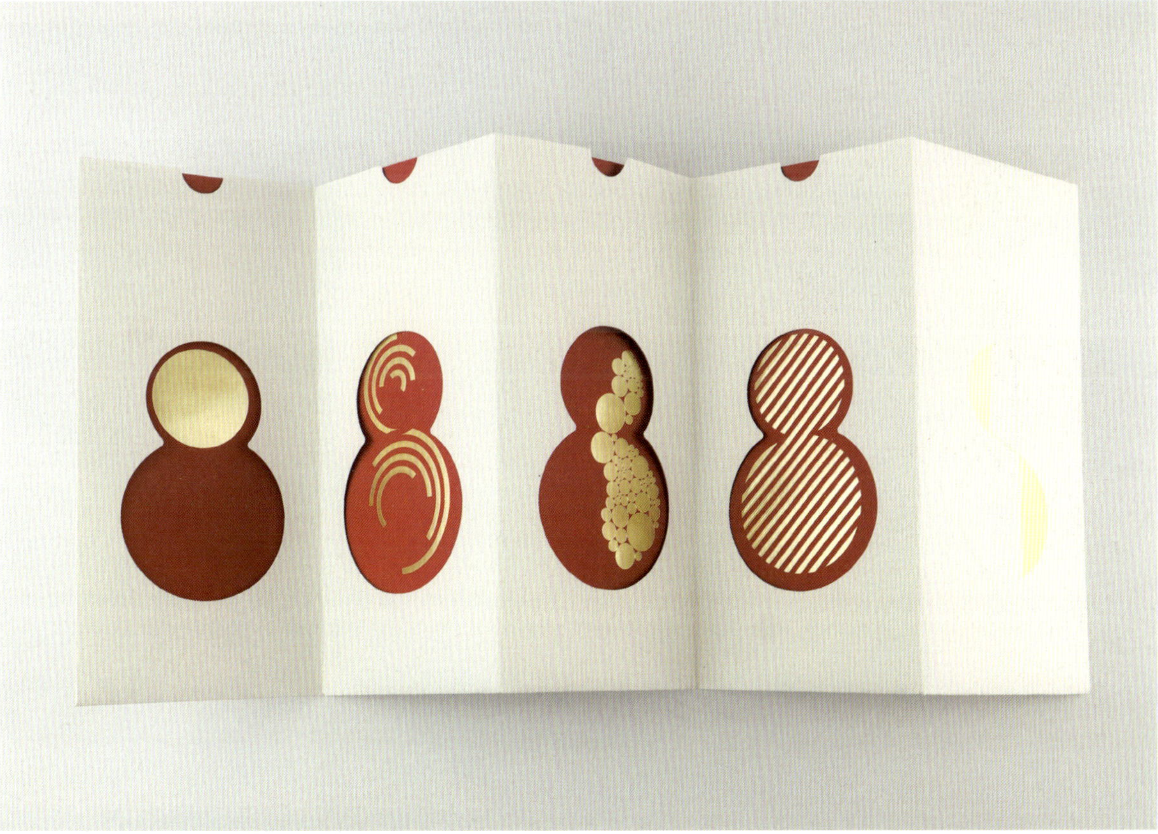

八 (ba) of the number 8 in Mandarin, is believed to be auspicious in Chinese culture. In rhyme with the word 发 (fa) which means to generate wealth, it is often used in festive greetings during the Lunar New Year. Coincidentally, a five-part digit 8 is similar to the infinity symbol ∞. Combined, the concept reiterates the two ideologies to signify a continuous cycle of fortune, unfolding a year of longevity in prosperity.

조

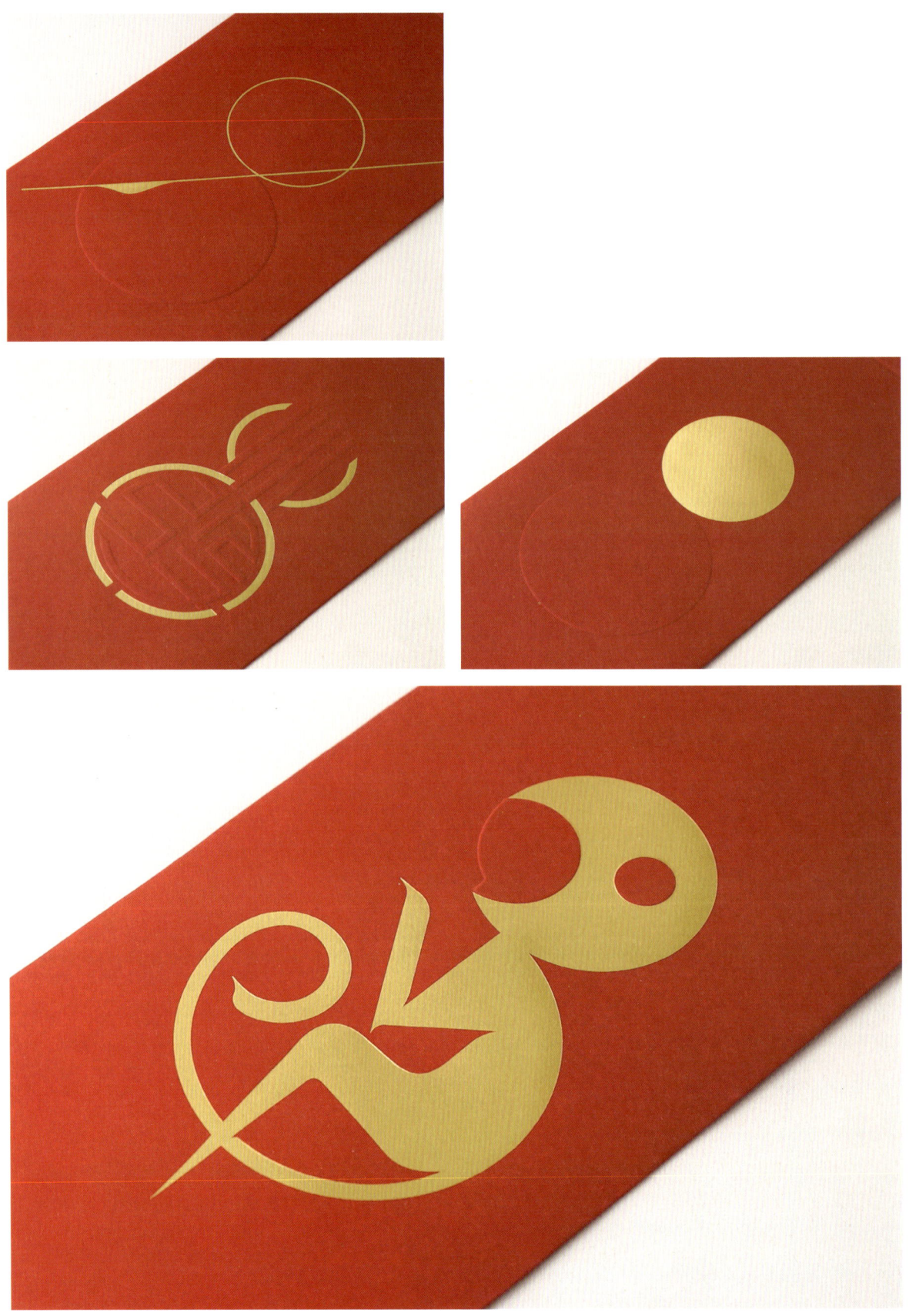

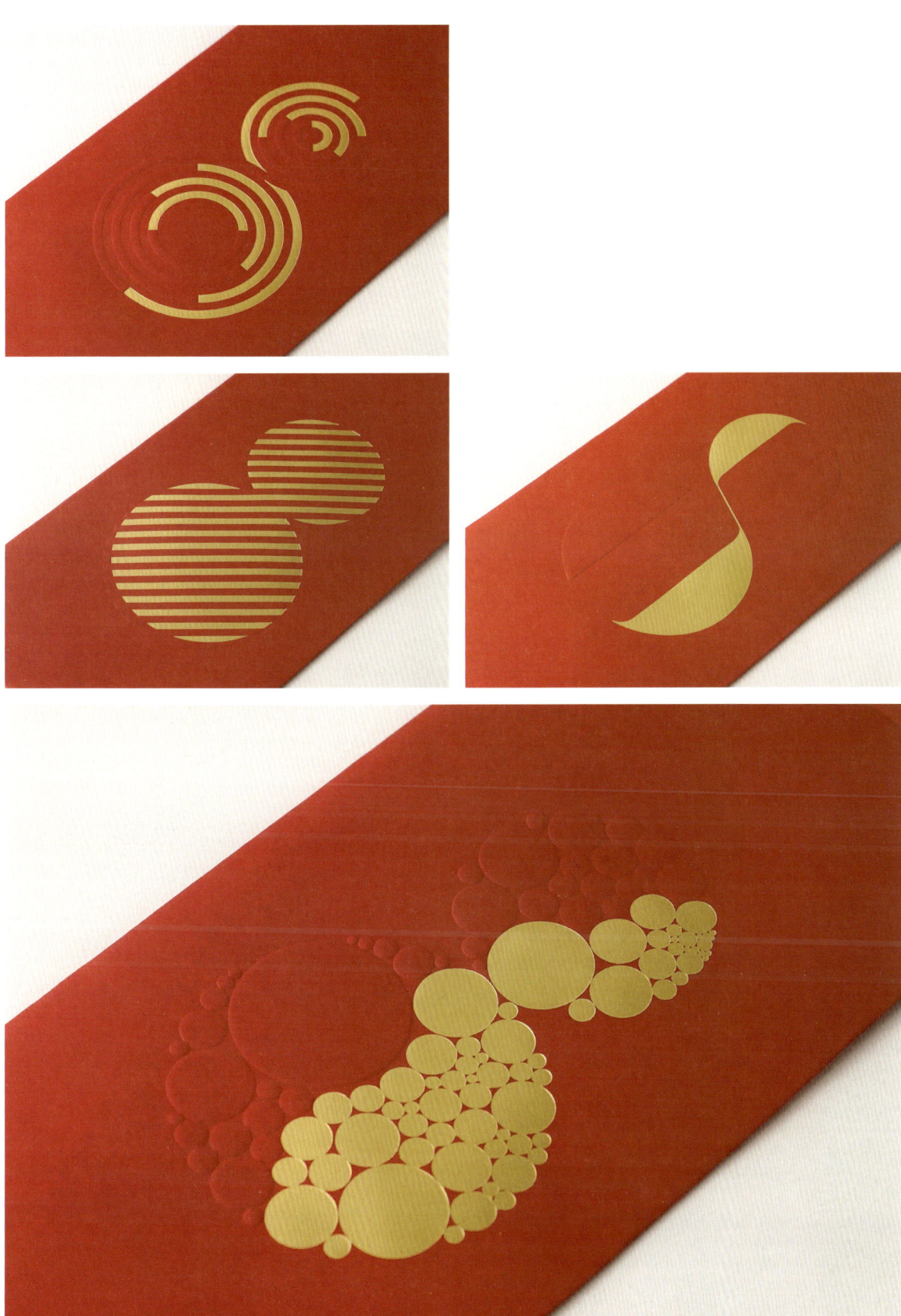

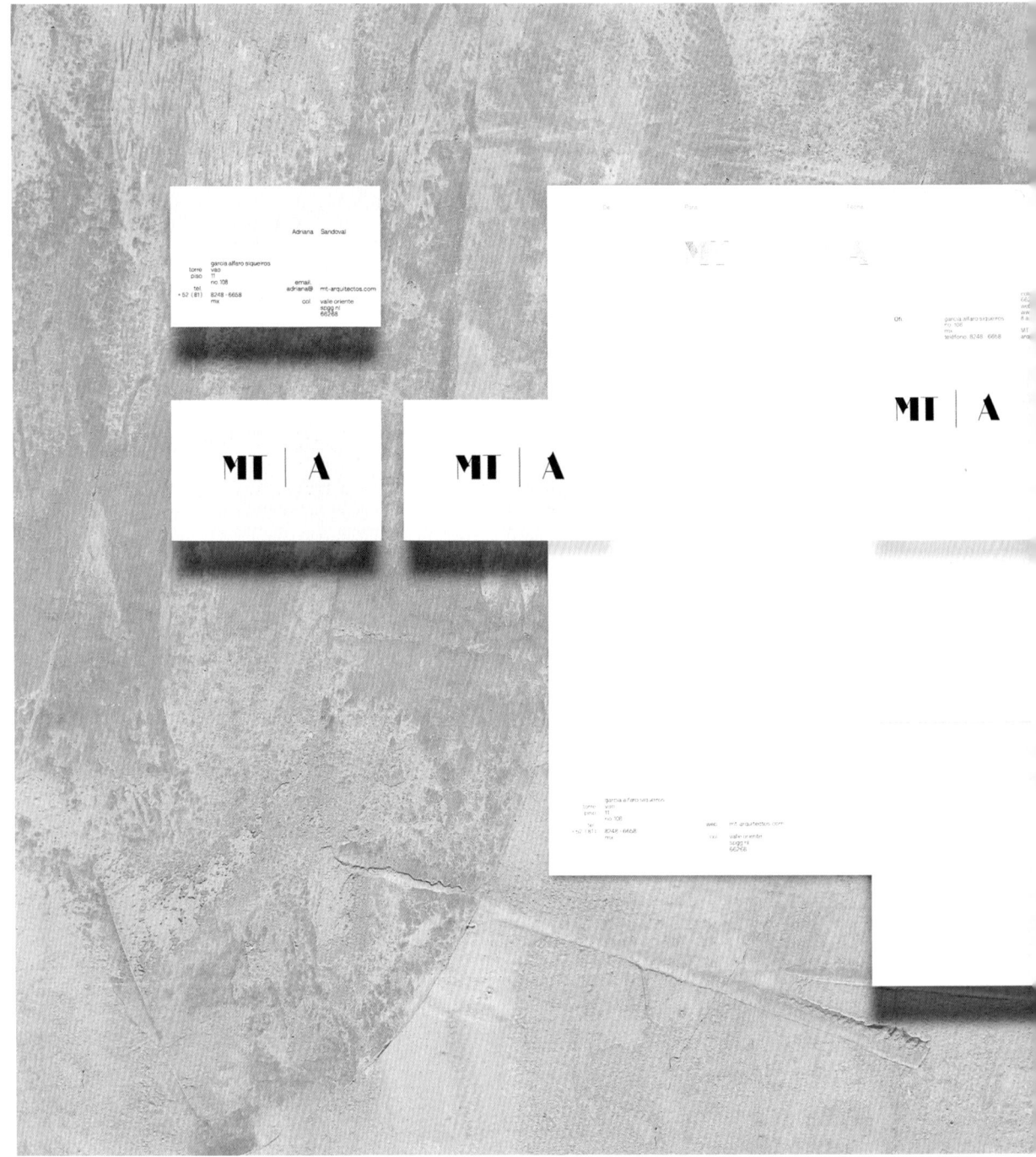

MT Arquitectos

Studio: Anagrama

For the MTA´s rebranding, Anagrama created a new identity based on the reflection on the brand´s evolution. Efforts were centered on designing a typographical logo inspired by the architectural supporting elements from previous projects accentuating bold features to highlight the brand´s personality in line with a clean and elegant identity.

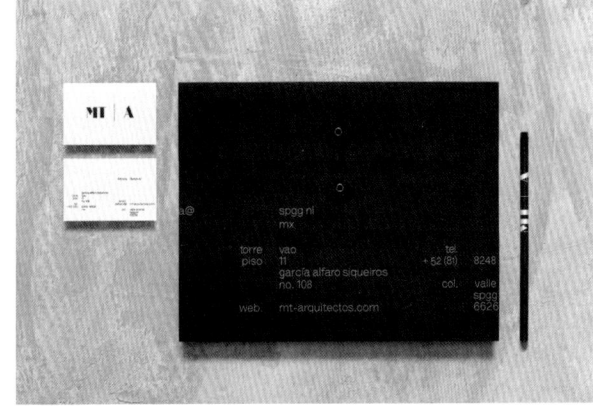
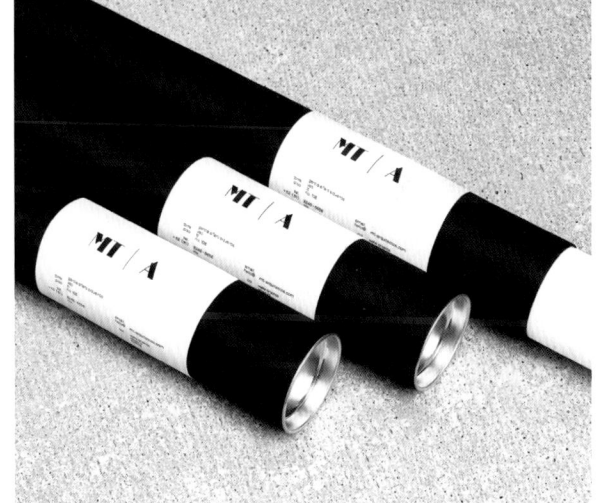

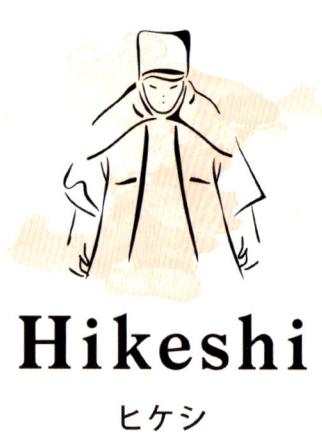

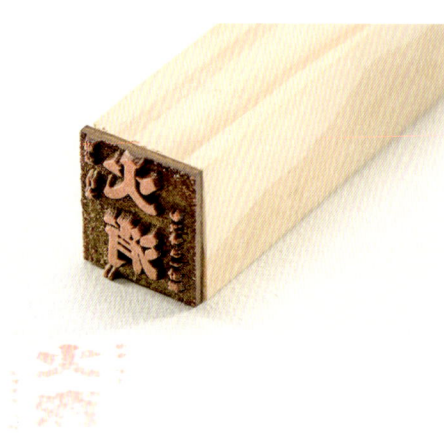

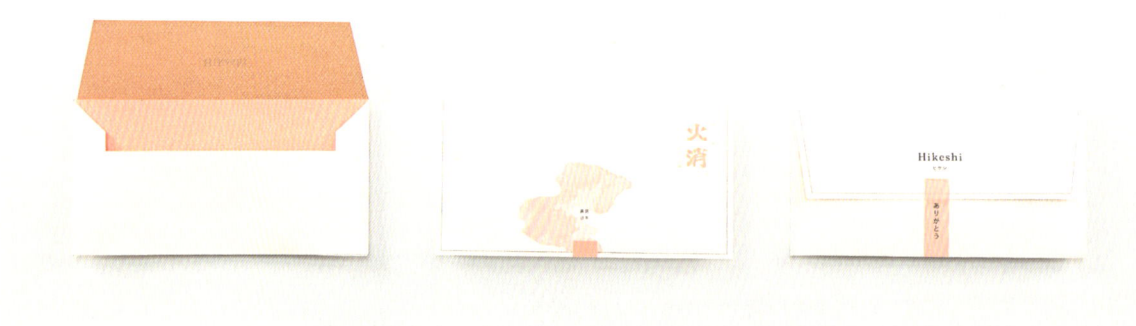

Hikeshi

Studio: Futura

For the branding for Hikeshi, a high quality clothing line that belongs to the Japanese brand Resquad, the general concept was inspired by the Edo Period in Japanese history. Futura designed a series of illustrations featuring fire fighters from this period, who were considered as high ranked as samurais. The typographic selection and color palette turn the brand into something modern, while the material, the composition and the combination of elements altogether make Hikeshi a timeless brand.

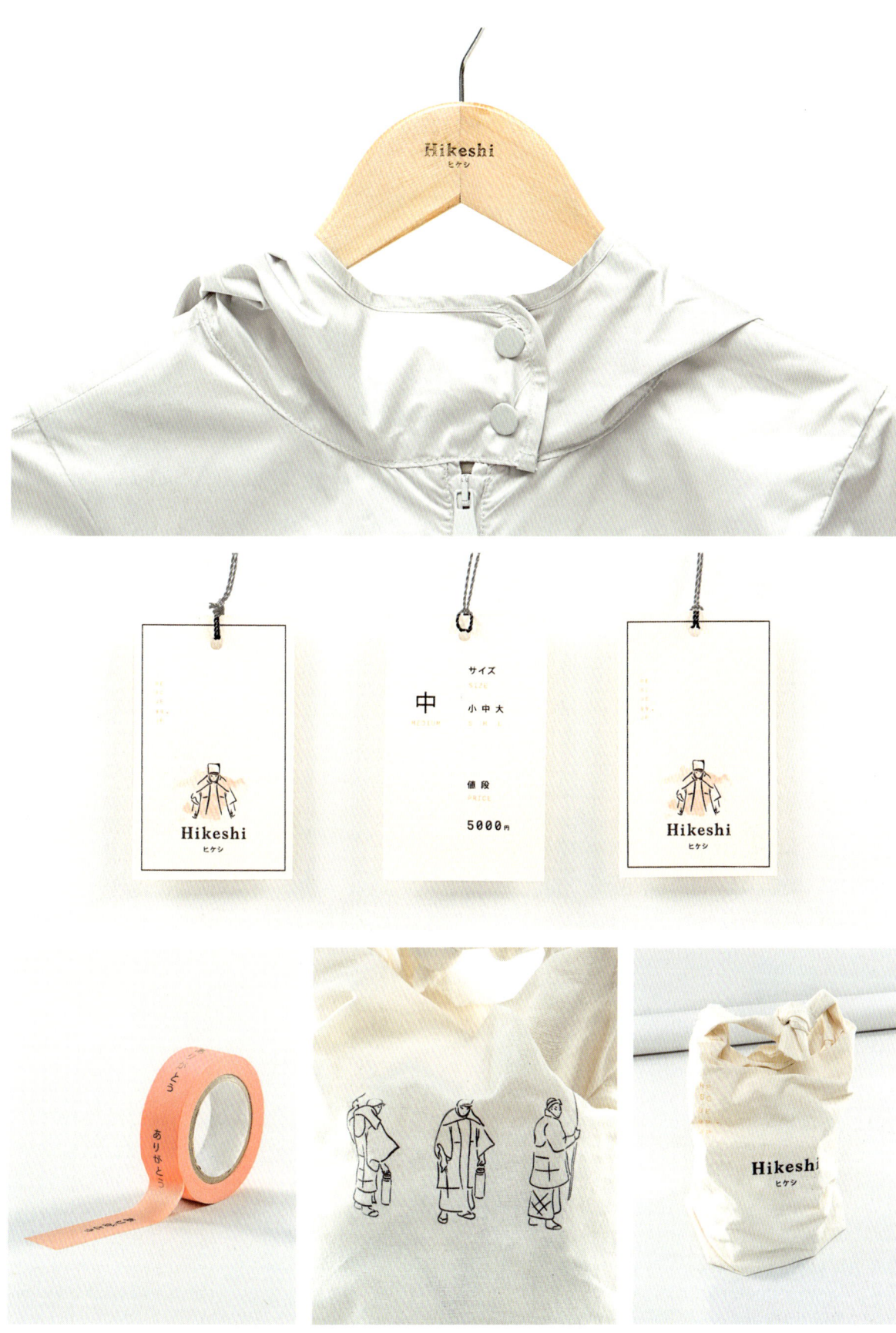

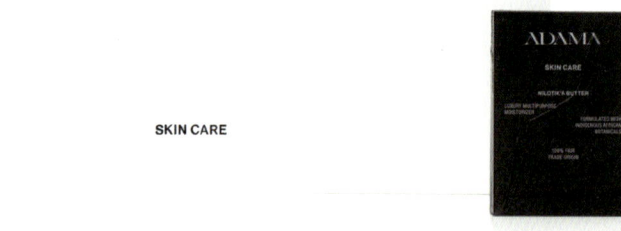

SKIN CARE

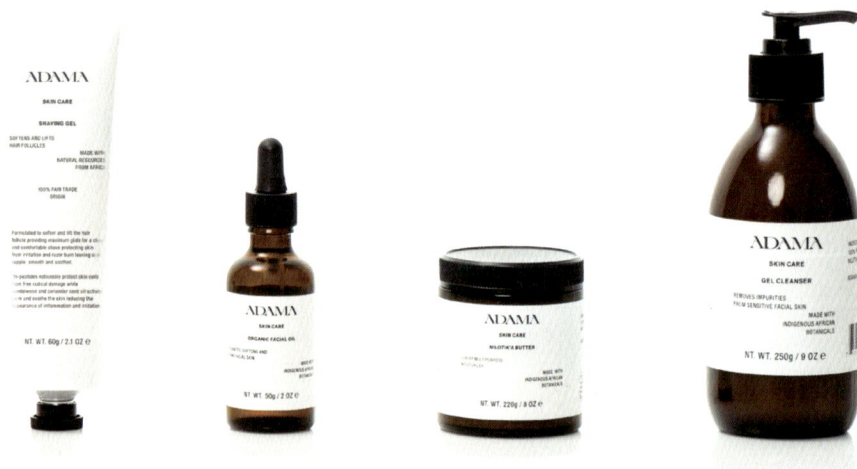

Adama

Studio: Anagrama

A delicate packaging featuring embossed roots was developed to enhance and compliment the healing attributes of Nilotik´a tree, the essential ingredient of the products. Black and white colors were employed to reflect Adama´s elegance and purity while details in gold emphasized the superiority of its botanical products.

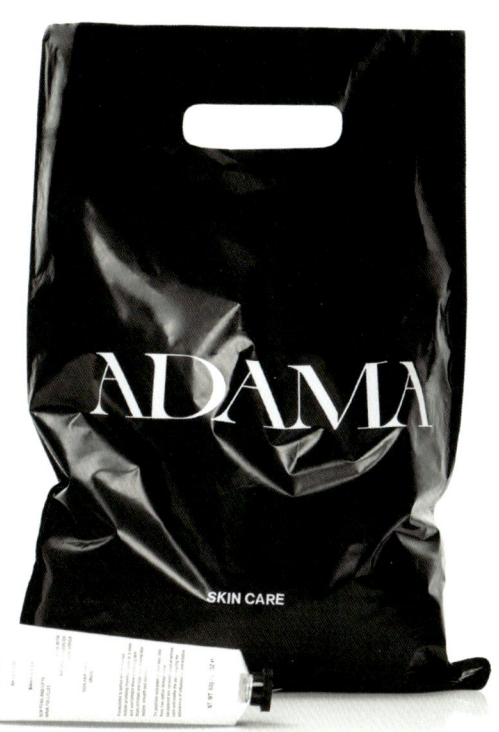

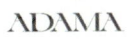
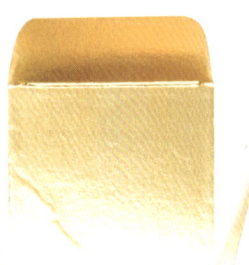

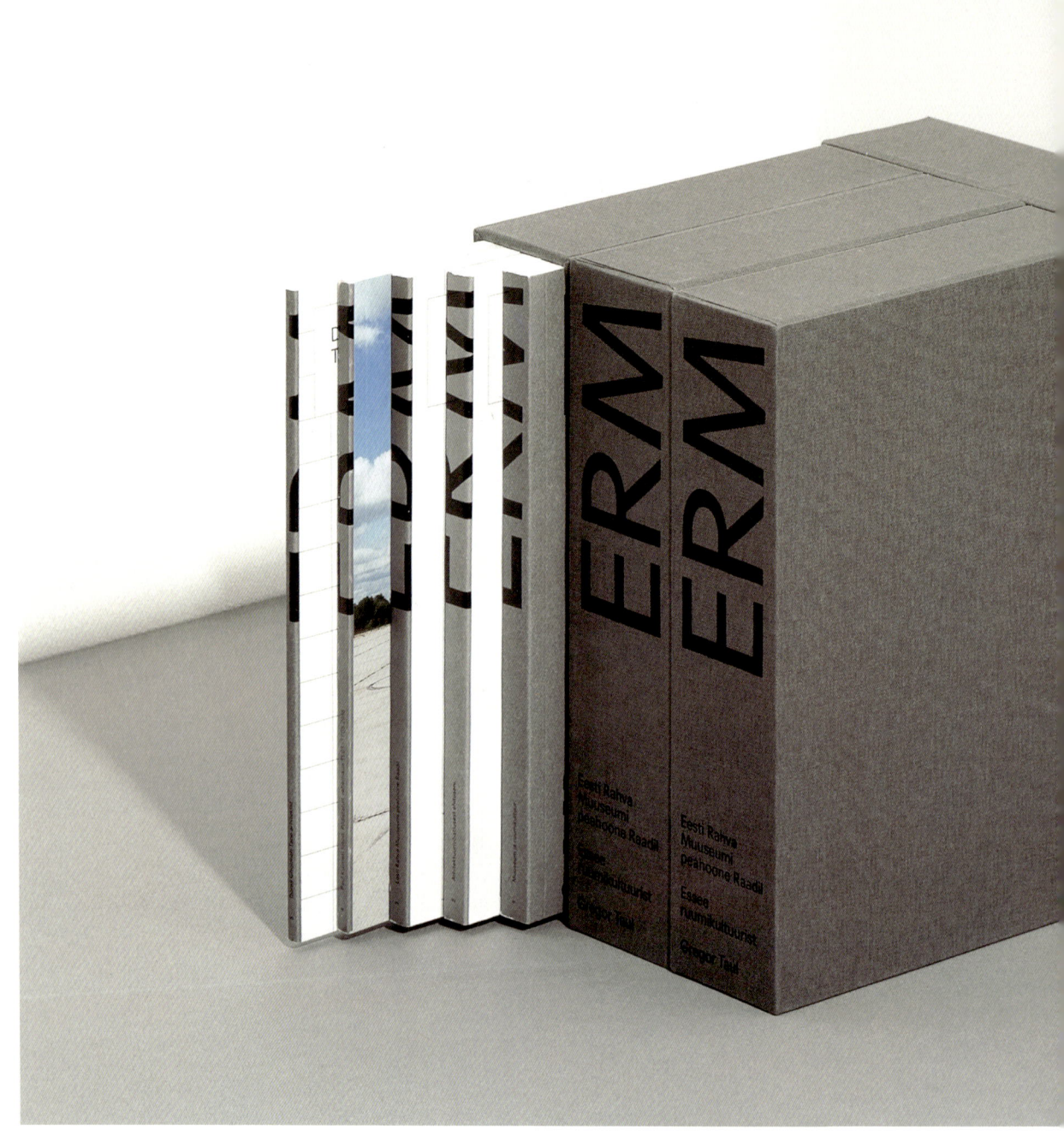

Book on The Estonian National Museum's Main Building

Designer: AKU

ERM tells the story of the newly built national museum of Estonia, and also features Gregor Taul´s essay The Estonian National Museum´s Main Building at Raadi: An Essay on Spatial Culture, accompanied by plenty of visual materials. The book has five volumes, each of which discusses a slightly different theme, but together forms a whole. They are all packed into a gray fabric slipcase, revealing the book title *ERM* on the spines. The special edition comes with a 3D-printed white slipcase, inspired by the form and surroundings of the museum´s building.

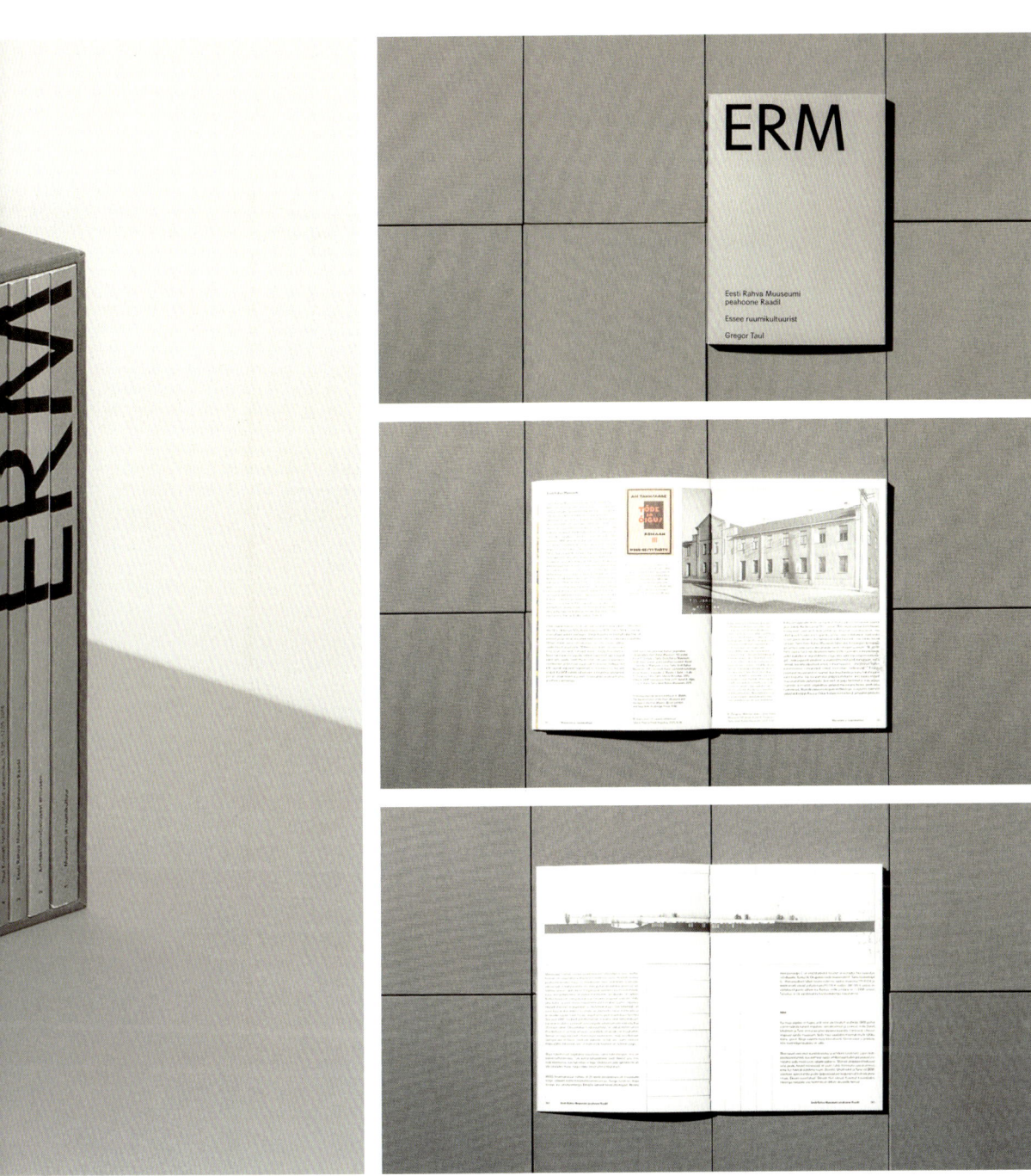

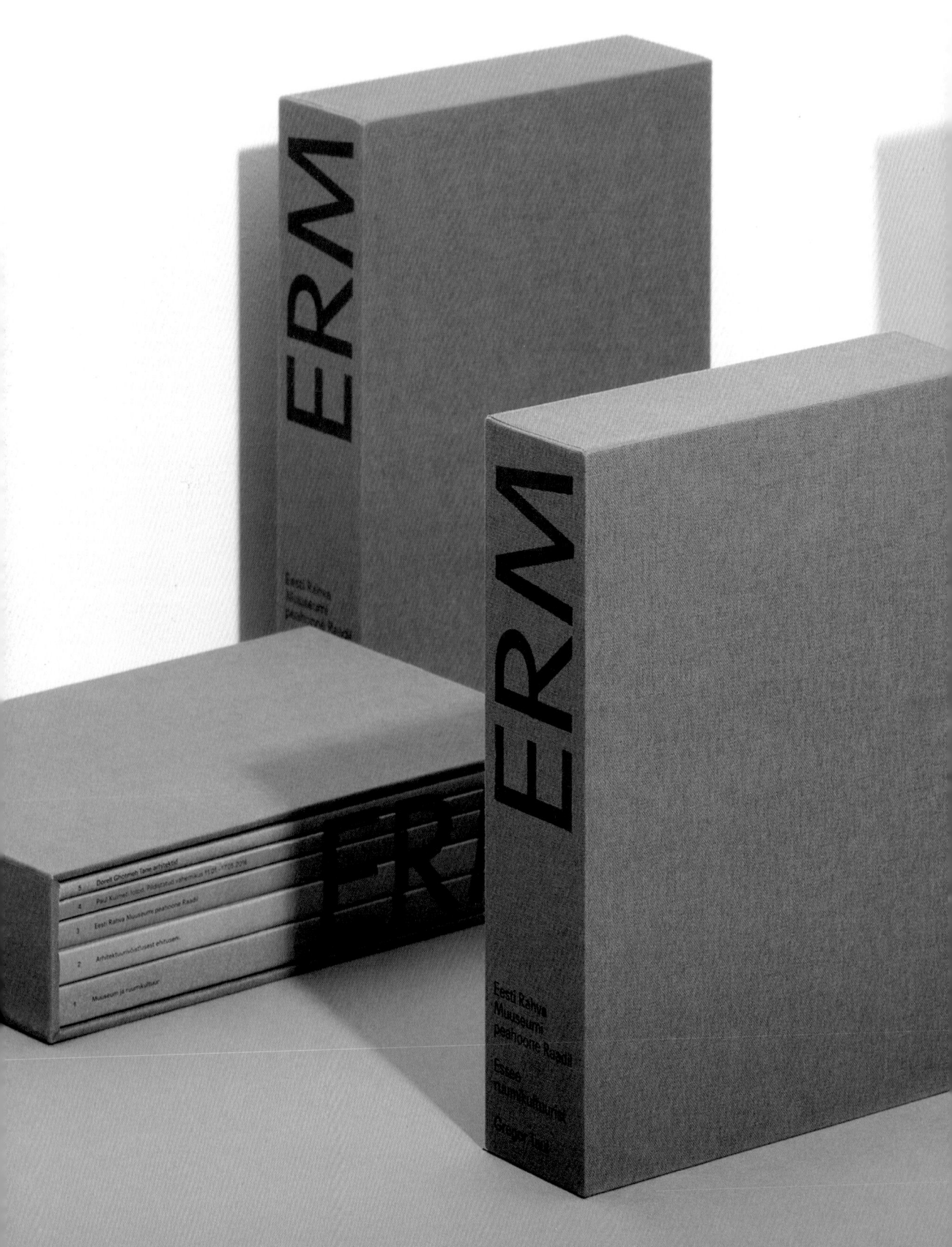

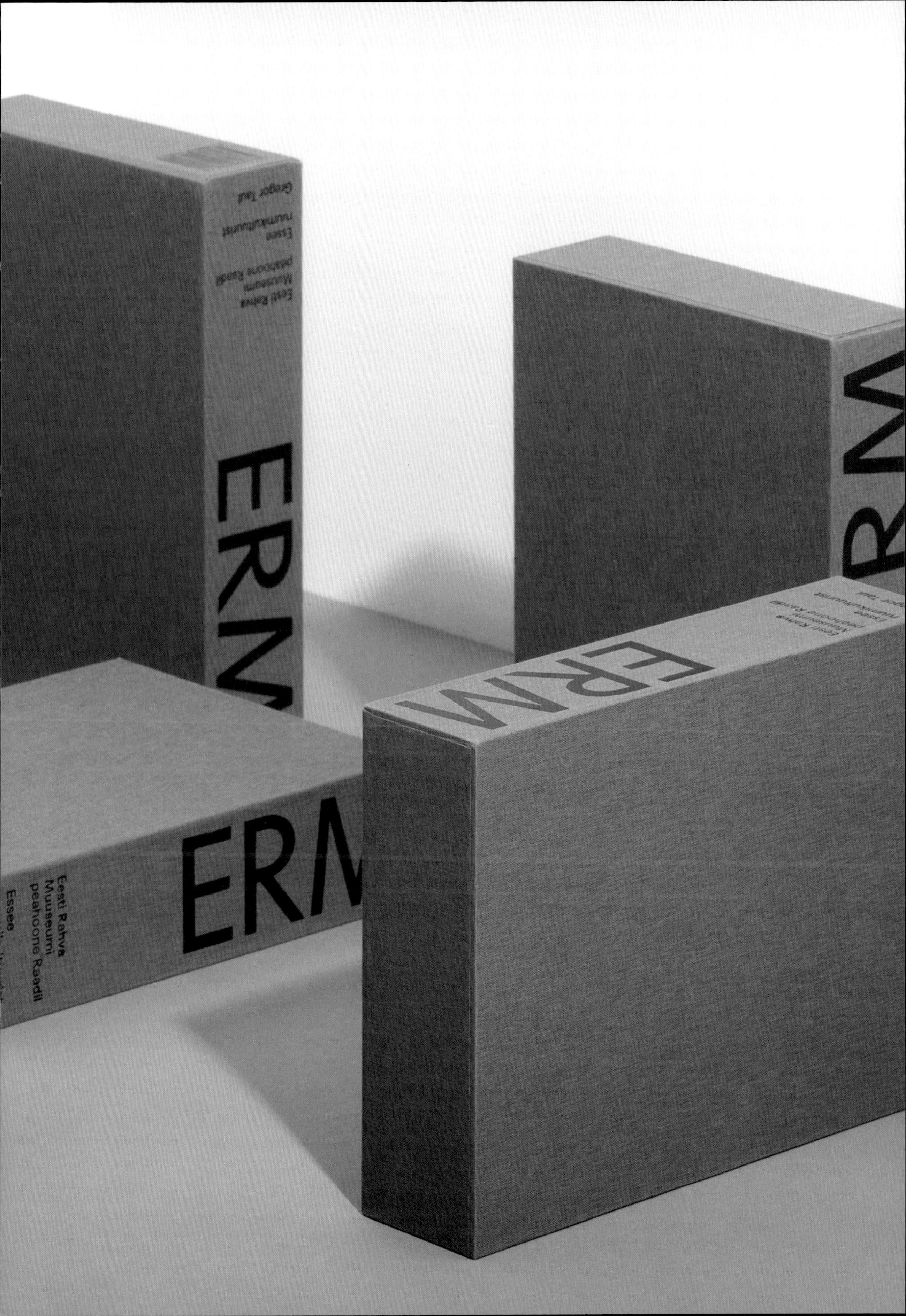

Eesti Rahva
Muuseumi
peahoone Raadil

Essee
ruumikultuurist

Gregor Taul

ERM

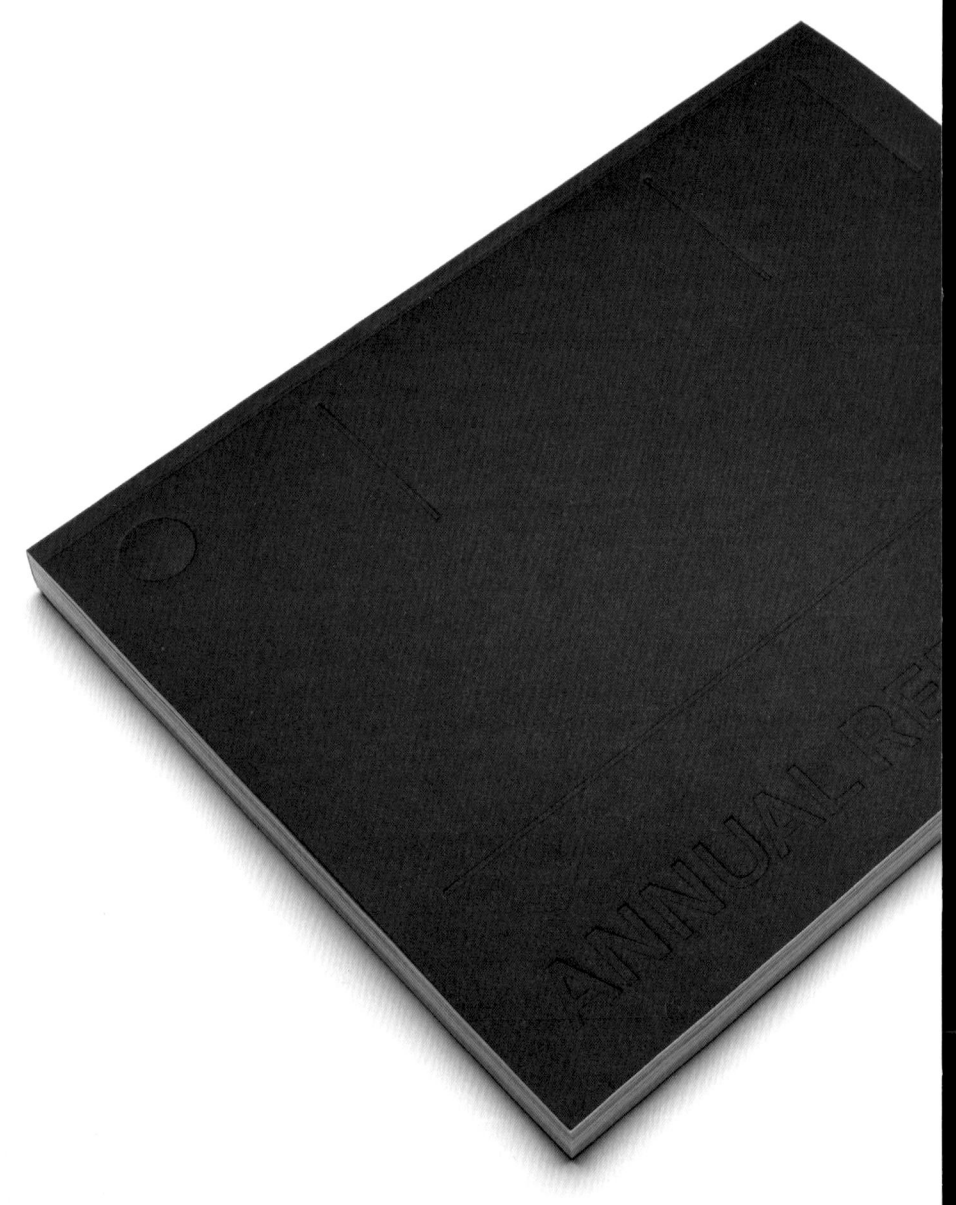

SNGP Annual Report

Studio: Ermolaev Bureau | Designer: Vlad Ermolaev

This work is a part of the new visual identity for an oil and gas company. Graphic compositions leading the visual identity system are based on the point, vertical and horizontal lines that embody the company's major businesses. Photos, toned to fit the company's signature color palette of navy blue, blue and red, were combined with graphic elements to discover the beautiful environment in which the field is located.

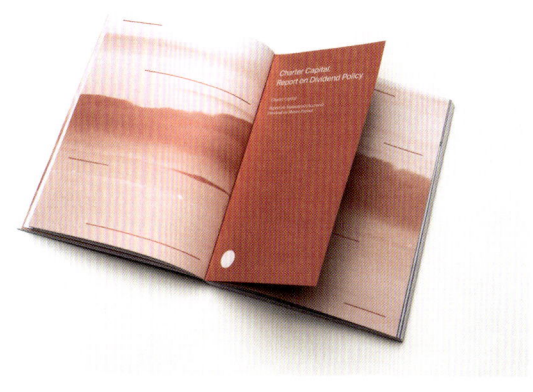
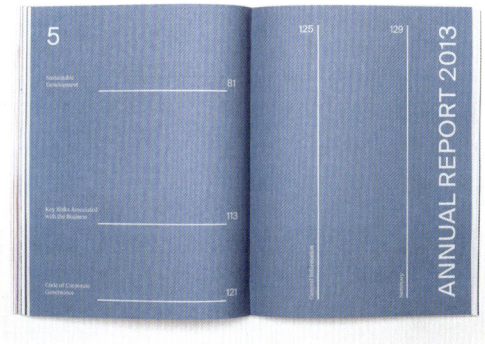
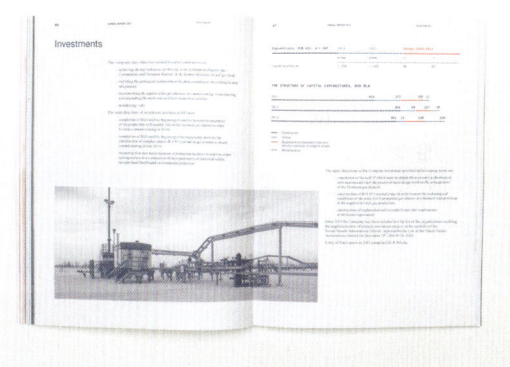
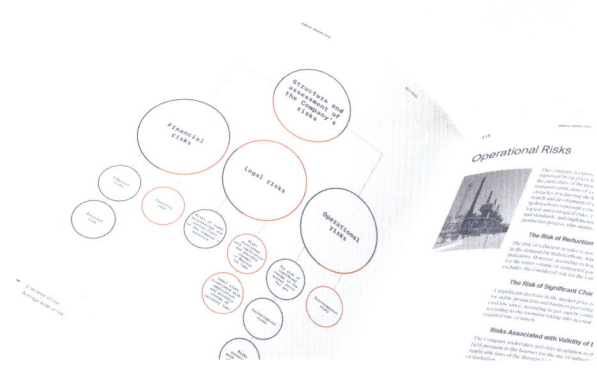

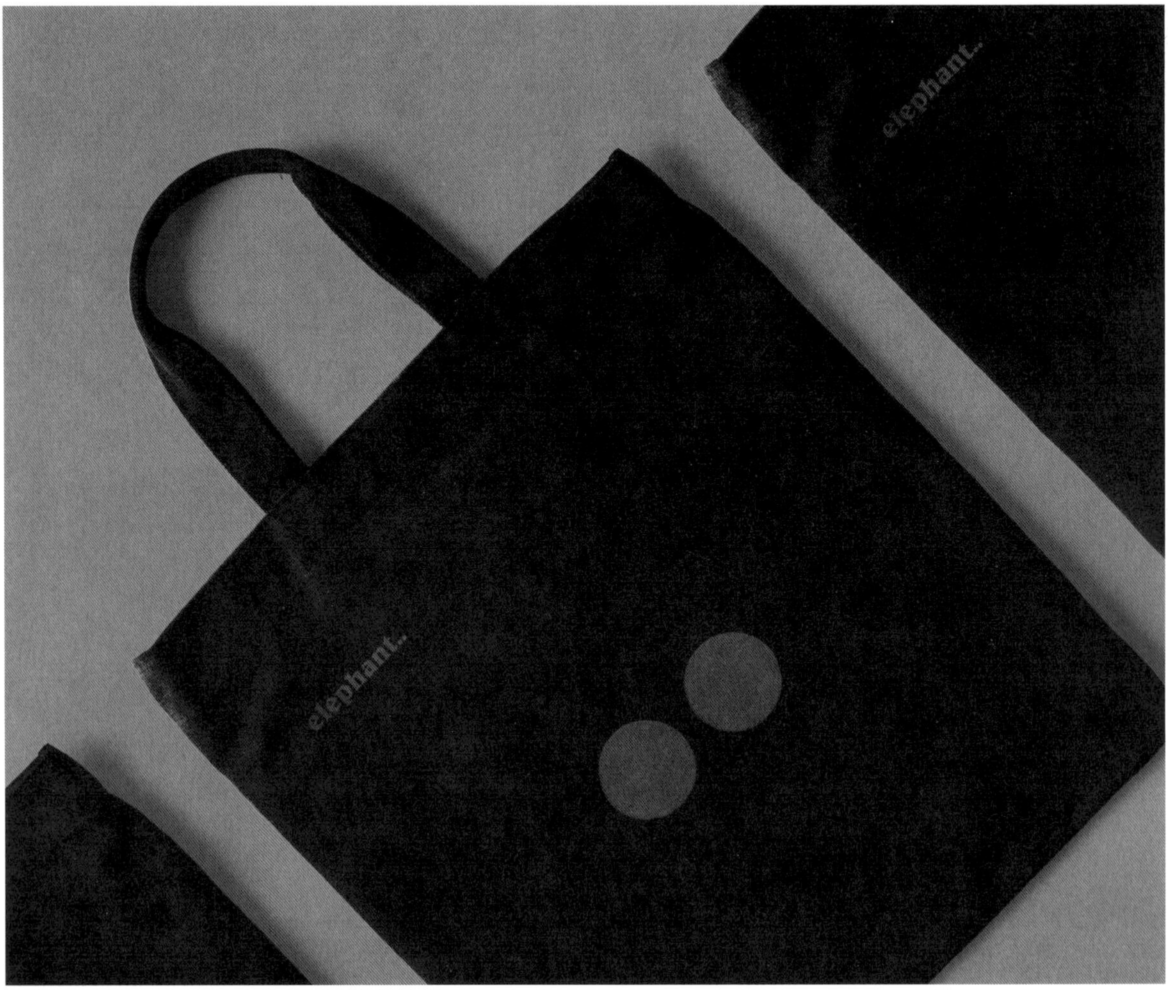

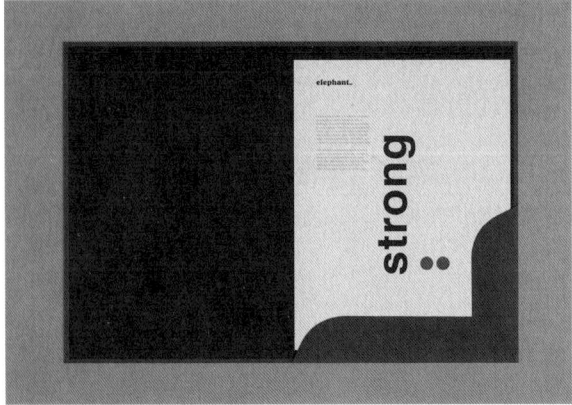
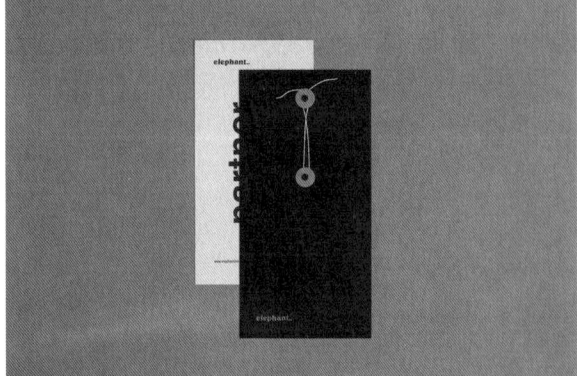

Elephant

Studio: Fagerström Studio | Designer: Puli Arancibia

This work is for a consulting agency specialized in developing marketing strategies for B2B companies. The naming and visual identity endowed the brand with a unique personality and a set of values.

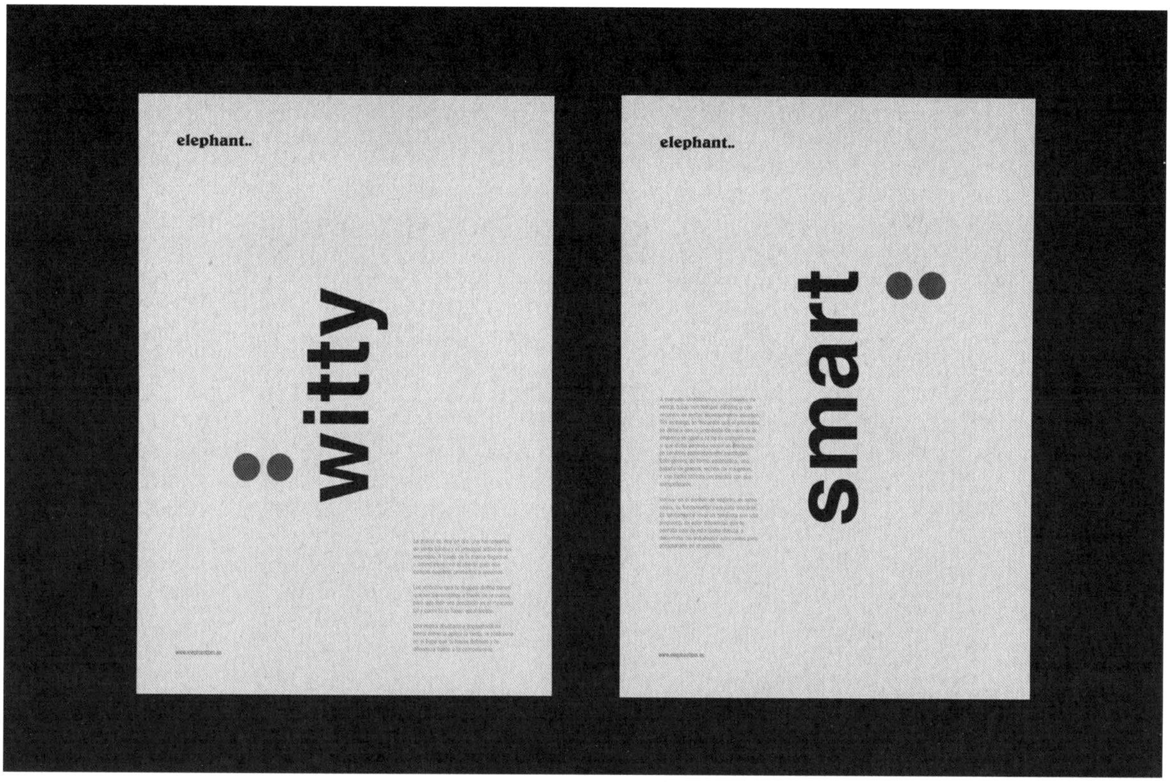

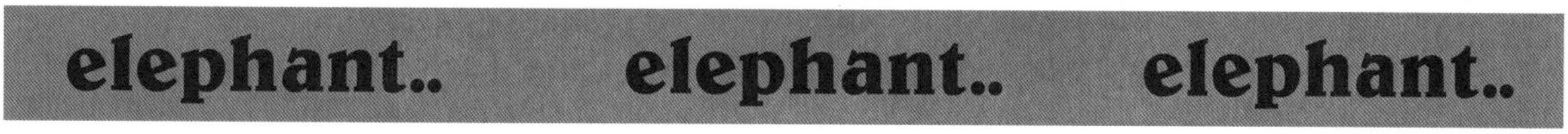

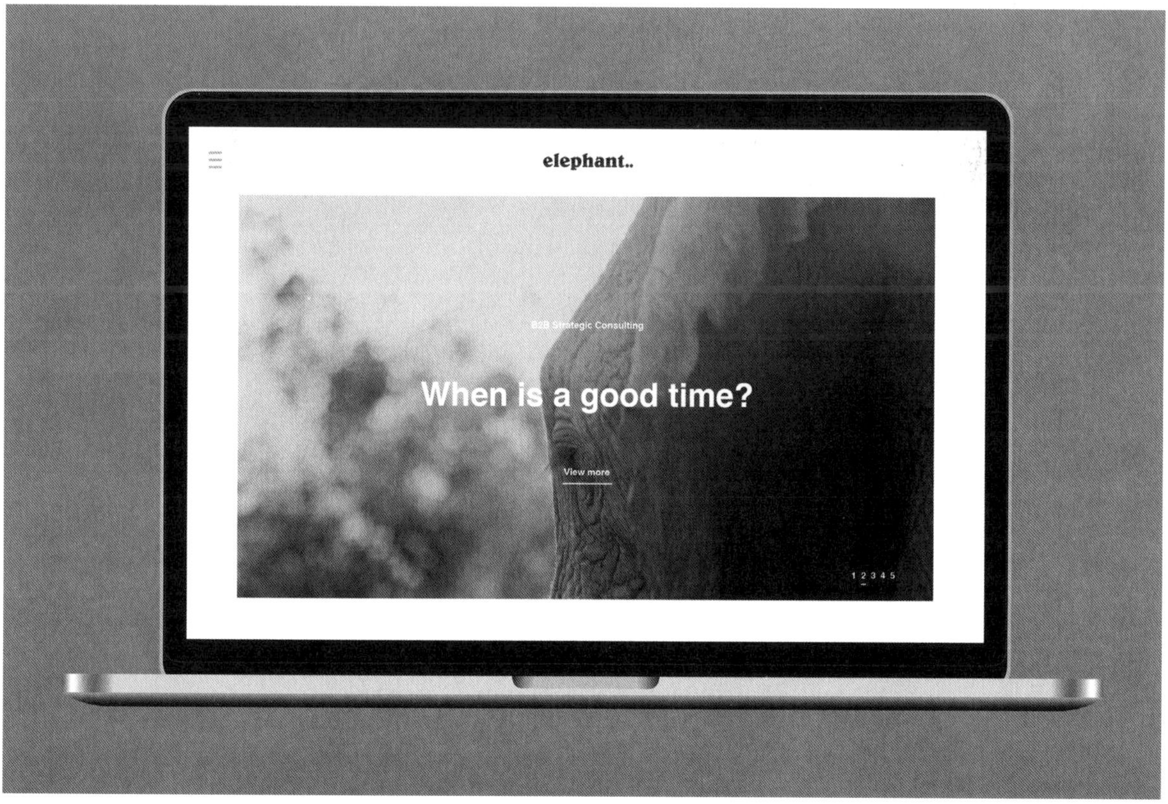

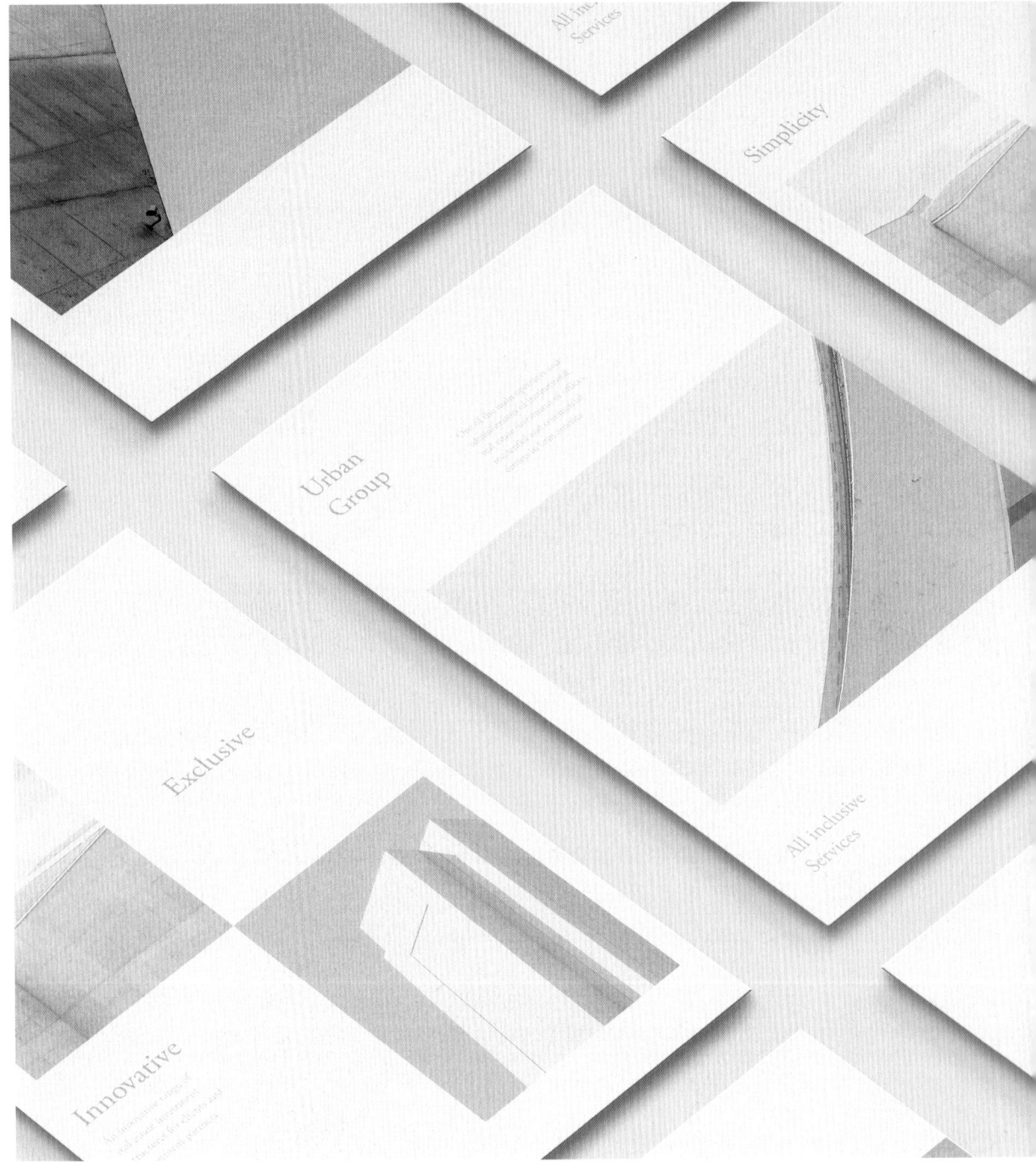

SDC

Studio: Fagerström Studio | Designer: Puli Arancibia

Combining meticulous and detailed work with a strong creative concept, a solid, recognizable and unique identity was created for Sara del Campo, an all-inclusive real estate rental system focused on the young public and offering service that goes beyond renting.

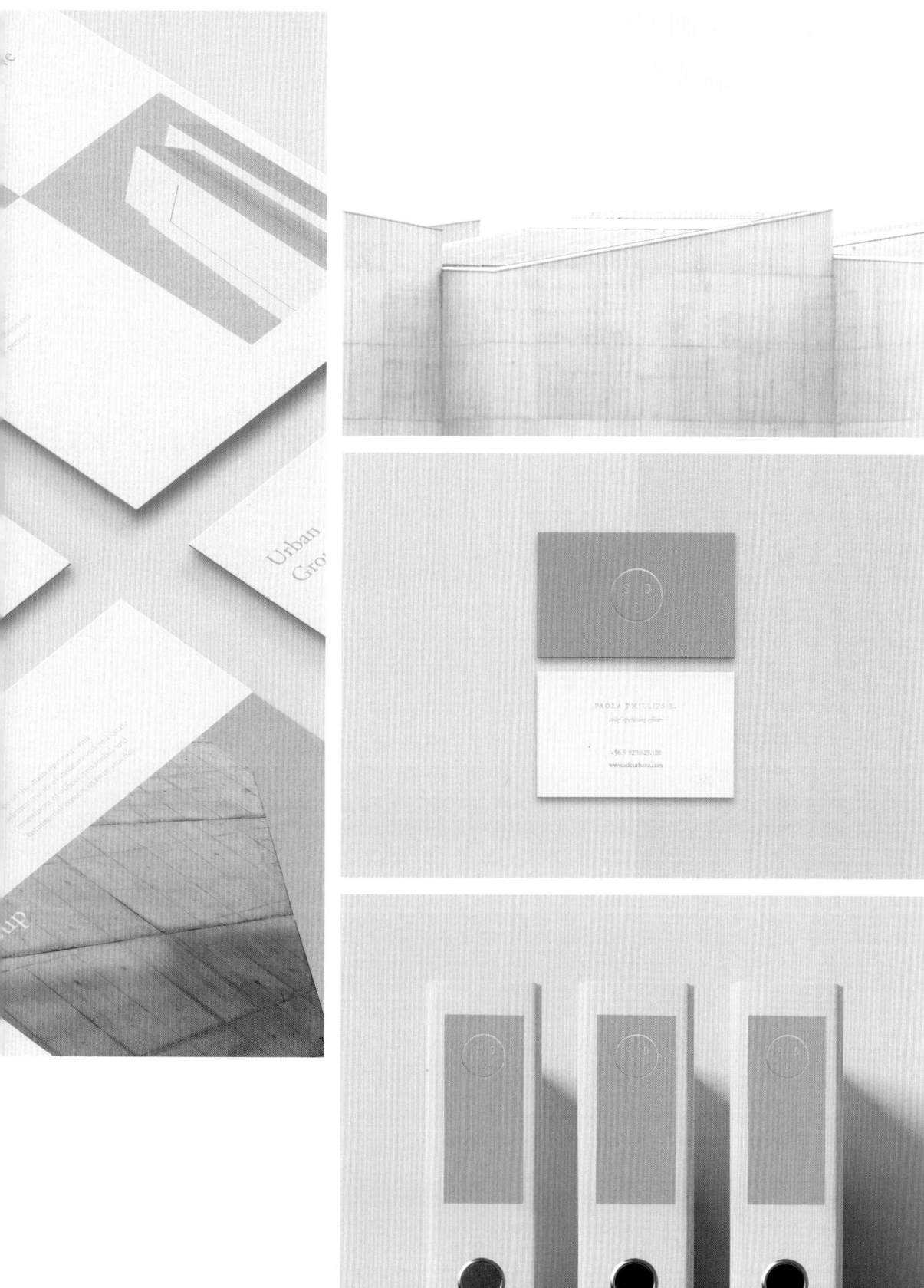

Hälssen & Lyon X
Ayzit Bostan—The Teabag Collection

Studio: KOREFE. Kolle Rebbe Form und Entwicklung
Designer: Christian Doering
Photography: Imke Jansen, Mitja Schneehage

KOREFE worked together with handbag designer Ayzit Bostan to create five limited-edition tea bags in the style of the world's most iconic handbags to thank long-standing customers for their ongoing commitment. The selection was handcrafted with cordless silk and permeable cotton and designed to fit perfectly with the personality of each brew.

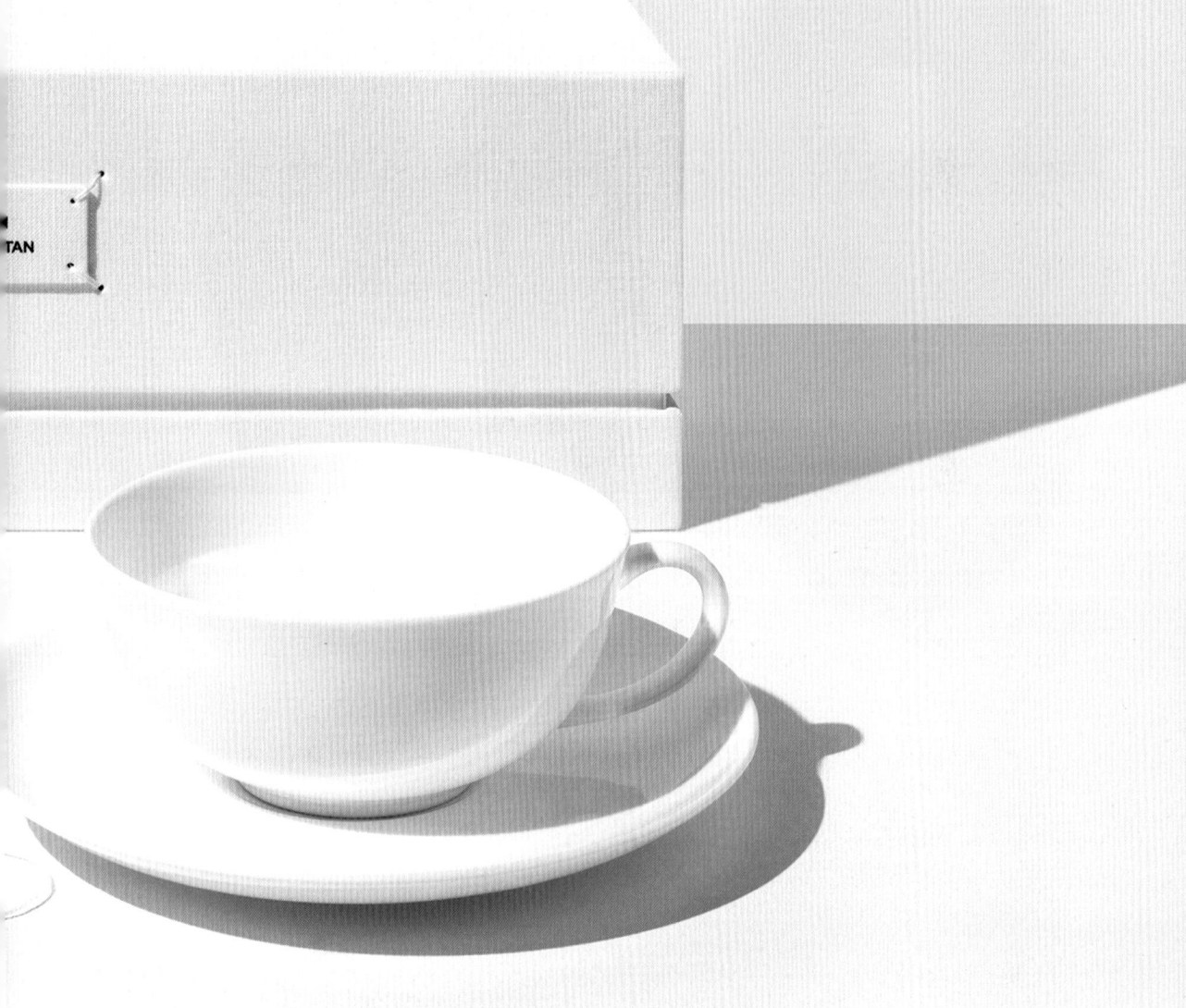

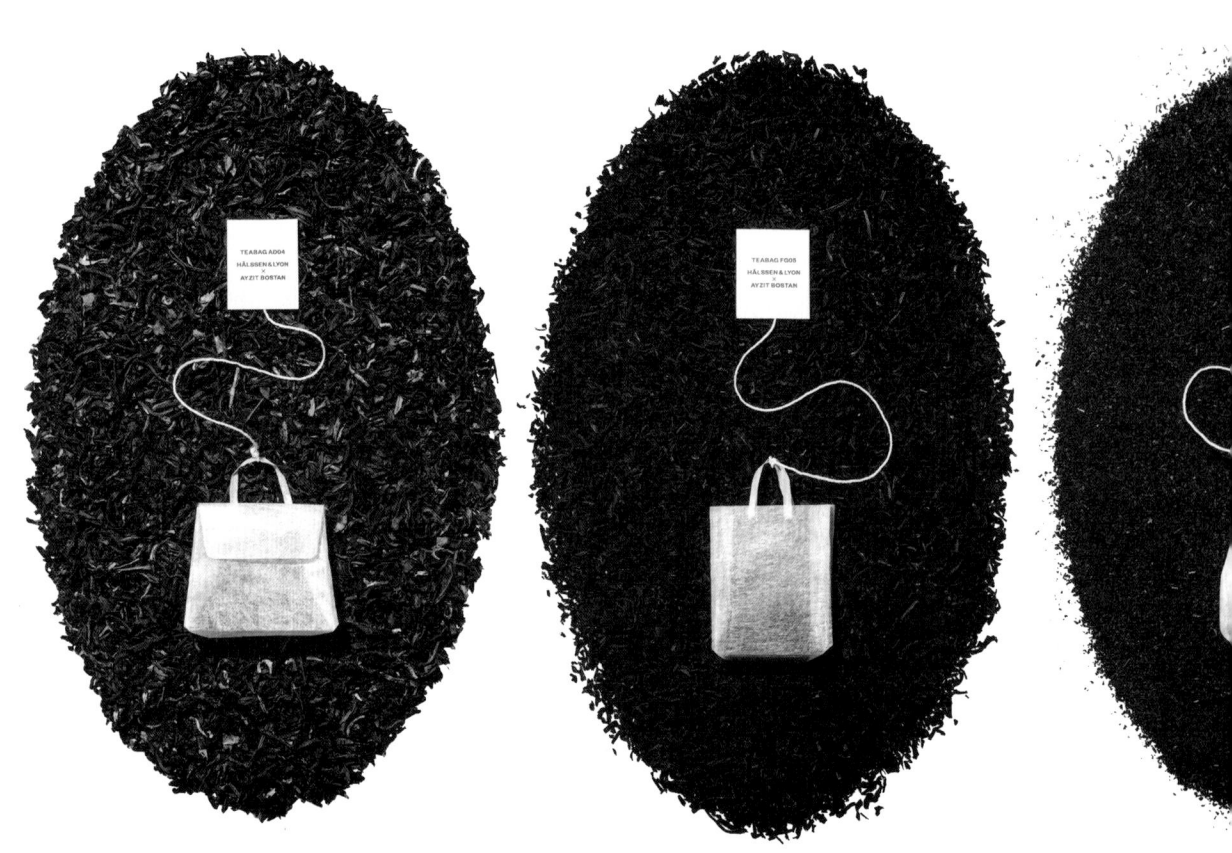

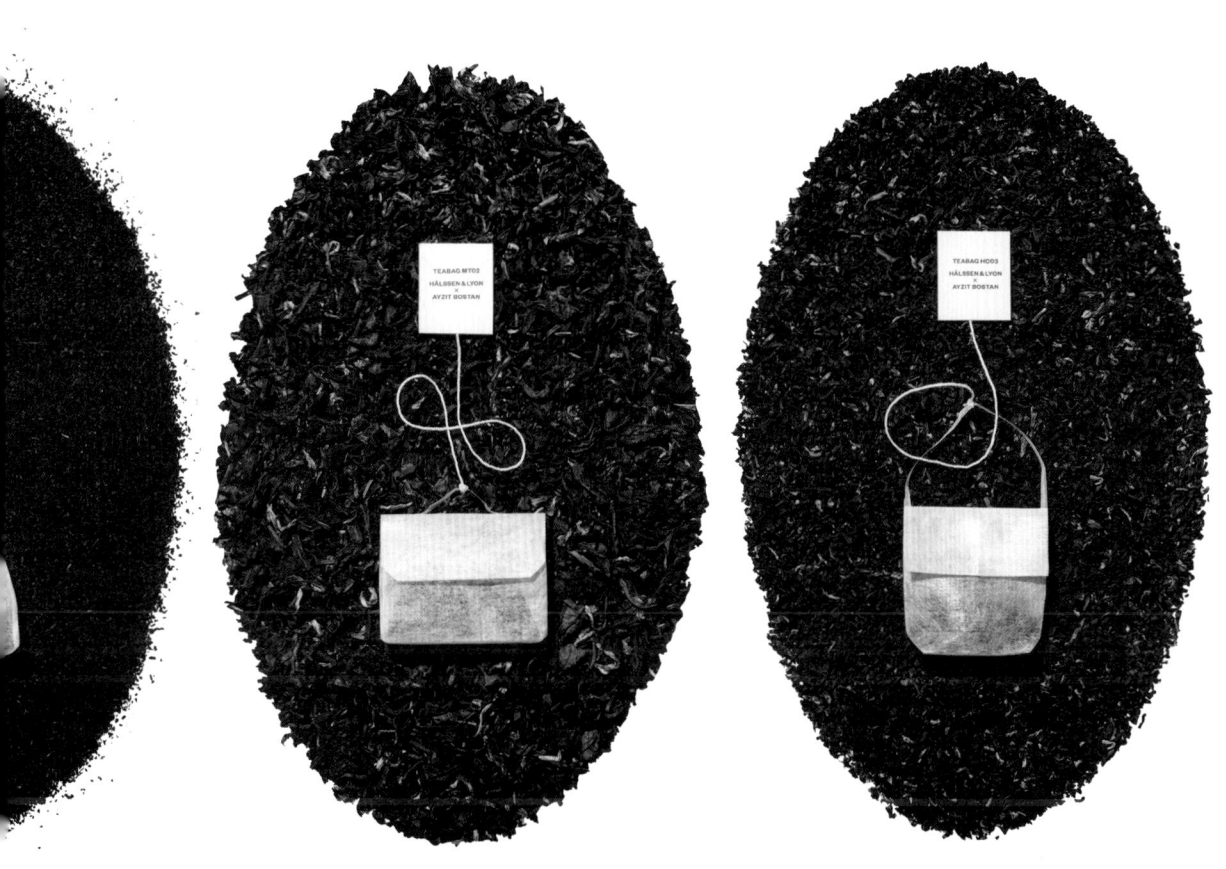

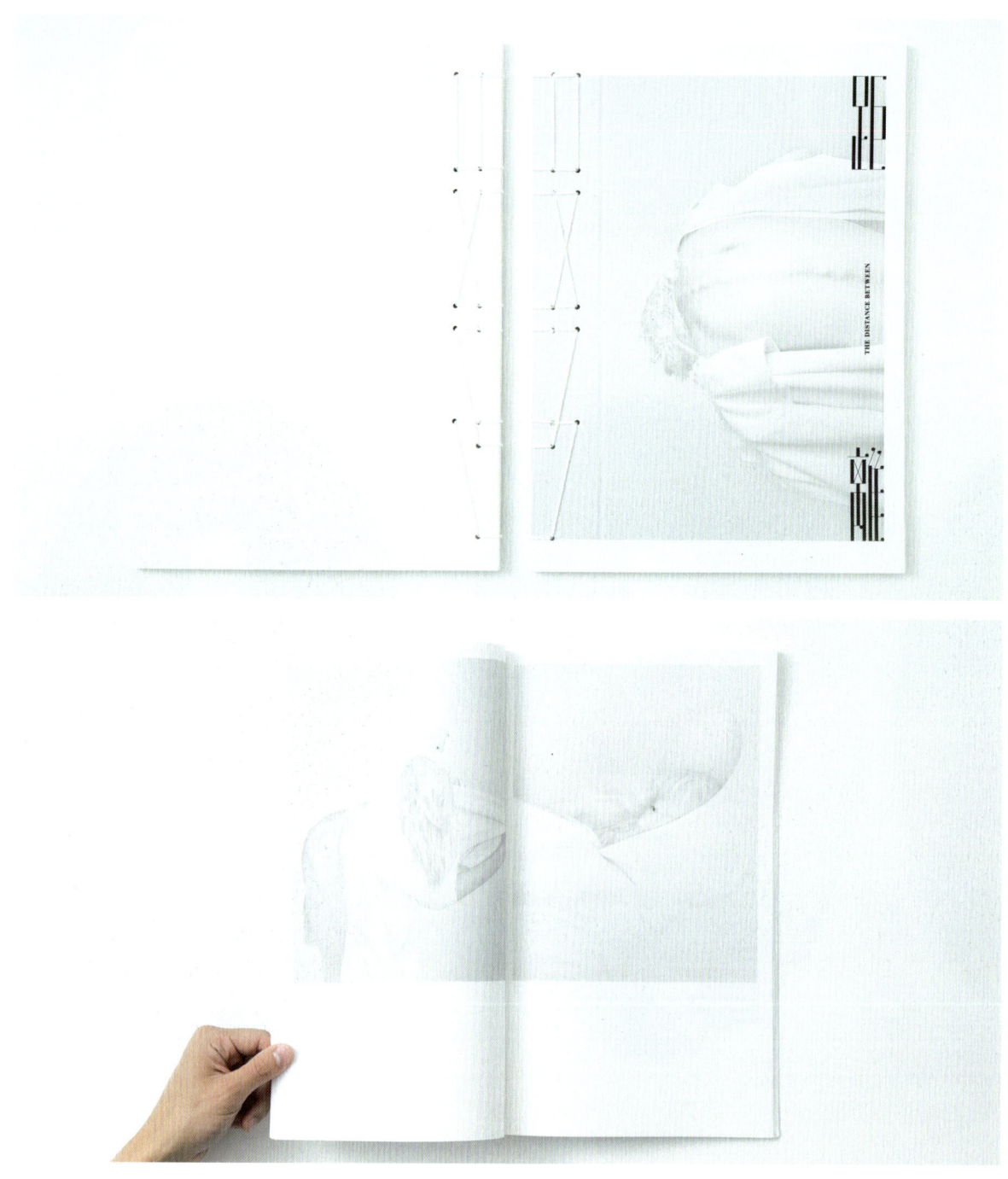

The Distance Between

Designer: nomocreative

The Distance Between is a creative photography project on the relationship between clothes and people. Thread stitching is used to imply the weaving relationship between them. The image featured on the white cover gives a hint of the topic as well. Inside the book, photos were carefully chosen and presented with text under the half-open pages. This special binding creates an interaction between readers and the book.

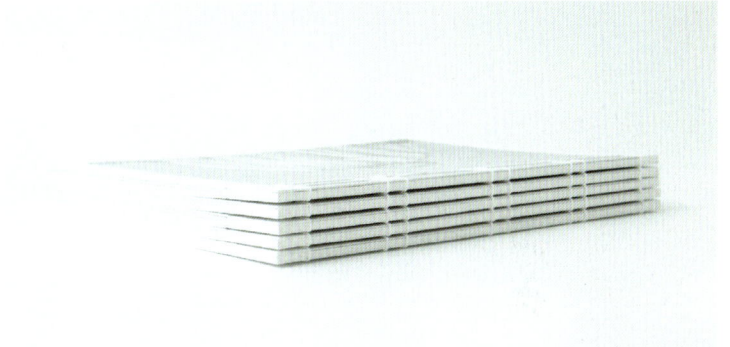
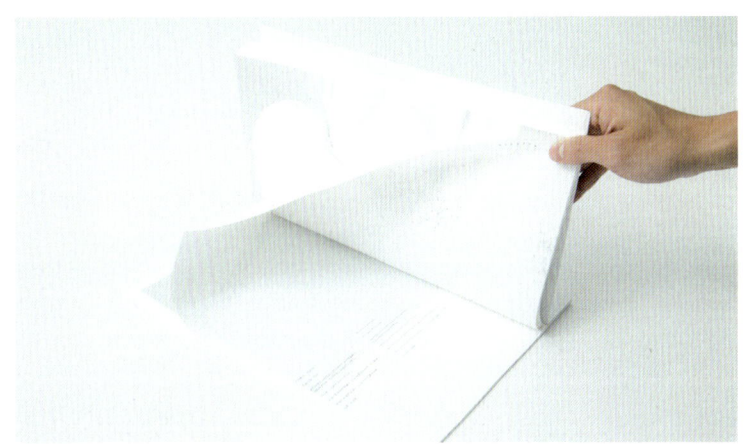
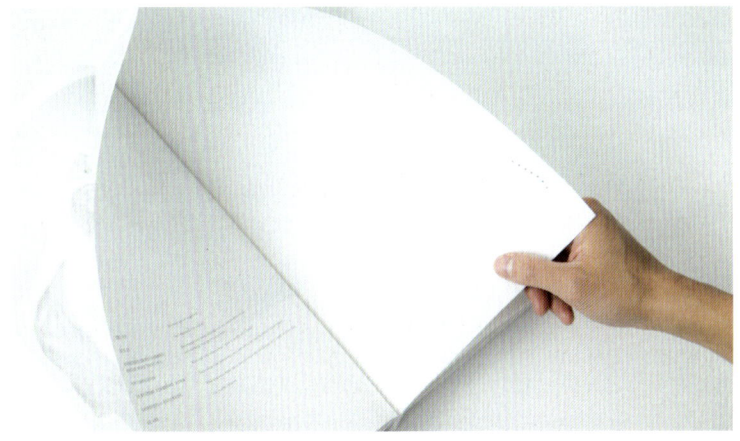

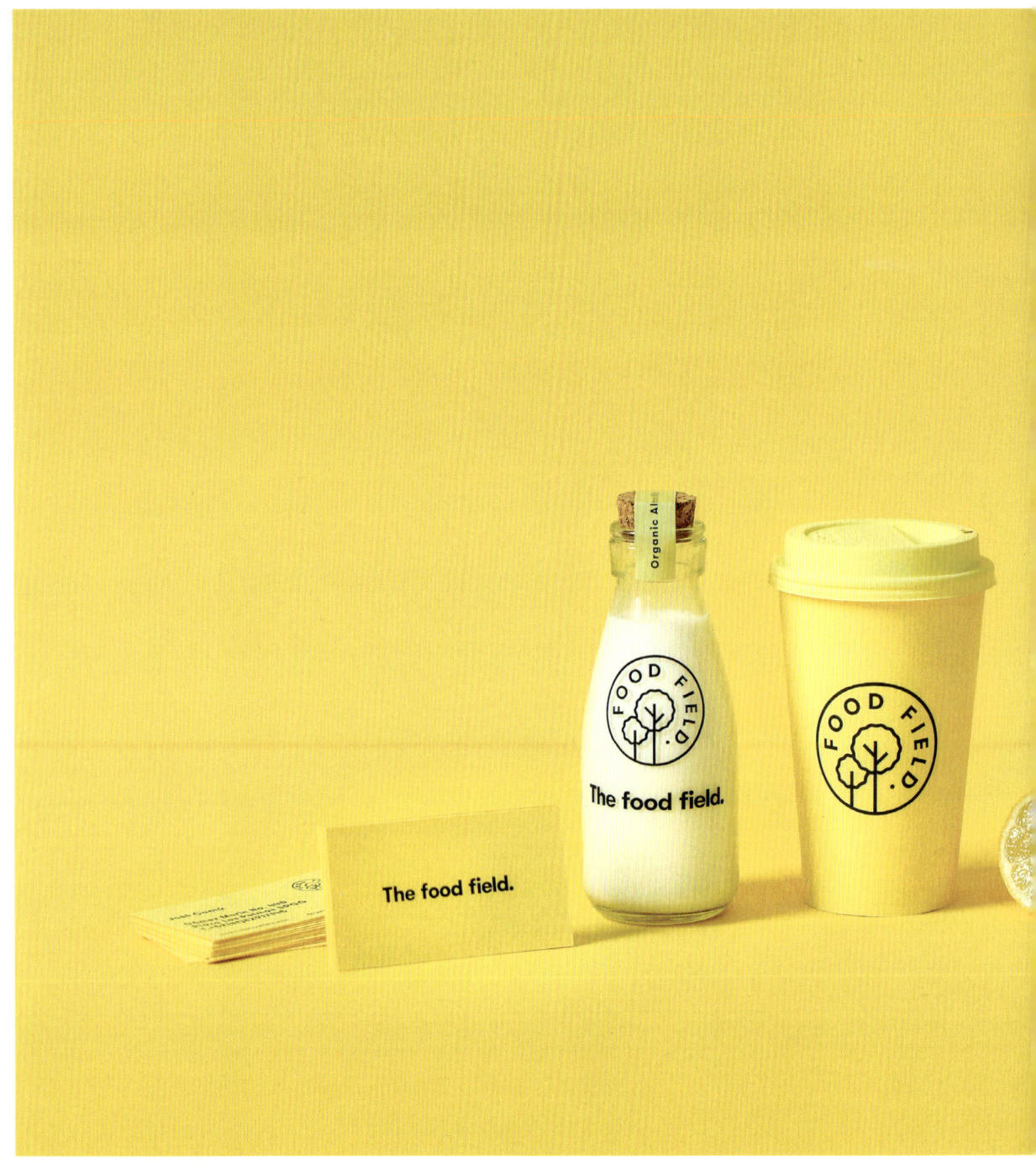

The Food Field

Studio: Parámetro Studio | Photographer: Ana Hinojosa

This comprehensive visual identity was created for an organic food store in México. To avoid an obvious green palette, a set of 3 different shades of yellow that symbolize the dawn and the start of a fresh new day was used. The logotype is accompanied by a simple geometric icon that can easily be used to mark their wide range of food products.

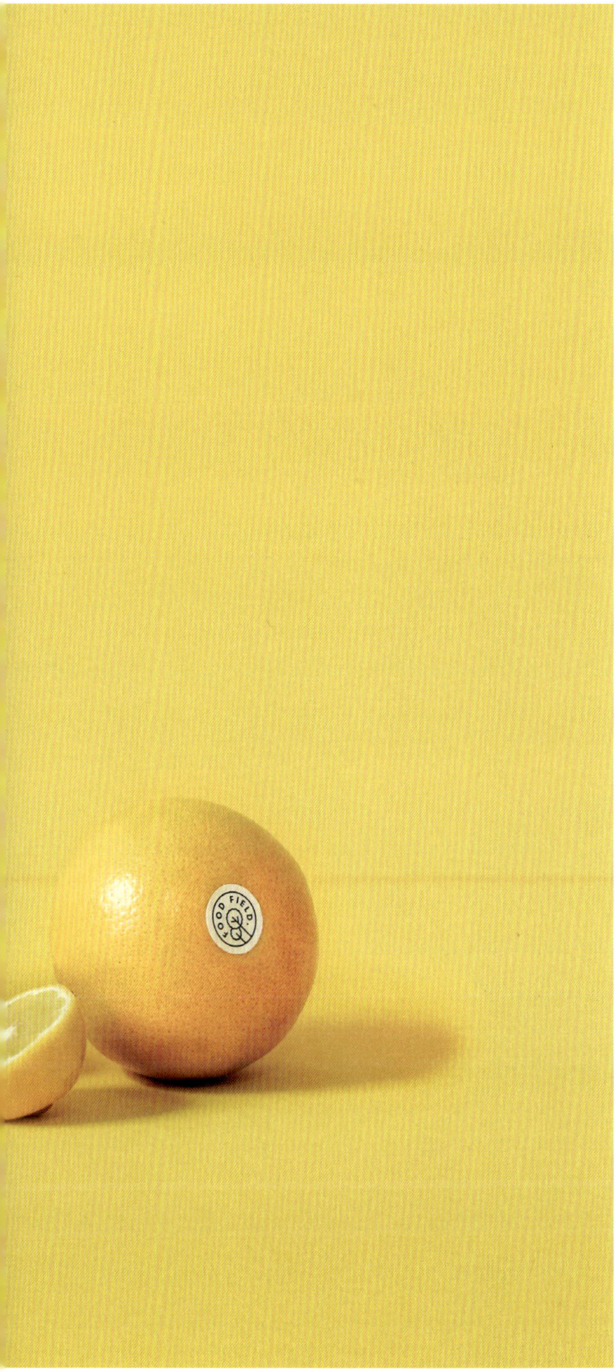

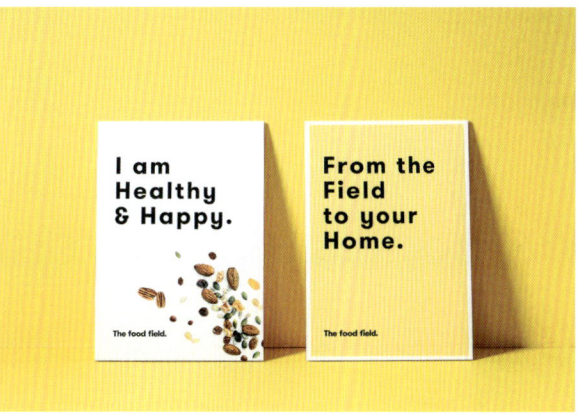

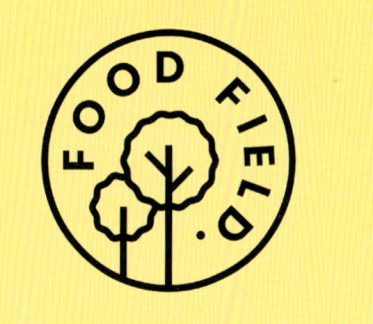

The food field.

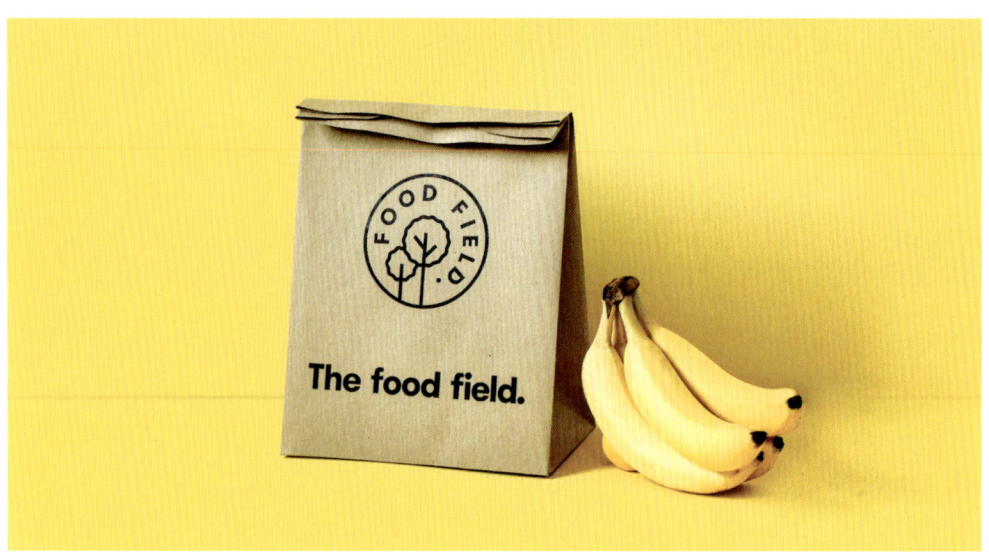
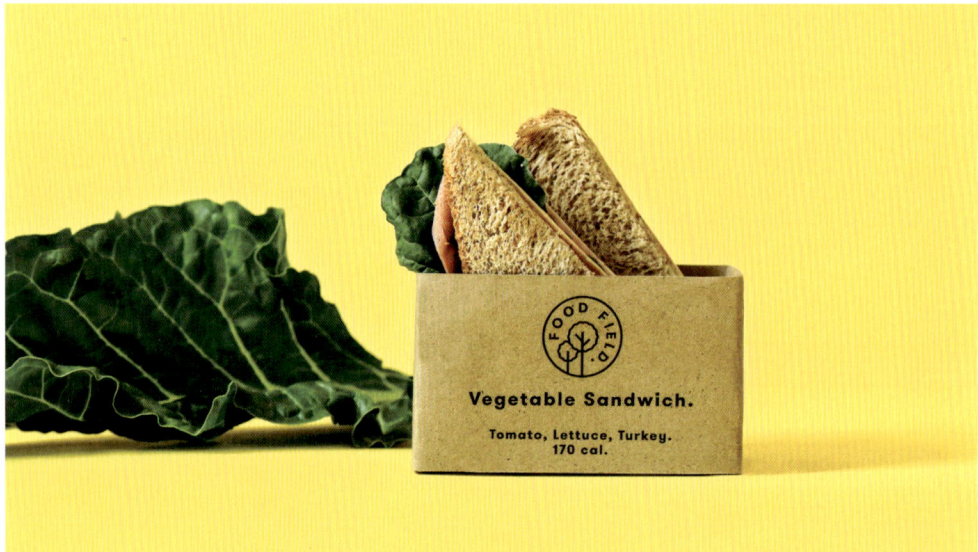
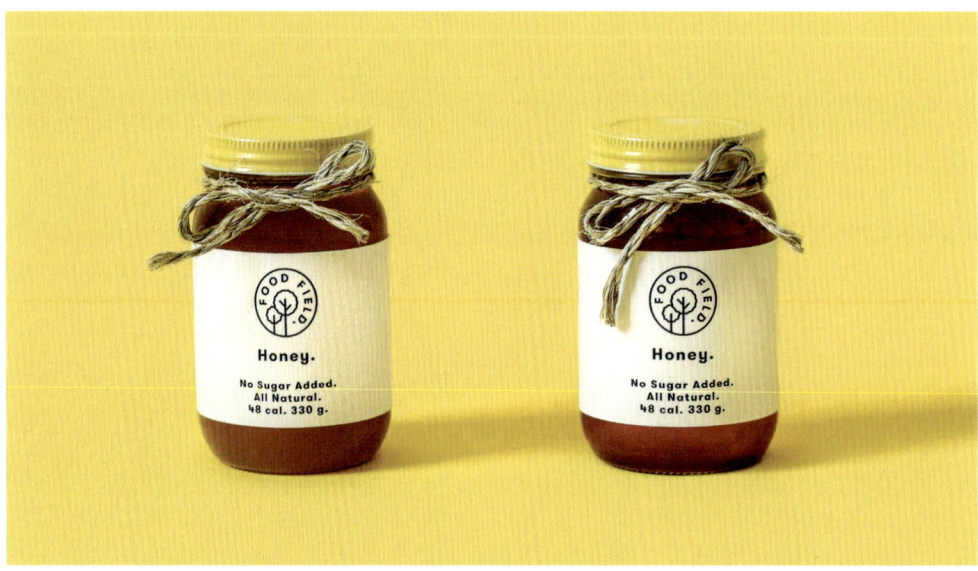

Sandwiches.

Vegetable. Tomato, lettuce, eggplant.	85
Turkey. Turkey, mustard, lettuce, bell pepper.	99
Chicken. Chicken, pesto, mozarella, arugula, chipotle.	115
Chicken Salad. Chicken salad with vegetables, lettuce.	110
Roast Beef. Roast beef, manchego cheese, lettuce, bell pepper.	115
Anchovy Caprese. Anchovy fillet, capers, mozarella, lettuce, eggplant.	99

Soups.

Tomato.	40
Broccoli.	40
Soup of the Day.	35

Healthy Drinks.

Strawberry.	50
Lemonade.	50
Lemonade + Cucumber	55
Green Mix. Pineapple, celery, kale.	60
Super Juice. Mixed berries, ginger, chia seeds, lemon.	65

Healthy Snacks.

Trail Mix.	25
Sweet Potato Chips	30
Almonds and Raisins.	20
Spicy Amaranth.	35
Amaranth with Chia	35
Dried Apple Chips.	40
Spicy Dried Pineapple.	25
Spicy Lentil.	25
Sunflower seeds.	20

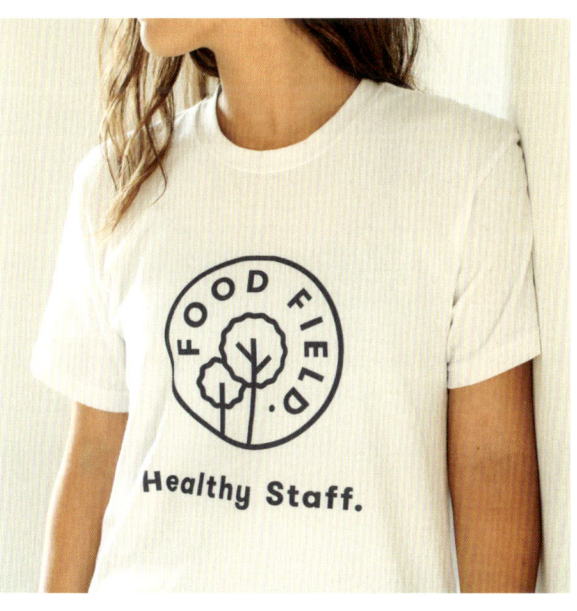

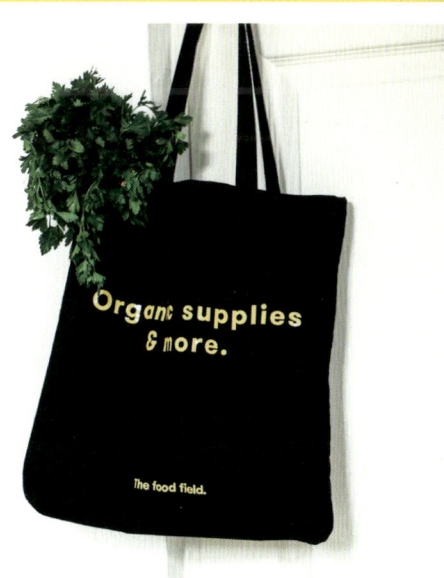

Bunny Hill

Studio: Comence Studio | Designer: Pavel Emelyanov

As the starting point for the brand identity design, a simple and clear logo featuring smooth and round shape was created for the loving and caring online shop Bunny Hill. The color white, inherent in the traditional Swedish design, imparted a shining, warm and friendly atmosphere. There were also a refreshing packaging concept and an official website.

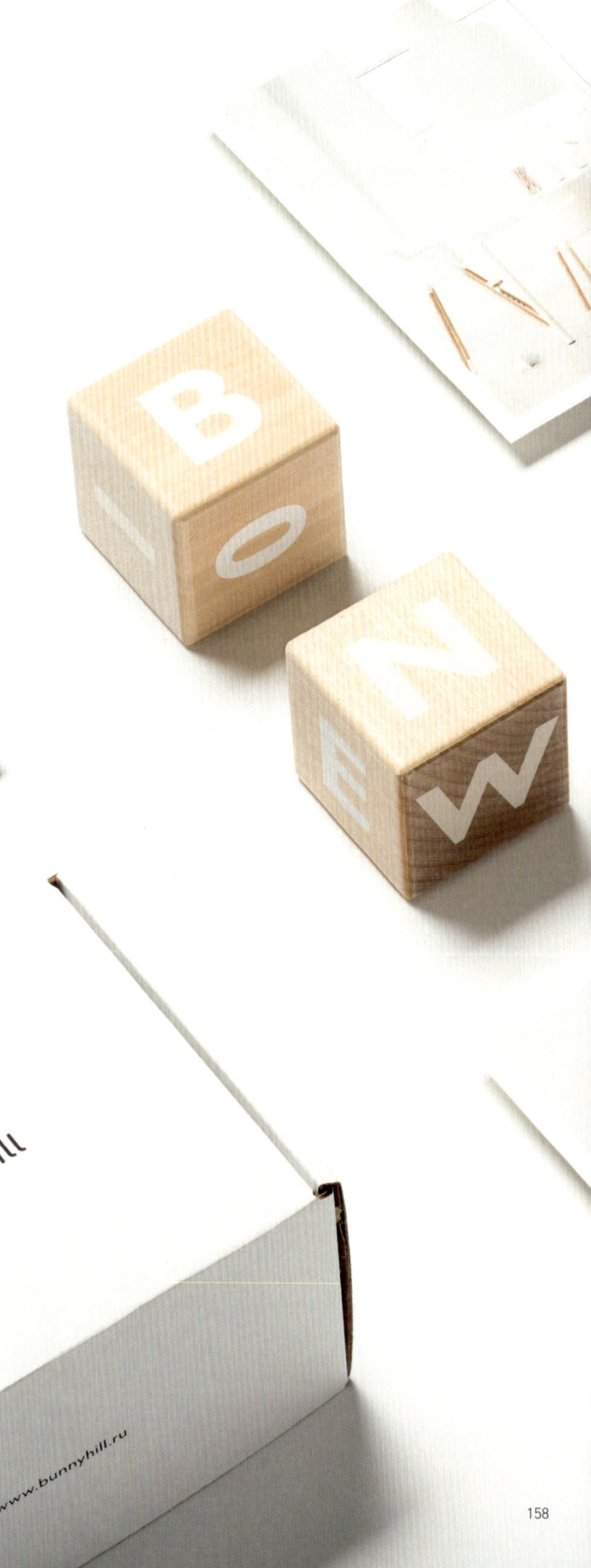

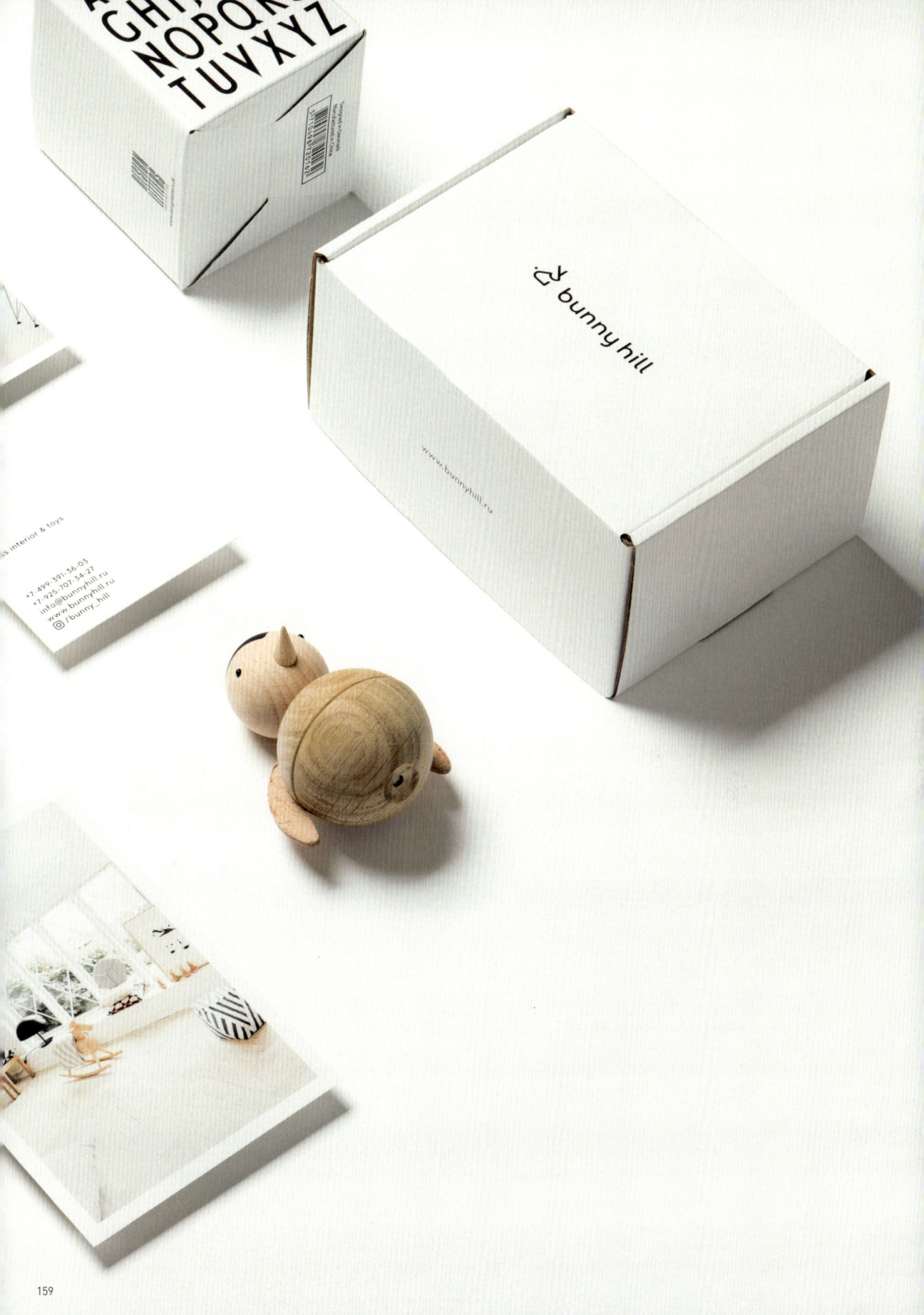

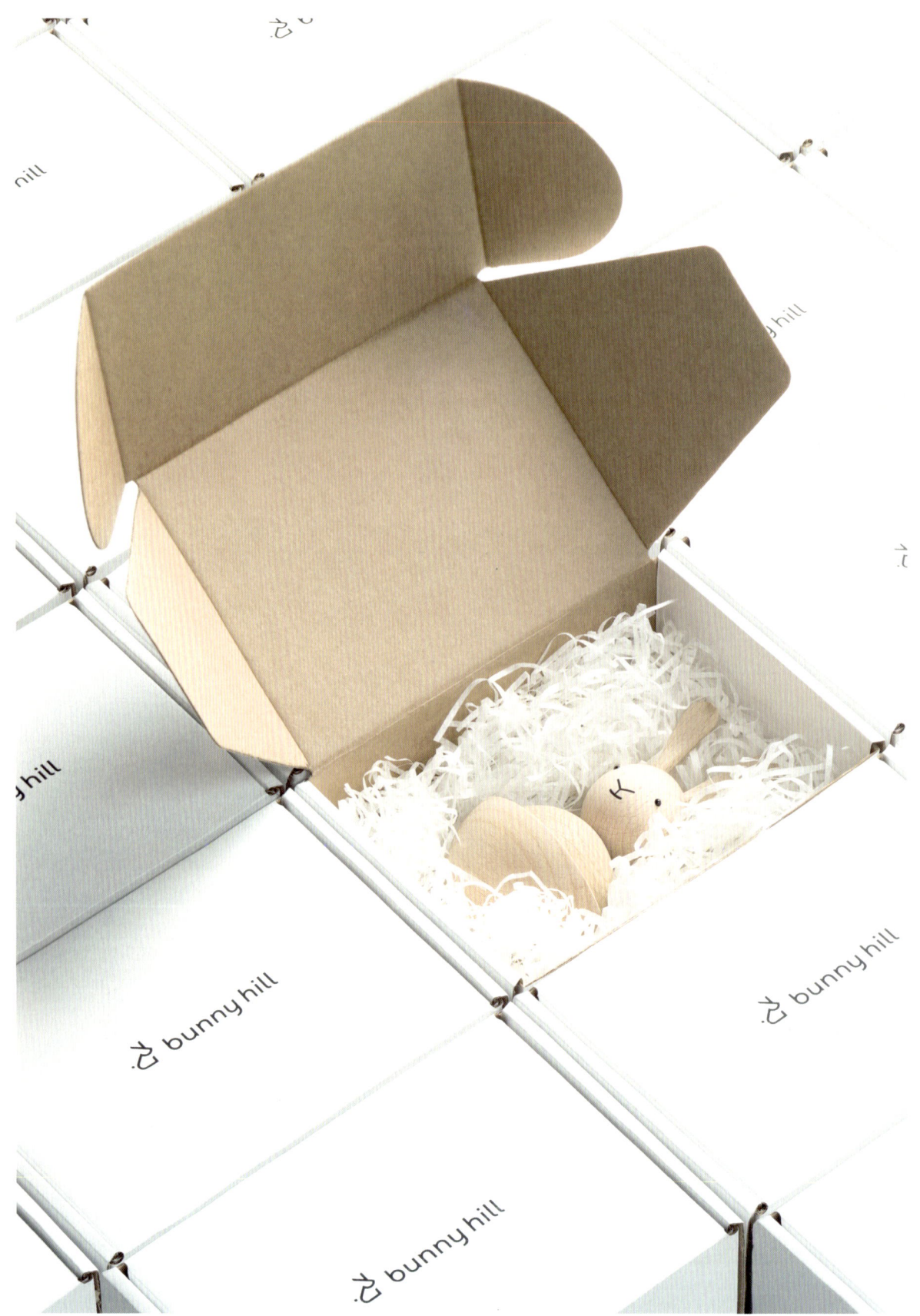

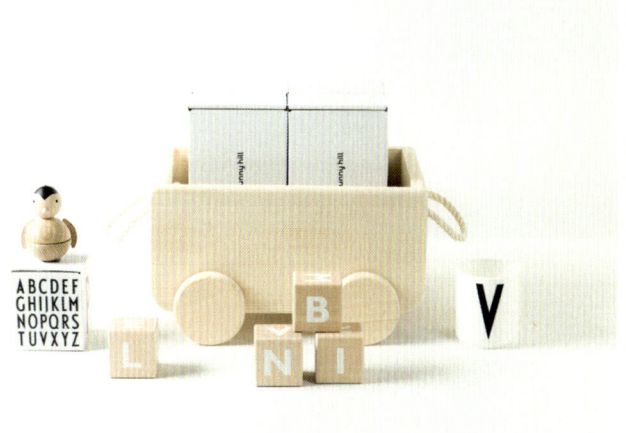
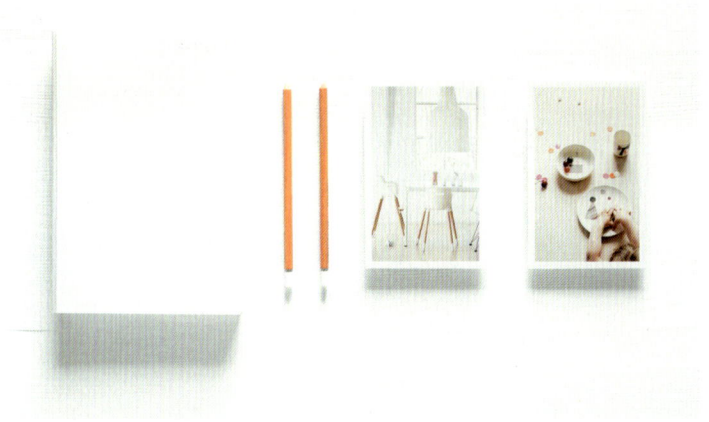
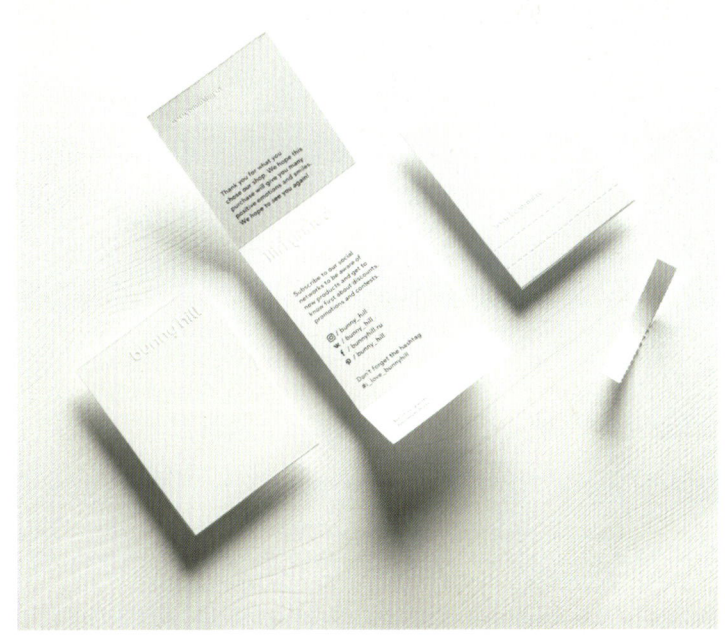

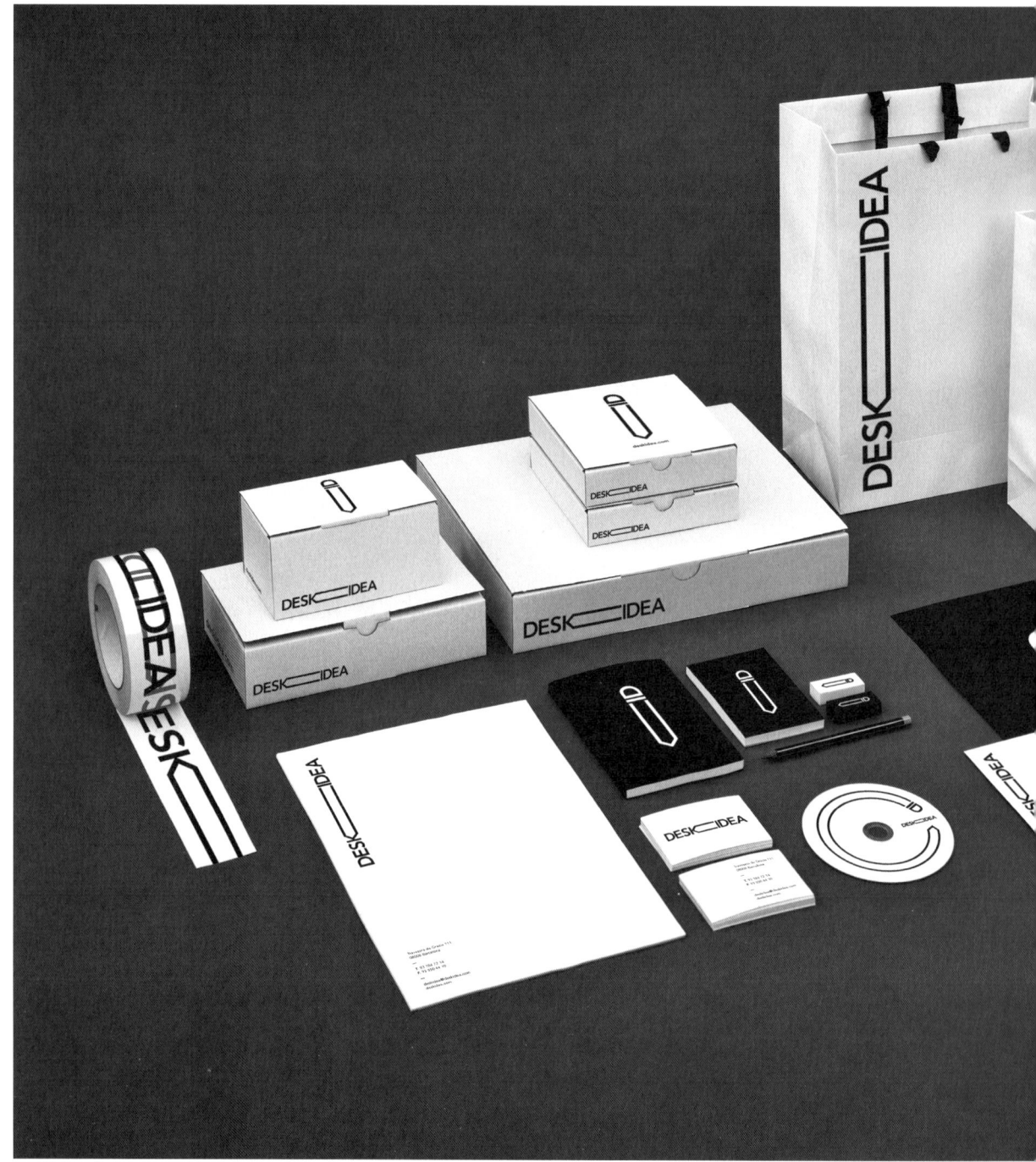

Deskidea

Designer: Alex Dalmau

Deskidea is a Barcelona-based e-commerce supplier, who aims to generate a major sense of simplicity for clients from the very first purchase from their website to the use of their products in the office. The brand identity was designed to boost such values and the graphic solution came from the name itself, Deskidea.

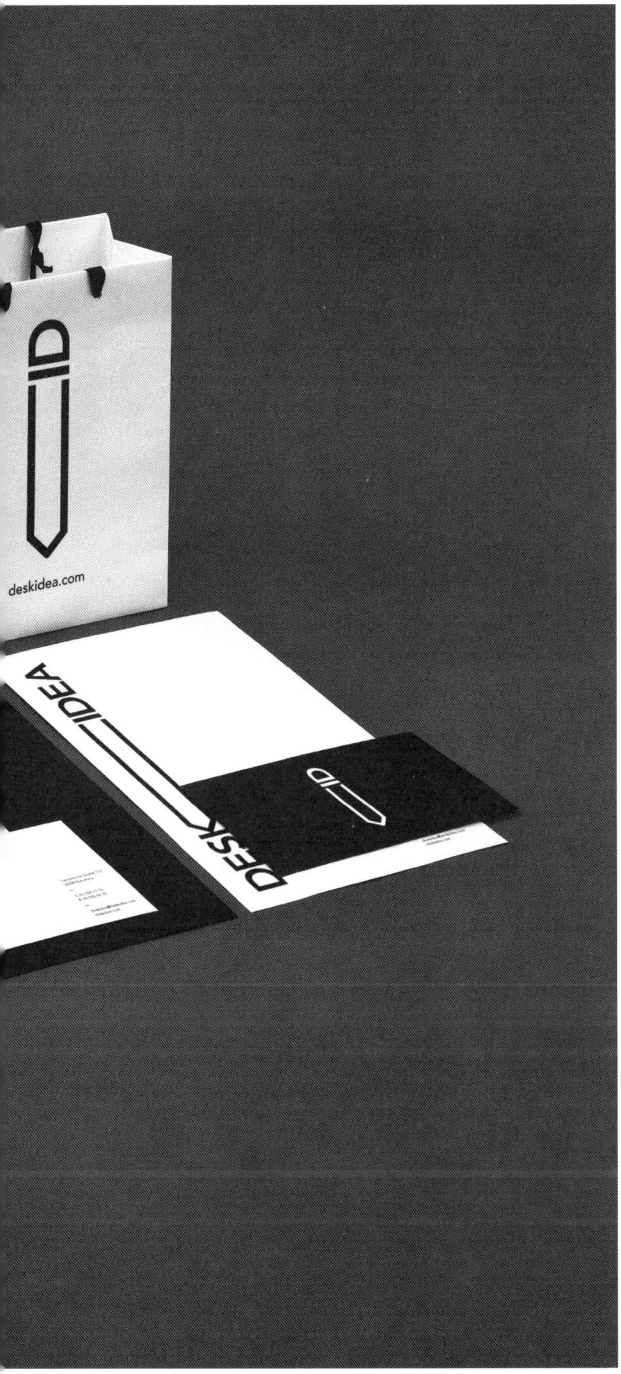

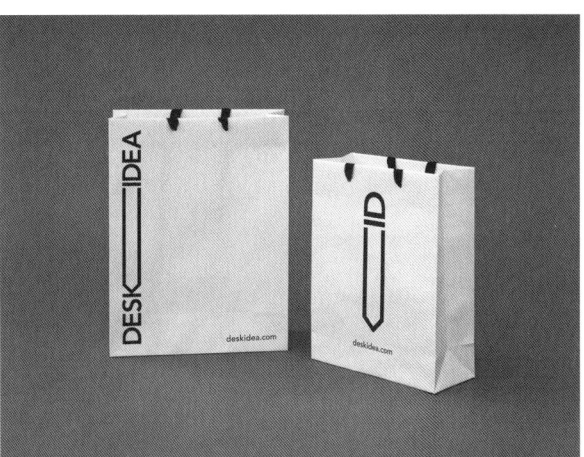

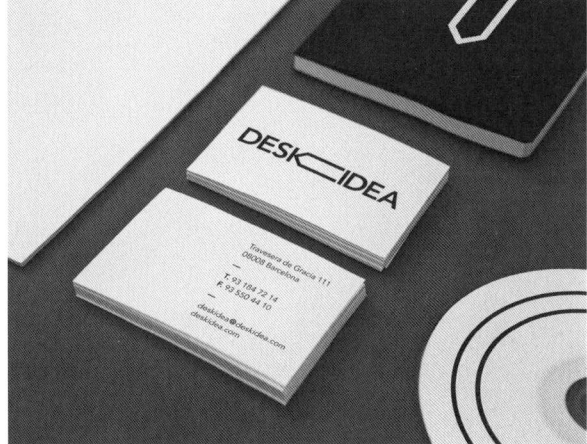

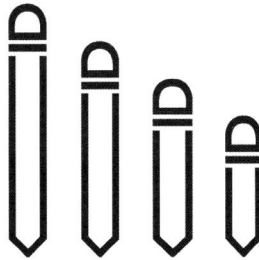

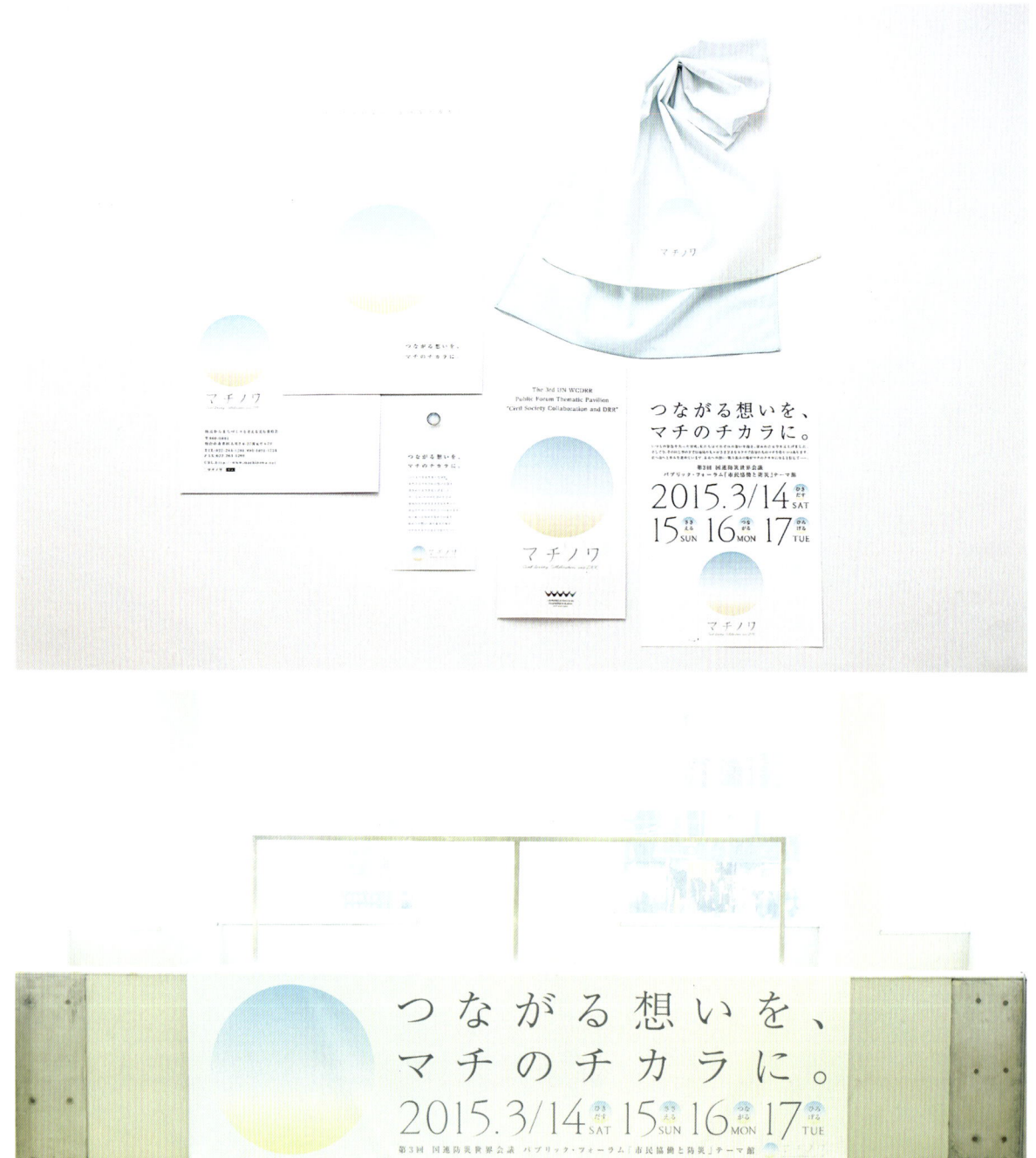

Thematic Pavilion—Civil Society Collaboration and DRR

Studio: Luck Show

This is a visual identity for the thematic pavilion of "Civil Society Collaboration and DRR" as part of the public forum of the UN World Conference on Disaster Reduction. Based on the understanding of the reconstruction after earthquake, Luck Show created a special Japanese towel and many other promotional materials to frame the image of the pavilion, where discussions on disaster prevention would take place.

つながる想いを、
マチのチカラに。

いつもの景色を失った翌朝、私たちはそれぞれの想いを抱き、澄みわたる空を見上げました。そして今、その同じ空の下では地域の人々がさまざまな
カタチで自分たちのマチを作りつつあります。前へ前へと歩みを進めています。未来への想い・取り組みの輪がマチのチカラになると信じて──。

第3回 国連防災世界会議 パブリック・フォーラム「市民協働と防災」テーマ館

2015.3/14 SAT (ひきだす)　15 SUN (ささえる)　16 MON (つながる)　17 TUE (ひろげる)

2015年3月14日〜18日の期間、仙台市で世界の防災戦略が議論される第3回国連防災世界会議が開催されます。パブリック・フォーラム「市民協働と防災」
テーマ館は、東日本大震災の経験や教訓を生かした防災や復興に関する市民や団体の取り組みを、参加者とともに共有し国内外に発信する場です。
開催期間：2015年3月14日(土)〜17日(火)　会場：仙台市市民活動サポートセンター　仙台市青葉区一番町4丁目1-3
主催：防災からまちづくりを考える実行委員会　URL：http://www.machinowa.net　マチノワ 検索

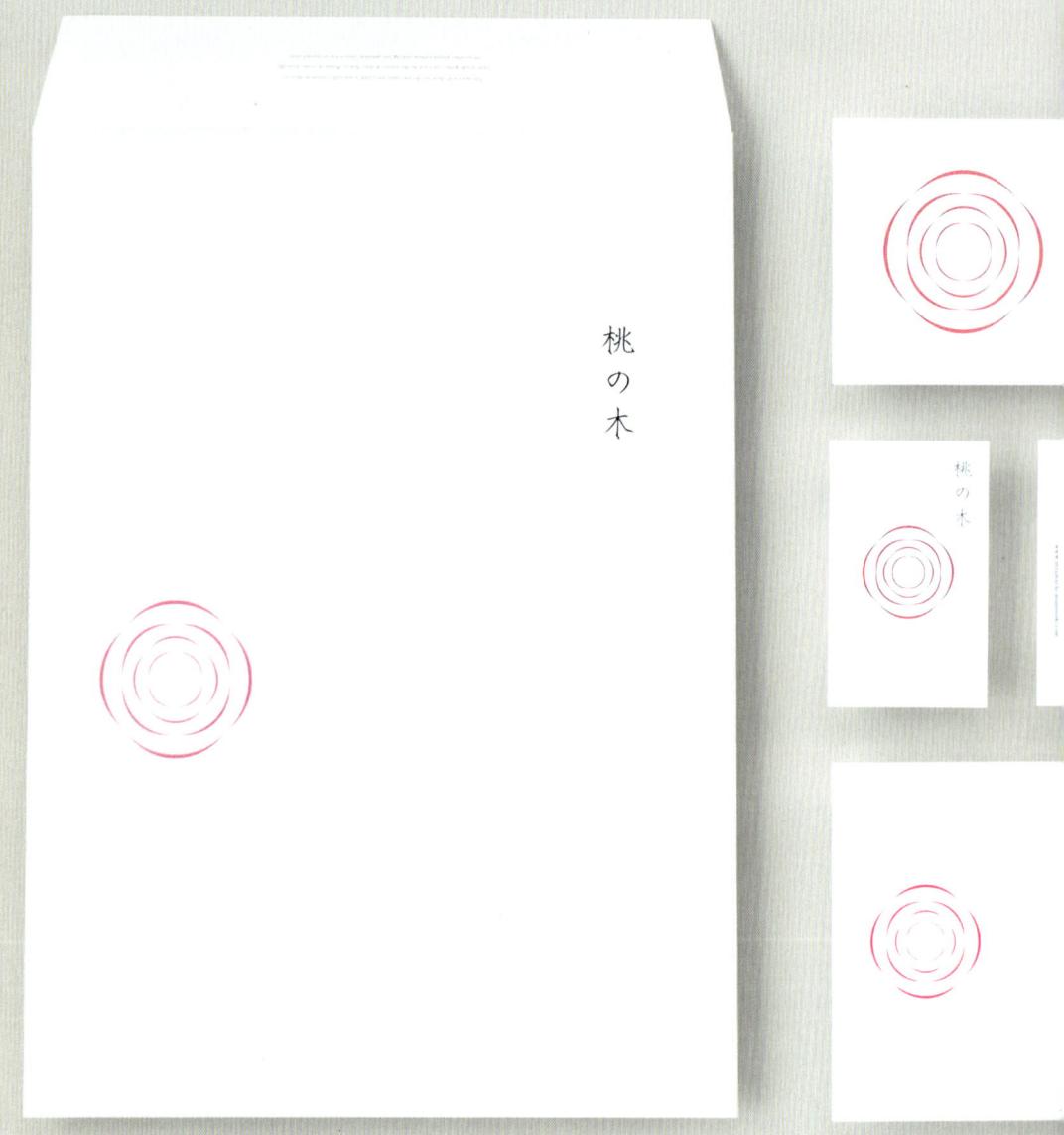

Momonoki

Studio: 6D-K | Designer: 6D Shogo Kishino, 6D Miho Sakaki

Momonoki, which means "peaceful tree" in Japanese, is a renovated Chinese restaurant. 6D-K designed a one of a kind set of logo, business cards, shop cards, envelopes, etc.

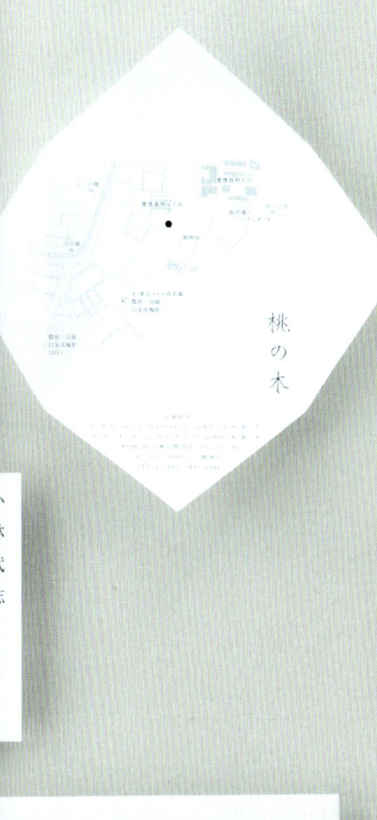
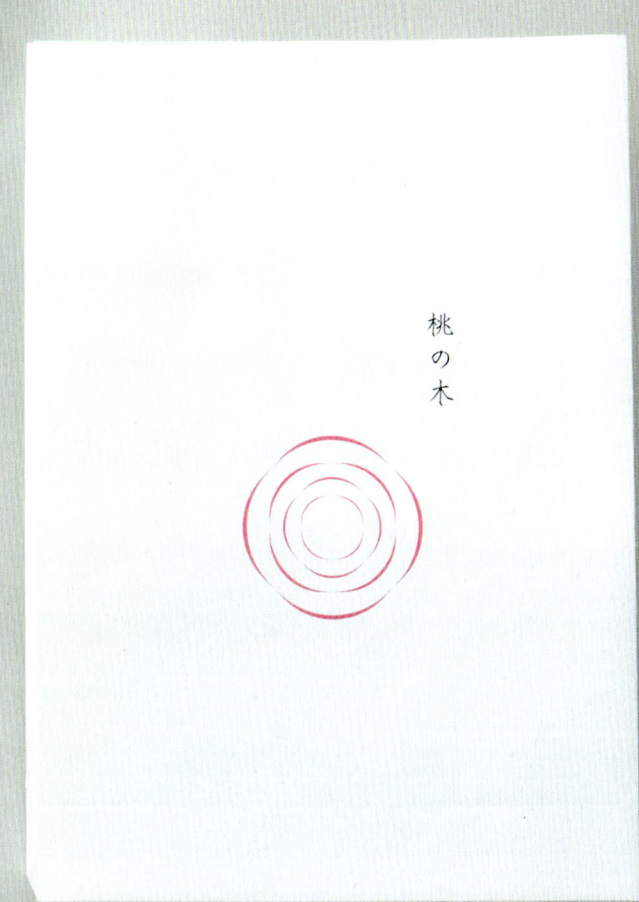

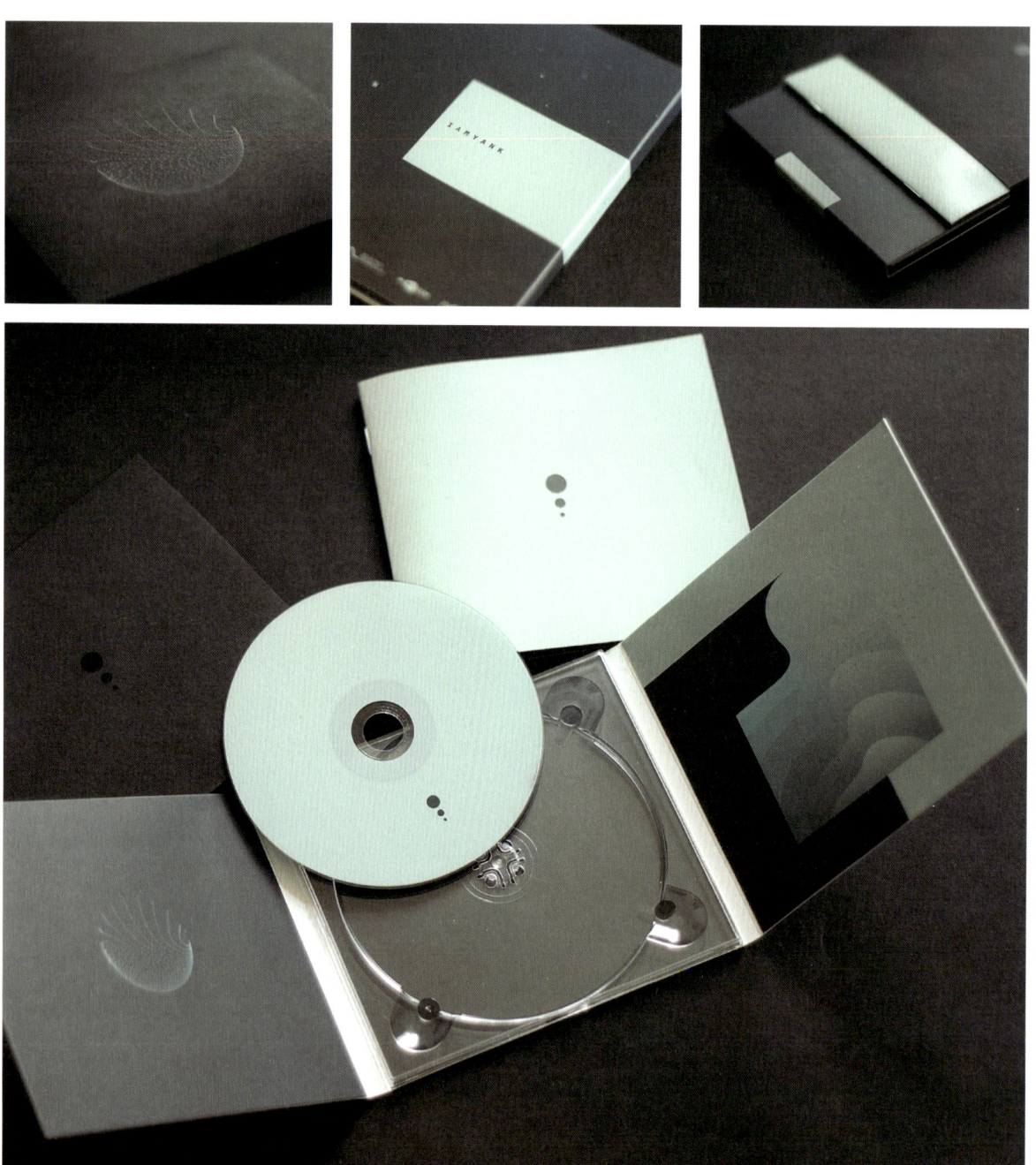

Hiraeth

Designer: Tamas Birinyi

The identity design and art direction for the first IAMYANK LP, "HIRAETH" is to reflect the dreamy, magical music in this album, which collects all the influences that inspired the multi-instrumentalist producer and songwriter. It renders dark places, weird sounds mixed with peaceful soundscapes into a melancholic journey.

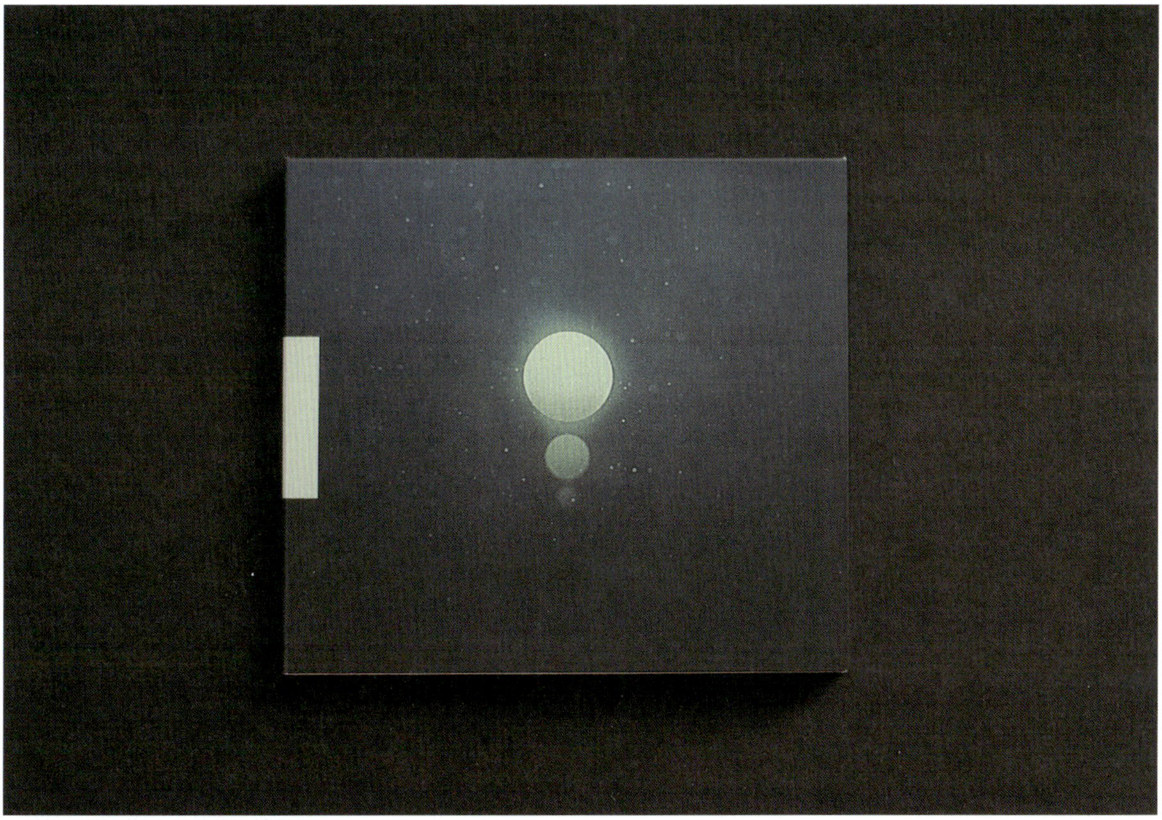

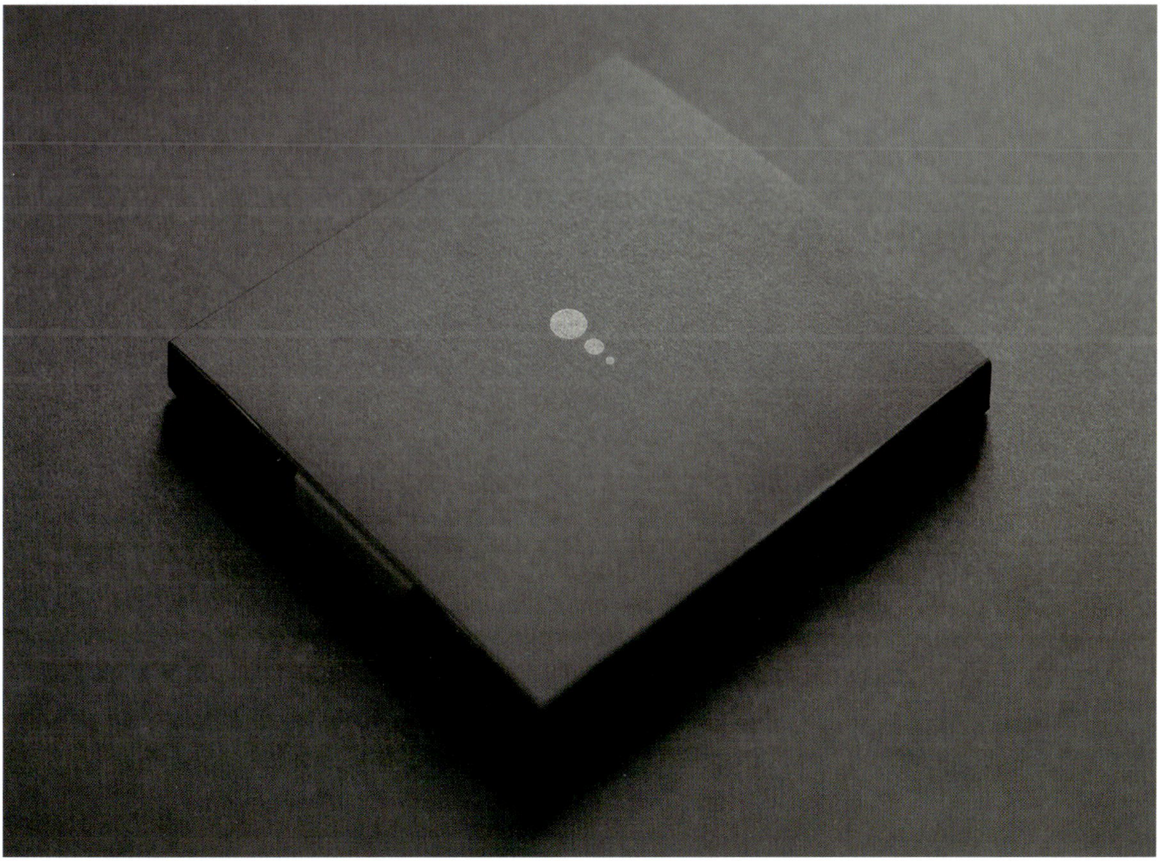

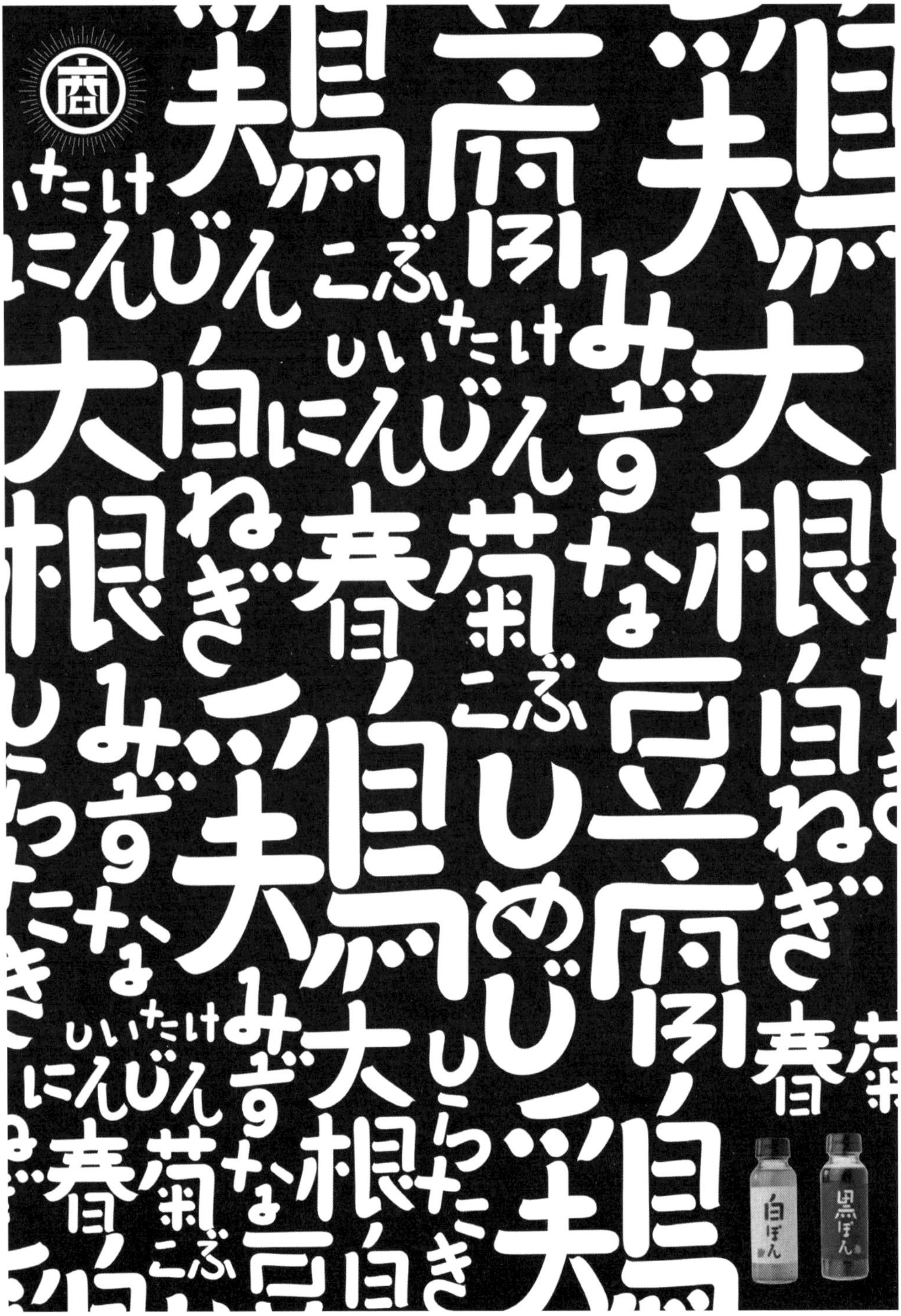

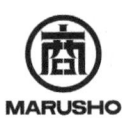
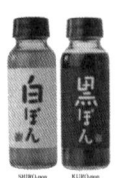

ShiroPON & KuroPON

Studio: Sekiura Design | Creative Director: Ruriko Sekiura | Designer: Michitomo Sekiura

The typography and logo used in this project is composed of 12 limited elements. Such limitation, however, enriches the design expression and conforms to the simple but high-quality products.

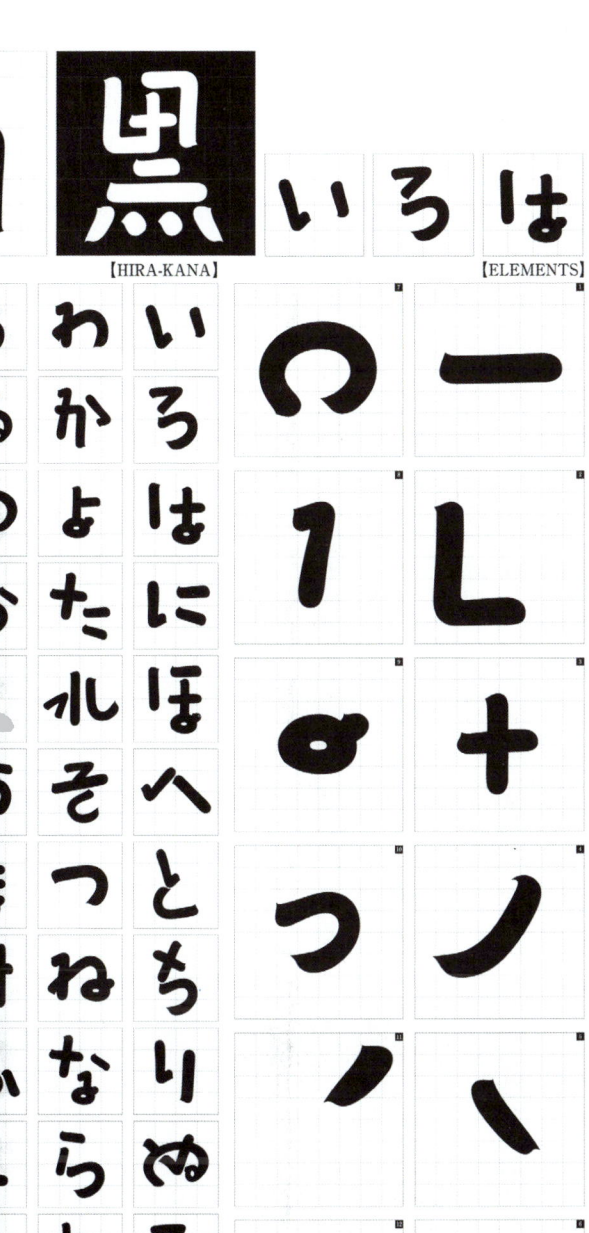

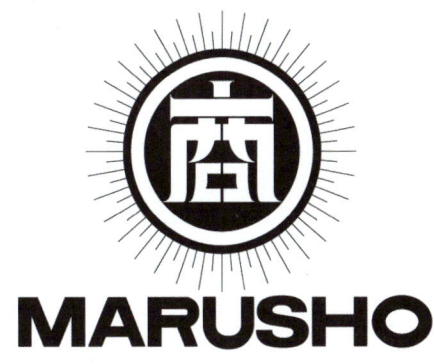

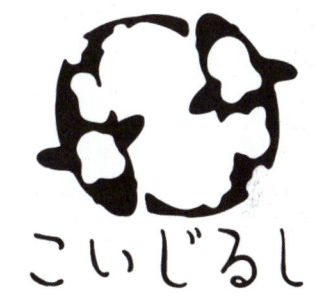

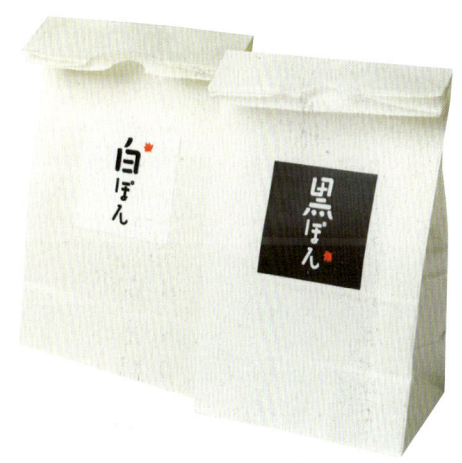

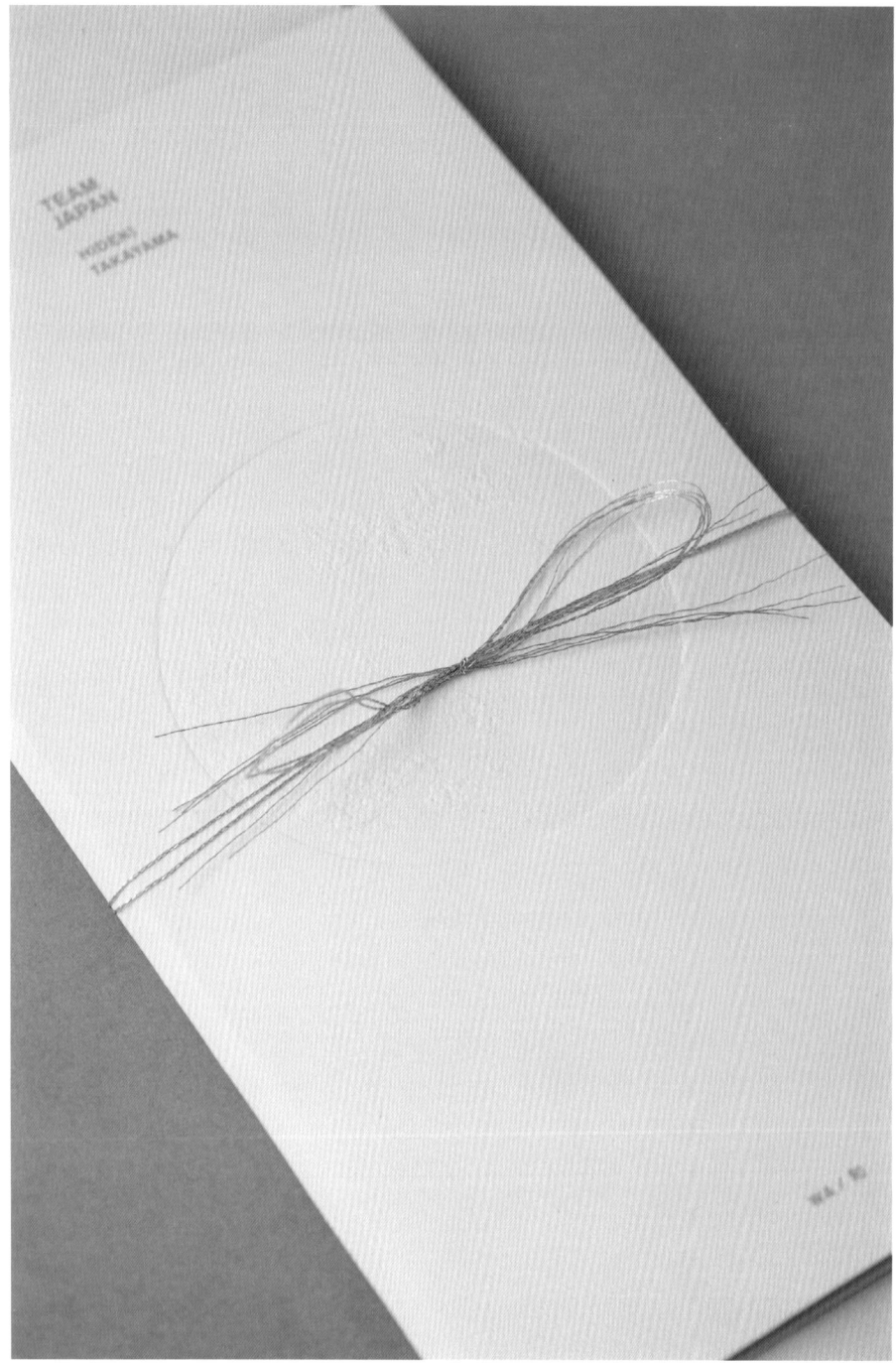

Menu for Team Japan for Bocuse d'Or

Studio: artless Inc | Art Director: shun kawakami | Designer: nao nozawa

This project was the menu for team Japan for Bocuse d'Or Asia-Pacific 2014. A simple, modern design was combined with authentic Japanese washi paper to create a modern impression whilst embracing traditional Japanese sense of beauty. Every detail of the menu, such as the accordion-styled booklet and embossed moon on the cover, were based on this authentic Japanese style.

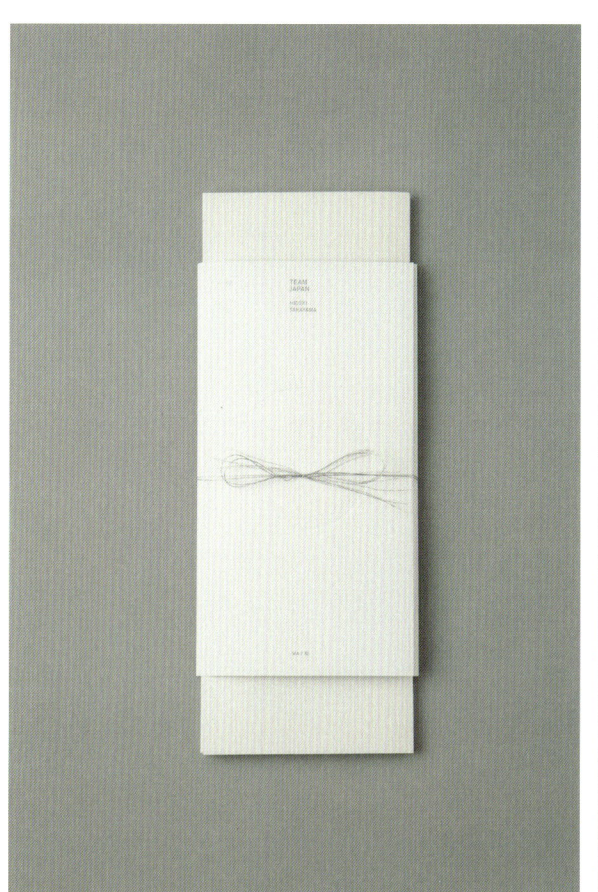
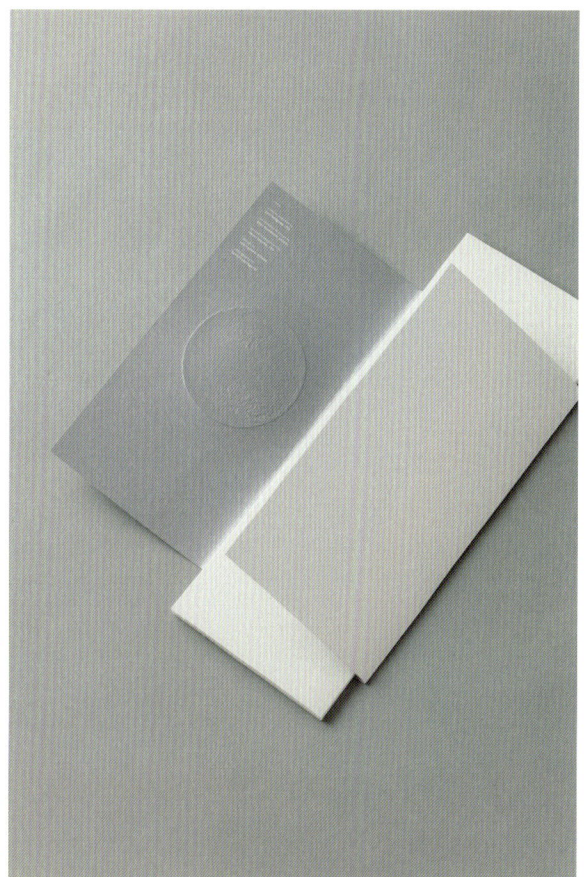

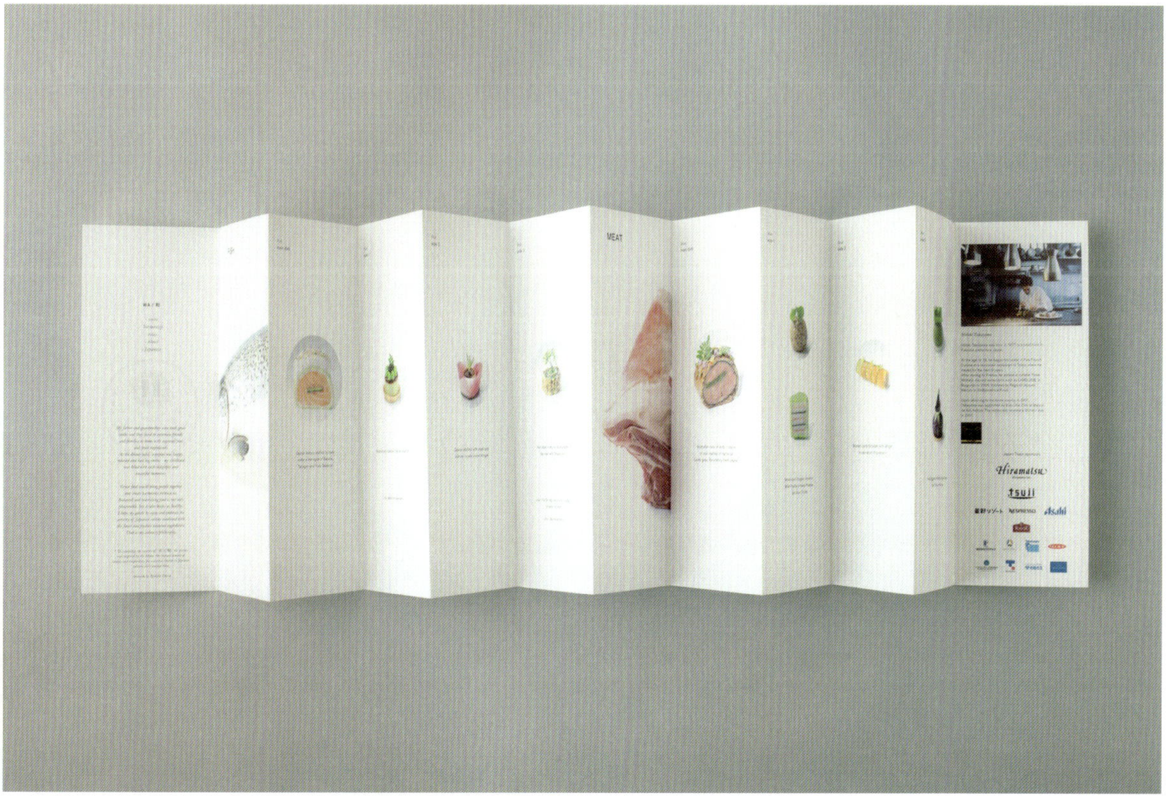

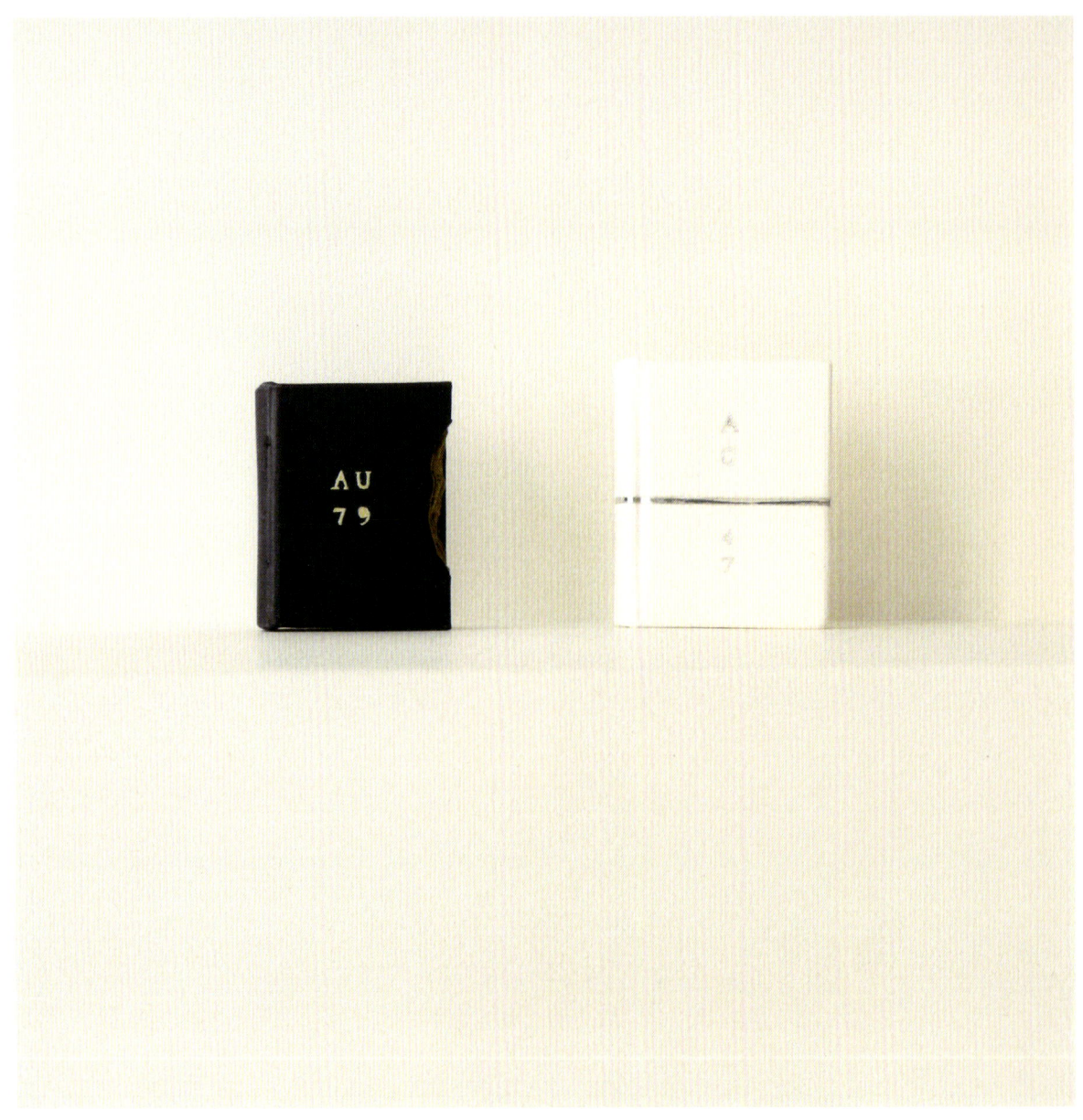

Booksmith: Gold & Silver

Designer: Furze Chan

Gold and silver are two of the most impor tant metals in human history. They are rare and expensive. Using a similar appr oach of making fine jewelery, two small book s with the sizes of 2.6 x 3 x 1. 4cm and 2.3 x 3. 4 x 0.9cm respectively, were made to represent gold and silver. The book covers were decorated with hand-cut paper titles .

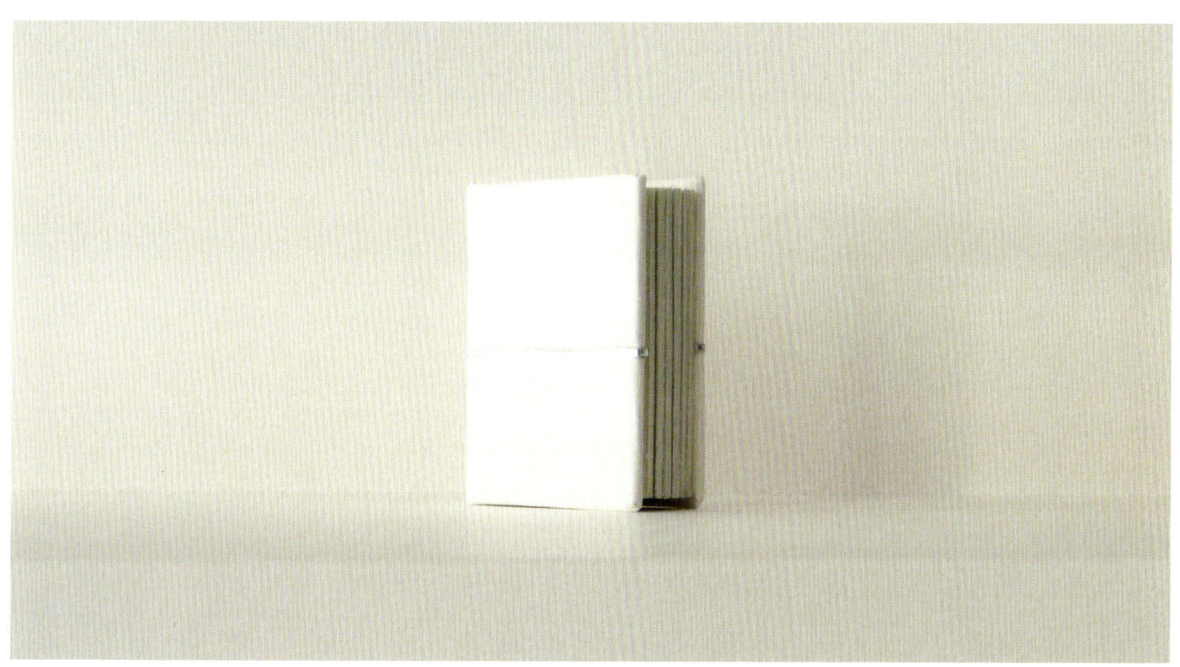

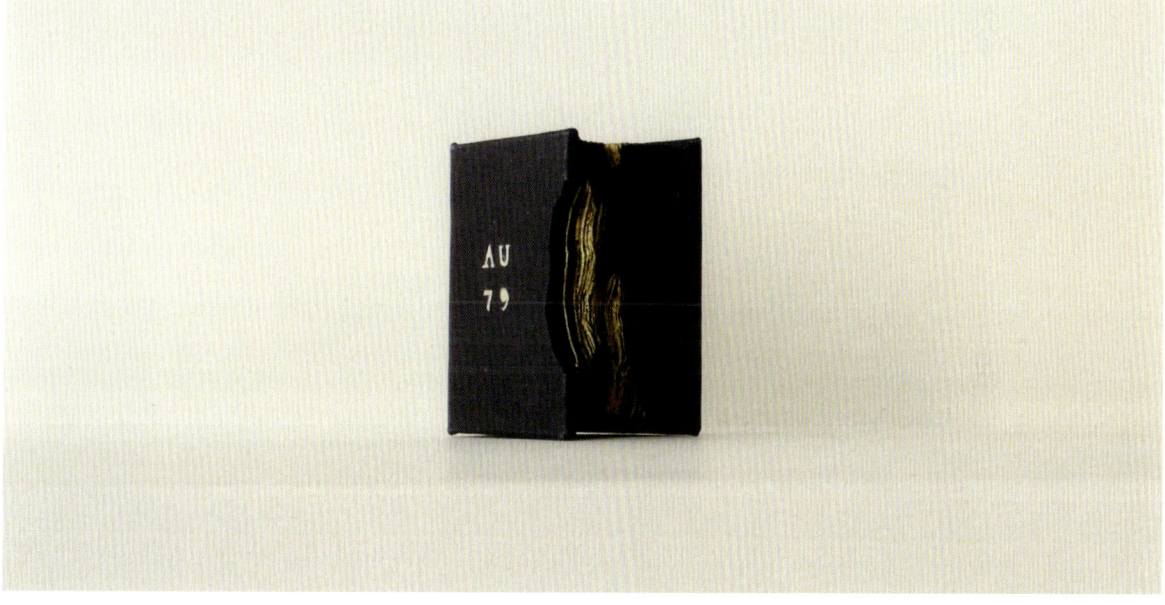

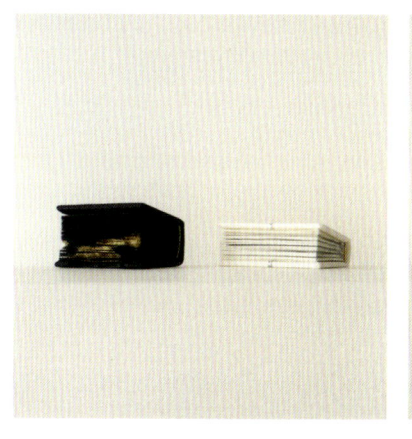
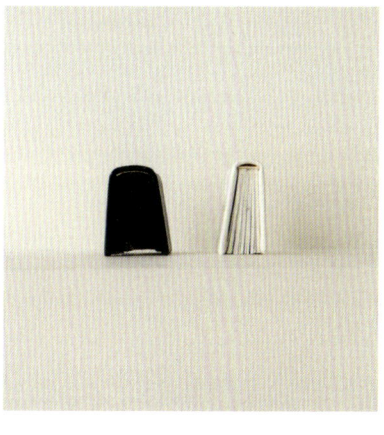
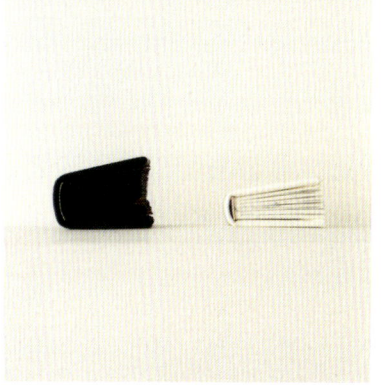

Deux Toiles
Bathroom Amenities

Designer: Wonchan Lee

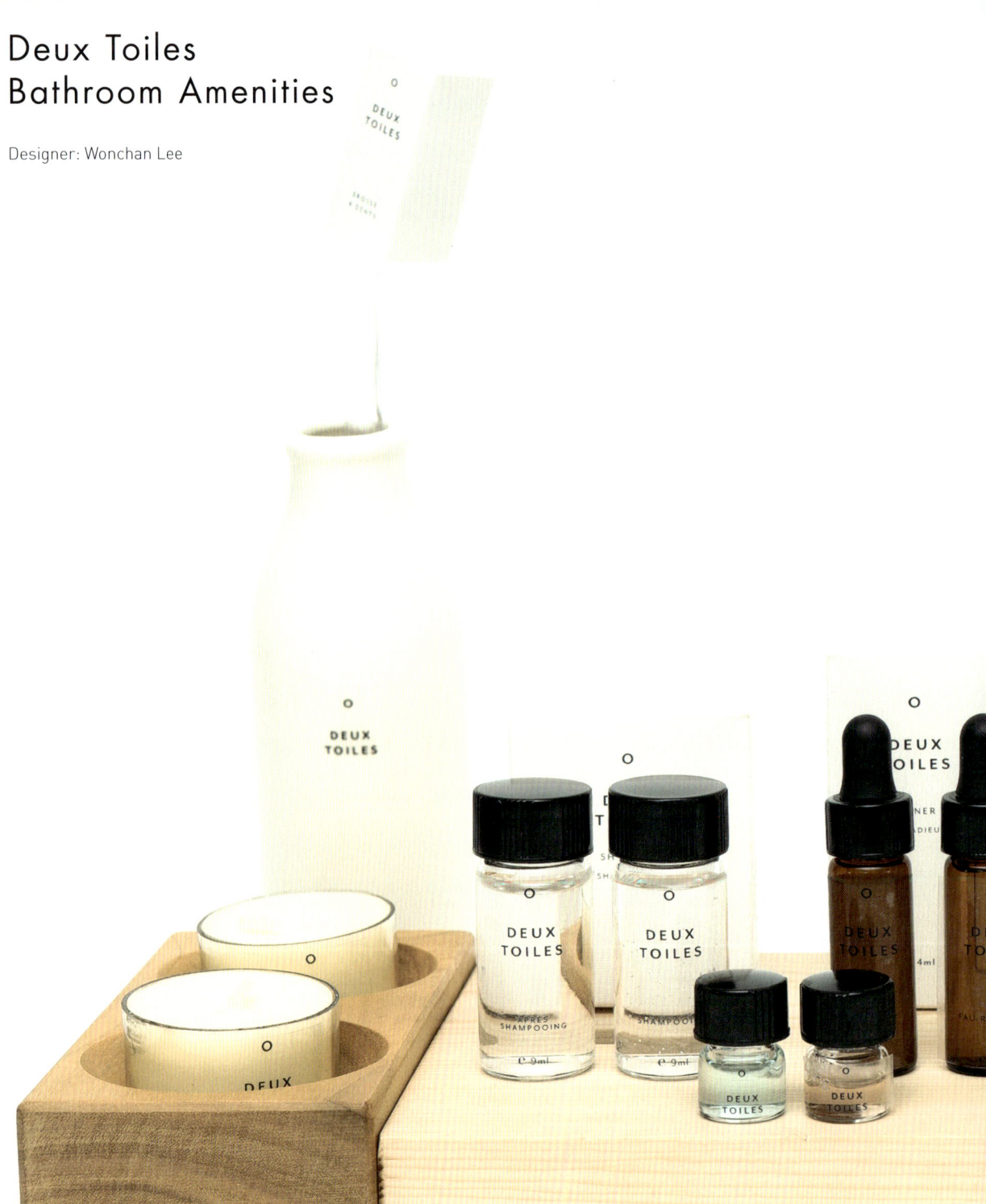

Deux Toiles is a high-end bathroom amenity range for The Cullen, a boutique hotel located in Melbourne, Australia. Inspired by the artist Adam Cullen (1965-2012) who was a contemporary artist, the designer came up with a concept for the range that has an individual identity to attract the customers the range that them with something to remember the hotel by. The name, Deux Toiles means "two canvases" in which the customers could draw their memories by using the products.

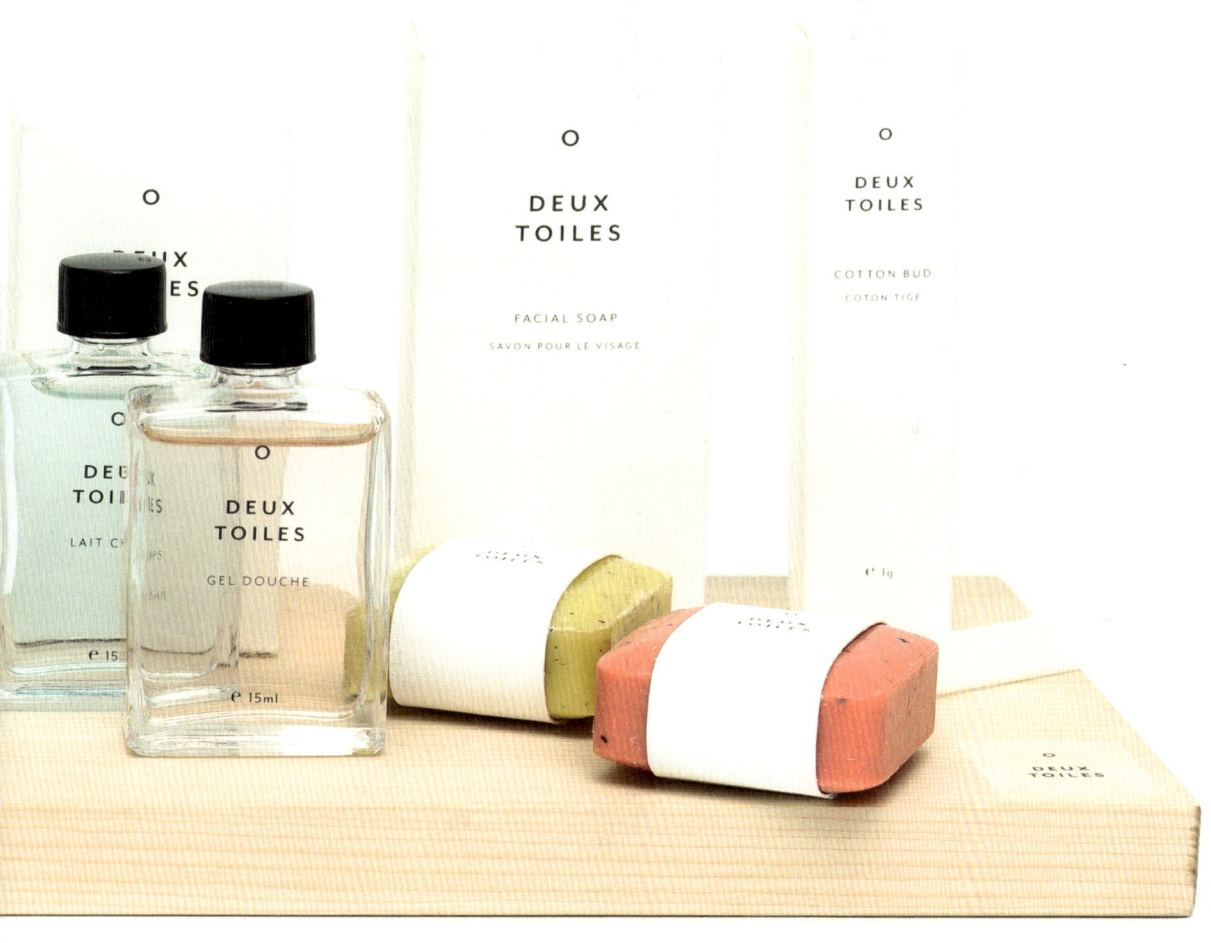

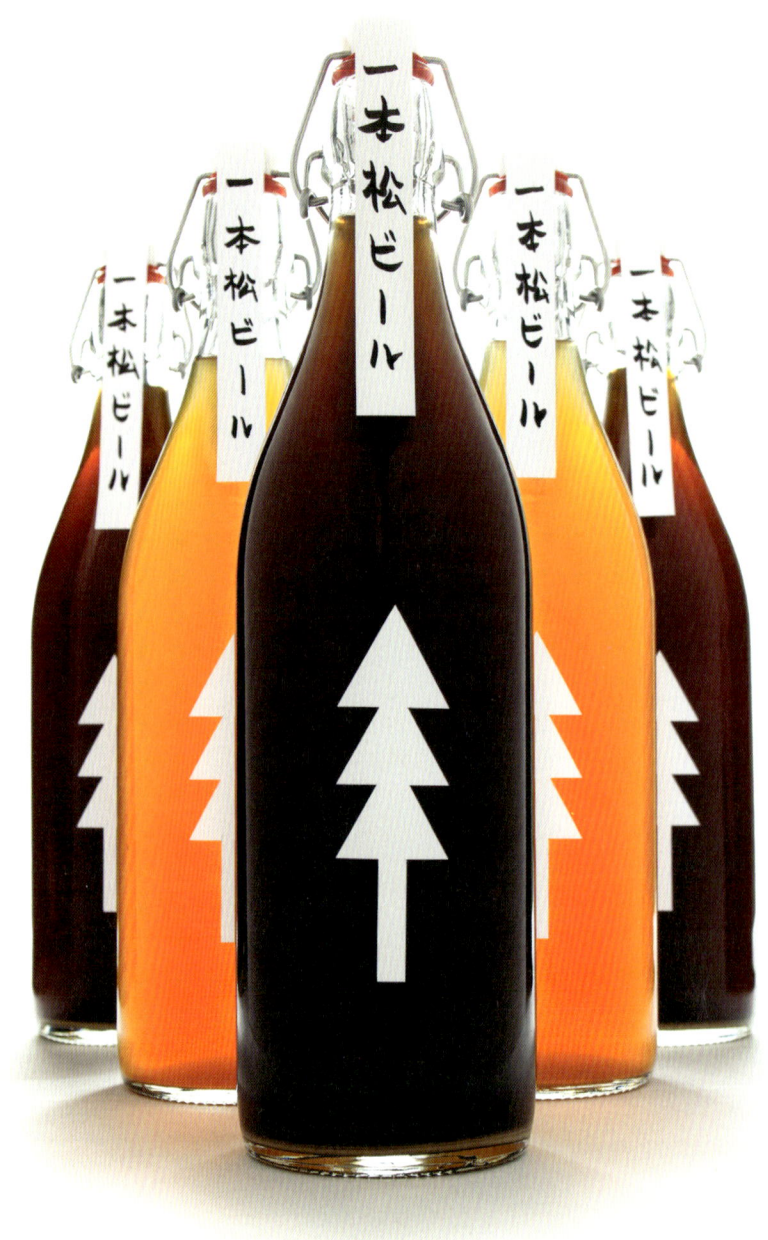

IPPON MATSU BEER

Designer: Kota Kobayashi

In the city of Rikuzentakata, a single pine tree stands as a testament to sur vival after the tsunami of 2011. This beer's name means "One Pine Tree" and its design is a symbol of charity and hope f or Japan's brighter future. A scroll-like, handwritten label seals the top with its story written on the inside. The label is a solitar y pine made of three triangles facing up, symbolizing the wish f or progress in the reconstruction ef forts.

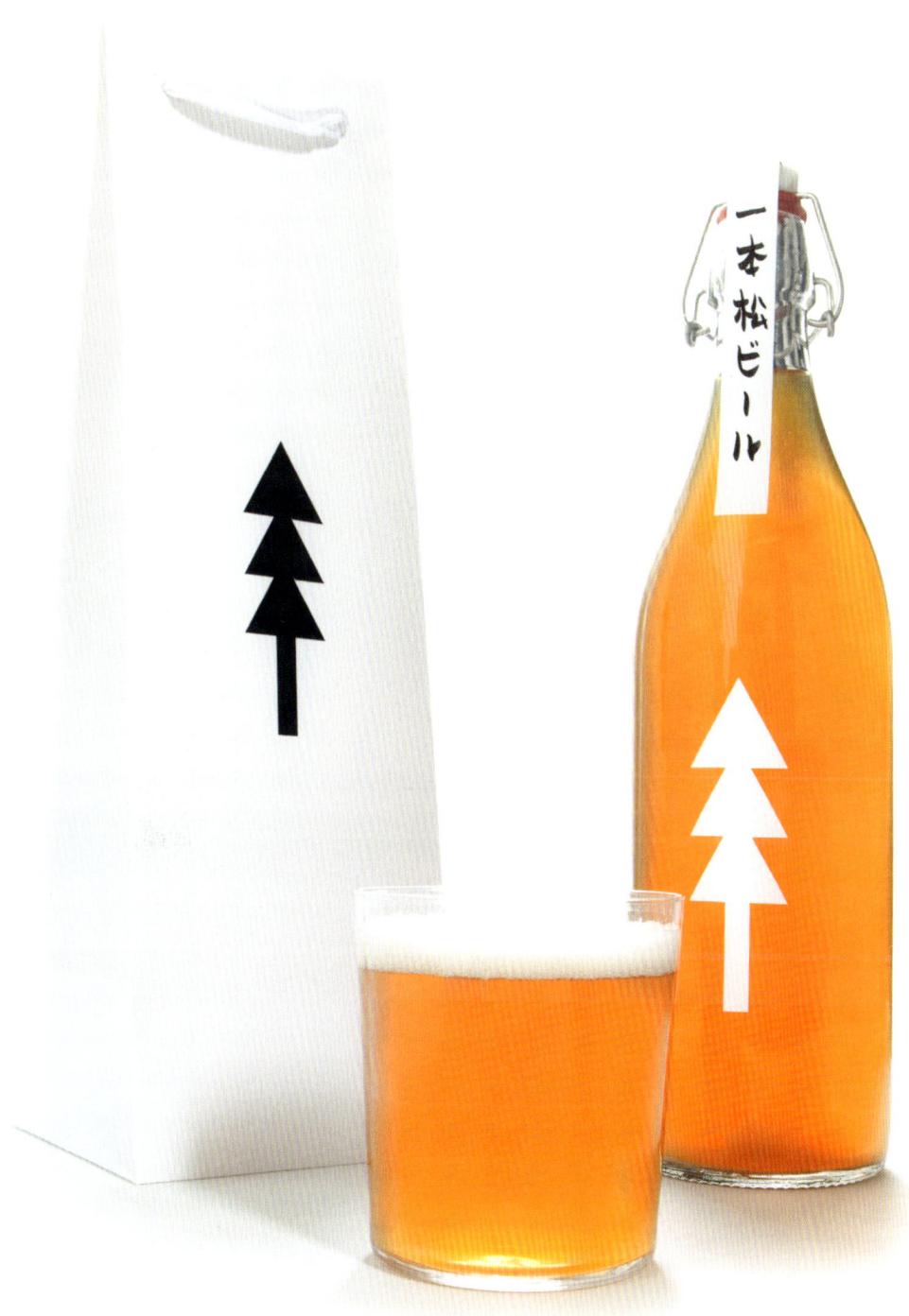

Salt Only

Studio: KD | Designer: Junya Kamada

The name of the product means "salt only". By using simple graphic and color scheme, the package design emphasizes the naturalness of the tomato source which is only made of tomato and salt.

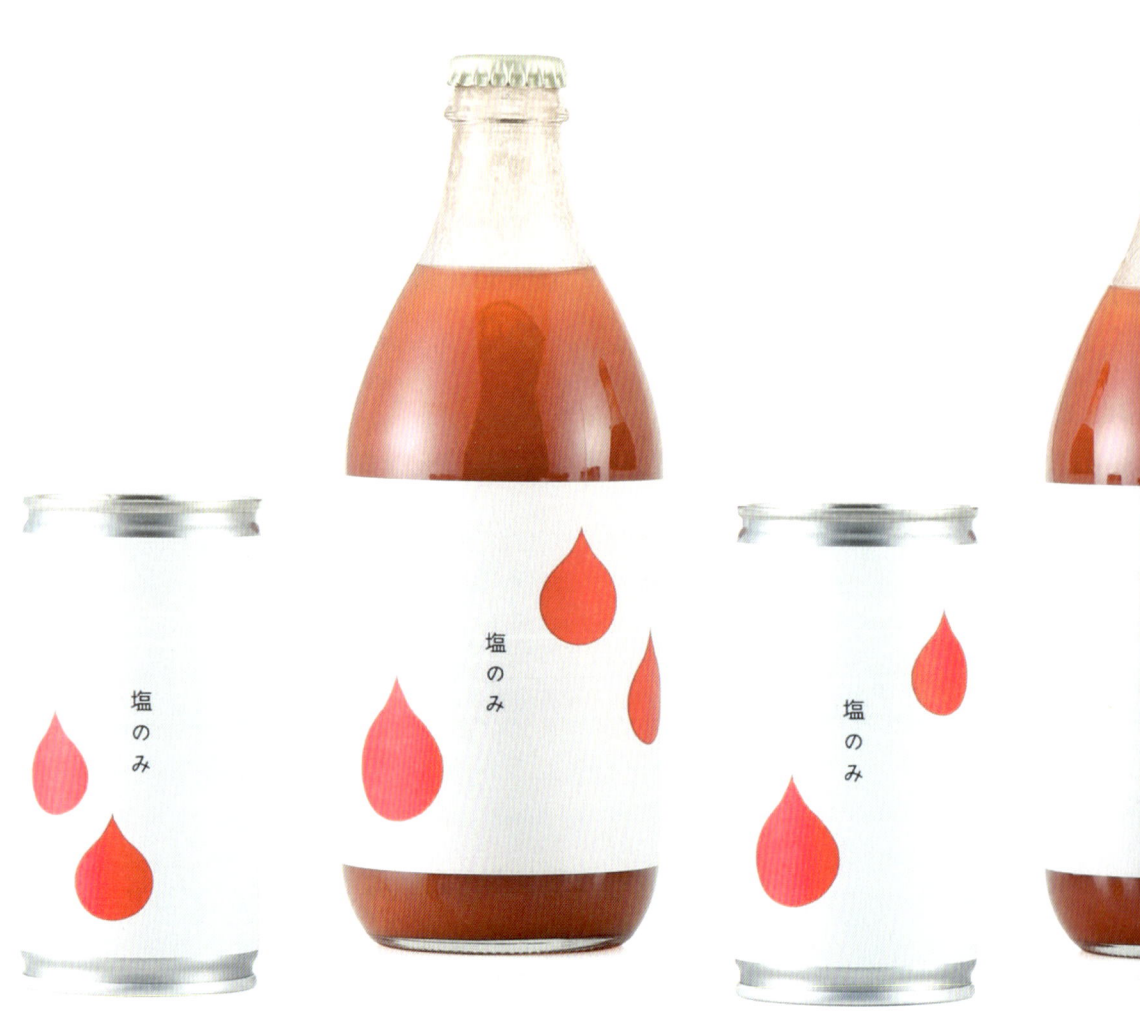

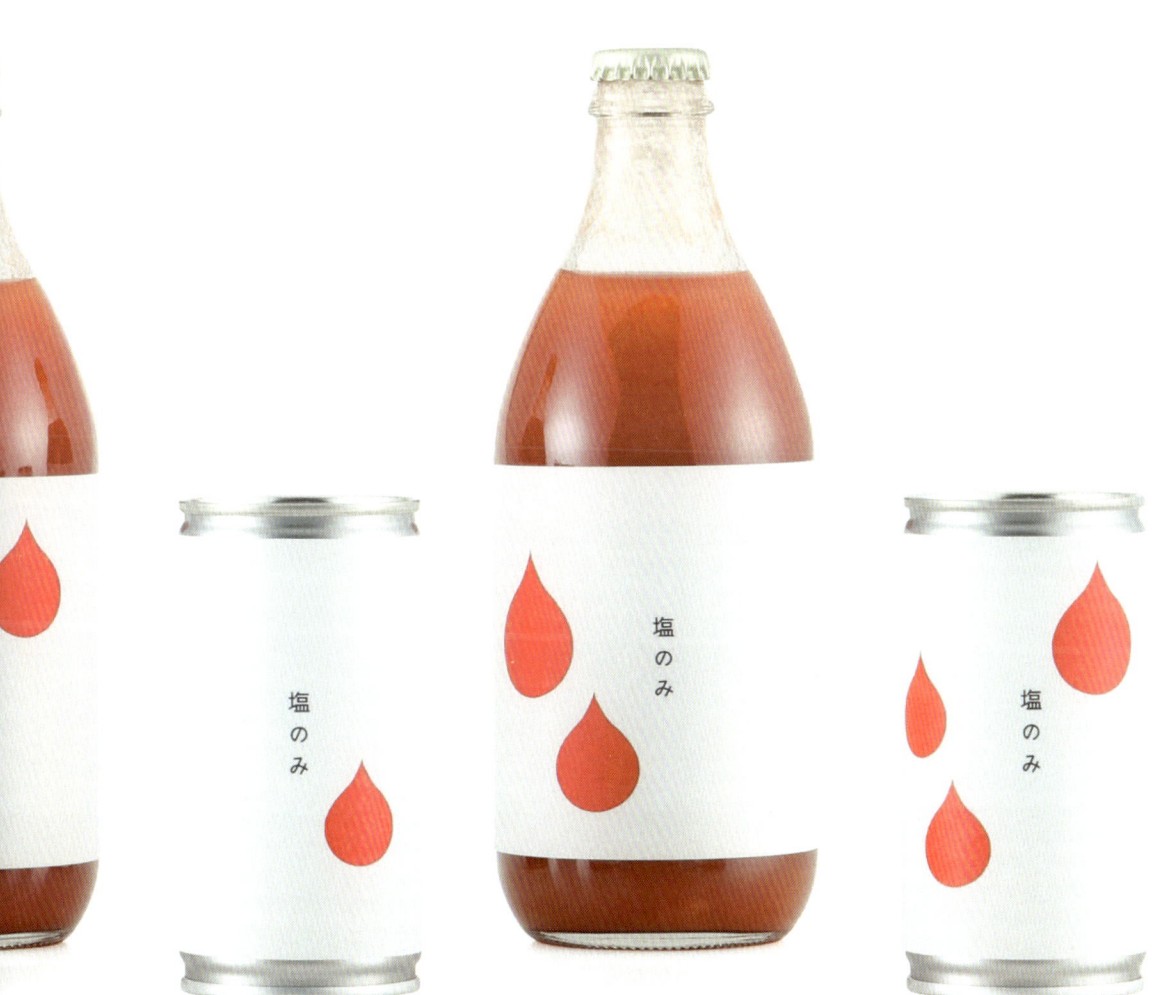

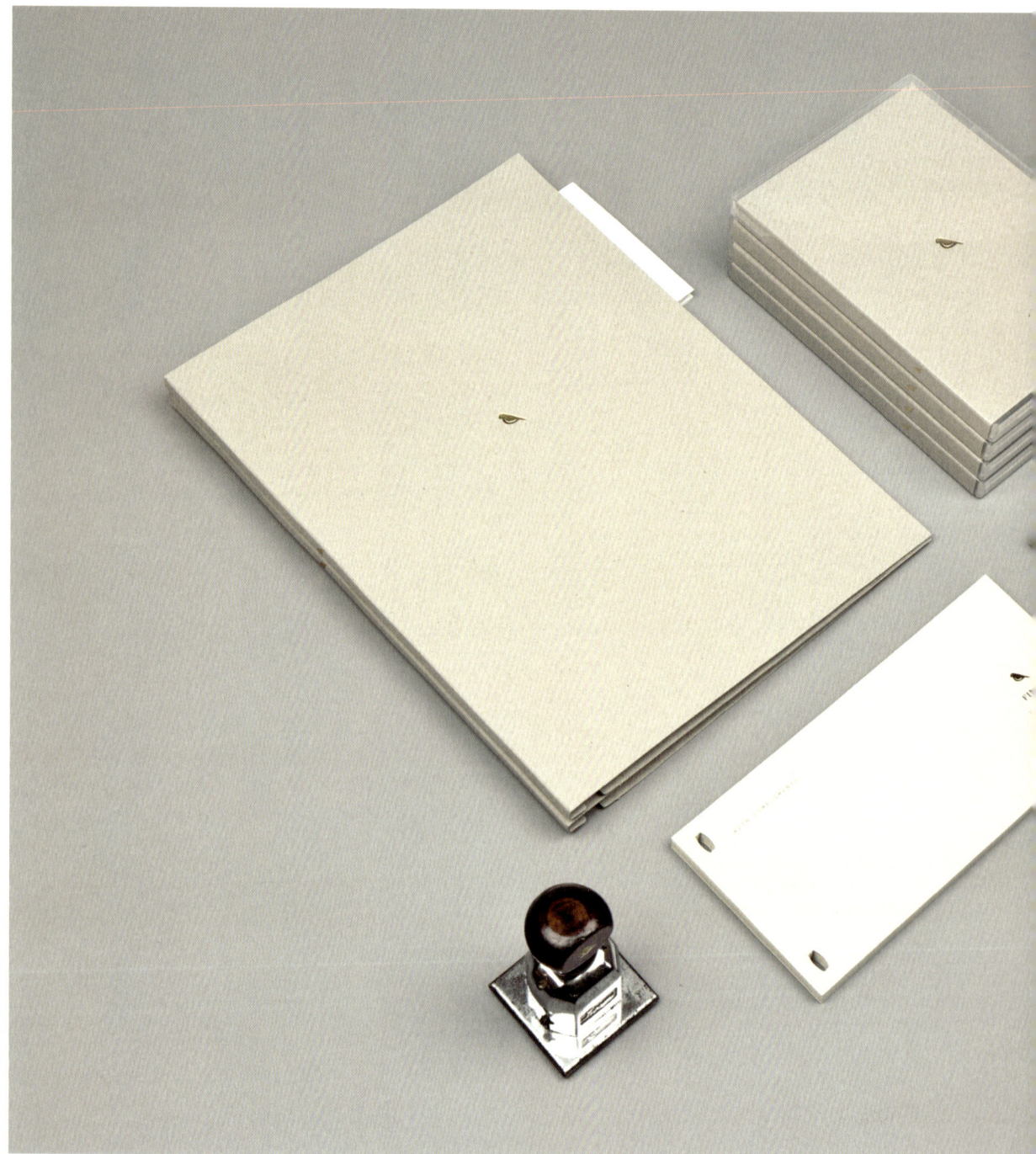

Finch

Studio: Maud

Finch is a new production company made up of some very talented Australian creatives. The brief was to develop a brand that can reflect the skill and respect these people command in the industry, without being overbearing or grandiose.
Using traditional production techniques, such as foiling, hand stamping and natural, recycled stocks, Maud created an honest, intriguing aesthetic that is humble , while still retaining a sense of value and craftsmanship.

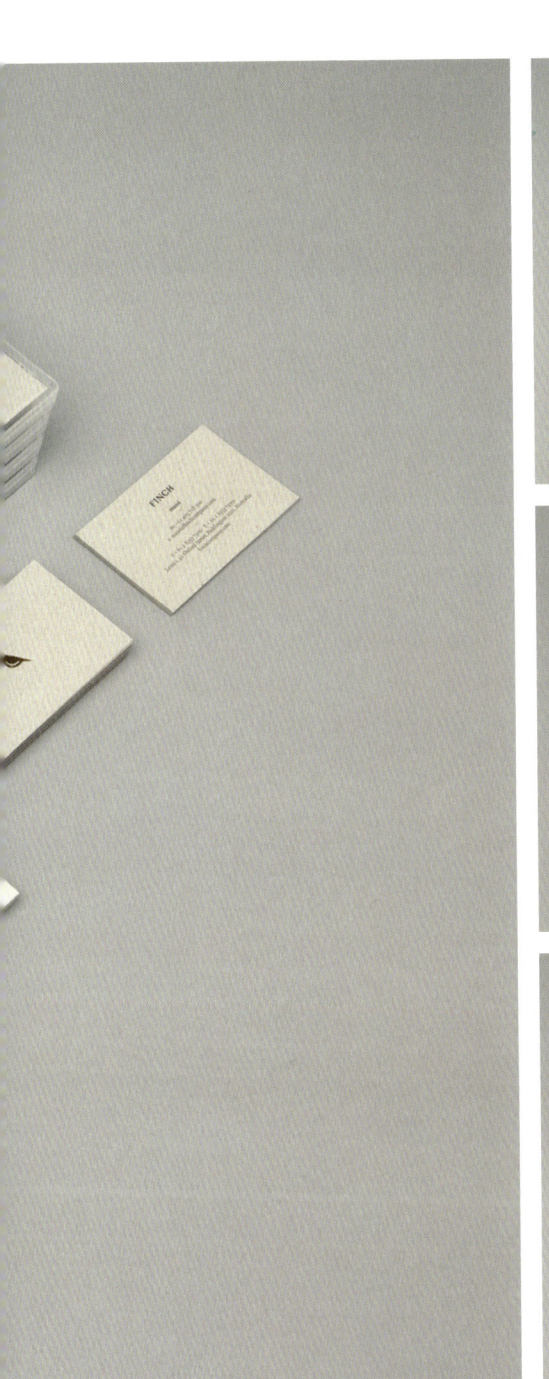
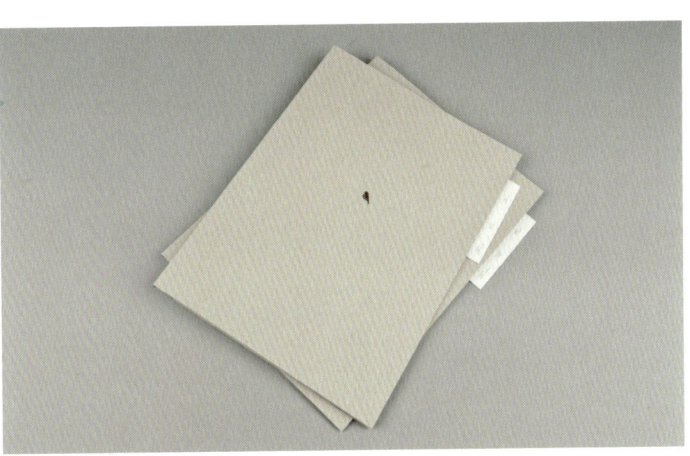
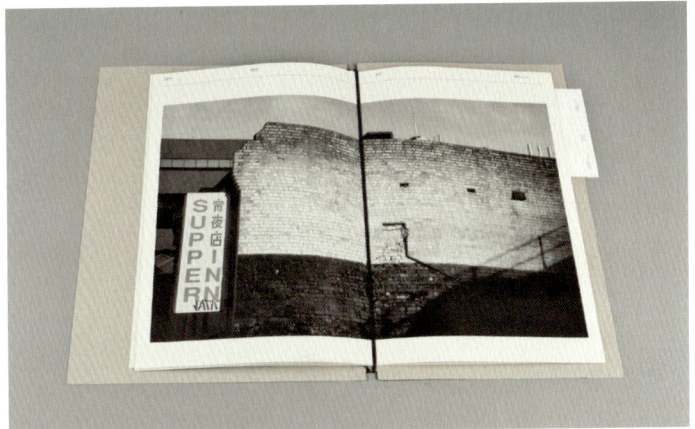
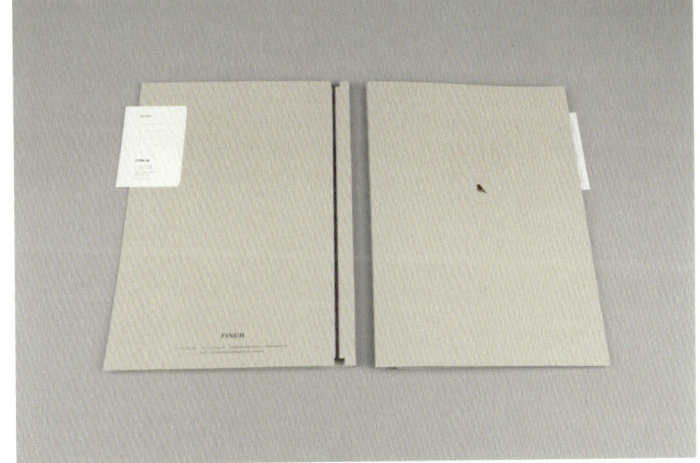

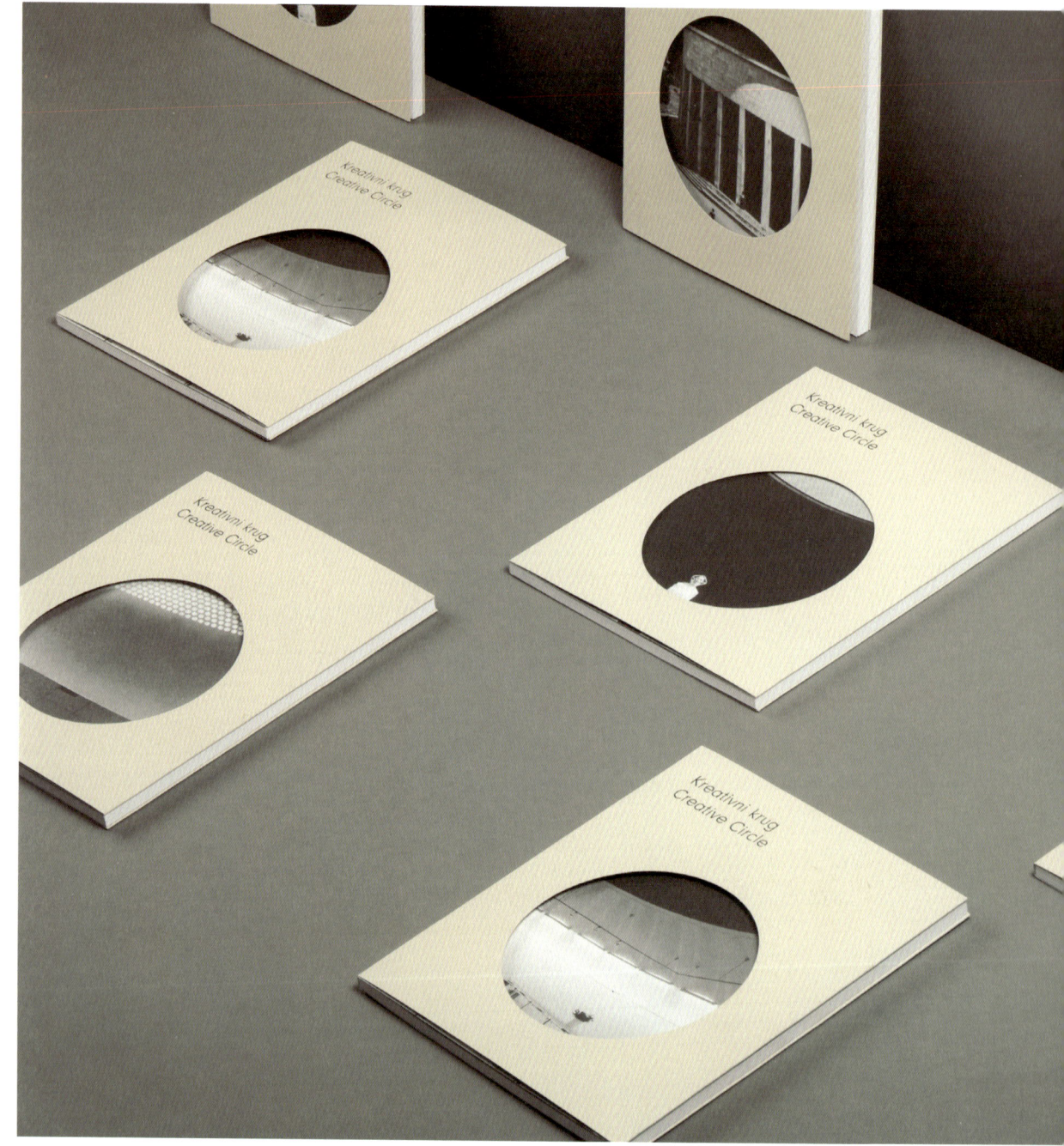

Creative Circle

Studio: Bunch | Creative Director: Denis Kovac

This publication provides a brief history of Croatian Society of Artists with a photographic journey of a monumental pavilion designed by pre-eminent Croatian sculptor Ivan Mestrovic in 1938. The building was converted into a mosque during World War II. Restored in 1993, the pavilion now serves as an exhibition space f or all f orms of visual ar ts. The brochure consists of four covers showing different stages of the pavilion's history. Each cover is pr esented through die-cut circle reminiscent of the pavilion's form.

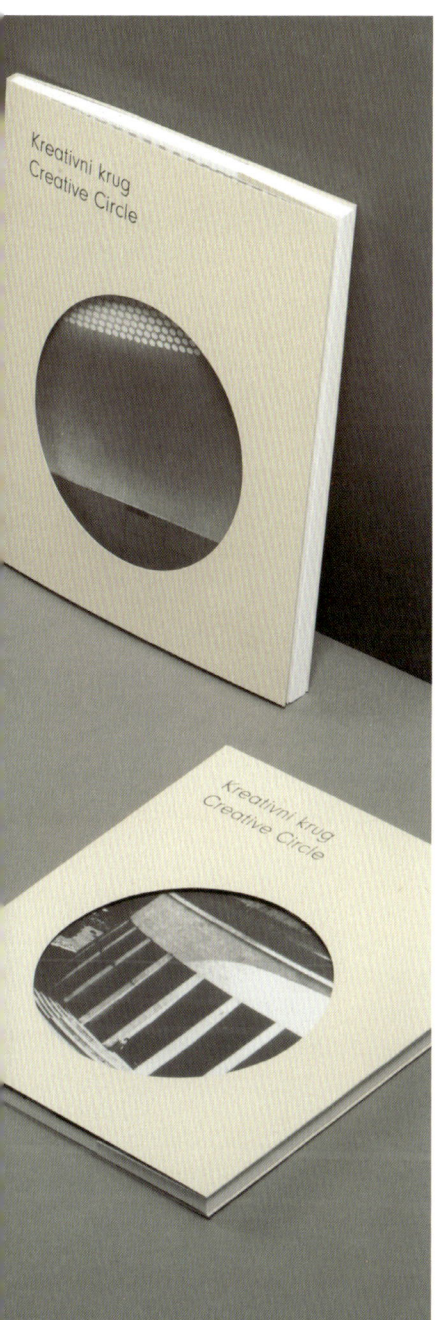
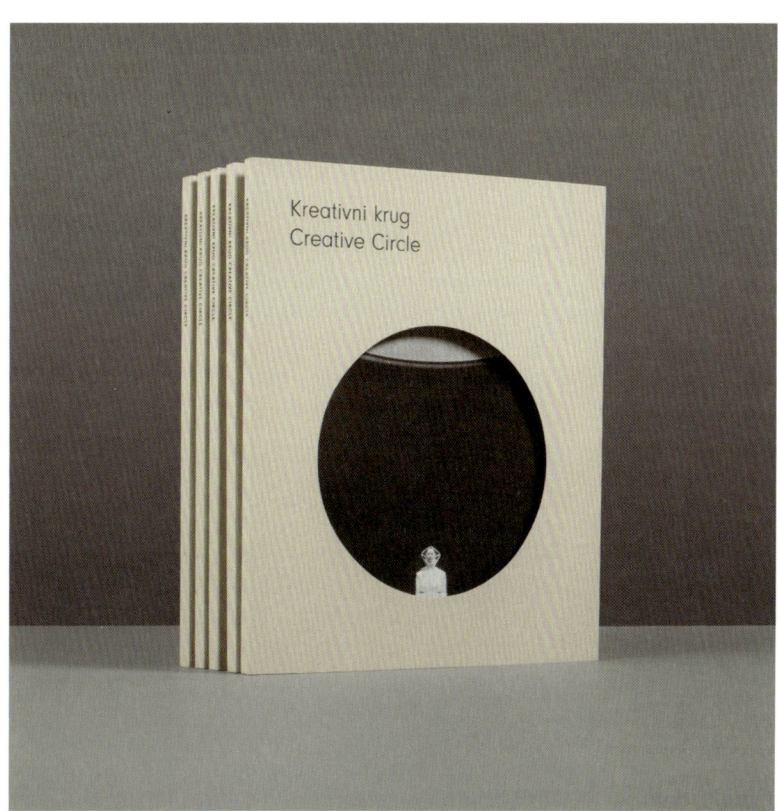
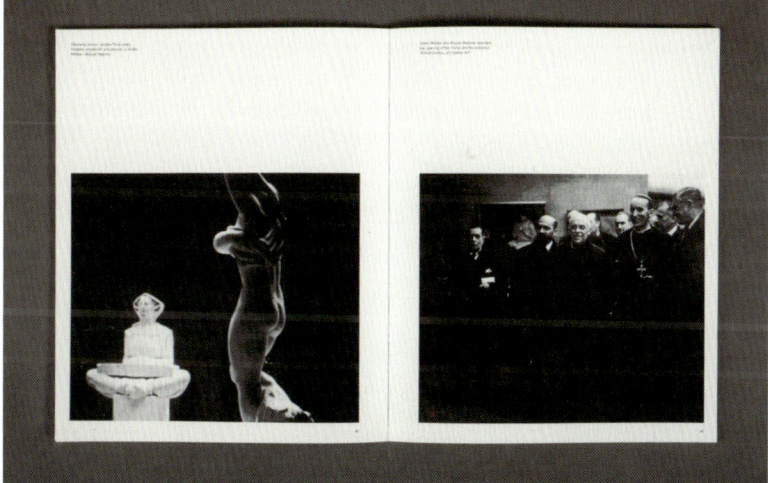

Stawell Chambers

Studio: Motherbird

Located on Little Bourke St Melbourne, Stawell Chambers is an architecturally significant Melbourne building. Having recently being refurbished, Motherbird was approached to create an identity to give the premises a new life. After researching the history of the building, a brandmark was created around 3 shapes in the buildings facade, forming an identity that is contemporary yet historically relevant.

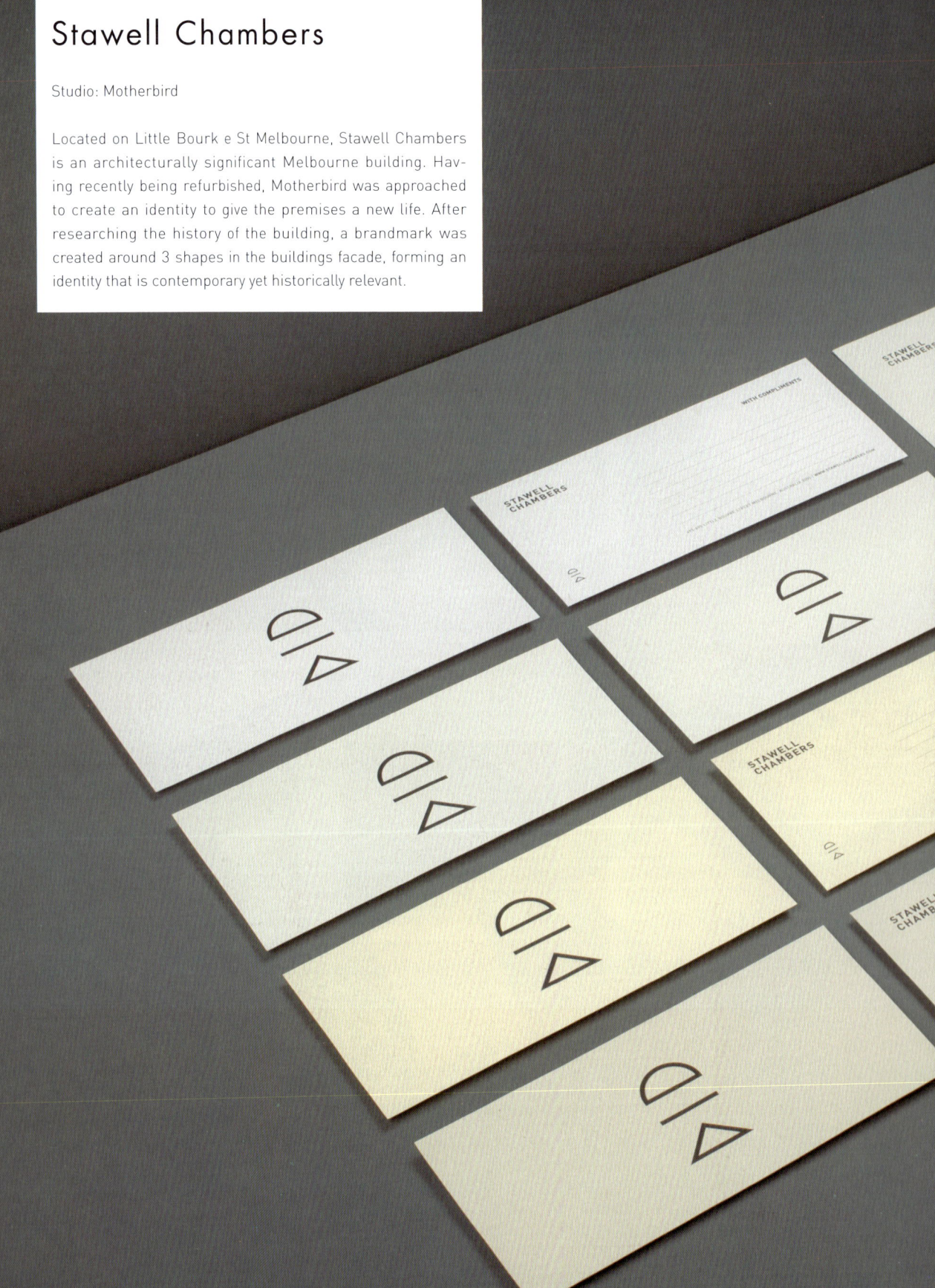

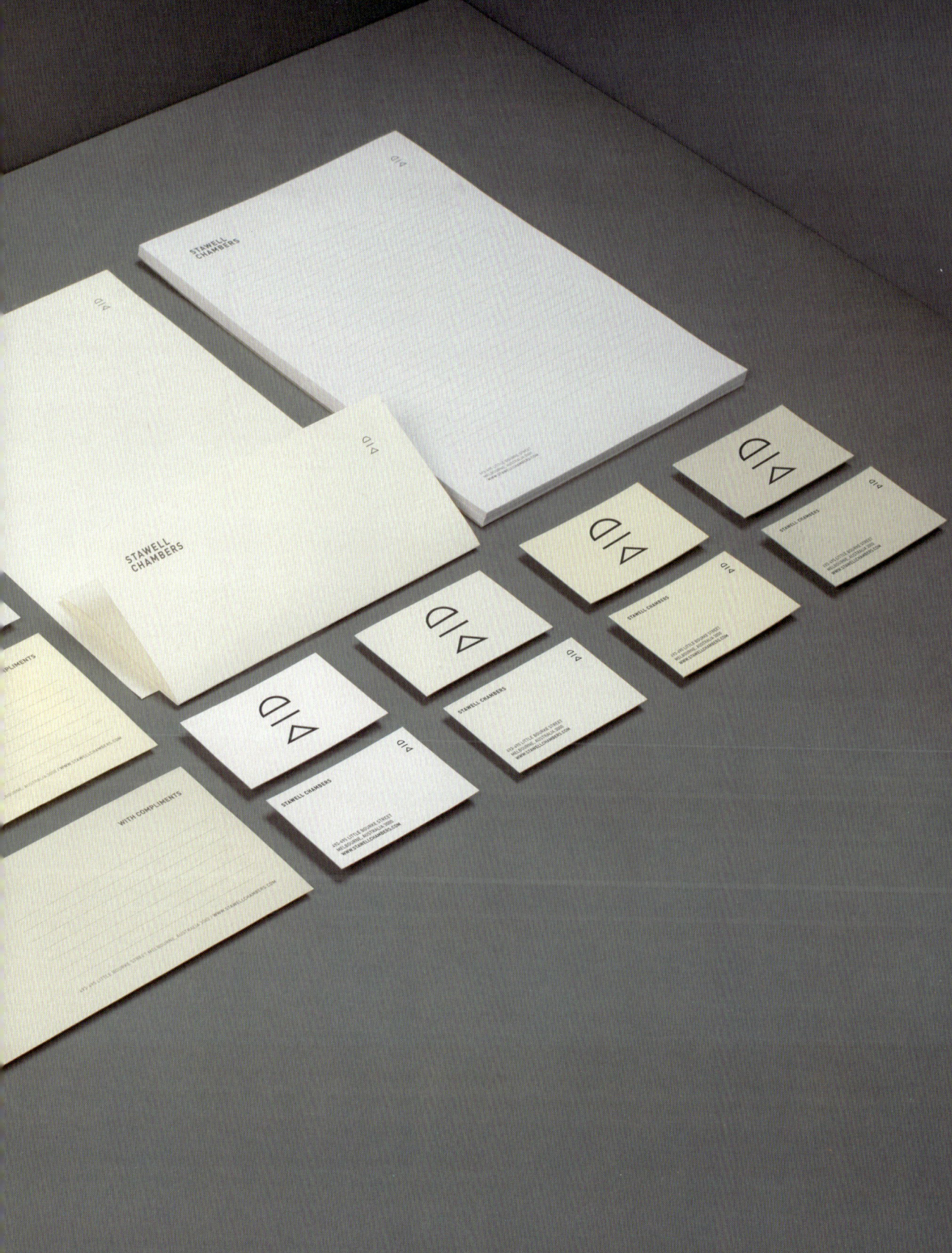

GF Smith — Master Specifier

Studio: SEA Design | Creative Director: Bryan Edmonson | Designer: Danny McNeil

The latest design for GF Smith is the ultimate toolkitf for professionals in design and print, for it reflects varying priorities in selecting paper. Housed in a pale grey onepiece clamshell box, the six books guide the user through the paper selection process, with the choice of color from black to white .

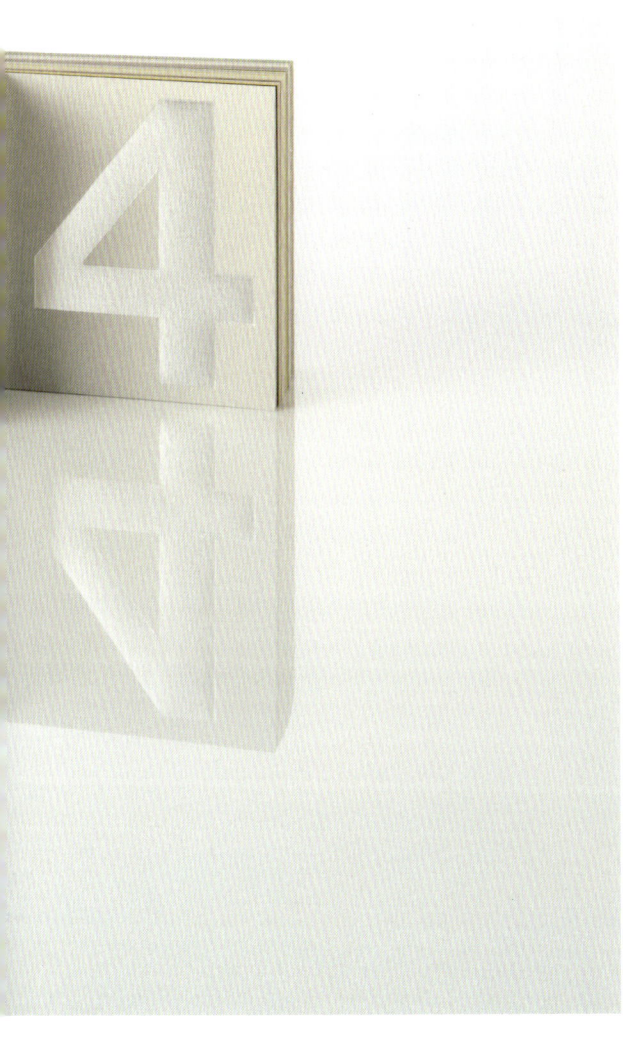
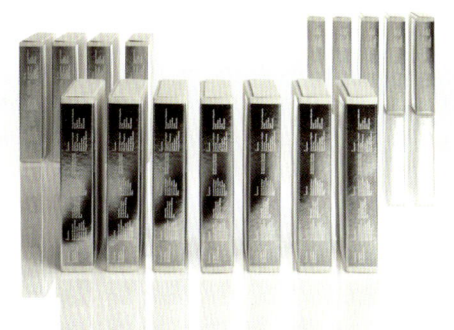
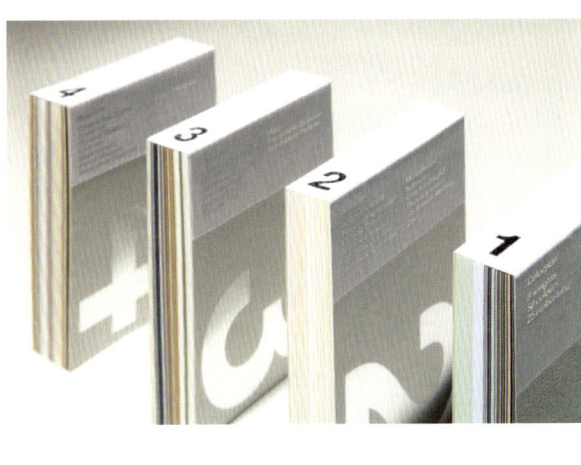
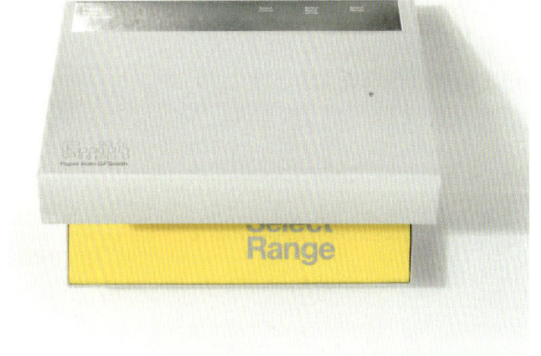

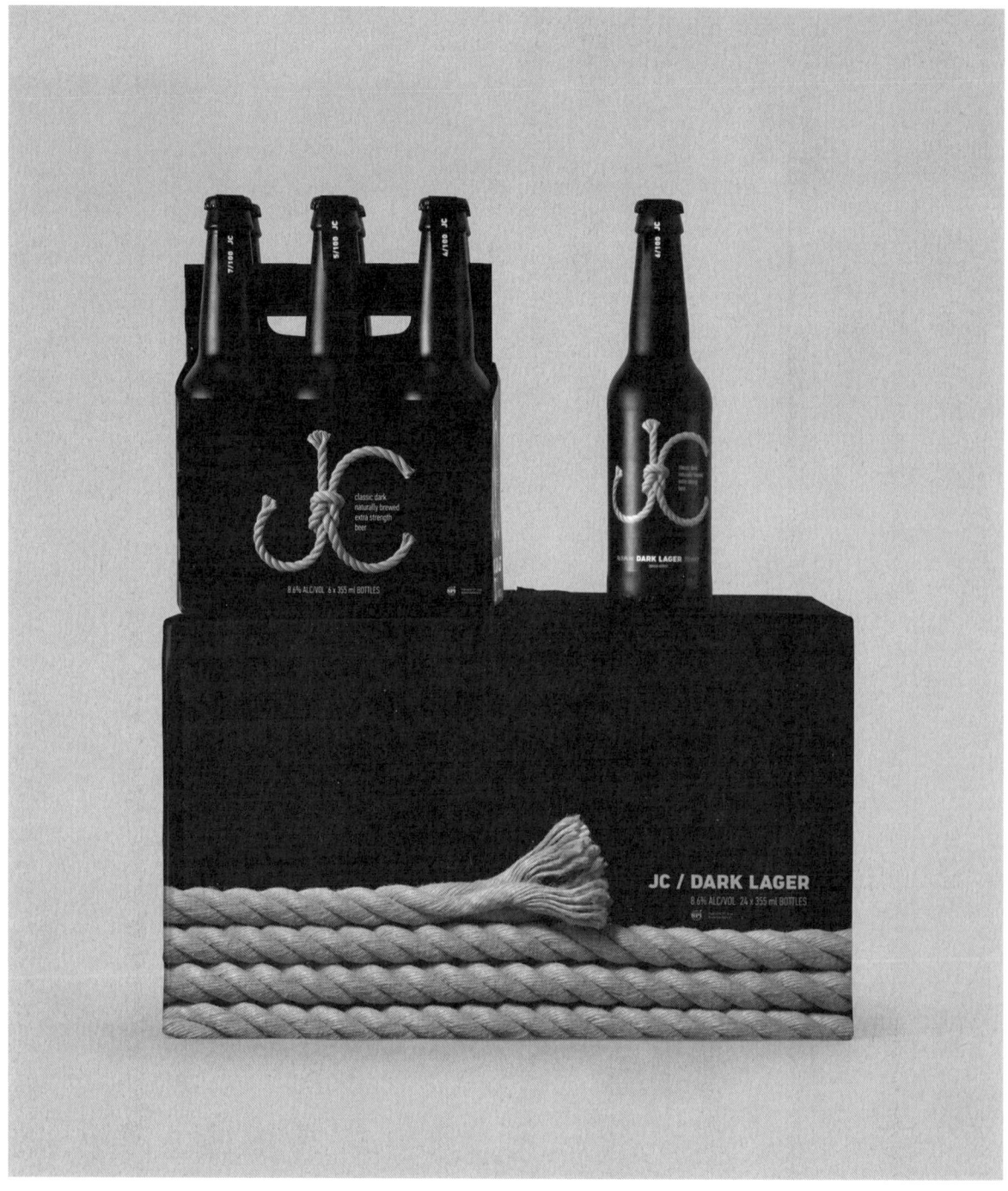

JC Beer

Studio: Tomatdesign | Creative Director: Andrey Tarakanov | Designer: Denis Bashev

Tomatdesign developed the name, logo and packaging design for a limited, personalized edition of beer, brewed specially for exclusive event of SPI Group company, with the participation of the famous French wine-maker Jean Claude. Having the most honoured guests being fans of yachting, Tomatdesign developed the design concept with this preference in mind.

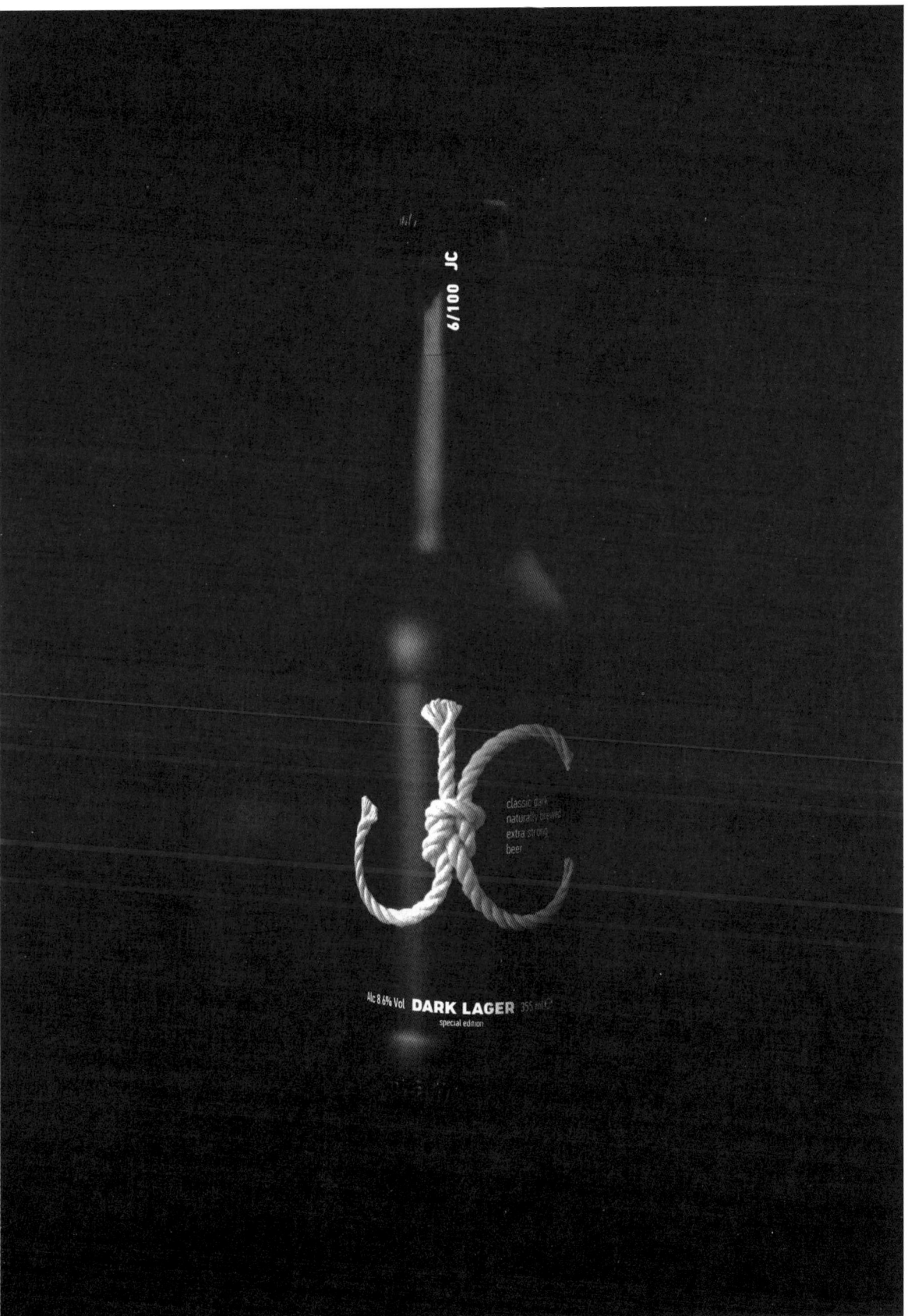

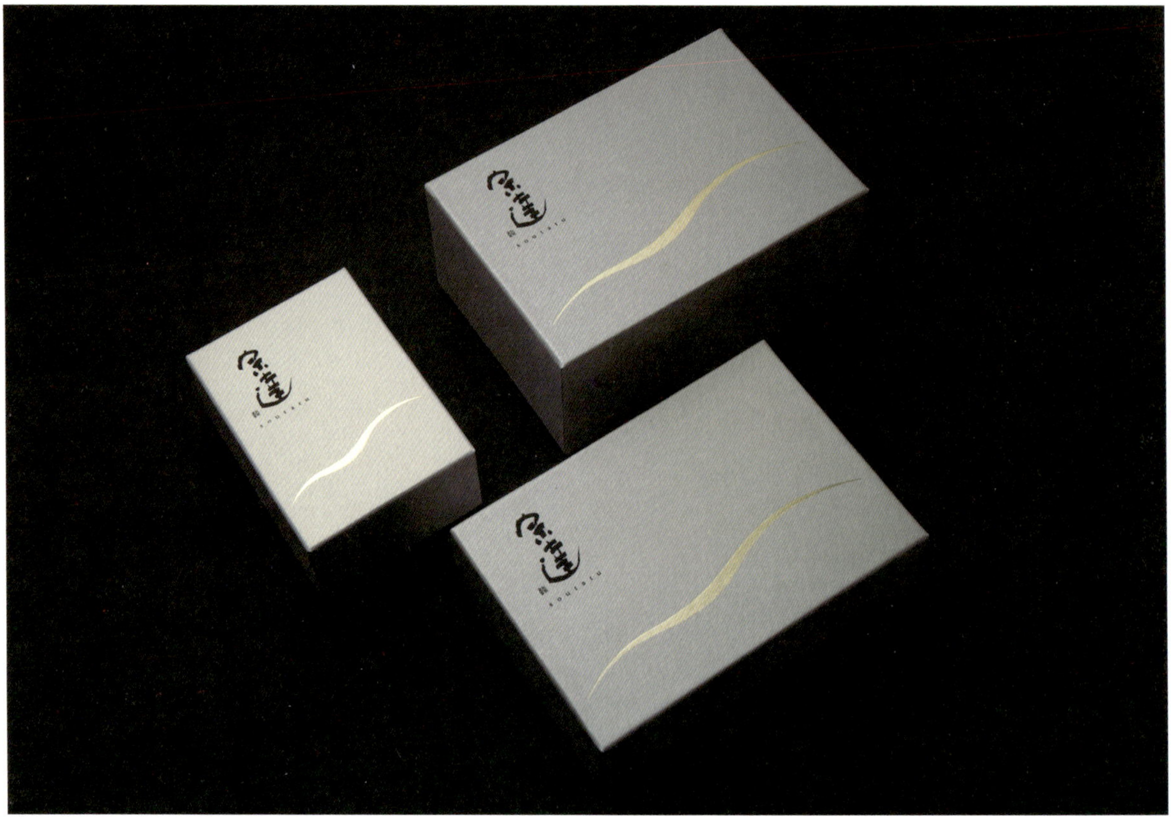

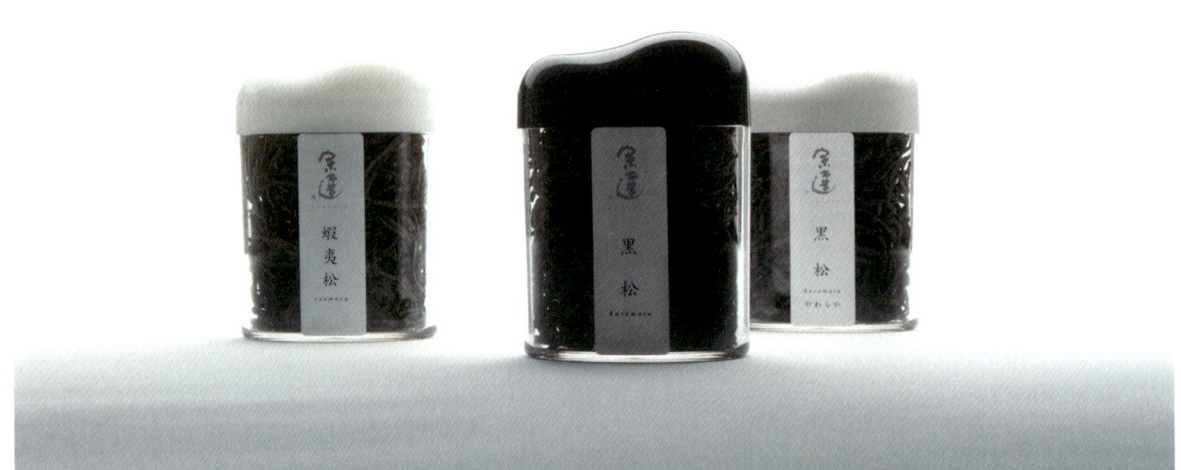

Soutatu

Studio: Ken Miki & Associates | Designer: Ken Miki

Through the use of modern style to convey Japanese tradition, this project aims to imply the high quality of the products.

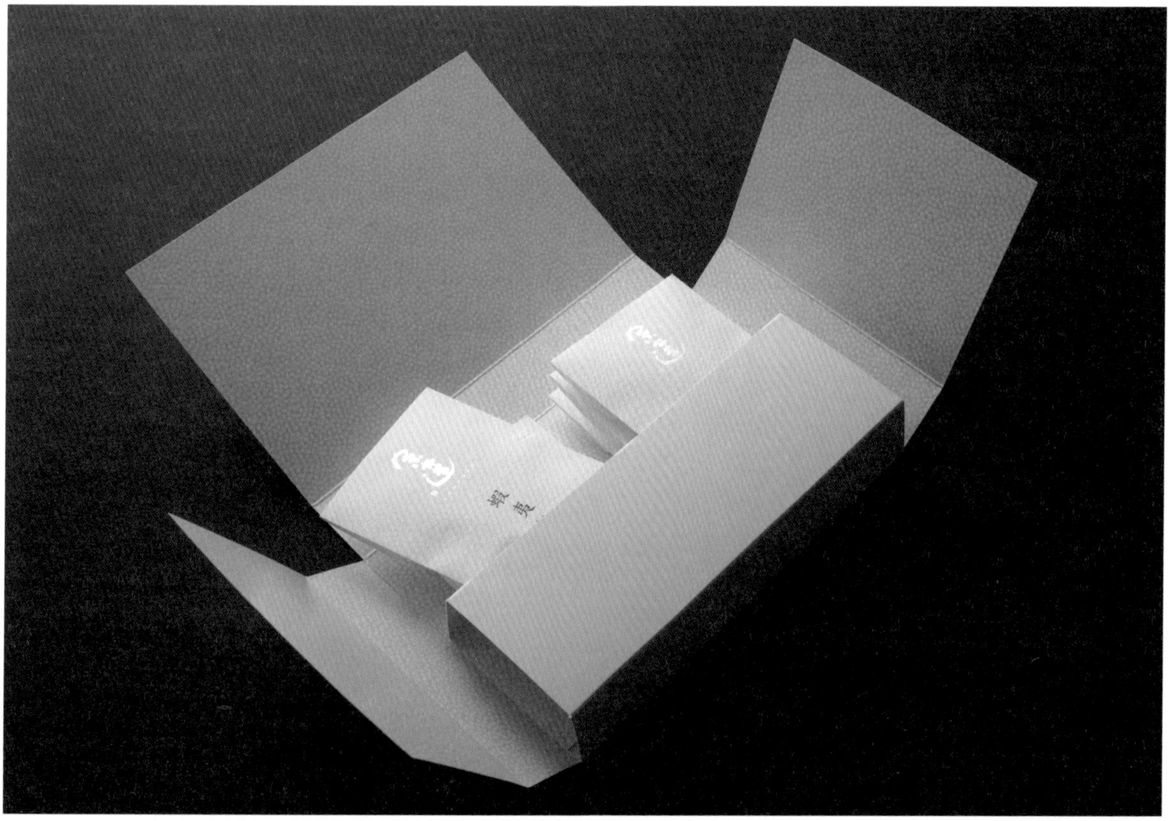

193

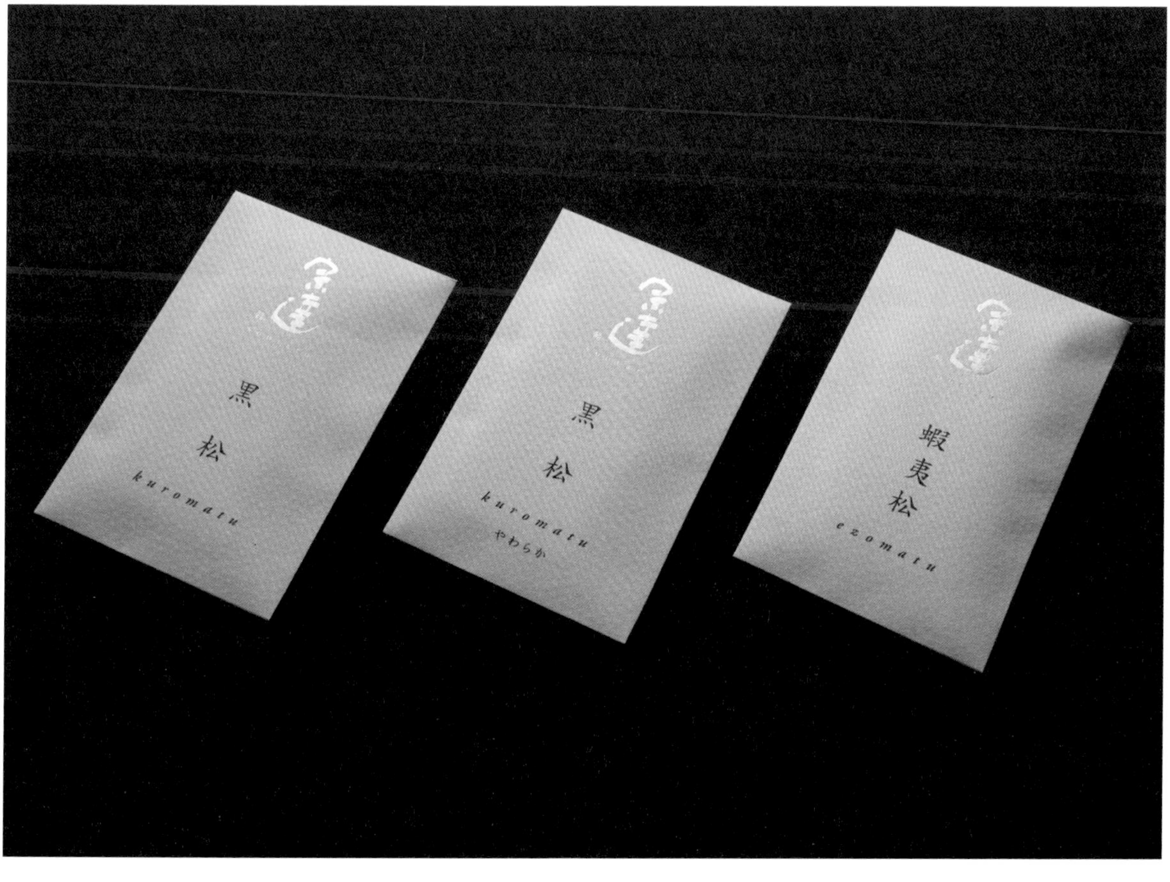

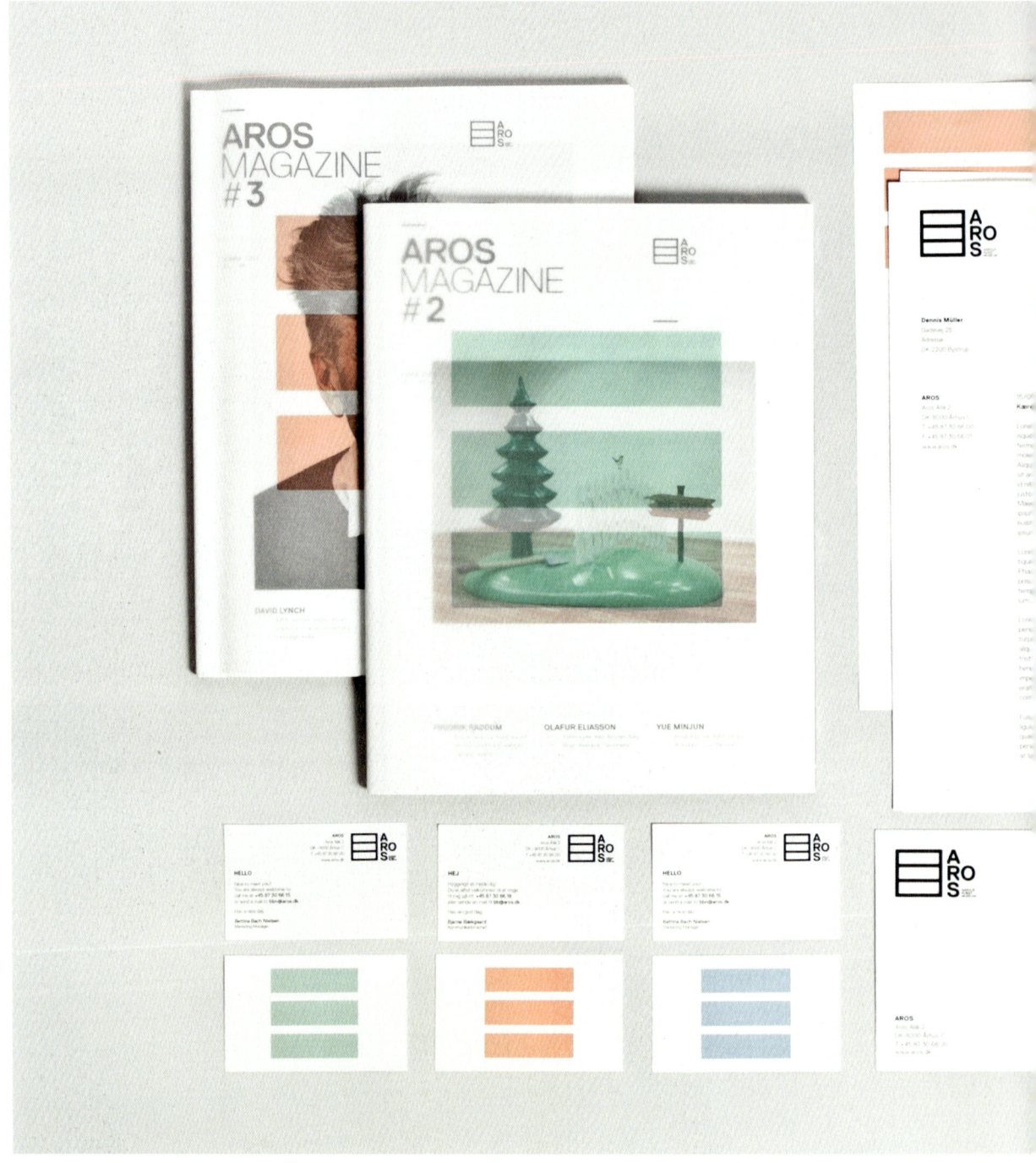

AROS

Studio: WAAITT™ | Creative Director: Dennis Müller

The identity is based on both the history and concept of the building of AROS (Aarhus Museum of Modern Art), its values and the visitors' experience in the museum.

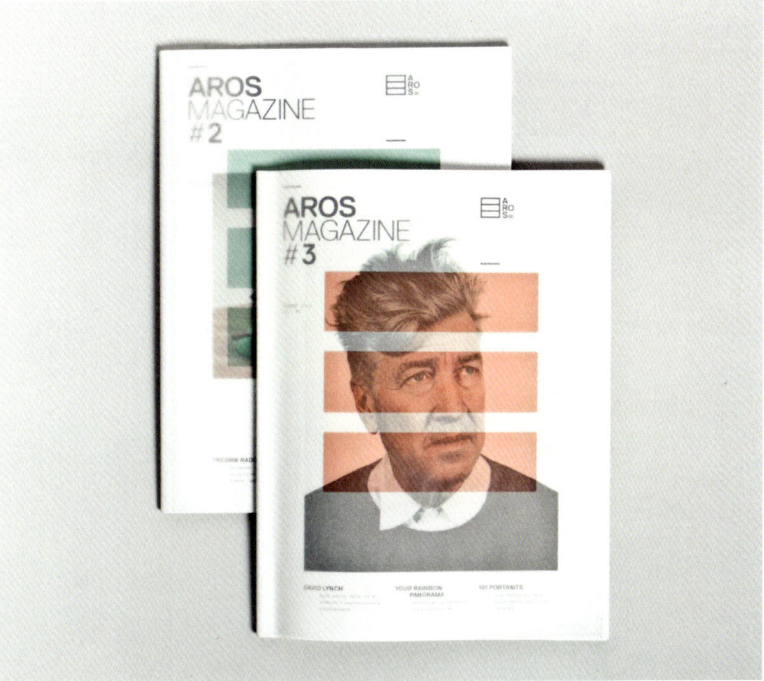
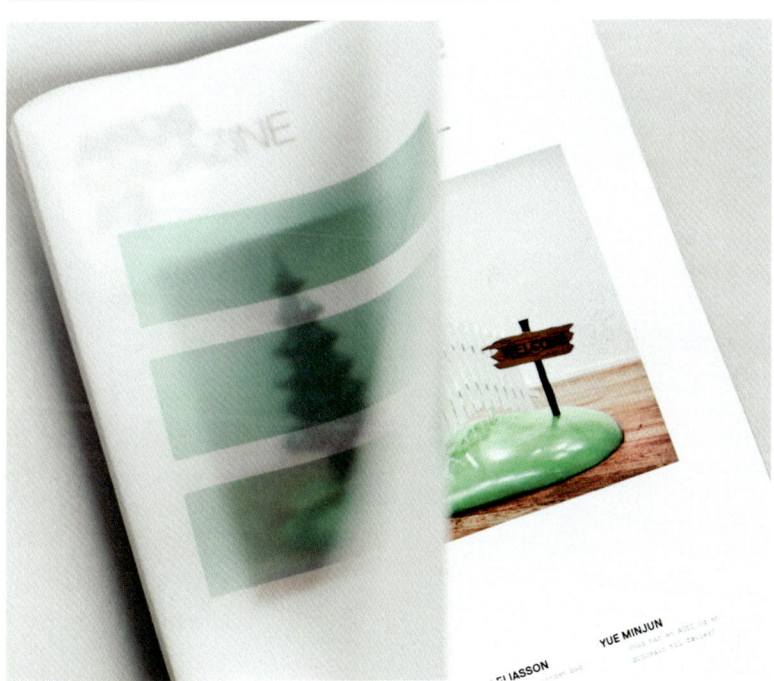

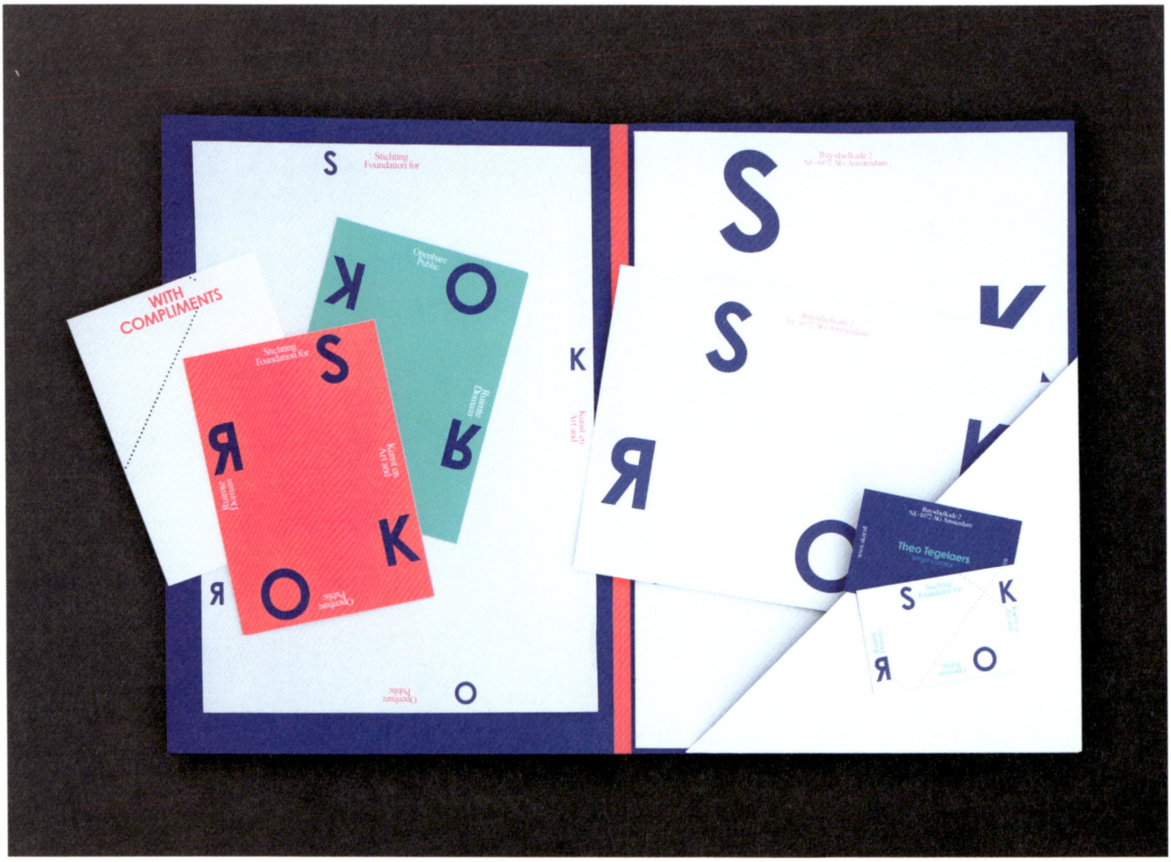

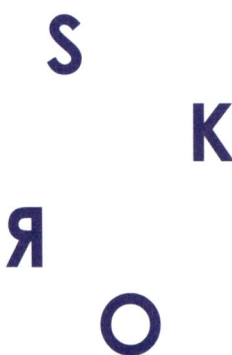

SKOR

Studio: Lava | Designer: Menno Cruijsen, Ruben Pater

SKOR is a Dutch foundation for art in public space. As their name indicates, the foundation focuses on the development and realization of art in public space. These projects react to socio-economic changes in society and new developments in contemporary art, urban design and the public. SKOR mediates between artists, commissioners and the public. The interaction with the public is an essential feature of their view on art in public space.
Lava's strategic starting point is an intention to reinforce SKOR's authority in the art of public place with this design. Using the letters of SKOR, a literal space was created on the page. Just as public space is in constant change, so do the letters of SKOR.

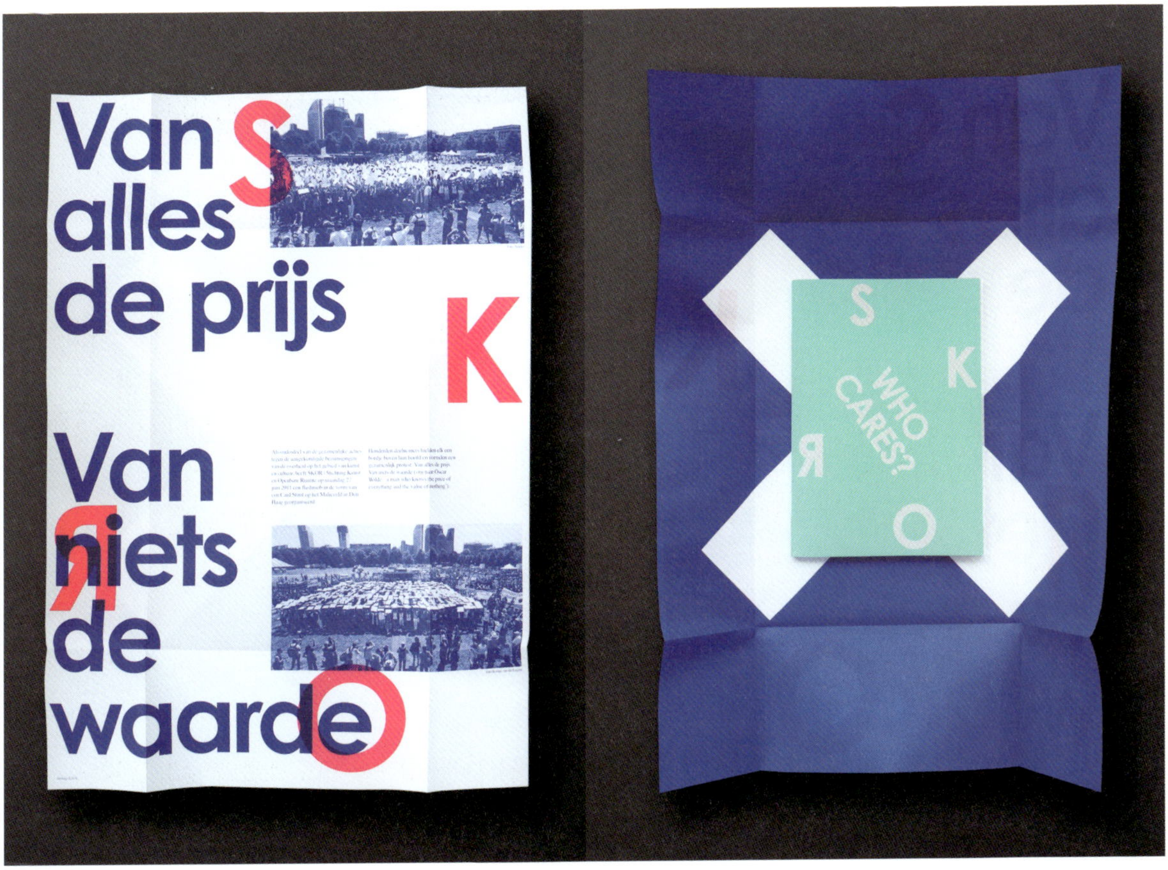

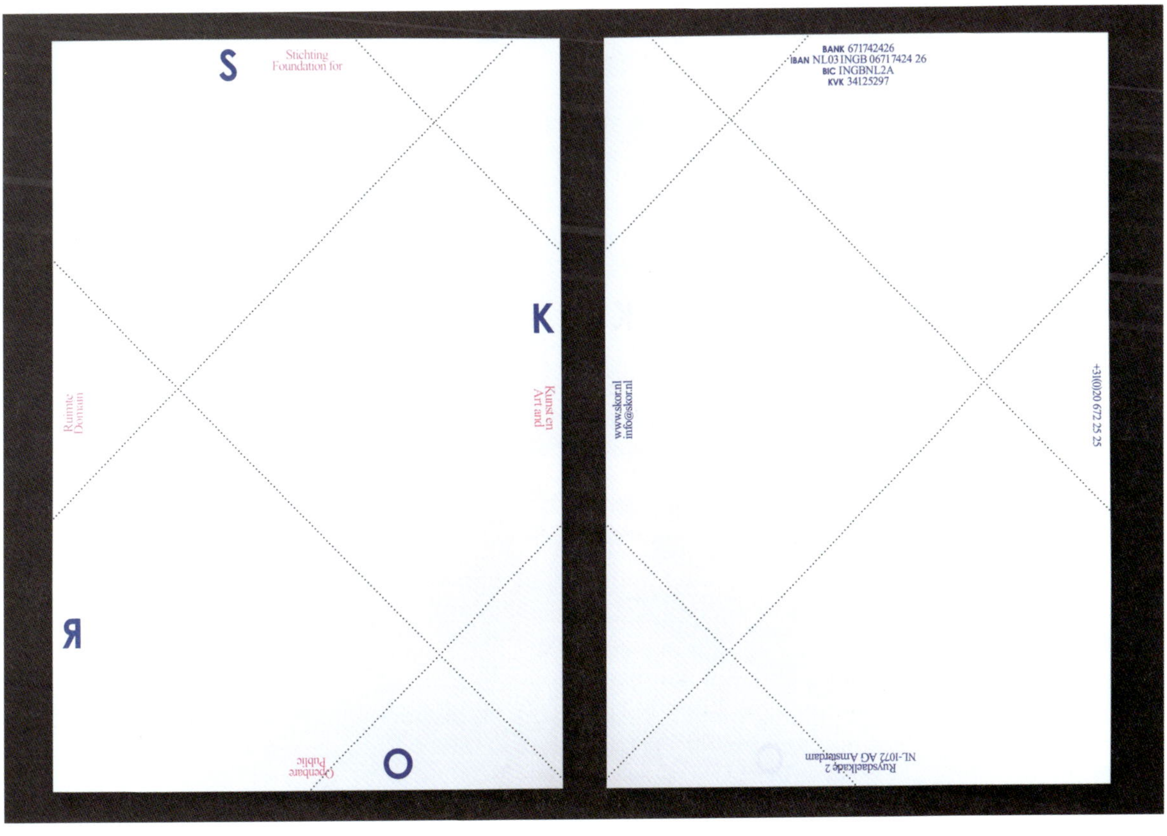

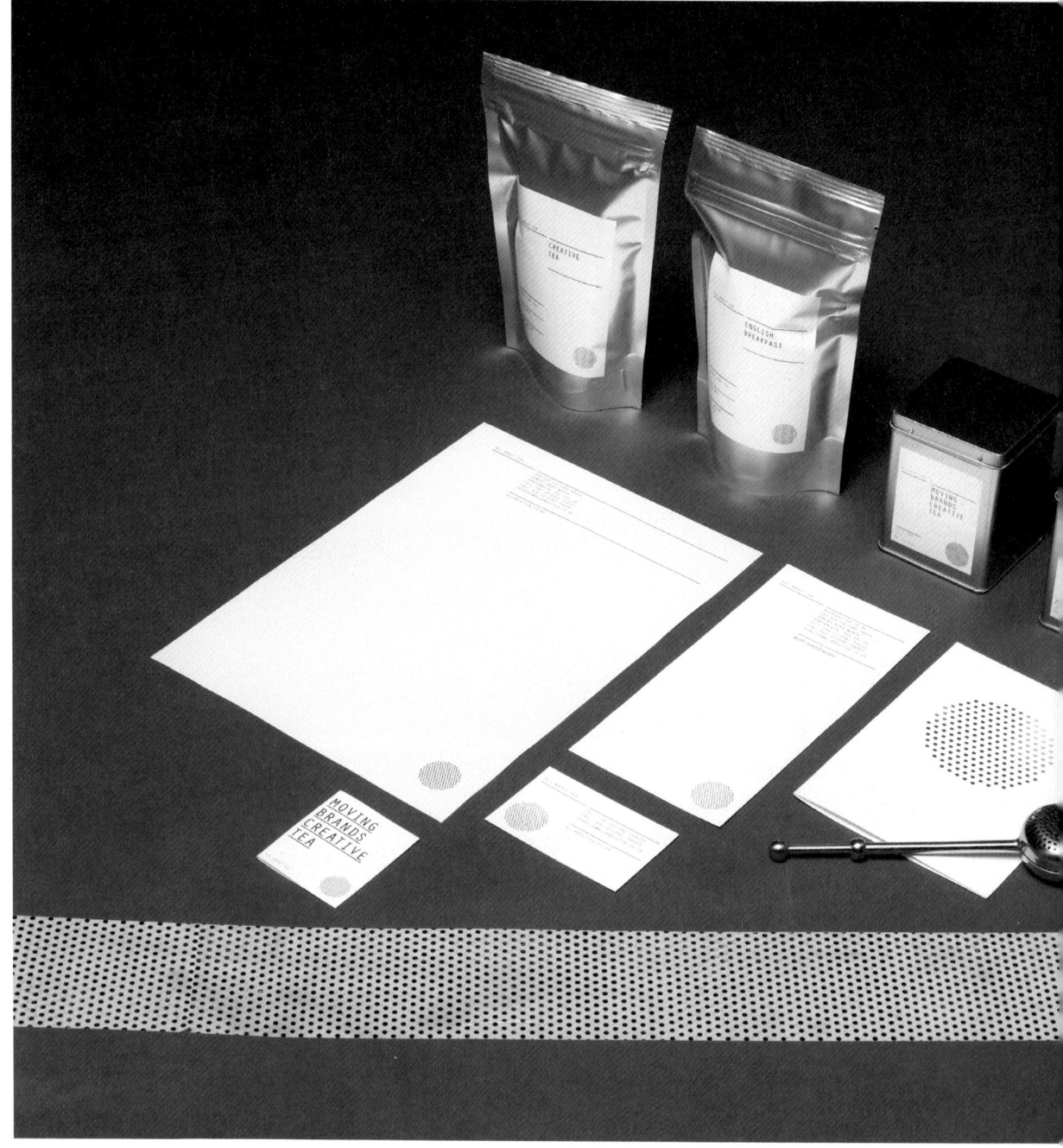

All About Tea

Studio: Moving Brands | Creative Director: Ben Wolstenholme | Designer: Marian Chiao

All About Tea is an expert wholesale tea distributor based in Portsmouth, UK. Moving Brands were task ed to create a new identity that would stand out among all others. The mark represents the process of making tea: the blending and the straining. The shape of the mark references a seal or stamp—an iconic industry standard - and is used in this way as a stamp of quality across the various applications . In all print applications these dots are laser-cut, inspired by the factory elements and tools involved in the making and distr ibution of tea.

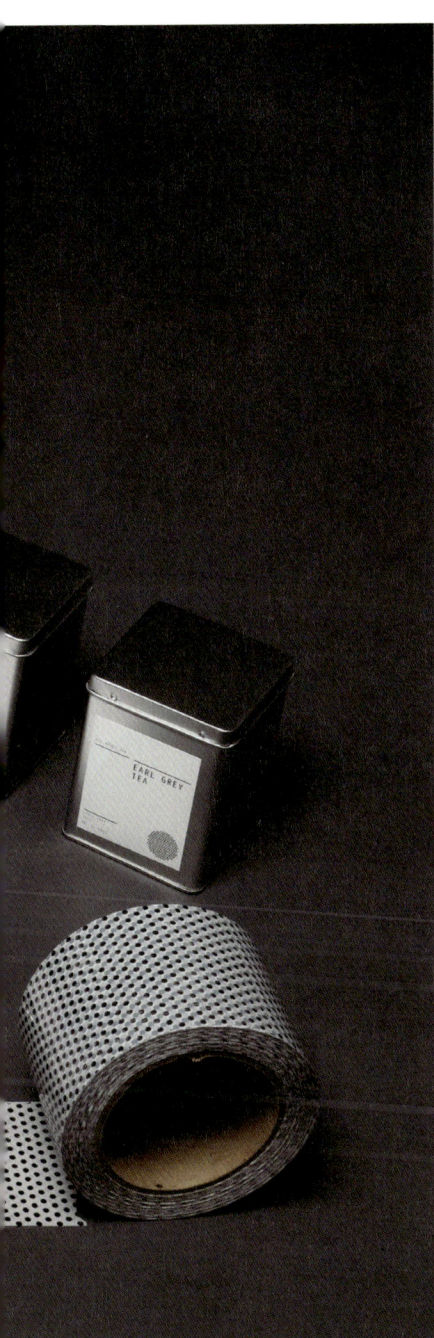

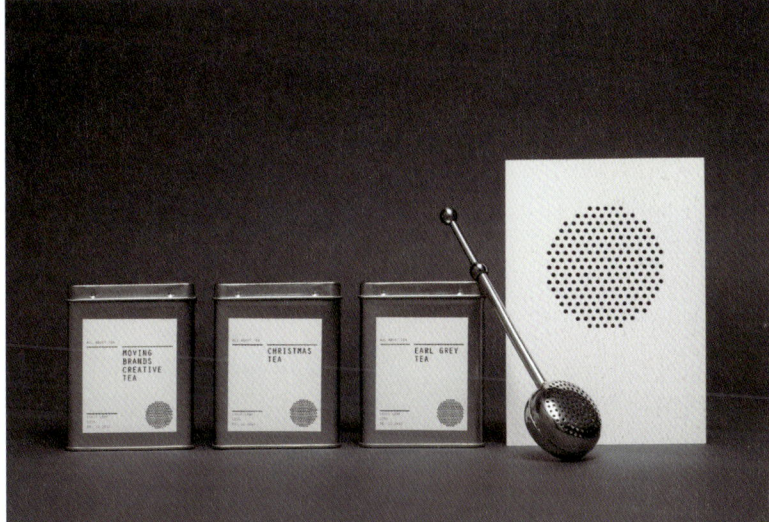
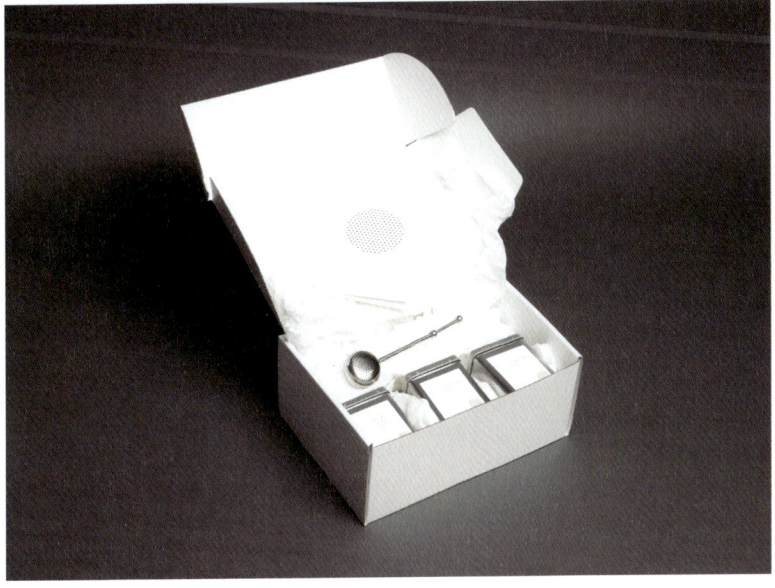

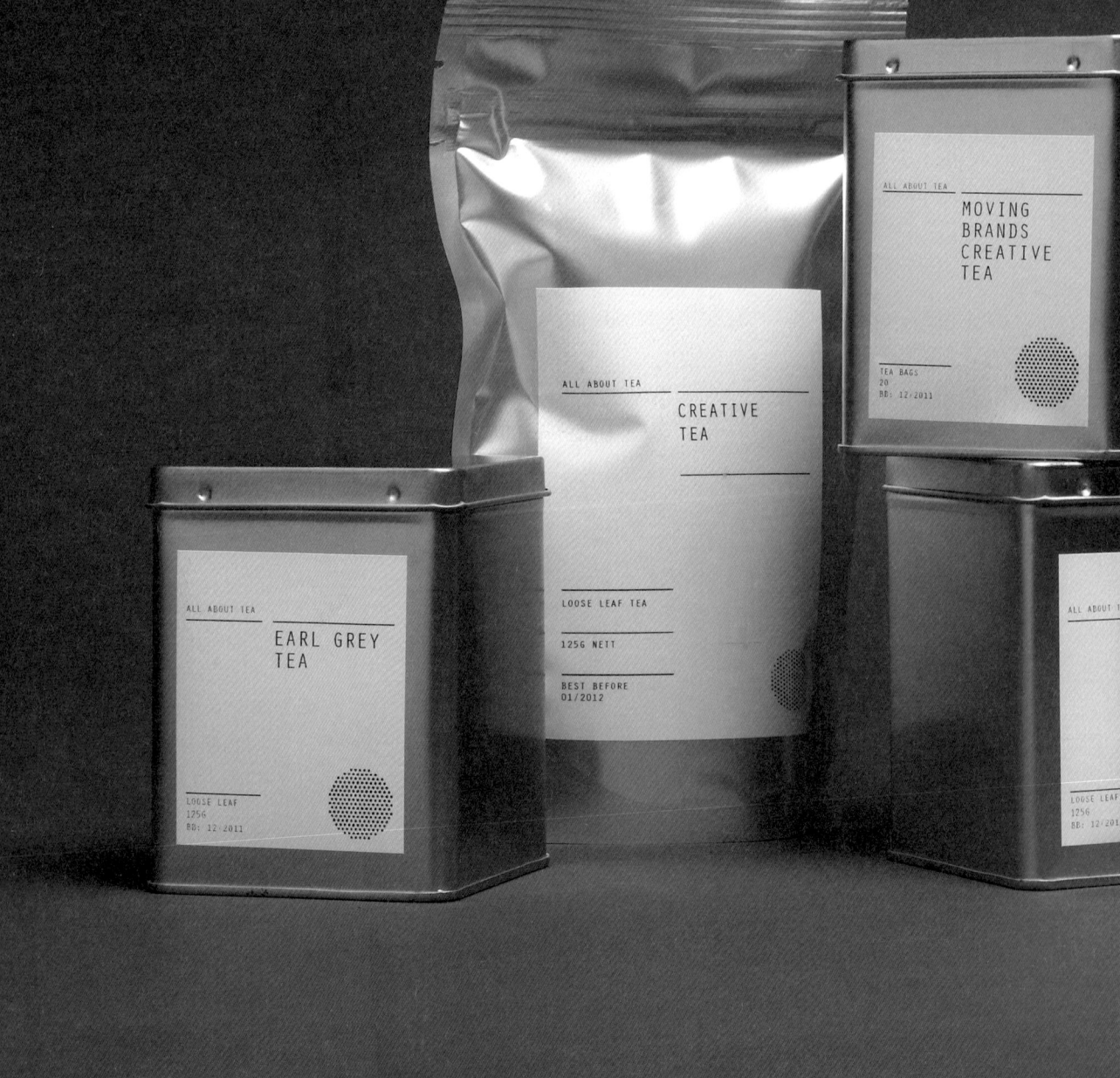

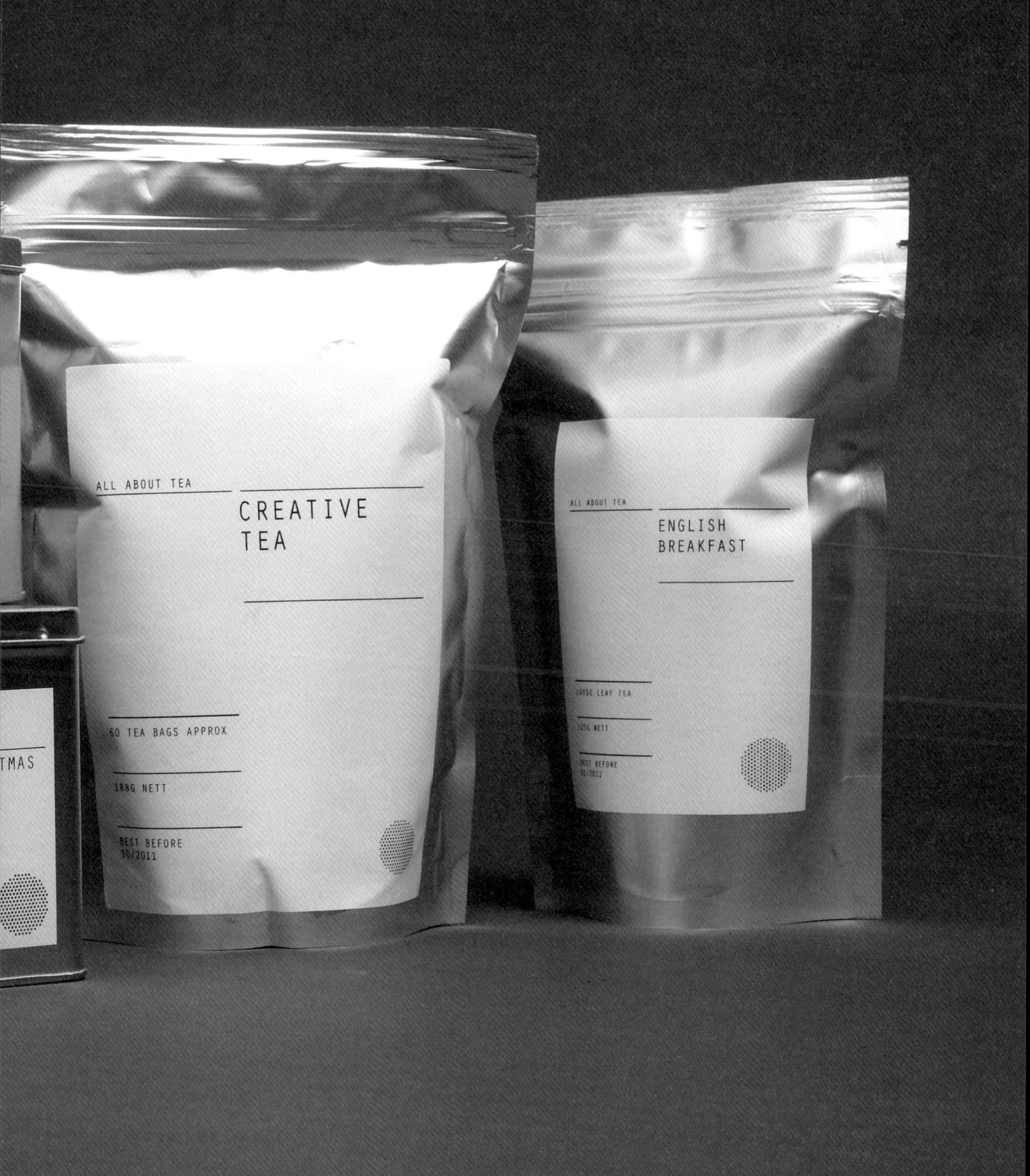

ALL ABOUT TEA

CREATIVE
TEA

60 TEA BAGS APPROX

188G NETT

BEST BEFORE
10/2011

ALL ABOUT TEA

ENGLISH
BREAKFAST

LOOSE LEAF TEA

125G NETT

BEST BEFORE
10/2012

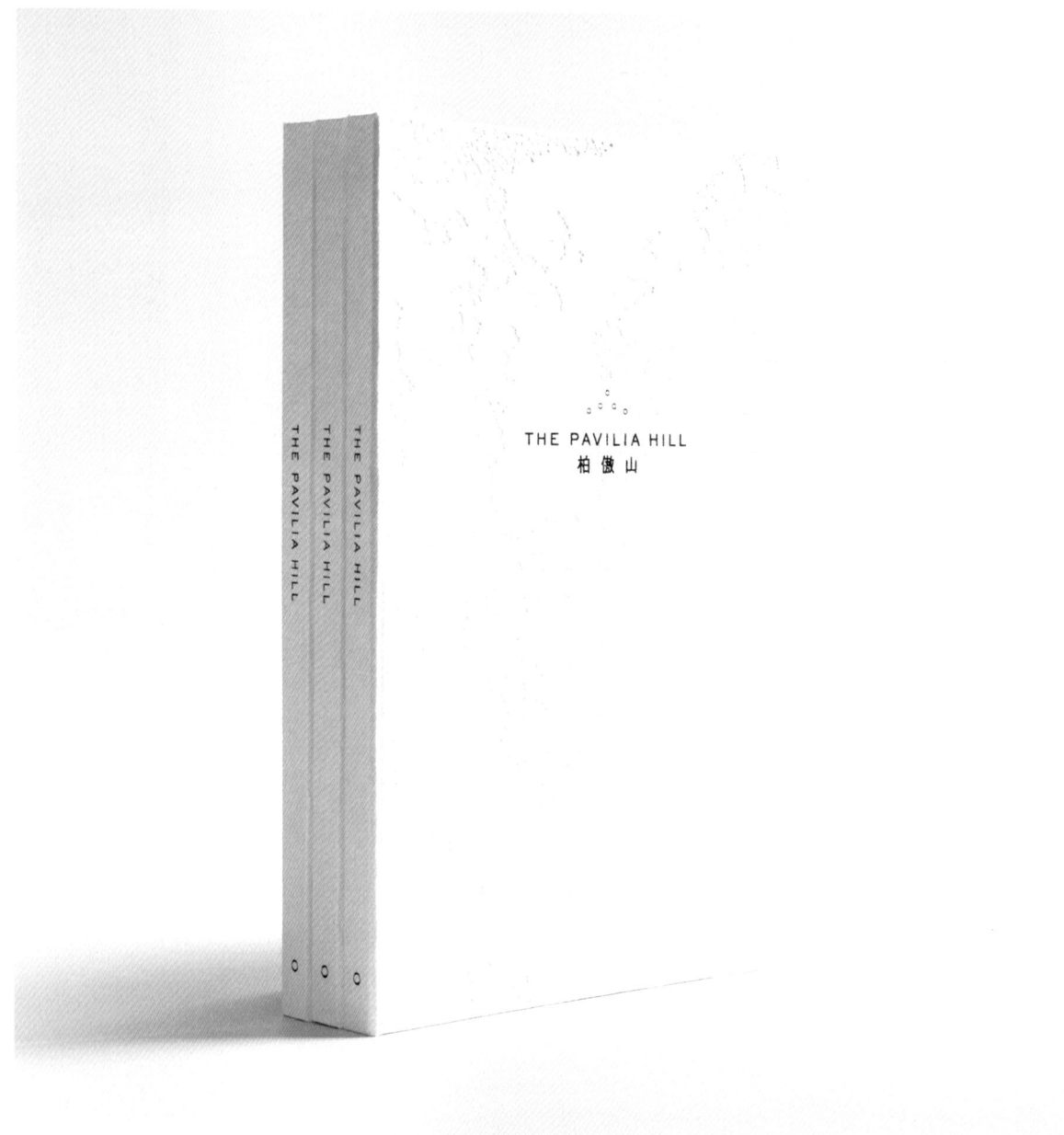

The Pavilia Hill

Designer: Toby Ng Design

The Pavilia Hill is a luxury bespoke residence in the heart of Hong Kong, whose design pays tribute to nature and artisanship. Its interior and landscape were designed under the guidance of Wabi-Sabi.
Based on the principles of Wabi-Sabi, the book design team created a visceral and texturally rich book to reflect the serenity of the main feature of this residence: the tranquil Zen gardens by Japanese Zen priest and landscape architect Shunmyo Masuno. A raw stone texture was chosen for the book's hard cover, to resemble the special stone sculptures' sublime presence in The Pavilia Hill. In addition, by deploying various printing methods in combination with a selection of 10 types of texturally rich and luxurious paper, the final effect is a striking visual impact and sensual experience for readers.

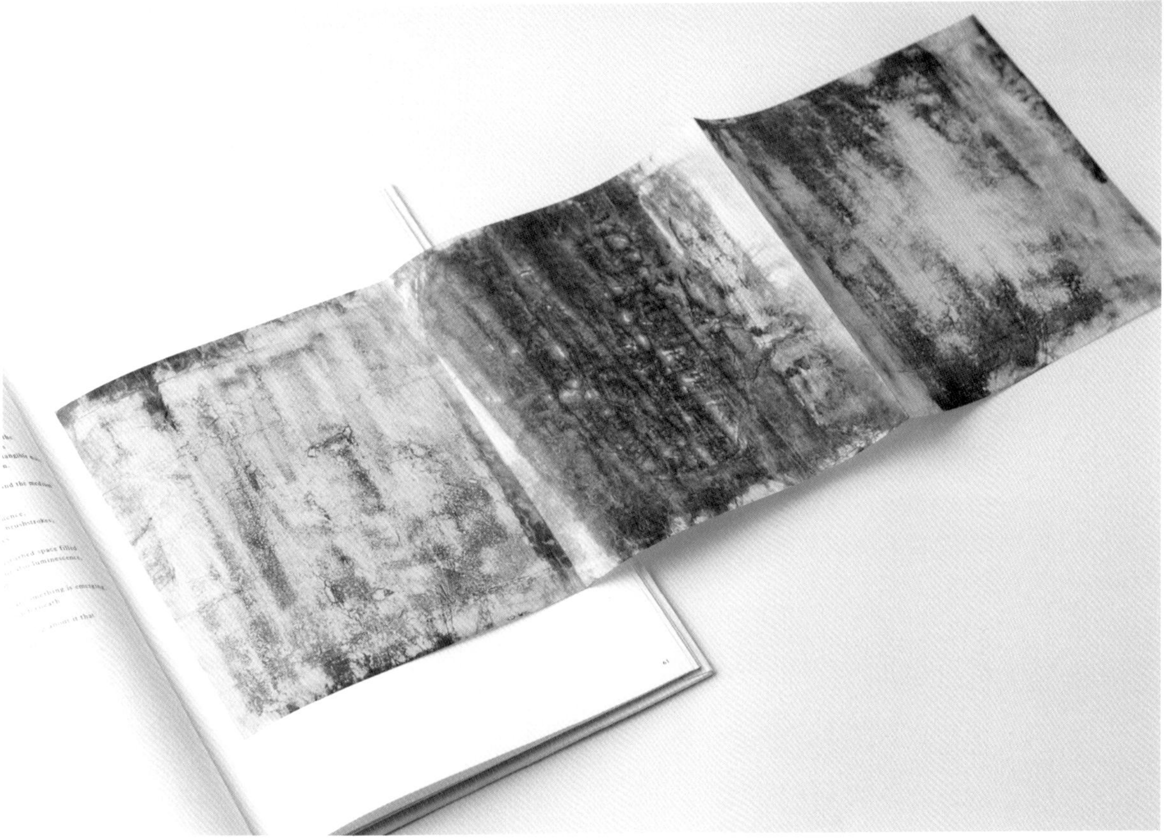

203

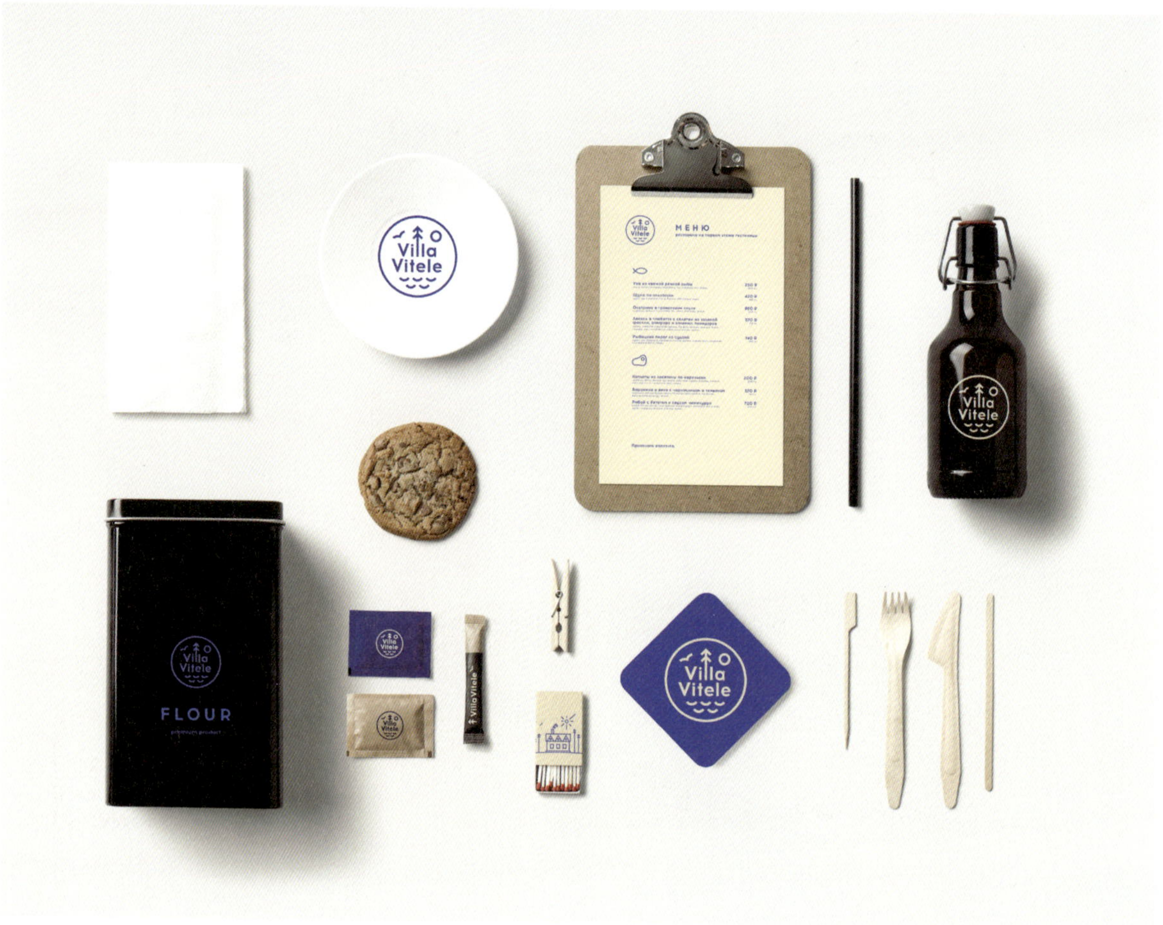

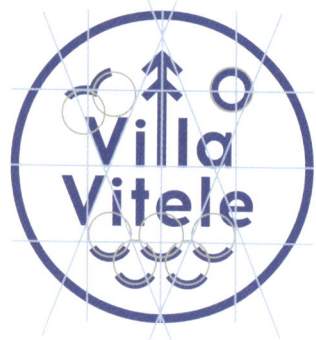

Villa Vitele

Designer: Axek Efremov

Villa Vitele is a hotel and restaurant complex located in Karelia, Russia, right where the Vidlitsa river flows into the Lake Ladoga. Much impressed by the simple purity of Karelian nature, the designer used the images of tall pin trees, water and sand as the feature elements in the logo design to invite people to enjoy the beauty of nature. Villa Vitele's unique blue lake and gray sand inspired the refreshing palette.

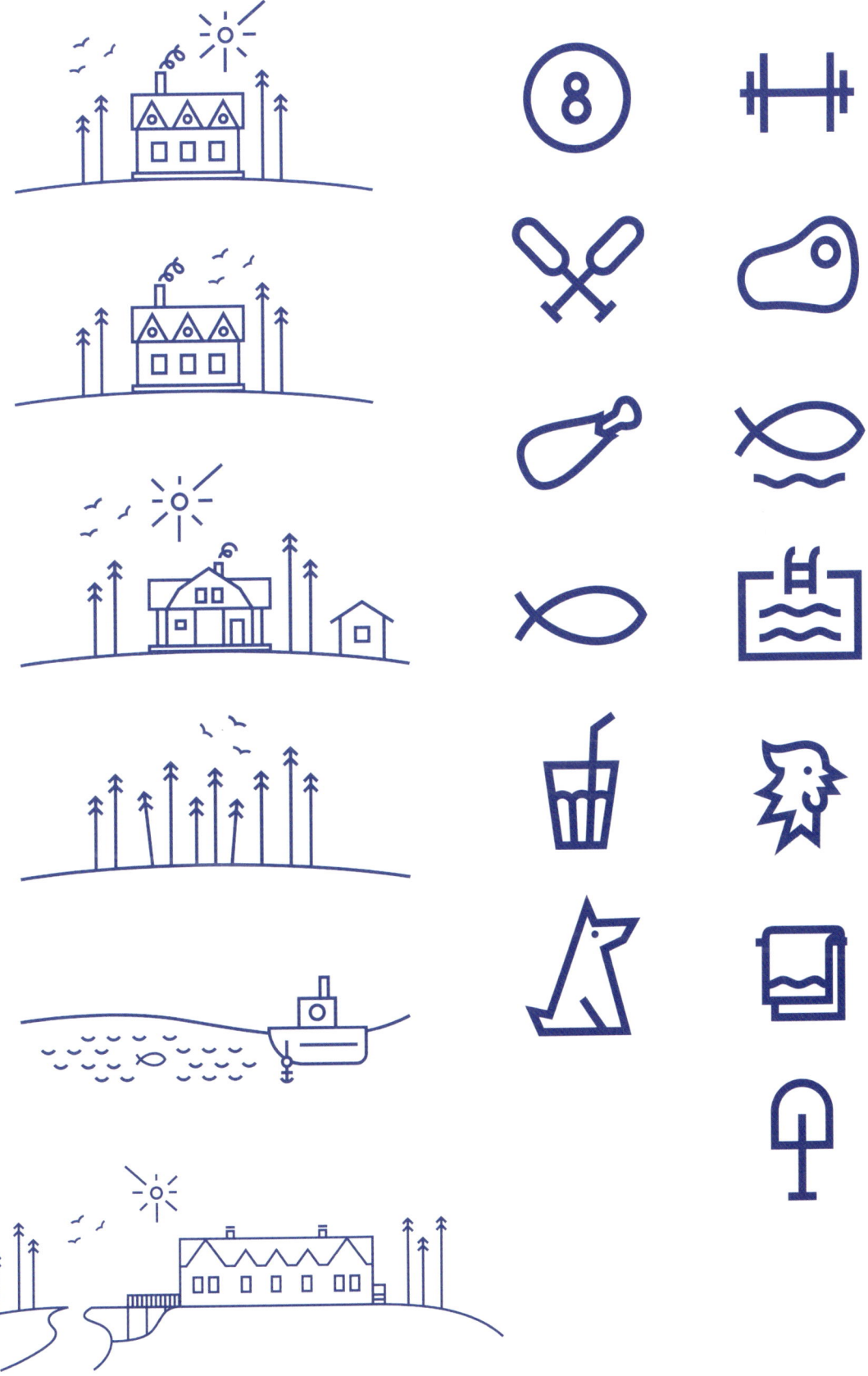

INDEX

#

6D-K
www.6d-k.com
166

A

ABEKINO DESIGN
www.abekinodesign.jp
54

Agata Yamaguchi
www.agatayamaguchi.com
40

AKU
www.aku.co
138

Alessio Rattazzi
alessiorattazzi.ch
18

Alex Dalmau
alexdalmau.com
162

Anagrama
Anagrama.com
124, 132, 136

artless Inc
www.artless.co.jp
172

Axek Efremov
www.behance.net/axek
204

B

BCOME
bcome.jp
16

BULLET Inc.
bullet-inc.jp
70

Bunch
www.bunchdesign.com
184

Buntesamt
www.buntesamt.de
14

C

canaria
www.canaria-world.com
72

CFC Studio
www.contentformcontext.com
74

Comence Studio
www.comence.ru
158

D

Daigo Daikoku
www.daikoku.ndc.co.jp
22

E

E.Co.,Ltd.
www.e-ltd.co.jp
114

Ermolaev Bureau
ermolaevbureau.com
120, 142

F

Fagerström Studio
www.fagerstrom.studio
144, 146

Furze Chan
artwork.furzechan.com
174

Futura
byfutura.com/en
134

H

Haller Brun
hallerbrun.eu
92

I

Ingrid Picanyol Studio
www.ingridpicanyol.com
50

K

KD
www.kamadajunya.com
48, 180

Ken Miki & Associates
ken-miki.net
192

Kong Studio
www.kongstudio.com.sg
128

KOREFE. Kolle Rebbe Form
und Entwicklung
korefe.de
148

Kota Kobayashi
kotakobayashi.com
178

L

Lars Kjelsnes
heydays.no
30

Laura de Miguel
www.laurademiguel.com
90

Lava
www.lava.nl
196

Luck Show
www.luck-show.com
164

M

Madelyn Bilsborough
madelyn.myportfolio.com
80

Mainstudio
mainstudio.com
60

Maria Szczodrowska
www.behance.net/mariaszczodrowska
58

Maud
www.brucemaudesign.com
182

Motherbird
www.motherbird.com.au
186

Moving Brands
www.movingbrands.com
198

N

Nakajima Design
www.nkjm-d.com
38, 39

Nendo
www.nendo.jp
98

NIPPON DESIGN CENTER
www.ndc.co.jp
42, 112

nomocreative
nomocreative.com
152

nottuo Inc.
nottuo.com
106

O

omsky studio
omskystudio.com
110

One Thousand Times
x1000.co
82

P

Parámetro Studio
www.parametrostudio.com
154

Planning ES
www.es-co.jp
46

R

room-composite
www.room-composite.com
96

S

SEA Design
seadesign.co.uk
188

Sekiura Design
sekiraracom.tumblr.com
170

Shanba Design
www.facebook.com/shanbadesign
56

Studio Naam
www.studionaam.com
102

T

Taku Satoh Design Office Inc.
www.tsdo.co.jp
94

Tamas Birinyi
behance.net/btworks
168

tegusu Inc
tegusu.com
62, 66

Toby Ng Design
www.toby-ng.com
84, 202

Tomatdesign
www.tomatdesign.ru
190

W

WAAITT™
www.waaitt.dk
194

Wonchan Lee
www.wonchanlee.com
176

Y

Yuta Takahashi
www.yutatakahashi.jp
78, 88, 118